TEN YEARS' RESIDENCE AT THE

COURT OF TRIPOLI

This edition is published by Darf Publishers, London

First published 1846
New impression 2002

British Library Cataloguing-in-Publication Data
A catalogue record for this book is available from the British Library

Letters written during a Ten Year's Residence at the Court of Tripoli
Published from the originals in the posession of the family of the late
Richard Tully, esq.

ISBN 1850779279

Dar El-Kutub No. 11468 / 2002

DARF Publishers
277 West End Lane
London NW6

LETTERS

WRITTEN DURING A TEN YEARS' RESIDENCE AT THE

COURT OF TRIPOLI

PUBLISHED FROM THE ORIGINALS IN THE

POSSESSION OF THE FAMILY OF THE LATE

RICHARD TULLY, Esq.

THE BRITISH CONSUL

Comprising Authentic Memoirs and Anecdotes of

THE REIGNING BASHAW

HIS FAMILY AND OTHER PERSONS OF DISTINCTION

Also an Account of

THE DOMESTIC MANNERS OF THE

MOORS, ARABS, AND TURKS

A NEW EDITION WITH INTRODUCTION AND NOTES
by SETON DEARDEN

INTRODUCTION

THE literature of the Barbary Regencies is scarce and diffuse, and its principal sources still lie buried in the consular archives of Britain, France, Holland, and Italy, and among the surviving records of the Sublime Porte. The French, it is true, with their special interests in Tunis and Algiers, and the Italians in Tripoli, have produced a sizeable body of research material, but it is usually specialist in approach and, alas, not infrequently coloured by prejudice or colonial propaganda. In English we have little but the fugitive accounts of travellers such as Lyon, Blaquiere, and Beechey ; the stories of Christian slaves like Lucas and Pananti ; and we have this book.

It is indeed strange that in the long, bloody, and often theatrical vicissitudes of the Barbary States—" *sombres melodrames avec çà et là les scènes de comédie les plus bouffonnes,*" as Augustin Bernard calls them —there should be such a dearth of record, that the letters of an English lady to a friend, the casual diary of daily life as seen from a British consulate, should be so unique that there is scarcely a subsequent study of the period which does not quote them. In fact they provide almost the only consecutive picture of the inner life of the Regencies that we possess.

This lack of literature derives from the fact that these small, remote dependencies of the Ottoman Empire were comparatively unknown and uninteresting to the West. Though they harassed and perplexed the European powers for more than 300 years, they played no other part in European life or culture. Such influence as they had was hostile, negative, marginal ; they were, in fact, nothing more than a discreditable footnote to the history of the times. The contemporary world, going about its occasions, considered them not as states, or political entities, with a corporate life of their own, but as something added to the hazards of trade and travel ; alien shapes emerging on the horizons of anxious sea captains ; sources for fireside tales of pagan licence and enforced bondage ; pests, drawn from behind the mysterious curtain of Islam to haunt the Mediterranean seaways. A reproach, perhaps, to the conscience of civilized nations ; but nothing more.

This was not without reason. For of what importance, indeed, of

5

what interest, were little obscure Arab dynasties with their illiterate and barbaric princes, their disreputable courts, their customs which combined the oriental extravagance and tyranny of the Grand Signior, with the fanatic seventh-century laws of the prophet Mohammed ; flourishing alone in a hothouse world surrounded by sea and deserts ? What traveller wished to visit their archaic cities on the desolate fringe of the North African coast, which looked landwards only on to the barren waste of the Sahara desert, the unprofitable mountains of the Atlas, or the enigma of Central Africa ; and what merchant, seeking new markets or trade routes, was drawn to lands where the poverty of the economies, and the hostile and treacherous character of the inhabitants (that fiery fusing of Turk, Arab, and Berber blood), made any enterprise both hazardous and unrewarding ?

And so, cut off from the West, without roots, the dead hand of Islam lying heavy upon them, the Regencies remained, unknown and unsought, owing to their continued existence only to the general turbulence and insecurity of Continental relations. Since they had no real resources but plunder and ransom to support their spendthrift economies and lax administrations, they could only thrive in situations brought about by the continual quarrels of the European states. In time of war, when the protection of trade routes was uncertain, and reprisal difficult, the Barbary corsairs sallied forth from their harbours upon the seaways of Spain, Italy, and Greece, taking sides between the contending powers, swooping on the defenceless shipping of the smaller maritime states, or raiding their coasts for slaves. Peaceful passage for small nations could only be bought by heavy subsidy, and was, even then, only indifferently honoured. Yet subsidies must constantly be paid or vital trade suffered ; and thus plunder and ransom filled their coffers. Conversely, in times of peace, they sank into comparative obscurity and penury. And so, since European relations were rarely peaceful during the sixteenth, seventeenth, and eighteenth centuries, the Barbary States continued to exist, and even to thrive. They lasted, indeed, until the final struggle between Britain and France ended early in the nineteenth century and, at the Congress of Vienna in 1815 determined action against piracy and Christian slavery was resolved, and Anglo-French fleets entered Barbary waters and imposed conditions which sounded their doom. No longer able to support their despotic rulers, they were reduced to their natural poverty, and disappeared from their shadowy place on the stage of Mediterranean history. With the final collapse of the Ottoman

Empire they fell, Algiers in 1830 and Tunis in 1881 to France ; Tripoli in 1911 to Italy.

§

The Regency of Tripoli, the setting of this book, was the most important of the three Regencies which owed their nominal suzerainty to the Sublime Porte. Its Bashaw, or ruler, carried a seniority of " Three Tails," a rank equivalent to that of the governors of the three greatest provinces in the Sultan's dominions ; those of Cairo, Budapesth, and Baghdad.

Tripoli's importance was derived from its link with Egypt and its geographical position on the great Hajj route from the west to Mecca, and the trade routes between Africa and Europe. In area the Regency extended from the eastern limits of Cyrenaica—possibly at the escarpment of Sollum—westwards along a winding sea coast to the frontier of Tunisia at Ben Gardane ; a distance of nearly a thousand miles. In its eastern section, the province of Barca, the country consisted of the fertile mountainous area of the Jebel Akhdar flanking the sea coast almost to Benghazi. West of this to Misurata was five hundred miles of desert and salt marsh, the Bay of Sirte ; and from Misurata to Tripoli, and in parts to the Tunisian border, a strip of fertile coastal land contained the main towns of the Regency. Southwards of this coastal strip stretched the desert, broken by the mountains of Gharian, the Berber stronghold, and again south of these, the Sahara.

The Regency's strategic value on the trade routes arose from this fortuitous geography. From Tripoli there was a comparatively short, and therefore safe, sea route to Europe by way of Malta and Sicily ; and the Regency stood at one of the narrowest crossings of the Sahara desert ; thus providing the centre for three caravan routes ; the first running due south through the oases of the Fezzan to Lake Chad ; the second turning south-west through Ghadames and Ghat to fabulous Timbuktu ; and the third which led south-east through th Jefara oases, by Socne and Zella to Wadai, Darfur, and the rich Sudan. In Roman and Byzantine times these caravan routes had carried a large volume of traffic from Africa to Europe ; but Arab mismanagement, the collapse of oases, and nomad raiding had reduced their value to little but channels for the transport of black slaves from the south, gold dust, ostrich feathers, ivory, and some gums. The country's other exports were wool, leather, meat, esparto grass, and vegetables to Malta, and salt from the salt-pans near Zuara to Venice. The great granaries which had supplied Rome in ancient times, and whose traces still remain all over the country, were gone.

The people of the Regency were equally varied in race. In the towns of the populated coastal fringe lived a mixed seafaring population of Turk, Arab, and Moor, Jewish-European, Jews, and Levantines. Arab peasants and Beduin semi-nomads cultivated the fertile oases of the coast. In the mountain areas, the Berbers and some Jews lived on cultivation. About the desert areas moved the large Bedouin tribes, of mixed Arab stock, who had entered the region from Arabia in earlier invasions. Of these the most important were the Ulad Suleiman (the almost pure Arab tribe of the famous chief, Ahmed Seif el Nasser) whose *dira* stretched from the Gulf of Sirte to the Fezzan ; and the Ulad bu Seif (a Berber admixture). At Beni Ulid, a mountainous area south of Tarhuna, a large and warlike Berber confederation, the Orfela, lived in comparative immunity.

This mixture of peoples was the result of a variegated past. The history of the Regency from earliest times was one of continued occupation. The original inhabitants, the Berbers, the Garamantes of Herodotus—a race whose origins are still a mystery, had suffered a succession of invaders—Roman, Vandal, Byzantine, Arab, and Christian. In the seventh century they had accepted Islam and provided some of the finest troops of the Arab armies in Spain. Islam had remained the religion in spite of subsequent occupation by Norman troops and the Knights of Malta.

In the sixteenth century the Regency in the hands of the Knights of St. John finally fell to the Turkish pirate captain, Dragut, and was annexed to the Ottoman Empire. Ottoman troops occupied the province and Ottoman rules of government were imposed, a regular tribute being paid to the Sublime Porte. For nearly two centuries the province lay under direct Turkish rule, governed by a Turkish Dey appointed by the Grand Signior and supported and administered by Turkish officials and a body of Janisseries, or European Moslem soldiers. But history here followed a familiar pattern. With the passage of time the ties with far off Constantinople became gradually looser, as a series of weak Sultans, with policies of *laisser faire* succeeded one another. Contacts became rare and confined to superficial courtesies, visits of Turkish inspectors dwindled ; tribute shrank and then practically ceased. Meanwhile a new rising power was making itself felt. The Turkish trained Janisseries had intermarried with Arab and

Berber women and created a new factor, the Cologhli, or Turkish soldier of mixed blood, who, not only succeeded in occupying posts of importance in the administration but had a natural sympathy and support from the indigent population. The Dey endeavoured to keep down the growing power of the Cologhlis by the importation of more Janisseries and a policy of intrigue. But in 1711 one of the leading Cologhlis, Ali Karamanli, whose family had come to Tripoli with Dragut, had risen, supported by other Cologhlis and a section of the population, deposed the Dey, slaughtered the Janisseries in the manner described so vividly by Miss Tully, and seized power. This was the beginning of an Arab dynasty that, with varying vicissitudes and much blood and intrigue, was to rule the Regency for 125 years. It is ten of these years, from 1783 to 1793, that forms the background to this book.

§

As has been seen, the establishment of despotic rule and a costly mercenary army made it necessary for the Regency of Tripoli to turn to other sources of revenue than the taxation of an impoverished population and trade. Slavery and plunder were necessary to support the country's economy ; and the Tripoli pirates became, from the sixteenth century, an active feature of Mediterranean life. Until 1655, when Blake's fleet first entered Mediterranean waters, the Barbary corsairs had been a constant scourge to English shipping. Trade was frequently interrupted and English sailors languished as slaves in the bagnios of Tripoli, Tunis, and Algiers. Blake's sharp lesson in England's growing sea power resulted in a treaty of commerce and peace between England and Tripoli, signed in 1678, and the first British Consulate was set up in the Regency. The French had established diplomatic relations forty-five years earlier ; and other countries followed. In 1783, the period of this book, there were some eight consular representatives, which included the Netherlands, Sweden, Denmark, Spain, and the Italian States.

The functions of these consulates were partly to foster trade, but also to secure the free passage of merchant vessels through Barbary waters and to redeem those vessels and their crews whose capture violated the Bashaw's treaty engagements. In Mr. Consul Tully's day, before the rivalry of Britain and France had reached its apogee, the political aspects of the Consul's life were confined to preserving a state of good relations with the Bashaw, or ruling prince, and sustaining the prestige of his country in the eyes of the local administration and his diplomatic colleagues. The hostility of the French and British Consuls, and their political manœuvres, which later became a constant theme in the history of the Regency, had not yet arisen. A great British Consul (whose story will be told elsewhere) was to follow Tully in later years when Napoleon's armies were overrunning Europe ; and in Tripoli, which became an important strategic centre in the southern Mediterranean (it was among other things the victualling station for Malta), there was a long struggle of prestige and power between the representatives of the two great Continental powers.

In the period covered by this book, however, the Consul's main tasks were the protection of his own nationals and their trade, the redemption of slaves, and the support of those weaker colleagues whose countries were allied to his own. An understanding of Miss Tully's narrative will be clearer if this is borne in mind.

In his protective role the Consul was supported by an international agreement which gave him wide powers. The status of Europeans in the Turkish empire was preserved by the Ottoman Capitulations of 1761. These, among other rights, gave to the Consuls the power of jurisdiction over their own countrymen in all civil and criminal cases ; and to the latter both liberty of movement about the Sultan's dominions, inviolability of domicile, and freedom from restriction in commerce and religion. In effect, these rights gave great influence to the Consul. He alone had the mandate to dispense justice to his fellow-countrymen, though he could call upon the local government to enforce his judgments if necessary. Consuls, as magistrates, therefore, had a unifying and controlling influence over their nationals and could bring, in proportion to the size and importance of the countries they represented, a varying pressure to bear on the Bashaw and the local administration. Consuls of the large maritime powers, such as Britain, France, and Holland, were virtually rulers in their own right. Behind them was always the invisible threat of sea power, to which a maritime Regency was particularly vulnerable. In times of trouble it was often sufficient merely to threaten the Bashaw with a naval visit. Sometimes this failed and it was necessary to summon a frigate to lie off-shore with its guns trained on the castle while an indemnity was extracted or a treaty enforced. The story of the Regency is frequently punctuated by the bombardment of the town and the capitulation of the Bashaw.

The influence of consular representatives was naturally in proportion to the speed and effectiveness with which they could summon outside aid ; and the smaller and weaker powers, such as the Italian states, suffered accordingly. The Bashaw did not scruple to break engagements with these and to treat their representatives at times with disrespect or contumely. Their fortunes waxed and waned with the political situation, the state of the Bashaw's finances, or the rapacity of his moods. It was a common practice, therefore, for the smaller powers to invite the British, French, or Dutch Consuls to act as their representatives. To counter this, it was the policy of the Bashaw and his government to foster and exploit any rivalry between the European powers, and keep the consular representatives divided by intrigue or the allotment of favours. The Karamanli family pursued this policy with some success ; profiting, as the European scene changed, first by exploiting the natural rivalry between Britain and Holland, then Britain and France, and finally Britain and America.

The policy of the Bashaw could in fact be summed up in the words of the Bashaw of Tripoli in 1736 when the British, Dutch, and French Consuls protested to him about the seizing of a Venetian ship in defiance of a treaty. " The Barbary Corsairs are born pirates, and not able to subsist by any other means ; it is therefore the Christian's business to be always on their guard, even in times of peace."

In the arbitrary, uncertain regime of the Karamanlis, the foreign consulates, inviolate from the Bashaw's whims or summary justice, safe from the dangerous tides of fanaticism and hatred which so often swept the city, were by long tradition become sanctuaries where redress from injustice might be obtained ; safety from pursuit might be secured ; succour in times of want granted. The tradition of sanctuary is firmly rooted in the North African consciousness. Certain spots and certain objects—particular mosques or tombs of holy men ; the Bashaw's person, his clothes, or his horse, all, if attained, gave immunity to a suppliant. So the flags of Britain, France, and Holland, fluttering high above the consular houses, became symbols, not only for Briton, Frenchman, or Hollander, but for the oppressed Levantine, the tormented Jew, and even the Arab or Moor flying from blood vengeance or summary justice. Nor was it easy for the Consul, in a country where prestige depended on a show of power, to avoid at least the gesture of protection to all comers. And thus these houses, small citadels in the shifting perilous world of Islam, were often, as Miss Tully's letters show, the scene of bloody escapes and adventures.

§

The old British consulate in which Miss Tully passed her ten years in Tripoli still stands, though it has been forsaken, fallen into dilapidation and reduced, when last seen by the writer in 1949, to acting as shop and store for a Maltese coffin maker. It is a large building of two storeys, standing in the narrow lane, filled on one side by bakers' ovens, which runs north from the arch of Septimius Severus, near the city's Marine Gate, to the former entrance of the Jewish quarter which, in Miss Tully's day, was shut from the Moslem section of the city at nightfall by heavy gates. Entering the house from the street, double doors led into an arched passageway, lined with stone benches, the *skiffer* so often referred to, which in turn opened into the large central courtyard. Here, round a fountain and basin and small plots of earth from which grew orange trees, jasmine and verbena, stood the dark rooms in which the consular servants and the Cologhli dragomen, supplied for protection by the Bashaw, lived. A kitchen, deep storerooms, and the consular prison surrounded a flight of broad steps which led to the commodious rooms above, built Turkish fashion to face inwards. On the first floor, galleries overlooked the courtyard, while the rooms within had smaller windows, protected by wooden grilles and iron bars, which looked out on the narrow street below. From the central gallery a small flight of stairs led up to other storerooms and on to wide balustraded roof where, between the rows of coloured peppers spread to dry and the brown heaps of grain airing in the sun, the family could walk and sit in the cool of the evening, and catch the sea breeze. From here the visitor had a view of the harbour, the Bashaw's castle, the Marine Gate which led to the jetty, the arch of Severus, and the decaying city walls.

A house near, or if possible, overlooking the harbour was essential to all Consuls, whose frequent preoccupation was the arrival and departure of shipping. The sound of the signal guns from castle and ship would be followed by the appearance of every Consul on his rooftop or balcony, telescope in hand, to fix the colours of the incoming vessel. With what varied emotions would the strip of bunting swim into focus ! Should it be the crescent flag of the Tripoli corsairs, it might be a jubilant vessel tacking in with a cargo of plunder, its narrow decks lined with the white despairing faces of newly captured Christian slaves. It then became the duty of the Consul to put on ceremonial uniform and proceed in state, accompanied by his dragomen, to the Diwan, where the slaves and their captors were assembled. Here in the great hall, filled as the eye of imagination can see it with a motley assembly of Arab and European pirates, slave-dealers, armourers, officials, and prisoners, the Bashaw in pomp and preceded by his three Horse Tails would come to supervise in the division of the slaves, select his own tithe, and redeem those claimed by the Consuls.

Piracy was ruled by a code of unwritten regulations. Slaves of nations in treaty relations with the Regency were redeemed, unless they were taken in the actual service of a power not in treaty relations. Thus, passengers in a ship of a power not in treaty relations could be released if proven to be nationals of a friendly power. Seamen serving in the same ship remained as slaves. It was the business of the Consuls to scrutinize the lists of captures and make their claims.

The scenes at these Diwans, of which Pananti has left us a picture,[1] must have been charged with emotion. Despairing Christians, men, women, and children, thrust rudely into bondage, chained and dragged rudely into this terrifying assemblage, must have eyed the row of ceremonious Consuls with mixed feelings according to their nationality. As the names were called out by the Great Kehya, the Bashaw would claim his tenth, choosing usually those with technical skills which might be of use in the castle bagnios. From time to time a Consul, rising, would interrupt and claim a slave. There would be a debate, a gesture by the Bashaw, the pronouncement of the magic words "you are free" by the Grand Kehya, and then and there an armourer would strike off the chains, and another slave was free.

More frequently the visiting vessel would be a merchant ship bringing mail, supplies, European faces, news from the capitals of Europe. For people cut off for long periods from the world of Europe these must have been red-letter days. Or again, and often most welcome of all would be the colours of a frigate of war, bringing official despatches, sometimes distinguished visitors, and always bringing with it that precious but constantly waning commodity—prestige.

§

Beyond the consulate within whose walls the style, the civilization, the decencies of the eighteenth century were preserved, spread the

---

[1] *Narrative of a Residence in Algiers.*

great rambling city of Tripoli, an anachronism of the sixteenth. In Miss Tully's time the city was at its lowest ebb from neglect and over-crowding. The French Consul [1] reported that the city walls were in parts so ruinous that they lay open to the outside like gates ; and in the castle the Bashaw's artillery was sited on such rubble that the firing of the signal gun often caused the ramparts to collapse. Beechey, the traveller, described the city as " encumbered with the rubbish of houses fallen into ruin and with the superfluous produce of those which were yet standing ; while the swarms of little naked and dirty children, and numerous groups of hungry and half-starved dogs almost blocked up the space which was left. . . . The dust, together with the heat of the sun, and the myriads of gnats and flies which assailed us in every direction were no grateful addition to these inconveniences." [2]

Although the town wall, as it stood in the eighteenth century, has mostly disappeared under Italian town planning, the outlines of the north and east walls can still be traced and most of the west and south walls remain. These walls, high, sloping ramparts of stone, completely surrounded the town which, on its south and west side was washed by the Mediterranean. The bay of Tripoli here makes a right-angled bend south, and then west and on the corner a great reef of rock runs out eastwards into the sea, forming a natural well-protected harbour, easily ringed by forts and difficult of attack. North of this the walls ran to the extreme north-eastern corner, where the Bashaw's castle stands ; a tall irregular series of battlements roughly square in shape, cut off both from the sea and the city by high walls. Within this heavily guarded enceinte, which turned few windows outwards, and entry to which could only be made through a heavily protected gateway, lay an intricate mass of courtyards, rooms, and passages on different levels, separated from one another by heavy iron doors. Here lived the Bashaw himself, his staff, and guards ; his slaves and his carefully screened women's quarters where dwelt his wife and concubines. Here also, in separate quarters, cut off from one another by guarded doors, lived his two sons and their families. The castle, which Miss Tully was to know so well, was, and still is, a dark, gloomy maze of buildings, through which the visitor stumbles along narrow smelly passages which turn and twist haphazardly and then suddenly open into bright courtyards surrounded by balconies,

[1] Vallière.
[2] *Proceedings of the expedition to explore the Northern coast of Africa.* Murray, 1828.

decorated pillars, and walls bright with Chinese tiles. Yet the bright-ness of these courtyards, so often the scenes of bloody drama, only seem to intensify the general impression of imprisonment and despair. A curious place, this castle, where sudden gleams of beauty only serve to make the walls without seem even higher ; a place of viciousness, stifled hopes, in which there still seems to linger the ghosts of concen-trated passions, fears, and crimes unspeakable.

From the Bashaw's castle an aqueduct, long vanished, led to a distant well. Beyond this again the city walls continued, making a sharp bend west and then south, to face the great maritime plain of sandhills and gravel called the *pianura*, which stretched away to the arid Jefara desert and the distant ridge of the mountains of Garian. Eastwards of the Bashaw's castle, along the bay and reaching almost to the city gates, was the Menschia, a narrow green oasis, stretching along the sea's edge for some ten miles and inland for some three ; a pleasant place of tall palm trees interspersed with green patches of vegetables and peppers, walled gardens planted with apricot, orange, and pomegranate trees, and discovering, as to-day, in its depths the little whitewashed mud villages of the peasants leading from one another by small sandy tracks lined with high mud banks topped with the green leaves of the Indian fig. Here many of the Tripoli notables kept summer houses, and the Consuls, when the security of the country permitted, would go for rides and picnics.

The city itself was a rabbit-warren of narrow lanes, arched bazaars, and overhanging buildings. Few windows gave on the streets, unless heavily shuttered with curious overhanging wooden grilles, masking the inside from the passer-by and protecting the women from his glance ; and, except for the bazaars and coffee shops, the streets had a forbidding and decrepit appearance. Opposite the town gate, open-ing on the Menschia and near the castle, was the great Karamanli mosque, reached by a viaduct from the castle and profusely decorated with tiles and arabesques. Behind this was the slave market where Christian slaves, after division among their captors, were offered for sale. These slaves were most often Neapolitans, Spaniards, or Portu-guese. Negroes from Fezzan and Bornu were in a bazaar adjoining. A long, vaulted place this bazaar, still standing. Here once a week the slave sales were held ; Christians, men and women, unless privately bargained for, as was usual, stood on small daises while the salesmen turned them about and showed either masculine sinews or feminine charms. The blacks were usually dragged, like cattle, up and down the lines of seated coffee-drinking buyers while bids were made. Most travellers' books speak of the pitiful scenes witnessed here ; husbands separated from wives, mothers from children, and dragged off by new purchasers to the life of the labourer, the servant, the concubine, or for resale in Tunis, Algiers, Egypt, or Constantinople.

The hand of fanatic Islam pressed hard on the city ; there were nearly twenty mosques, always possible centres of excitement and emotion ; and such was the temper of the Moslems that any religious procession, Friday gathering for prayers, or religious feast day, such as Yom al Ashura or the Id el Kebir, might be the occasion of an out-burst against Christian or Jew. Wild, often half-mad dervishes wandered about the city unchecked, because of the *baraka*, or blessed-ness, accorded to madness, and might vent unchecked their rage or delusions upon any passer-by. Thus the Christian, and even more the unprotected Jew, walked in constant fear of assault. Jews were easily marked down. They wore special black garments, were obliged to remove their shoes on passing mosques, and were not permitted to mount animals in the city. All the wealthier Christians, and all consular representatives, were provided with guards, without whom they never walked or rode abroad. The Tripoli Jews had no rights and no privileges but those they had bought.

Of the Tripoli city population of some 25,000, about 5000 were Jews of the Sephardic rite. They were mostly refugees from the Spanish oppression of the fifteenth century. Although they had succeeded in getting into their hands much of the trade and the finance of the city (they had the monopoly in the export of esparto grass, ostrich feathers, and saffron) they were in fact forced to lead a life of sad restriction. The dirtiest tasks were allotted them ; such as the collection of ordure and the public execution of criminals. For offences they were sometimes burned alive ; or, a common punish-ment, nailed by one hand to a synagogue door and smeared with honey to die in the sun and flies. Nevertheless, they contrived to prosper ; and part of Miss Tully's narrative deals with the hold the Jews succeeded in obtaining over the Bashaw through a concubine named Esther. It will be seen what was her fate.

§

The administration of the Regency, references to which frequently appear in the letters, was based on the Turkish system, adapted to meet local conditions. Control was kept in the hands of as few persons as possible ; and all senior officials were linked, if it could be arranged, by consanguinity or marriage to the Bashaw himself. After the Bashaw, as supreme head of state with unlimited powers, came his eldest son, the Bey, who was commander of the military forces and responsible among other things for security in general. He commanded both the Janissaries and Cologhlis, or mercenary troops, and the Arab irregulars who were recruited for defence in time of war. He was responsible for the maintenance of order throughout the country, and the collection of tribute from the tribes. Under his command were a number of officers, called Aghas, chief of whom was the Agha of the Janissaries.

The Bashaw's other two sons were appointed governors of adjoining towns.

The corsair fleet of small vessels was under the Rais of the Marine and chief of the customs (called in Miss Tully's day the " Doganier," or custom's official). He was responsible for all matters concerning the port. Under him was the Rais of the Navy, who commanded the pirate fleet at sea. The Rais of the Marine at this period was a renegade Neapolitan, married to one of the Bashaw's daughters ; and he wielded great influence in the Regency. It was a post which could only normally be held by a renegade European, since it demanded some education and considerable intelligence and courage. Raiding had to be carried out with due regard to the Bashaw's treaties with the various maritime powers ; but since the Regency depended on the major part of its income from slaves and plunder, raiding must be continuous and successful.

On the civil side, the most senior and influential official was the Great Kehya (Miss Tully calls him Chiaia : the word in Turkish means superintendent), the private counsellor of the Bashaw, the dispenser of the Bashaw's justice, and in most things his civic representative. His office stood at the end of the large entrance *skiffer* in the Bashaw's castle. Here he sat daily checking all visitors who came to see the Bashaw. He was also *chef de protocol*, political adviser, and tutor of the Bashaw's eldest son, the Bey. He was assisted by an aide, the Little Kehya. This post, again, was always held, if possible, by a blood relative of the Karamanlis. The responsibilities of these posts naturally required men of great wisdom, knowledge of the customs of the country, and also knowledge of European mentality and procedure. A further responsibility of the Kehya was supervision of all matters concerning the tribes, and the execution of all the laws and ordinances of the Bashaw, including the punishment of wrong-doers. The Little Kehya, who was assisted by a chief clerk called the Katib, was commander of the Bashaw's personal bodyguard and attendant of the castle.

The Bashaw's secretariat was officered by the Khojas, or senior clerks, who also provided such Ambassadors or Consuls as the Regency sent abroad, since they were trained in the Bashaw's complicated diplomacy.

The finances of the Regency were administered by two Khas-nadars, or treasurers. The Bashaw's private treasure was kept in a single strong room of the castle, of which only the Bashaw and the Great Khasnadar-had access to the key. At night this key, with the great key of the main gate, were handed over by Khasnadar and Kehya to the Bashaw, who kept them in his bedroom, thus securing the castle from treacherous entry overnight. Fear of treachery, indeed, was the motive in both the choice of men for these important posts and for the somewhat unusual distribution of the tasks allotted them. Thus, although the little Kehya was responsible for the castle guard, the Khasnadar had the supervision over all the Bashaw's slaves ; to put both sections of the castle staff under one command would be to invite a possible *coup d'etat.*

The constables and law officers were known as " *shawishes* " (Miss Tully's chaoux). These also acted as messengers and guards. They were assisted, in cases where the Bashaw's direct interests were in-volved, by the hampas (Turkish : *hampa,* a companion or adherent), who were mostly Janissaries, renegade Christians, or negroes. In the centre of the city was a guard and police post under an Agha, staffed with more *shawishes.* These were used for town supervision ; and the police post was called the Sandanar.

The civil administration of the city was enforced by the *Sheikh el Beled,* and executed by a number of sub-officers called *Kaids.* The racial minorities and the city guilds were represented by *Kaids.* Thus in Tripoli there was a *Kaid* of the Jews, another of the Christians, a third of the wine trade, a fourth of the city bakeries. *Kaids* also were charged with the administration of the sub-districts outside the city, and of the various tribal areas.

Moslem law, which extended over a wide field of civil and social rights and contracts, was executed, as to-day, by the Qadi, or religious magistrate, who was assisted on points of religious interpretation by the Mufti. The Bashaw himself, as the mood took him, would dispense justice; in this case he was assisted by either the Qadi or the Great Kehya.

As a further measure of control, two *shawishes*, with the names of dragomen, were attached from the castle guard to each consulate. They served a dual purpose. They accompanied the Consul or his family as they went about the city (if the Consul went beyond the gates, the guard was increased to three). They also acted as the Great Kehya's informants on all that went on in the consulate. Thus the Great Kehya kept a finger on all the consular activities. No Consul could refuse these unwanted guests. To do so would be to relieve the Bashaw of responsibility for the safety of the consular entourage; indeed it would be easy for the Bashaw, in this semi-lawless country where the Christian was a hated and despised interloper, to arrange an incident which would quickly bring the Consul to a condition of complaisance. Miss Tully gives a graphic account of what could happen to a Consul, even with a guard, when he was careless or unlucky.

Such was the city, and such, in brief, its administration. In 1788, the fortieth year of the reign of Ali Karamanli, grandson of the founder of the dynasty, its condition, after years of neglect, was ruinous. Indeed the fortunes of the Regency as a whole had never been lower. The Bashaw, aged, vaccilating, and vicious, had relinquished much of his authority, and seemed to live only for drink and women. He rarely left the castle, or appeared in the city, and passed his days in what the Arabs call a condition of *keyf*, while the mother of his three sons, Lilla Kebierra, strove to keep the peace between them, and a Jewess, known locally as " Queen Esther," and numerous concubines, absorbed his affections and consumed his substance.

" He rules," wrote the contemporary French Consul, Vallière, " but is not obeyed. . . . Master of large estates which yield him nothing, he lives in extreme want, which under a wise administration could easily be converted into abundance. Shut up in his harem, where he indulges his passions with his negresses, and his lust for drink from his private distillery, he builds nothing, repairs nothing, lets all collapse. . . ."

The country had been further impoverished by a severe and protracted struggle between Ali Karamanli and a pretender to the throne, who had been supported by the Bey of Tunis. The constant skirmishing on the Tunisian frontier, the repeated alarms, the stream of money which had to be paid out to wavering tribesmen to keep them loyal, had all contributed to the virtual economic collapse of the Regency. The pirate fleet lay idle and the Bashaw's treasure chest was virtually empty.

Meanwhile the Bashaw's three sons—Hassan, the Bey, Ahmed (Hamet), and Yusef—were engaged in that intermittent struggle for the reins of power which forms the theme of much of Miss Tully's story. Hassan, the oldest, emerges as perhaps the best character of the three. In the short life which lay before him he showed himself as capable, energetic, and, by the standards of those days, an honest ruler and administrator. He realized that the economic future of the Regency, then at its lowest ebb, depended to a large degree on the state of security in the tribal areas. So long as the caravan routes were threatened by raiding and the cultivated areas of the Regency deserted because of insecurity, there would be little hope of improving either the marginal food supplies of the Regency or the export trade. Much of his effort, as commander of the troops, was spent in trying to pacify the restless Arab tribes of the interior. He had improved relations with the Bey of Tunis and, with his assistance, succeeded in quelling the tribes on the Tunisian frontier ; and there is little doubt that he might have succeeded elsewhere if he could have given himself wholeheartedly to the task. But he was hampered by the constant political intrigues against him of his younger brothers.

These, according to custom, had been appointed governors of Zuara and Misurata towns. But they were rarely at their posts, and spent much of their time, surrounded by large and dissolute bands of retainers of Moorish and negro blood, squabbling with each other and their father, committing depredations on the country peasants, or intriguing in the castle against their elder brother.

To leave them thus meant to expose his father's weak, distrustful, and treacherous nature to intrigues which might get out of hand. Hassan, therefore, had to leave the pacification of the country in order, vainly as will be seen, to rescue his inheritance for himself. The resultant failure in security led directly to a fall in foodstuff stocks and later famine.

Of the younger brothers, Ahmed, the elder, later himself to fall a victim of his younger brother's intrigues, seems to have inherited from his father a character of weakness and complaisance, very suitable to his younger brother's purpose, which was to divide his elder brothers from each other and from his father, and remove them one by one from his path.

Yusef Karamanli is an interesting character ; ambitious, remorse-less, and cunning. From an early age he must have determined to succeed his father as Bashaw, and Miss Tully's letters ably describe how he set out to do this by intrigue and murder. Eventually he succeeded and ruled the Regency for over forty years with skill and vigour. He had many of the qualities of the successful Arab rulers of the past ; overweening ambition, swift ruthless decisions, great charm of personality and powers of persuasion—"beautiful, rash youth"—his eldest brother called him ; faculty for attracting and keeping the affections of the common people ; cunning—he had great powers of dissimulation, and would stoop to any trick (see how he moved about the castle sometimes disguised as a woman) to gain his ends. He is both the evil genius and the hero of this story.

Chief factor in his favour was his father's maudlin devotion to him, which was in contrast to Ali Karamanli's indifference and even dislike to his eldest son. Time and again in this book it will be seen how Yusef, outraging the rules of duty and loyalty both to his father and eldest brother is forgiven and indulged. The climax is reached when, in circumstances of the utmost treachery and cruelty, he murdered the Bey in front of their mother—an episode still related with horror by the Tripoli Arabs—and was forgiven by his father. Miss Tully's description of the circumstances and scene of this murder are obviously taken from first-hand observation ; the spot where the murder took place can be readily recognised from Miss Tully's account ; and is still shown to visitors to the castle.

And so, when these letters open, the stage is set for the "sombre melodrames" which follow. The weak Ali Karamanli, torn by suspicion, intrigue, love, fearing perhaps for his own life ; the Bey, majestic, affable, calm, cheerful," as Miss Tully sees him, spinning out his short span of life, in part ignorance of the forces moving against him ; and the tigerish Yusef plotting revolution, fratricide, and prepared to stoop to any barbarity to attain his ends. These are passions, and these are scenes which must have repeated themselves endlessly in the annals of oriental despotism ; but surely it is rare to have them described so freshly and so graphically by a cool and inquisitive foreign observer.

§

Apart from the struggle for power between the Karamanlis which forms the *leitmotiv* to the book, there are three other events which more or less dominate the narrative. These are the famine of 1784, the appalling wave of plague in 1785, and the occupation of Tripoli in 1793 by the Georgian adventurer, Ali Bourghol.

The first disaster was the direct precursor of the second; and both resulted, as has been seen, from the ruinous condition of the country's economy. Failure of the wheat and barley crops from lack of rain is a regular cyclic feature in Libya; and stocks of grain have from time immemorial been built up to tide over the bad years. But insecurity and the flight of peasants from the cultivated areas had left the grain depots in a state not capable of carrying the population over a whole year of grain shortage. A similar condition occurred in Tripoli in 1948 when the writer witnessed the results of a famine which was brought on by the shortsighted policy of the British administration. Scenes which Miss Tully describes were repeated in all their piteousness. The tragic march of hungry Arab families from the outer areas to the city was accompanied by a tale of deaths, the exact number of which will never be known. But several hundreds perished; and the scenes at the *meljaa*, or refugee camp, erected by the exertions of the Tripoli Arabs themselves, were indeed distressing.

So must have been the famine of 1784, from which even the city could provide no relief. The resulting debilitation of the population made it an easy prey to the wave of plague which succeeded the famine in the following year.

It is here that Miss Tully's pen is at its most harrowing. The corpses in the streets, the smell of corruption everywhere, the consulates shut up from the world for long months while the dead and dying lay around their walls. The Jews burying their dead inside their own houses. Out of the population in the city, some 10,000 are known to have died, including half the Jewish population and nine-tenths of the Christians. The two sons of the unhappy Bey died, together with all but one of the Bashaw's senior ministers. In the Menschia outside 25,000 Arabs were buried while the plague raged.

The next tragedy to strike the Regency was the murder of the Bey in 1790 by Yusef Karamanli and the subsequent civil war which broke out between the Yusef and his father and brother. The resultant anarchy, in which Yusef aided by tribesmen and supported by his Cologhli adherents blockaded Tripoli, cut off food supplies, and further precipitated the economic collapse of the Regency, led directly to a move from the Sultan in Turkey, which was to plunge the unhappy country into an even more disastrous episode.

A Georgian adventurer from Algiers had fled to Constantinople after a quarrel with the Dey, and, seeking for further fields to conquer, had told the Sultan of the unhappy condition of the Regency of Tripoli. Since no tribute had been received from Tripoli for several years, the Sultan was willing, unofficially, to lend his aid in sending this Georgian, Ali Bourghol, to Tripoli to depose the reigning Karamanli and occupy the throne in the name of the Sultan until a proper Dey could be appointed.

Ali Bourghol, with a small fleet mostly manned with renegade adventurers and Turkish irregulars, arrived off Tripoli in 1793 to find the struggle between Yusef Karamanli and his father at its height. With the Bashaw's forces divided, his resources slender, and his general purpose infirm, it was easy to land, occupy the castle, depose the Bashaw, and take the throne on the Sultan's mandate. The Bashaw was exiled ; Yusef fled to Tunis, and Ali Bourghol began a short reign of rapine and robbery which is described with horror by all contemporary accounts. The plunder taken, the executions carried out, and the cruelty and extortion practised by the invader made anything done by the Karamanli regime seem mild by comparison.

It is at this point that Miss Tully's narrative ends. The British Consul and his family embarked, their departure probably being hastened by Ali Bourghol's refusal to see any foreign representatives unless they approached him in audience chamber barefooted and without their swords. The consular corps refused ; the Dutch Consul fled, and the Tullys, whose departure was already in hand, hastened it ; and left Tripoli no doubt with relief. Ali Bourghol was later driven out by a rising of the populace aided by Yusef Karamanli and Tunisian soldiers. His meteoric rise, however, did not end here ; some of his plunder found its way to Constantinople, and the Sultan, pleased, appointed him as governor of Egypt. His career of cruelty and extortion was terminated, however, shortly afterwards. He was murdered by the Mamelukes.

§

It was to the opening scenes of this Karamanli drama that Miss Tully arrived in 1783, when Richard Tully, the Consul, with his family returned to the Regency. According to the records, he had been Consul since 1772 and was now returning for a second tour of duty which was to last for ten years. Tully himself emerges but little from the narrative, and there is very little information available about him;[1] indeed Miss Tully is not concerned to delineate any of the members of her family. Her eye is outside it, and her pen, ever poised to record events in the city, was laid down perhaps when she turned to consider the familiar faces about her. It may be, of course, that the unknown editor who produced her letters himself removed the domestic passages ; at any rate they have not come down to us.

Her narrative consists of a series of letters written from Tripoli to an unknown correspondent between the years 1783 and 1793. She clearly arrived with this task in mind ; and set herself not only to describe political events in the Regency as they transpired, but to touch in a background of history, habits, and customs such as she felt necessary to instruct and edify her correspondent.

She was admirably placed to collect her information. The consulate, as has been seen, was naturally a centre for visitors of all types ; it was the Consul's duty to keep himself *au courant* with all that passed in the city ; and what was easier for a woman with unlimited time at her disposal and few distractions than listening to and noting the gossip and anecdotes of Arab women friends and servants ? In the East all gossip finds its way, as if by a force of gravity, to the *harem* ; and the *harem* has played a far more important part in the Moslem world than can ever be known. The harems of Tripoli were open to Miss Tully ; and she must have been indefatigable in her search for information. She seems too to have had the useful gift of making her informants talk. The accounts she gives of the various castle episodes never seem the disjointed, exaggerated accounts of hearsay and surmise ; they always seem clear and connected narratives of events, carefully retailed at first hand and as carefully set down on paper.

" I believe," she wrote on arrival, sitting in her shuttered, stifling room in the consulate, while the hot sandstorms of June raged about outside in the close, stinking city, " that I shall be able, during my stay here, to present to you a series of events not unworthy of your perusal. . . . I purpose simply to relate facts as they occur, without the least embellishment. . . ."

And so she does. Cool, dispassionate, with a sharp eye for detail and an ear for a story, she writes her letters without art and with true simplicity, exactly as they occurred. This is the reason for her value to subsequent historians. But it is not only for the historian that her book holds an unfailing interest. It has a distinct value to the student

[1] Except that he was sadly underpaid and heavily in debt.

of Islam. Her account of the life of the Moslem women in the city, and particularly the *harem* of the Bashaw, dreaming away their years in the shuttered depths of the castle, a prey to intrigue, love, and hate —all the hothouse emotions of life in a narrow world of stifled passion and long leaden hours of boredom—is of great interest. As a woman she had constant and easy access to a world that not even the hardiest and most assiduous of male travellers could have penetrated. Far easier, indeed, for a man to attain were the jungles of Equatoria than the narrow courtyard, barred from the sky by huge iron lattices, in which Lilli Halluma, " Queen Esther," the sinister Mezeltobe, and the countless women, relatives, and concubines of the Bashaw lived. Even so Miss Tully could have learned little if she had not the good fortune to be accompanied by her nieces, who had both spoken Arabic from their birth, and were well known since childhood to the royal family.

Life cannot have been easy for her during those ten years. The eye of imagination sees her stepping out into those turbulent, filthy lanes of the city with her dragoman, her parasol, her cool, alert eye. Clouds of dust rise under the blazing sun, and a myriad flies attack her, rising from the offal and ordure in the streets through which she picks her careful way to the castle. A fleeing slave ; a mad marabout foaming at her across the street ; a sudden brawl, a tribesman's head stuck on a street pole ; a Jew nailed in agony to a synagogue door—past all these she must often have made her way, observant, curious, yet unmoved. Perhaps she soon became inured to shocks and boredom. " Since our long quarantine," she writes, " having been close prisoners for thirteen months, from the beginning of June 1785 to the end of July 1785, we have availed ourselves of every opportunity to enjoy our liberty." She can write this with equanimity ; but what a picture it conjures up. The small consular house, surrounded by disease and sudden death ; the lack of hygiene, lack of water, difficulties in obtaining food ; thirteen months cut off from the outer world.

They were harder than us, these eighteenth-century forebears of ours ; and not so nice in matters of hygiene and cleanliness. But even for them life must have been hard. Miss Tully, apparently uncomplainingly, was to spend ten years of her life in a town of some 25,000 illiterate, fanatical, and primitive Arabs, whose language she knew not (her small inaccurate vocabulary of Arab phrases at the end of the book is mostly phonetic versions of what she must have heard from the servants) : surrounded by disease, dirt, lack of water, constant insecurity, daily seeing or hearing of deeds of violence and cruelty, sometimes at the very doors of her house, inured to the tragic spectacle of the suffering of her enslaved fellow-Christians ; without variety in companionship (there cannot have been more than a dozen European women in the city)—lack of news, boredom. All these must have been hers. Yet she always seems unruffled.

This book indeed raises one's curiosity about its author. What became of her after she sailed from Tripoli on that memorable day in August 1793 ? Who discovered her letters : they were not published until twenty-three years after the events described in them ? To whom were they originally addressed ? Who edited them ? Where are the originals ? All this one would like to know. Once published her book was a rapid success, and in the first three years went into as many editions. It was translated into French in 1819 and again in 1912. I believe there is also a Dutch edition. The letters are a source for every subsequent authority on the period ; and are extensively used by Feraud and Micacchi.

We shall probably never know much more of her. Yet self-effacing though she is, she must always loom in our imaginations as we turn her pages. But her story awaits, and as we open the first pages let us think of her in that month of June 1783, sitting at her table in the old consulate in the Zenghet el Yehud, writing her first letter to England. June is a bad season in Libya. At intervals in the month the southern sky glows with a lurid yellow light ; the people of the city hurry where possible within doors and hasten to fasten windows and shutters. And then, with a swirl, a scalding wind, carrying a fine yellow dust from the desert is upon one ; burning the skin, irritating the eyes, parching vegetation so that it seems to dry and crackle before the eyes ; drying up the watercourses, withering all it touches, forcing its way through every crack and crevice in the buildings, covering everything with a fine, yellow powdery dust. The old consular house must have been insufferable on those days. Indifferent to it all, she takes up her pen. Her mind is far away on her correspondent in England. The curtain goes up ; the Karamanli drama begins.

SETON DEARDEN.

Baghdad, 1956.

NOTE

THE text followed here is that of the First Edition, published in 1816. The Preface, in particular, was altered in later editions, and by no means improved. The author, described as "sister of late Richard Tully Esq," is, in later editions, designated as "sister-in-law." I have referred to her throughout as "Miss Tully" for convenience.

The editor of the first edition burdened his pages with long, often inaccurate and frequently inapposite footnotes, usually geographical or historical. These have been removed. Miss Tully's own notes are retained and are indicated by the letter T.

The author's original spelling of names, Arabic words, etc., has been retained. Correct versions of them can be found either in the Introduction or the footnotes. The Appendix, which would otherwise lose its charm, has been untouched.

PREFACE

TO

THE FIRST EDITION

THE authenticity of the following letters cannot be questioned. They were written by the sister of the late RICHARD TULLY, Esq., his Brittanic Majesty's Consul at the Court of Tripoli, between whose family and that of the Bashaw, it will be seen that the closest intimacy subsisted for many years.

Notwithstanding the length of time which has elapsed since the events occurred that are here narrated, yet as, in the parts of Africa to which they refer, the natives neither admit nor even know of innovations, their manners remaining from age to age invariably the same, this circumstance cannot affect what is related or described.

The volume will be found an object of particular curiosity, from the lively and artless manner in which it lays open the interior of the Court of the Bashaw of Tripoli. It contains, we believe, the only exact account which has ever been made publicly known of the private manners and conduct of this African Despot, and details such scenes and events, such sketches of human weakness and vice, the effects of ambition, avarice, envy, and intrigue, as will scarcely appear credible in the estimation of an European.

It has also been the object of the author to present a faithful picture of the manners, ideas, and sentiments, of the Moors in general—a task that could not possibly have been effected, except under peculiar circumstances, from the almost utter impracticability of any Christian, male or female, being introduced into the interior circle of Moorish families of distinction, and still much less that of the Bashaw.

As a proof of the close intimacy that subsisted between the family of the Author and that of Ali Coromali, the late Bashaw, it may be mentioned that the Consul, finding it necessary to repair to England with his lady for a short time, the Bashaw and Lilla Halluma (called by her subjects Lilla Kebbierra, or Queen of Tripoli) entreated them to leave their two children under their protection till they should return, assuring them that nothing the country could produce, should be spared to render them happy. Lilla Halluma offered to consider them as *bint el bled* (daughters of the country), and guard them as her own children ; adding, that she would promise in the most solemn manner "by the Prophet," that neither their religion nor manners, should be in the slightest degree interfered with, while their parents were absent.

It may be supposed that, friendly and condescending as this offer was, it could not be accepted with propriety, considering the opposite tenets and manners of the parties ; but the offer clearly proves the confidential intimacy and habitual intercourse that subsisted between the families, and which consequently gave rise to such frequent interviews as left not the slightest events unknown to the author of the journal.

The Consul's daughters also being both born in Tripoli and speaking the Arabic language from infancy, were easily and even eagerly admitted into close habits of intimacy with all the female part of the Royal Family, by which means they frequently promoted reconciliations between the Moors and the English residents, and created such an attachment on the part of the Bashaw towards our nation, as induced the natives to regard the latter at that time with peculiar marks of attention and respect. Many incidents will present themselves, in the course of the following sheets, to confirm the truth of this statement.

These particulars will sufficiently account for the detailed manner in which are related not only the anecdotes of the castle, but those of many persons of distinction, with a narrative of the late intestine commotions originating in the conduct of the present Bashaw, and which will be found to exhibit many singular customs and incidents attendant on a Moorish war.

The state of Tripoli, from the moment the journal closed to the present time, owing to the change in its government, the ferocity of Useph Bashaw its present sovereign, and the severity of the laws imposed by him, preclude the possibility of similar minute accounts being again collected, at least till some very distant period, and then chance must bring together coinciding circumstances, equally as strong as those here mentioned, to afford the necessary means of information.

But considering the natural jealousy of the African character, and the inveterate prejudices which peculiarly characterize the Moors, it is hardly within the bounds of human probability that any traveller through the country, or even a resident clothed with a diplomatic authority, will be admitted to that social and familiar state of observation which was possessed by the author of these letters. At this time, therefore, when the attention, not only of the British public, but of the great part of the civilized world, is turned with eager curiosity towards the coast of Barbary, in the expectation of seeing there a nearer approximation to the enlightened principles of other nations, with regard to the personal rights and liberties of mankind ; at this eventful and teeming period, which has already yielded so many triumphs to justice, and which indicates still more extensive and permanent blessings to follow over all the earth ; an accurate, and, as it were, domestic picture of that country in general, or of any of its sovereignties in particular, cannot fail to fix the consideration of every one who has the exalted interests of humanity near to his heart.

Under existing circumstances, therefore, in the relative situations of Europe and Africa, these letters will prove no less important to the political inquirer than amusing to the public at large ; laying open much that will materially assist the comprehensive views of the statesman, blended with all the rich entertainment that so greatly distinguished the correspondence of Lady Mary Wortley Montague.

LONDON,

July 1, 1816.

ROYAL FAMILY OF TRIPOLI

ALI COROMALI . . .	The late Bashaw.
HASSAN BEY	The eldest Son.
SIDY HAMET	The second Son.
SIDY USEPH	The third Son and present Bashaw.
LILLA HALLUMA . . .	Wife of Ali Coromali.
LILLA HOWISHA . . .	Wife of Hassan Bey.
LILLA UDUCIA . . .	Eldest Daughter of the late Bashaw Ali Coromali.
LILLA FATIMA	Second Daughter.
LILLA AISHA	Third Daughter.
LILLA ZENOBIA . . .	Daughter of Hassan Bey and Grand-daughter of Ali Coromali.

LETTERS

WRITTEN DURING A

RESIDENCE AT TRIPOLI

July 3, 1783

I AM induced to believe that I shall be able, during my stay here, to present to you a series of events not unworthy your perusal. I am the more confirmed in this belief from the peculiar facilities afforded me by a constant intercourse with the Bashaw and his family. I purpose simply to relate facts as they occur, without the least embellishment, as that, I conceive, would not increase the interest which they may probably inspire.

Previous to entering the Bay of Tripoli, a few miles from the land, the country is rendered picturesque by various tints of beautiful verdure : no object whatever seems to interrupt the evenness of the soil, which is of a light colour, almost white, and interspersed with long avenues of trees ; for such is the appearance of the numerous palms planted in regular rows, and kept in the finest order. Their immense branches, coarse when near, are neat and distinct at a distance. The land laying low and very level, the naked stems of these trees are scarcely seen, and the plantations of dates seem to extend for many miles in luxuriant woods and groves. On a nearer view, they present a more straggling appearance, and afford neither shelter nor shade from the burning atmosphere which everywhere surrounds them. The whole of the town appears in a semicircle, some time before reaching the harbour's mouth. The extreme whiteness of square flat buildings covered with lime, which in this climate encounters the sun's fiercest rays, is very striking. The baths form clusters of cupolas very large, to the number of eight or ten crowded together in different parts of the town. The mosques have in general a small plantation of Indian figs and date-trees growing close to them, which, at a distance, appearing to be so many rich gardens in different parts of the town, give the whole city, in the eyes of an European, an aspect truly novel and pleasing. On entering the harbour, the town begins to discover dilapidations from the destructive hand of time, large hills of rubbish appearing in various parts of it. The castle, or royal palace, where the Bashaw resides, is at the east end of the town, within the walls, with a dock-yard adjoining, where the Bey (the Bashaw's eldest son, and heir to the throne) builds his cruisers. This castle is very ancient,[1] and is enclosed by a strong high wall which appears impregnable ; but it has lost all symmetry on the inside, from the innumerable additions made to contain the different branches of the royal family ; for there is scarcely an instance of any of the blood royal, as far as the Bashaw's great grandchildren, living without the castle walls. These buildings have increased it by degrees to a little irregular town.

The arrival of Christians in the harbour occasions a great number of people to assemble at the mole-end and along the sea-shore, the natural consequence of an African's curiosity, who, never having been out of his own country, finds as much amusement at the first sight of an European, as his own uncouth appearance affords to the newly arrived stranger. It consequently, after our arrival here, was not easy for us, during some minutes, to draw off our attention from the extraordinary group we perceived. It was noon when we disembarked, an hour when, on account of the extreme heat at this season, no Moor of distinction leaves his house ; but a number of the Bashaw's chief officers, some of them from the Bashaw, and some on their own account, came to welcome Mr. Tully on his return to Tripoli. This being the first time we had seen assembled together so many persons, splendidly arrayed in the fashion of the east, their appearance was rendered more striking. Their long flowing robes of satin, velvet, and costly furs, were exhibited amidst a crowd of miserable beings, whose only covering was a piece of dark brown homespun cotton, or a lighter web, resembling a dirty blanket, but which (by a wretched contrast) heightened the lustre of those who passed among them towards us. Of these brilliant figures I shall only describe three, who spent nearly the whole of the day with us ; these were Mustapha Scriven (the prime minister), and two ambassadors, Hamet Coggia [2] and Hadgi Abderrahman. The two latter have been at most of the courts of Europe ; their address is easy and polite, and they are perfectly well-bred and well-informed. Hamet Coggia is by far the more enlightened of the two, differing from a Christian in little more than his habit. Though an old man, he is still very handsome, and has a very

---

[1] Guidi, the Italian historian, states that although built on Roman and Byzantine foundations, the castle was completely rebuilt during the Spanish occupation in the sixteenth century.   [2] Ahmed Khoja.

fine figure. He speaks English perfectly well ; visits much at the Christian houses ; is easy in his manners ; and at dinner gives English toasts and sentiments, and seems quite at home. Each of these persons had several attendants, consisting of Moorish officers and servants, as well as black slaves. The dresses of the latter and their rattling arms, were equally striking from their noise and brilliancy ; for when these attendants were summoned near, little more could be heard than the din of the arms, with their long pendant silver chains.

The first minister had on a short jellick,[1] or jacket, of crimson satin, embroidered with gold down the front, made like a waistcoat sewed up before and behind, and put on by introducing the head through an opening at the neck. Over this, he had a short caftan of purple velvet, open before, and with sleeves down to the wrists, slashed so as to turn up and shew a different coloured stuff embroidered with silver : down the slash was sewed small gold-thread buttons close together, each button finished at top with a coral bead ; and the same kind of buttons were also on each side of the front, which was of gold and silver thread about four inches wide. A thick girdle, made of gold and silver, fastened these two dresses at the waist. Over these, he had on another caftan made full, and long enough to reach the ground, of pale yellow damask, with light green satin cuffs richly embroidered round the edge with gold and silver, slashed and turned up ; and over all, he wore a transparent white woollen bernuse, a sort of wrapping cloak immensely wide with a number of white tassels. He had this over the right shoulder and brought under the left arm : it hung gracefully over the dress and swept the ground as he walked along. This part of his habit had a beautiful effect, being as thin as gauze, and displaying clearly all the colours under it. He had on a very large white turban of the finest muslin, with a green shawl passed carelessly over it and brought round the neck. Yellow half boots, and over them slippers of the same colour (which are taken off on going into an apartment), and a pair of long white muslin trousers, reaching nearly to the ankle, completed his dress. People of less consequence wear trousers of white cotton, or of blue or brown coarse cloth, and less ample. Handsome ones are about seven yards wide. The size of the turban increases here according to the rank of the wearer. Two or three of the highest in the suite that followed these persons had turbans of a very moderate size compared to those of their chiefs. The others had red cloth caps, round which was

---

[1] *Kajalik* (Turkish). The correct Arabic name is *Sidrea*.

rolled two or three times a coloured shawl twisted, with one end brought round the neck, and the other flung over the left shoulder. These shawls are worn of the very finest texture by people of consequence, but only when they ride or hunt ; and then the young men wear them to cover nearly the left eyebrow, and so high on the right side as to discover the ear. A young Moor thinks himself quite irresistible with his shawl worn in this manner ; but it is sometimes fatal to the wearer, serving for the instrument of death, as it takes less time to tighten one end of it as it hangs round the victim's neck, than to strangle him with the fatal cord, sent to him from the Bashaw.

Hamet Coggia, who, the day before we arrived, was appointed ambassador to Morocco, had on a dress very different from the rest : instead of the number of coverings I have just described, a bernuse of the finest scarlet cloth, with gold lace at least six inches wide entirely round it, wrapped him completely up. These bernuses cost a considerable sum of money, and are a present from the Bashaw to each of his ambassadors at their departure on an embassy. From this description you will conceive that the Tripolitan dresses, almost covered with gold and silver, and with so much rich drapery over them, make a most superb appearance.

The city of Tripoli is, or rather has been, surrounded by a prodigiously strong wall, and towers, which are now in bad order ; but persons of judgment in these matters say, that with repairs only, it might soon be made one of the strongest fortifications. The sea washes this town on three sides ; and on the fourth a sandy plain, called the Messea,[1] joins it to the rest of the country. On the east it is divided from Egypt by the dreary deserts of Barca, where none reside except occasionally the wandering Arab.

Not far from this spot, it was, that idolators paid divine worship to their deity Jupiter Ammon,[2] under the figure of a ram ; and here stood the famous temple dedicated to his name, which few could approach, on account of the burning sands, which still divide the inhabitants, or islanders, of this sandy ocean from the rest of their species. Ages pass without a traveller attempting to cross these burning seas. This city is much less than either Algiers or Tunis, neither of which states have been Moorish kingdoms quite four hundred years. About the year 1400, three different bands of soldiers, under

1 *Menschia* (Arabic), which means usually an inhabited cultivated area.
2 The author is referring to the oasis of Siwa.

the protection of the Grand Signior,[1] settled at Tripoli, Tunis, and Algiers ; and from them these people sprung. This state soon became very flourishing, and continued so till the rigorous siege it sustained from the Spaniards, who attacked it, under the general Don Pedro de Navarra. Since that period, though harassed by the Spanish and the English, and latterly by the French, it has continued in the possession of the Turks and Moors, and governed by a Turkish bashaw. It was tributary to the Porte for a long series of years, until freed from this yoke : it afterwards remained entirely under a Moorish sovereign. The town is so uneven with accumulated rubbish, on which they often build without removing it, that the thresholds of some of the street doors are on a level with the terraces or tops of houses not far from them. The streets are narrow, but nearly double the width of those at Tunis and Algiers. There is only one kind of vehicle used here for conveyance, and that kept only by a few of the great Moors, for the females of their families. It is a sort of palanquin, entirely enclosed with linen, and placed on the back of a camel. The one belonging to the Bashaw is very richly and elegantly adorned, inside and out, and is merely for the purpose of conveying the ladies belonging to his own family to their country residences. None of the ladies belonging to the royal family ever walk in the streets, except when they go to their mosques, to fulfil a vow, or make an offering, which they frequently do on various occasions, but with the greatest circumspection. They go out as late as eleven or twelve o'clock at night, attended by a considerable guard from the castle. A number of black female slaves and Moorish servants form a large body, in the very centre of which the princess or princesses walk, with their own particular attendants or ladies encircling them. The guard continually announces them as they go, to give timely notice of their approach. They have with them a great number of lights, and a vast quantity of burning perfume, which is carried in silver fillagree vases, and also large silver ewers of rose and orange-flower water, to damp the burning perfume, which, during their walk, produces a thick cloud around them, composed of the finest aromatic odours. Either of these accompaniments, besides the vociferous cry of the guards, is fully sufficient to indicate the approach of the royal party, in time to leave the way clear for them ; and this is particularly necessary, as their law decrees no less a punishment than death for any person who may be in the streets and remain there while their ladies are passing by, or for any

---

[1] The Sultan of Turkey.

man who may look at them from a window. Of course, every place
is perfectly free from spectators before they come near to it.

Women of a middle station of life generally go out on foot, but
hardly ever without a female slave or attendant. They are then so
completely wrapped up, that it is impossible to discover more of
them than their height, not easily even their size. They have a covering called a baracan, which is about one yard and a half wide, and
four or five in length. This conceals them entirely, and they hold it
so close over their face, as scarcely to leave the least opening to see
their way through it.[1] The Jewesses wear this part of their dress
nearly in the same way ; but they hold it in such a manner as clearly
to discover one eye, which a Moorish woman dares not do if she
have a proper regard for public opinion, as her reputation would
certainly suffer by it.

Merchandize is usually carried on the backs of camels and mules ;
and the dust they raise, in these dry sandy streets, is intolerable. The
town stands on a foundation of rock. Here and there are a few remains of pavement, some of which are very ancient, and appear
evidently to be Roman. They do not excel here in shops, the best
of these being little better than booths, though their contents are
sometimes valuable, consisting of pearls, gold, gems, and precious
drugs. There are two covered bazars, or market-places ; one of
which is very large, and built in four aisles, meeting in a cross. These
aisles are fitted up with shops, built on each side of them, containing
every sort of merchandize, and having a way in the middle for purchasers to walk in. Several parts of this place are nearly dark, and
the powerful smell of musk makes it very unpleasant to pass
through it. The other bazar is much smaller, and has no shops in it.
Thither only black men and women are brought for sale ! The
very idea of a human being, brought and examined as cattle for sale,
is repugnant to a feeling heart ; yet this is one of their principal
traffics.[2]

In consequence of the ruinous state of this city, the Bashaw incurs
a great deal of displeasure from the Grand Signior, who rather than
see it in the hands of the Christians, will garrison it again with a Turkish
force. Heavy tributes used to be paid the Grand Signior from hence,
which for many years he has generously excused ; and if the Bashaw

---

[1] This costume is worn in Libya to-day.
[2] According to contemporary travellers, between three and four thousand black
slaves were brought yearly by the slave caravans to Tripoli.

were to keep the place in order, the Porte would leave him in quiet possession of it.

The exterior of the great mosque, where the deceased relations of the royal family are buried, is extremely handsome. It stands in the main street, near the gate of the city which leads to the country, and almost opposite to the palace. Before the door of this mosque there is a second entry of neat lattice wood-work, curiously carved, with two folding doors of the same work : a great number of beautifully coloured tiles, with which the bottom of the lattice work is set, gives it an appearance of delicate neatness very pleasing to the eye. Over the doors of all the mosques are long sentences from the Koran sculptured and painted ; those over the door of this mosque being more richly gilt and painted, and the sculpture much handsomer than in any others in the town. There is another mosque at no great distance, having a door of most curious workmanship, carved in wood by the Moors. We stopped to look at it, but could not enter the building, it being the time of divine service. The appearance of the Moors at prayer was as solemn as it was strange. They were at that part of the service which obliged them to prostrate themselves and salute the earth : the whole congregation was accordingly in this posture, absorbed in silent adoration. Nothing seemed capable of withdrawing their attention for a moment from the object they were engaged on. The eye was alternately directed from earth to heaven, and from heaven to earth again, uncaught by any objects around, unheeded even by each other. They seemed wholly enwrapped in the prayers they offered up in this humble manner from the ground. There are no seats in the mosque, no desks, nor hassocks, nor pews : the people stand promiscuously together, without distinction of rank or dress. The women are not permitted to attend public worship : they go to the mosques only at midnight.

The coffee bazar is where the Turks meet to hear and tell the news of the day, and to drink coffee : it is filled with coffee houses, or rather coffee kitchens, which within are very black with smoke, and in which nothing but coffee is dressed. No Moorish gentlemen enter these houses, but send their slaves to bring out coffee to them at the doors, where are marble couches, shaded with green arbours. These couches are furnished with the most rich and beautiful mats and carpets. Here are found, at certain hours of the day, all the principal Moors, seated cross-legged, with cups of coffee in their hands, made as strong as the essence itself. The coffee served to the ladies of the castle has sometimes in it a quantity of cinnamon, cloves, and nutmeg. The Moors, when at these coffee-houses, are waited on by their own black servants, who stand constantly by their masters, one with his pipe, another with his cup, and a third holding his handkerchief while he is talking, as his hands are absolutely necessary for his discourse, he marks with the forefinger of his right hand upon the palm of his left, as accurately as we do with a pen, the different parts of his speech, a comma, a quotation, or a striking passage. This renders their manner of conversing very singular ; and an European, who is not used to this part of their discourse, is altogether at a loss to understand what the speakers mean.[1]

One of the grandest arches of antiquity stands yet entire at the Marine. The old arch, as the Moors term it, was built so long ago as A.D. 164, by a Roman who had the control of the customs. He erected it in honour of, and during the joint reigns of Marcus Aurelius and Lucius Ælius Verus. Marcus Aurelius, on the death of Antoninus Pius, with whom Lucius Verus likewise reigned, took him also as his colleague in the empire, though Lucius Verus had proved so vile a character that Antoninus did not nominate him at his death. When, in 161, these two emperors began to reign, they changed their names, which accounts for the great number of initials in the inscriptions on the arch. When this arch was built, there were few habitations nearer this place than Labeda, the Leptis Magna [2] of the ancients, which is about three days' journey from Tripoli. Lucius Verus was at this time rioting in the woods of Daphne at Antioch, and committing all kinds of outrages throughout Africa ; and the Romans having strayed to the spot where Tripoli now stands, to hunt wild beasts, found under this arch a welcome retreat from the burning rays of the sun at noon-day. It is thought by all good judges to be handsomer than any of the most celebrated in Italy, as the temple of Janus, though built of marble, and esteemed one of the finest of these edifices, has only a plain roof. This arch is very high, but does not appear so, being from the great accumulation of sands carried thither by the winds, exactly as deep beneath the surface of the earth as it is high above it. It is composed of stones so extremely large, that it seems wonderful how they were conveyed hither, considering there are neither stone nor stone quarries in this country ; and it is no less

---

[1] A singularly accurate observation. Bedouins to-day often use these gestures.

[2] Leptis, now completely excavated, stands near the town of Homs, about eighty miles east of Tripoli.

extraordinary in such a country as this, how they could be raised to form this immense arch. No cement has been used to fasten them together, yet so solid are they that the hand of time, in its continual ravages around it, has left this monument of antiquity uninjured. The ceiling is of the most beautiful sculpture, a small part of which only remains in view, as the Moors, blind to its beauties, have for some time filled it up with rubbish and mortar, to form shops in the interior of the arch. On the outside are enormous groups of whole-length figures of men and women, which those who are versed in antiquity can easily explain ; but they are too much worn away by time for others to understand them. So little inclination is there to search for antiquities, that those which remain are in general undis-turbed. Europeans are often tempted to bring these antiquities to light : and they might doubtless make great and useful discoveries ; but the Moors and jealous Turks will not permit them to disturb a stone, or move a grain of sand on such an account ; and repeated messages have been sent from the castle on these occasions to warn Christians of their danger.

Without the walls of the town are frequently found pieces of tesselated pavement, known to have been laid down two thousand years ago. At Labeda very considerable remains of Roman buildings are still standing nearly buried in the sands. So grand were the Roman edifices, that from Labeda, seven granite pillars of an immense size were for their beauty transported to France, and used in ornament-ing one of the palaces built for Louis XIV. At Zavia, which is but a few hours' ride from hence, an amphitheatre, built by the Romans, is still standing entire, with five degrees of steps : its interior is one hundred and forty-eight feet in diameter.[1]

When we reflect, that on the northern extremity of Africa, the Grecians founded Cyrene and settled other colonies, while the Phœnicians built the city of Carthage, afterwards conquered by the Romans, with all the kingdoms of Numidia, and that this is the same spot on which Tripoli, Algiers, and Tunis now stand, it is no wonder that Roman vestiges are yet to be found here, notwithstanding the neglect and destruction of the Arab, who is careless of the preservation of works of art. Tripoli was called by the ancients Tripolis, as being one of the three cities of Leptis, Œa, and Sabrata ; it is on the site of Œa, and was the birth-place of Apulius. I make no apology for reminding you of these historical facts, as by referring to them at

[1] This is the Roman city of Sabratha, about thirty miles west of Tripoli.

present, they contribute to interest you considerably more for the part of the world I write from. Most of the cities and towns in the kingdom of Tripoli exhibit many interesting remains which prove their antiquity. Bengazi, which is a very short distance from Tripoli, governed by a Bey, or viceroy, under the Bashaw, is the ancient city of Berenice, built by Ptolemy Philadelphus, 284 years before Christ. Near to Bengazi, at Derne, which is also governed by a Bey from Tripoli, in the village of Rasem, are considerable ruins of a tower and fortifications built by the Vandals. On the coast near Tripoli is the island of Jerbi, known to be the Meninx of the ancients. This island has been in the possession of the Bashaws of Tripoli from the time that the Moors, by burying nearly the whole of their own army and that of their enemy in the sea, drove from it the Dukes of Alva and Medina-Celi, in the fifteenth century. From the island of Jerbi they bring to Tripoli great quantities of fruit, of nearly the size of a bean, and of a bright yellow when fresh. This fruit is the produce of a tree which grows there, and is said by a French author to be the lotus of the ancients.[1]

The Moors call it the karroob, and with the seeds or stones of this fruit they weigh diamonds and pearls ; the value of the diamond is ascertained by the number of karroob stones. A considerable city in the neighbourhood of Tripoli, of the name of Bona, is built entirely with the ruins of Hippo Regius, and is little more than a mile distant from the place where that ancient city stood. The desert adjoining Tripoli, and leading towards Egypt, still bears the name of Barca, given it by the Romans on account of the fierceness of its inhabitants at that time. The couriers from Tripoli cross these deserts in their way to Grand Cairo, mounted on dromedaries, which the Moors esteem much swifter than a horse. The couriers are obliged to be fastened on with cords, to prevent their being thrown off by the fleetness of the animal ; and owing to the extreme difficulty of passing these dreary regions, the couriers can seldom quit their caravans, and are generally from twenty-five to thirty days on the way from Tripoli to Cairo.

On this part of the desert, towards Egypt, are islands of inhabitants environed by oceans of sand, which completely separate them from each other and from the rest of the world. None attempt to approach their habitations through the burning regions which surround them.

---

1 The carob tree : a leguminous evergreen. Bedouins eat the seeds, which are also reputed to be the " locusts " eaten by St. John the Baptist.

Among these islands, called by the ancient geographers, Oases, was that of Ammonica, where lived the worshippers of Jupiter Ammon.[1] But as the credit of that deity decreased, the road to Ammonica was insensibly lost, and it is not known whether such a nation now exists. Only a few islands in this part of the desert are known to the caravans, where they stop in case of extreme necessity for refreshment and repose, after the hardships of a journey more dreadful than can be conceived, and which would not often be completed, but by the help of the compass and a knowledge of astronomy. The vast and sudden shifting of the sands, levelling mountains in one spot and raising them in another, so completely varies the aspect of the way, that the traveller, bewildered, knows not where he is except by such aid. Other islands are also here, where the inhabitants will probably be insulated from the rest of the world to the end of time. Close to these deserts is Pentapolis, a country of the Cyrenaica, where stood the five cities of Appollonia, Cyrene, Arsinoë, Ptolemais, and Berenice. This part of Barbary, once called, from its great fertility, the granary of the Romans, is recently much fallen off. The failure of its produce is attributed to the want of rains, which were formerly much more copious and frequent in this country, than they have been of late years.[2] The steep mountains of Gouriana [3] are the only ones seen on a clear day from the city of Tripoli, and seem to be a long ridge of high black hills. These, and the sands, are inhabited by numerous tribes of Arabs, among which are those of the Tahownees, Acas, Benoleeds, Nowalles, Wargammas, and others. These Arabs form three classes ; the first, those who come from Arabia, the second the Arabs of Africa, and the third, the wandering Bedouins. The first two are equally warlike, handsome in their persons, generous in their temper, honourable in their dealings, grand and ambitious in all their proceedings when in power, and abstemious in their food. They possess great genius, and enjoy a settled chearfulness, not in the least bordering on buffoonery. Each of these tribes are governed by a chief, whose title is Sheik, by whose laws all those under him are directed, judged, and punished. Each family has a chief of its own kindred, whose authority in the same manner extends to life and death. Their trade is war. They serve as auxiliary troops to whoever pays

---

[1] The oasis of Siwa.
[2] The collapse of the extensive system of water conservation built by the Romans is the real cause.
[3] The correct name is the Jebel Nefusa. Gharian is the principal town.

them best : most of them are at present considered as being in the interest of the Bashaw of Tripoli. The Bedouins are hordes of petty wandering merchants, trading with what they carry from place to place. They manufacture a dark cloth for baracans, and thick webs of goats' hair, used to cover tents, which they sell to the Moors.

These Bedouins,[1] in the spring of the year, approach Tripoli from the Pianura,[2] adjoining the town. Here they sow their corn, wait till they can reap it, and then disappear till the year following. During the stay of these people in the Pianura, the women weave, and sell their work to the Tripolitans. They pitch their tents under the walls of the city, but cannot enter the town gate without leave ; and for any misdemeanour the Bedouins may commit, their chief is answerable to the Bashaw. Besides being divided into hordes, each family is governed by its own chief, in the same manner as those of the Arabs. Both the Arabs and Bedouins still retain many customs, described in sacred and profane history, and are in almost everything the same people as we find mentioned in the earliest accounts. I expect to see a great deal of them, and to write you more of their manners in future letters. The Sultans, or Kings of Fezzan and Borno, are both tributary to the Bashaw of Tripoli. The grandfather of the present King of Fezzan was, in 1714, brought prisoner to Tripoli, by Hamet [3] the Great, grandfather of the present Bashaw. The Moors of Fezzan and Borno are of a dark copper colour, almost black. They are many shades darker than the Tripolitans who inhabit the countries at a small distance from Tripoli ; for the Moors in the city and suburbs of Tripoli are, in general, white. To each of the cities belonging to the Bashaw he sends a viceroy with the title of Bey, and to the lesser districts a governor, who is denominated a Cyde. The disunion among the Moorish princes preventing the Bashaw from attending as rigidly as usual to those governments, the Cydes are suffered to neglect going out to their different cyderies till it is absolutely necessary for the Bashaw to receive his tributes, which are then, for want of time, taken by force from the people. Where the Cydes have remained at their posts, they have found the Moors loyal to the Bashaw, and have gathered the tributes easily ; while the Moors, who are harassed at other cyderies, have become troublesome and

---

[1] The author refers here to the semi-sedentary tribes. The true Bedouins in Libya are only goat and camel breeders.
[2] Pianura is the Italian for plain. This word frequently occurs. (T.)
[3] Ahmed.

dangerous to the state. Among these cyderies are those of the Messeah (including the villages of the Sucari and the Amrose), Tajura, Mezzurata, Messlata, Zavia, Zuarra, and others. Near the Messeah is a large district of land, under the jurisdiction, and in the possession of a priest. This district is called the Seide,[1] which was the name of its former priest, and means *lion*. It is a sanctuary which cannot be violated by the Bashaw himself. The life of a murderer within its walls is sacred. He may be starved out, by his friends being prevented from relieving him, but he cannot be taken thence by force.

🕮

July 29, 1783

The Moors' great fast of Ramadan is nearly finished : it has been dreadful to them on account of the violent heat at this time of the year. The batteries of the castle are fired at the beginning and termination of this fast, and the flags are hoisted on all the mosques and forts, the signal for which is one large cannon fired from the Bashaw's castle. This fast finished on the first appearance of the next new moon after it is begun, but does not exceed thirty days if the moon be not visible at that period. During the whole of this fast the true Mussulmans taste nothing from sun-rise till sun-set. A guard is appointed merely for the purpose of passing through every part of the city at dawn of day, which is the hour when the Moors announce their *adan*, or first prayers. This guard [2] warns the people in time, to make a hot meal before sun-rise, that they may be enabled to wait for food till sun-set. The people are summoned by a most uncouth noise made by this guard, who carries with him a tin vessel or box, with pieces of loose iron in it. These discordant sounds are substituted for those of bells, which are unknown here, not being allowed by the religion of the Moors. The *adan* (morning) is the time of the first five songs or prayers, which the Moors chant during the twenty-four hours, from the tops of their mosques, walking round on the outsides of them, with a flag of Mecca in their hands. The second prayer is exactly at noon-day. The third is at the middle hour between noon and sun-set, and is called here lezero.[3] The fourth is at sun-set,

---

[1] *Asad.*

[2] This *sahhar*, or wakener, is still a feature, though a dying one, of Moslem towns. He usually employs a drum and a door-knocker to awaken the laggard.

[3] *El asser.*

and the fifth at one hour and a half after sun-set, and is called the last marabut.[1]

These calls answer exactly to our bells and church clocks : it is the method by which the people are summoned to prayer, and of course announces the hour of the day. The good Mussulmans are so strict in their observance of this fast, that during a land wind, which happened three days ago, and which occasioned a confined burning heat that threatened suffocation, resembling what is felt from the mouth of the fiercest oven, no decent Moor was seen to break his fast, and lessen his anguish by tasting water, and there were several instances of their dropping down in the streets overcome with excessive thirst, in which cases the people present sprinkled water on their faces, but never attempted to wet their lips with it.[2] Those who can, sleep the greatest part of the day ; but the Bey and the rest of the Bashaw's sons divert themselves in riding out on the sands, almost every day during the Ramadan. After several hours' hard racing they retire to lazero, or afternoon prayer, to one of the Bashaw's palaces out of town, and undressing themselves bathe in a Gebbia [3] (a large reservoir of spring water in the garden, shaded with mulberry trees). This is all the refreshment they take in the most violent heats. They never fail to be in town by sun-set, the hour of breaking the fast. The gates of the consulary houses being always open at this hour, the Moors flock in five or six together, in order to drink the first moment they can. The servants, chiefly Moors, are ready in waiting, through religion and a fellow-feeling, to meet them half-way with a vessel of fresh water, and many who come are so exhausted as not to have voice left to ask for it, nor strength to stand to drink it : some have fainted in the skiffer,[4] or hall, before the servant could bring it to them.

The Jews have a fast of seven days and seven nights, which many pretend to have kept ; but as reason convinces us that nature is unequal to such a task, they are certainly mistaken themselves, or wish to mislead others. Several of them own candidly that they have attempted this long fast, but have not succeeded, which is most likely to be true with all of them. A very handsome Jewess, about sixteen years old, at present a servant in our house, endeavoured to sustain

---

[1] More correctly *el 'isha.*

[2] The hot wind called *ghibli*, since it blows from the south.

[3] *Jabia* : the water for which is drawn by a bucket, rope, and cradle worked by an animal.   [4] *Saqiffa*, or entrance, an Arabic word.

this fast unknown to us, as she knew we did not approve of a proceeding so opposite to common sense, which might probably cause her death. The girl grew extremely ill, but did not own, though often questioned, that she was keeping this fast. As she did not sleep in the house, we could not ascertain the truth ; till she was laid up at home about the fourth day, when nature unable to resist longer, she fell senseless on the floor. The inside of her mouth was covered with a very thick white skin, and her breath was shockingly offensive. Her friends immediately poured new milk and sweet oil down her throat ; and by the greatest precaution being taken in the quality and quantity of what she ate and drank for several days, she at last recovered, but for many weeks she was the exact colour of a lemon, though previously she had the finest complexion possible.

The Moors, after their long fast of thirty days, particularly in this extreme hot weather, watch with such anxiety and eagerness for the new moon which puts a period to it, that it is become a proverb in their language, when they ardently desire a thing, that they wish for it, as for the moon of Ramadan. The morning after this fast, the castle guns and those of all the batteries round the town announce the feast of Beiram, which lasts three days in town and seven in the country. All sorts of noise and rioting seem to make up for what they have suffered during the fast. Men go about dressed in all kinds of strange and awkward garbs, resembling nothing in heaven above or in the earth beneath. Though they call themselves by the names of lions, camels, etc. the greatest complaisance cannot lead you to make out the least similitude to any thing but a bundle of sticks and rags strangely packed up together. They go about dancing with reeds and other music. Swings are erected between two extremely high wheels in the streets, where the people swing for a small piece of money each. No fish can be procured during this feast, as the boats are all taken up in rowing the common people about the harbour. Though drinking wine is against the law of Mahomet, immense numbers of Moors get intoxicated with a liquor they call lakaby, which is extracted from the date tree, and which renders them very troublesome, as it literally throws them into a state of madness. In fact, during these three or four days it is dangerous for Christians to go into the streets. In the Consuls' houses, a table is set out in the courtyard and kept covered with fresh supplies of wine, oil, bread, and olives, during the three days of the feast, for as many hampers, couches, and black slaves belonging to the Bashaw, as chuse to partake of it, and the dragomen, or guards, call them in, in parties, according to their rank. During the feast, every night all the mosques are illuminated. The town not being otherwise lighted, but totally dark, shews to great advantage, the bright glare of several rows of lamps round the top of each high mosque. The coffee bazar, I before mentioned, is illuminated from one end to the other, during every night of the feast, till after one or two o'clock in the morning. We walked in it one evening during the Beiram, till after twelve o'clock ; it was, on each side, crowded with the first people in the place, most of them richly dressed. The perfumes of amber, orange flowers, and jessamine, were much too strong to be agreeable. From the immense quantity of lamps the whole place was as light as during the day. After they have broken the fast at sun-set the great Moors all assemble here for recreation, to talk of the news of the day, and to drink coffee.

It was one of these evenings, in this bazar, thirty years ago, and in the beginning of the present Bashaw's reign, that an odd accident happened, which in that hour determined the fate of Tripoli.[1] An Arnaut, who had been sent upon an expedition from the Grand Signior, with some small vessels, and between five and six hundred men on board of them under his command, put into the harbour of Tripoli for provisions, sometime before the fast of Ramadan. The government, though much more energetic than it is now, was still like the Moorish states, very weak. Many people were greatly discontented, and this man finding several of the chief officers displeased with the Bashaw, and ripe for rebellion, and having also observed that a part of the fortifications near the sea, for want of a few days' labour, rendered that part of the city easy of access, formed the extraordinary idea of attempting, with his handful of people, the capture of Tripoli by surprise ; and had not one of his emissaries committed the most grossly ignorant act that can be imagined, he would most probably have succeeded in this strange undertaking. He tampered with some of the great people, who tired of the reins of the Bashaw, or of the manner in which he held them, and instigated by the hope of gain from the spoils of the government, determined to favour his plan. Amongst these was the Sheik.[2] Without the concurrence of so capital a personage, it is not probable that the Arnaut would have undertaken this enterprise. Late one evening he landed the greatest part of his

---

[1] According to Feraud, the French historian, this event occurred in 1752, two years before the death of Mohammed Karamanli and the accession of Ali.

[2] *I.e. Sheikh el Beled.* See Introduction.

crew, under the walls of what the Moors call the Spanish castle, at the decayed part of the fortifications, and took possession of it. The guns on that side, which had lain neglected and out of use for years, exactly commanded the Bashaw's palace. These the Arnauts immediately set about putting in order. The port-holes since that time have been filled up and no guns placed on that side of the castle. This fort being left without a proper guard, the Arnauts found an easy admission. They got into it unobserved, and immediately proceeded to place in it a great quantity of ammunition from their ships, and about ten o'clock at night, during the Ramadan, when all the great Moors were assembled in the coffee bazar, the chief Arnaut sent one of his people with a message to his friend the Sheik, and ordered the man to take particular notice and bring word back, who of the great people were at the bazar. This man, probably intoxicated and not clearly understanding his master's project, when he got up to the Sheik, who was surrounded by everybody of consequence in the place, was struck by a most extravagant idea, and while he was delivering his message secretly pulled out a pistol and shot the Sheik dead at the instant. Such a violent step, of course, spread a general alarm. The man was dispatched in a moment by the hands of the people round him. The greatest part of the Arnauts were immediately cut to pieces ; the rest saved themselves by flying on board the ships in the greatest disorder. Their chief escaped, after several hours, to one of the Christian houses, where he remained concealed some days, and afterwards by the help of a disguise got into a vessel. Thus ended this ill-conducted conspiracy, the failure of which saved the Bashaw's throne for that time.

September 3, 1783

In all parts of Barbary, as at Constantinople, a guard of two dragomen are sent from the government to reside at the ministers' houses :[1] these guards accompany the family when they walk out. Here they are strengthened by an additional guard granted by the Bashaw, if the Christians wish to proceed to a distance from the city, as the Bashaw will not be answerable for the safety of the Christians on account of the Arabs, who are now particularly troublesome, owing to the scarcity of everything at this period, and the circumstance of enforcing the Bashaw's taxes on them. In Algiers, the Christian

---

[1] E.g. the consular houses.

families are obliged to let the dragoman dine at their own table. He is there a complete spy on all that passes, having it in his power to report what he pleases to the Dey, which is the cause of great disturbances and often endangers the lives of the Christians ; but in this part of Barbary the Christians are particularly well treated.[1]

In our walk this afternoon to the westward, we passed a great number of Bedouins from the deserts, I may say moveable villages of them. They are the first I have seen since my arrival, this being the season of the year when they approach to Tripoli to profit from the soil, it being too barren where they come from, to admit of the same cultivation it does here. Their tents are pitched very near the walls, in the green parts of the plain adjoining the town. They are divided into a prodigious number of tribes, and distinguished by the names of their chiefs. Each tribe forms a sort of village, and each family has a tent or portable hut of its own. They traffic with the people of Tripoli. Among the things they bring into town are woollen baracans, which they weave in their huts and grounds. Each Sheik, or chief, is answerable to the tribe of Arabs under him, and to the Bashaw of Tripoli, for the action of each individual. These Bedouins, like birds of passage, have no settled habitation. When the fine weather and corn fail them in one place they immediately forsake it, and travel on to a more fertile spot, carrying their families, houses, and cattle with them. A family of distinction amongst them will pitch four or five tents, so that nothing more striking can be imagined than the innumerable and differently shaped tents, now collected together on the Pianura, adjoining the town : they almost cover it. All the cattle of each family stand close by the tent, under a shade made of date leaves : they are placed in a row, and one thick spardate, or straw rope, passed along the bottom of their fore-legs, fastens all at once. The Bedouins sow wheat, barley, and other grain. They wait the growing and cutting it, and then depart for another part of the country.

The Bedouin men wear a thick dark brown baracan of wool, five or six yards long, and about two wide ; this serves them as their whole dress by day, and their bed and covering by night. They put it on by joining together the two upper corners with a wooden or iron bodkin, and these being first placed over the left shoulder, they

---

[1] This comparison between the treatment of Christians in Algiers and Tripoli is borne out by all contemporary sources. Ali Karamanli's treatment of Christian slaves was also comparatively benevolent.

afterwards fold the rest round their bodies, some of them putting it on rather gracefully. To those unaccustomed to wear it, it is not an easy matter to dress in it ; and a stranger is easily discovered by the folds of his baracan, so different from those made by the constant wearer of them. The women wear the same kind of baracan, which in general also serves them for their only covering : few of them wear a chemise with it. The baracan is a part of the Moorish dress ; but that for the ladies in Tripoli serves only as an upper garment. They wear them of silk and fine gauze in the house, and of the finest cotton and silk mixed, of a most beautiful white, to go out of doors, and over that a fine white woollen one. What an addition of drapery is here, which luxury has made indispensible for the Tripolitan female, while the Bedouin dresses herself completely with one out of four of these coverings. The Bedouin women wear the baracan extremely gracefully, much more so indeed than the Moorish women. They ornament their hair with bits of glass, tin, china beads, and coral. They plait the hair in a great number of very small tresses over the face, cutting it strait when plaited, just above the eyebrow : it has not, however, a bad effect, and makes some of them look handsome. Their skin is very dark, almost black : all of them have black eyes, amazingly white teeth, and in general handsome features. They have the barbarous custom of scarifying their faces, particularly their chins : they rub the wound with gunpowder immediately, which leaves ever after a black mark in the shape they have previously cut. Many of them prick with a needle very deep the figure they wish to print in the flesh ; a much longer and of course more painful operation : but the beauty of the ornaments they esteem a sufficient recompence for the dreadful torment they endure under it.

We went into one of the best looking tents, and had a great deal of conversation with the women in it. One of those we spoke to, had beads of different colours set in her face, particularly round her mouth and in the middle of her cheek. We found here women working hard at the loom. The chief manufacture among the Arabs is woollen baracans, and webs for their tents. This work is done by the women, who make no use of the shuttle, but conduct every thread with their fingers, and then with a machine they have in their hand, not unlike a comb, made roughly of wood, press down each thread as they lay it across : the texture by this means acquires a degree of strength and thickness, and a workmanlike appearance, quite peculiar to the hand of an Arab. We saw the young boys and girls attending the flock, the husband engaged in tilling the ground, and the wife grinding at the mill, working at the loom, or dressing provisions. She offered us her dish of cuscasu [1] with an air of sincerity, and seemed hurt when we declined tasting it : it was just cooked, standing on the fire, which was made up between two stones on the floor in a corner of her apartment. This particular dish is only to be met with amongst Moors and Turks. It is dressed entirely with the steam of the meat, and when made, as in Tripoli, of fine wheat, it is excellent : what the Bedouin offered us was very coarse, and almost black. Notwithstanding the work these women do, they never take off any of their ornaments, neither the bracelets for their arms or legs, nor the ear-rings, with which they may be said to be weighed down. They never omit dying their eyelashes black, painting their eyebrows, and carefully plucking out stray hairs from them, making them of the shape, length, and breadth which pleases their own fancy, without the least regard to the form they receive from nature : so that a Bedouin, as well as a Moorish lady in Barbary, having completely changed her face, when dressed and adorned, may easily escape being known by those who had seen her before. It may, therefore, be said that an African, wrapped up only in her woollen blanket in the deserts of Barca, is not more exempt from the vices of fashionable follies than the finest lady at a court of Europe. The Bedouins, like their neighbours the Arabs, from whom they scarcely differ but in name, pique themselves on their nobility. They call themselves descendants from the tribes of Sabeens, which passed from Arabia-Felix into Africa, conducted by their king Melic-Ifrique, who is said to have given the name to Africa. The Bedouin, who stopped to speak to us, seemed easy and affable : her companion was alarmed, and ran out of the way. Their tents are not very sumptuous within : they are raised from the sands, which, without any preparation, serves for the floor of the apartment : and when anyone rises from this soft floor with his large heavy flowing baracan, he naturally arises a cloud of dust, which for some time eclipses the whole family.

When the Bedouins or Arabs converse they sit down in a circle : the man who speaks first makes a smooth place with his hand on the sand ; then with his finger continues his discourse ; and again smooths this spot from time to time, to begin again with his strokes. They are so much accustomed to this, that in failure of a sandy spot, an

---

[1] The celebrated North African dish still made with semolina, meat and red peppers.

Arab talking to a Christian will take hold of his hand, and mark with his finger on the palm of it, or if that be not permitted, on his own, the strokes necessary for the points of his argument, and will then smooth it over again at certain periods. The Bedouins still retain many of the customs we read of in sacred and profane history. They are, in almost every thing, the very same people they were some thousand years ago. They greet each other with the old salutation of, "peace be with you," which is, in the Moorish, *salem-alieke*,[1] clapping at the same time the right hand on their breast. The Tripolitans carry the right hand from the breast to the forehead alternately several times, when they mean to be respectful ; but when two friends meet cordially, their manner of saluting is still more singular : they lock their right hands fast together, and kiss the back of each other's hand mutually very quick for some minutes. The Bedouins are, in general, tall, thin, and well made : the women do not seem to be of the same opinion as some ladies in Tripoli, who think if they are not too fat to move without help, they cannot be strictly handsome, and to arrive at this, they actually force themselves, after a plentiful meal, to eat a fine small wheaten loaf soaked in cold water.

The Pianura at present looks remarkably pleasant and rich ; but the greatest part of the year it is a sea of sand, shifting from place to place, with occasionally a mud covering on it, and small patches of ground that have been sown, yet looking as if they had been burnt with fire, owing to the extreme power of the sun, which leaves the stubble perfectly black. It just now makes a very different appearance : it is for the present a rich field, or little country of corn ; every corner of it being sown with bishna,[2] Indian wheat and barley. The Indian wheat [3] grows here from five to six feet high, and forms the most delightful alleys to walk in where the sand is not too loose ; but that is in general so inconvenient that we are obliged to confine ourselves to a part of the Tunis road, so called from its being the high road from Tripoli to that kingdom.

There is a lake close to the road, on which the salt lays thick on the edges ; [4] but there seldom falls rain enough to make it worth while to gather the salt by way of traffic. This lake is dry the greatest part of the year ; it is then clean, soft, and even as the finest carpet, and we walk on it frequently. At a great distance we saw the dark blue tops of the mountains of Gouriana, and these are visible only on

---

1 *Es salaam aleik.*   2 A kind of millet.   3 Indian corn is meant.
4 Known as *el mellaha*, "the salty." Now an airfield.

a clear day. In these mountains is a very curious village of Arabs. The habitations are at the very summit of the mountains, not to be easily distinguished but by those who inhabit them, as they are all built under ground in the mountains. A small entry, very narrow and long, is dug slopingly, which leads under the earth to the house, down which the cattle are driven, followed by the family. These Arabs are chiefly banditti ; and they are never disturbed nor attacked, as the narrow subterranean passages to their houses, where one man may keep many at bay, form a sufficient safeguard to them from the Moors. The length of the entry of these houses has given rise to a proverbial simile among the Moors ; every story and tale that is long and tiresome, they say, is like the skiffer (entry) at Gouriana, which has no ending.[1]

September 9, 1783

The houses of the principal people of Tripoli differ from those of Egypt, which, according to the customs of the east are mostly built three and four stories high : here they never exceed one story. You first pass through a sort of hall or lodge, called by the Moors a skiffer, with benches of stone on each side. From this a staircase leads to a single grand apartment, termed a golphor, which has (what is not permitted in any other part of the building) windows facing the street. This apartment is sacred to the master of the mansion. Here he holds his levee, transacts business, and enjoys convivial parties. None even of his own family dare enter this golphor,[2] without his particular leave ; and though this seems arbitrary, yet a Moorish lady may, in this one instance, be said to equal her lord in power, as he cannot enter his wife's apartments, if he finds a pair of lady's slippers on the outside of the door, but must wait till they are removed. Beyond this hall or lodge, is the court-yard, paved in proportion to the fortune of the owner. Some are of a brown cement, resembling finely polished marble, others are of black or white marble, and the poorer houses only of stone or earth. The houses, either small or large, in

[1] Until 1948 colonies of Jews and Berbers still lived in these underground houses, which locally are called *domus* (a name retained possibly from Roman times), mostly at a village called Tigrinna, near Garian. Since the departure of the Jews for Palestine, most have fallen empty.

[2] I cannot find the origin of this word *gulphor*, which is neither Arabic, Turkish, nor Persian.

town or country, are built exactly on the same plan. The court-yard is made use of to receive large female companies, entertained by the mistress of the house, upon the celebration of a marriage, or any other great feast, and also, in cases of death, for funeral ceremonies performed before the deceased is moved to the grave. On these occasions, the floor is covered with mats and Turkey carpets, and is sheltered from the inclemency or heat of the weather by an awning, covering the whole yard, for which the Moors sometimes incur great expense. Rich silk cushions are laid round for seats ; the walls are hung with tapestry, and the whole is converted into a grand sala. This court-yard is surrounded by a cloister, supported by pillars, over which a gallery is erected of the same dimensions, enclosed with a lattice-work of wood. From the cloisters and gallery, doors open into large chambers not communicating with each other, and which receive light only from this yard. The windows have no glass, but are furnished with jalousies of wood curiously cut : these windows produce a gloomy light, being admitted through spaces a quarter of an inch wide, and crossed with heavy bars of iron ; and as they look into an inward court-yard, they are well calculated to calm the per-turbated mind of the jealous Moor. The tops of the houses, which are all flat, are covered with plaister or cement, and surrounded by a parapet about a foot high, to prevent any thing from immediately falling into the street. Upon these terraces, the Moors dry and prepare their figs, raisins, and dates, and date-paste. They enjoy on them the refreshing inbat,[1] or sea breeze, so luxurious after a parching day, and are here seen constantly at sun-set, offering their devotions to Mahomet ; for, let a Moor be where he may, when he hears the marabut [2] announce the prayer for sun-set, nothing induces him to pass that moment without prostrating himself to the ground —a circumstance surprising to Europeans, if they happen to be in company with Moors, or walking through the streets at that hour. From the terraces the rain water falls into cisterns beneath the court-yard, which preserve the water from year to year in the highest perfection. No other soft water is to be had in this country. There are innumerable wells. Fresh water is everywhere found near the surface of the earth, but all of it is brackish and ill-flavoured.

---

[1] Arabic : literally, the breeze, which causes plants to grow, in contradistinction to the *ghibli*, which destroys.
[2] The author means the *muaddan*.

There are no rivers near, and consequently a long dearth of rain may possibly occasion a plague. The rains fall incessantly for many days and nights, and ceasing suddenly, not a drop more of water descends for several months together. The inside of the cisterns is made of a composition resembling marble, and often occupies as much ground as the size of the court-yard. The guard-house, which is known by the name of the Sandannar, is near the middle of the town, where an Aga, or captain, is always stationed with a guard. This Aga sends a party of soldiers through the town, accompanied by a pack of dogs in a starved state, who save the men the trouble of pursuing the people they wish to apprehend, for with a word the dogs rush forward, seize the unfortunate victim, and keep him pinioned to the ground till the guards come up.

One of the handsomest of the Moorish fendukes, or inns, is just finished, at the expense of the Bashaw's wife, who gains great credit with the Moors for this act of charitable hospitality, as within its walls all travellers find a free shelter. This building is very large, with a square area in which is a well and a gebia, or marble reservoir for water, for the convenience of the Moors to wash in before prayers and meals. Round the area is a number of small rooms, each for the goods or merchandize of the person or persons who may sleep in the apartments over it. The camels, horses, and mules of the travellers are ranged round the yard. When a stranger arrives, a Moor dusts the floor of an empty room, and spreading a mat, which is all the furniture allowed, leaves the guest in quiet possession of it. Those who can afford it, are expected, on quitting it, to leave a small gratuity to the porter, and none can get out or into the fenduke till the adan,[1] or dawn of day, when a Moor unlocks the gates. The baths, which are large, are built chiefly of marble, and every hour in the day till sun-set are crowded with ladies, who go there also to adorn their persons. They take their tirewomen and slaves with them. Each lady requires several attendants after she has bathed ; one of her women washes her hair thoroughly with orange-flower water, and another is ready to dry it with a powder she has just prepared of high scented perfumes, composed of burnt amber, cloves, cinnamon, and musk. She divides or plaits the hair into small tresses to the number of at least fifty—a long operation, giving a great deal of pain ; and additional sufferings are endured from the plucking out with an instrument all the uneven hairs of the eyebrows, and then painting with the

1 The dawn call to prayer.

greatest nicety the eyebrows and eyelashes with a black composition laid on with a silver or gold bodkin.[1]

In our walk to-day we passed the walls of a large building, where the great divan, or council, met in the time of the Turks, when Tripoli was under the dominion of a Turkish Bashaw, sent from Constantinople : this divan was a body composed of the Moors highest in power. The Bashaw acquainted the divan with the orders he had received from the Porte, which were usually to gather in tributes, and to guard against certain parties gaining too much power : at present the country being entirely under Moorish government, the great divan, which makes so considerable a part of the pageantry of Constantinople, is assembled by the Bashaw only on certain occasions.

Notwithstanding the despotism here, it is not difficult for the subject to approach the sovereign and make his grievances known. Often while the Bashaw is on his throne the cry of *Shar-Allah* (which means justice in the name of God !) is heard resounding through the palace. The oppressed Moor calls out these words as he approaches, before he comes into the Bashaw's presence. When this cry of justice is heard, the way is instantly made clear for the breathless suppliant ; and the sovereign, though leaving his throne, is expected to stay till he hears, and, if possible, redresses his grievances.

The people here may be said to walk upon gold. This precious ore is sifted for on the sea-shore, and taken up in very small quantities ; but whole veins of this rich metal are found inland as they approach to Fezzan. When it is found on the coast (which it is at several parts near Tripoli) the people gather up handfuls of it, put it into a wooden bowl, and wash it with several waters, till all the gold, which is so much heavier than the sand, remains at the bottom. This rich sediment is then tied in little bits of rags of about the size of a small nut, and brought in that state to Tripoli. These small parcels are known by the name of metagalls.[2] Each of them are worth exactly a Venetian sequin, or ten shillings and sixpence. The merchants who purchase these metagalls, melt a certain number of them into bars, which they call ingots, and they are known by the same name in India. These bars of gold are of various sizes.

---

[1] The author modestly omits the further operation of removing all body hairs with a sort of toffee paste called *aidi*, which is clapped on the skin and then pulled sharply off, removing the hair by the roots.

[2] Arabic, *methagall*, or gold weight.

November 1, 1783

I propose, my dear friend, to give you in this, the account of a visit we have recently paid to the Bashaw's family ; and as the interior of the harem and the castle of Tripoli have not yet been pourtrayed by any one admitted confidentially within its walls, I trust a relation of the hours we spend here will in general interest you. On approaching the castle of the Bashaw, you pass the first intrenchments, escorted by the hampers (the Bashaw's body-guards). The castle is surrounded by a wall upwards of forty feet high, with battlements, embrasures, and towers, in the old manner of fortification, and is of ancient architecture, much disfigured on the inside by irregular additions made by the present Bashaw to contain the numerous branches of his family. Having passed through the gate, you enter the first court-yard of the castle crowded with guards, waiting before the skiffer or hall, where the Chiah [1] sits all day. This is the highest officer belonging to the Bashaw, and the most in his confidence. He is invested with supreme power whenever the Bashaw is absent. No subject can approach the Bashaw on any affairs but through him. A number of guards with black slaves and Mamelukes attend him. Through this hall is a paved square with a piazza supported by marble pillars, in which is built the messeley [2] or council chamber, where the Bashaw receives his court on gala days. It is finished on the outside with Chinese tiles, a number of which form an entire painting. A flight of variegated marble steps lead up to the door of it. The nubar,[3] or royal band, performs with great ceremony before the door of the messeley every afternoon, when the third marabut announces the prayers of lazzero at four o'clock, and on the whole of Wednesday night, being the eve of the Bashaw's accession to the throne. No one on any account can pass the music while it plays, and the Bashaw's chaouxses must attend during the performance. The nubar is never played but for the Bashaw and his eldest son, when they go out with the army, or on any public occasion. Before it begins, the chief or captain of the chaouxses, who, in this instance, must be considered as a herald, goes through the ceremony of proclaiming the Bashaw afresh. The sounds of the nubar are singular to an European ear : they are composed of the turbuka, a sort of kettle-drum, the reed, and the timbrel ; the turbuka belongs to the Moors, and the reed and timbrel to the blacks.

[1] *Kehya* : see Introduction.
[2] Literally *mejlis*, or meeting-place (Arabic).
[3] Literally *noba* (Turkish). This can still be heard about the city of Tripoli on feast days.

The numerous buildings added to the castle from several streets, beyond which is the bagnio where the Christian slaves are kept. There are a number of Maltese, Genoese, and Spanish within it at present, but none of any other nation. No gentlemen are permitted to approach nearer the harem, or ladies' apartments, than the bagnio : hence you are conducted by eunuchs through long vaulted passages, so extremely dark, that it is with great difficulty the way can be discerned. On entering the harem a striking gloom prevails. The courtyard is grated over the top with heavy iron bars, very close together, giving it a melancholy appearance. The galleries round the courtyard, before the chambers, are enclosed with lattices cut very small in wood. The Bashaw's daughters, when married, have separate apartments sacred to themselves : no person can enter them but their husbands and attendants, eunuchs and slaves ; and if it is necessary for the ladies to speak in presence of a third person, even to their husband, father, or brother, they must veil themselves. The great number of attendants filling up every avenue, renders it almost impossible to proceed from one apartment to another.

We found some black slaves recently brought from Fezzan extremely troublesome, from their alarming fears created at the first sight of an European's dress and figure. A miniature on a lady's arm was taken by one of these new Fezzan blacks for a shietan, or evil spirit. Its resemblance on so small a scale to the natural figure was so strong, that on suddenly perceiving it she uttered convulsive screams, and it was only after much persuasion that she could be pacified. It is dangerous to come in their way with costly lace or beads : the first, if they are suffered to touch, they quickly pull to pieces ; and the latter they instantly bite through in trying if they are genuine pearls. On entering the apartment of Lilla Kebbiera, the wife of the Bashaw, we found her seated with three of her daughters. The eldest is married to the Dunganeer [1] who is at the head of the customs : the second to the Bey of Bengazi ; the youngest is expected to marry the Rais, or admiral of the port : these men are all renegados, as here they do not mix the blood-royal with that of their subjects. Often the princesses treat their husbands, so provided for them, infinitely worse than their slaves, particularly if their birth has been low, which happens sometimes. The husband consoles himself for the little notice his wife takes of him by the liberty he enjoys, and the daily increase

[1] Doganier : see Introduction.

of his wealth and consequence from his high station and connection with the sovereign's family.

The countenance of Lilla Kebbiera bespoke the character given of her. She is extremely affable and has the most insinuating manner imaginable. She is not more than forty ; but her age is not exactly spoken of, as it is against the Moorish religion to keep registries of births. She is still very handsome, a fair beauty with light blue eyes and flaxen hair. Her complexion is perfectly delicate, but has evidently suffered from grief and heavy fasts imposed by herself, owing to the loss of some of her favorite children, and the present unhappy disputes constantly arising between her three sons, fed by the demon of jealousy. On visiting this sovereign, the Consuls' wives are permitted to kiss her head ; other ladies in their company, or their daughters, her right hand ; her left [1] she offers only to the dependants. If any of her blacks, or any of the attendants of the castle are near her, they frequently seize the opportunity of kneeling down to kiss the end of her baracan, or upper garment. She is adored by her subjects, which is natural, as she is extremely benevolent ; her greatest fault is, not in spending, but in giving away, more than her revenues afford. Halluma is the name given her by her parents, and Lilla means, in Moorish, Lady. She is called in her family Lilla Halluma, but by her subjects she is stiled Lilla Kebbiera, the great, or greatest lady. The Bey, her eldest son, has been married several years. He married at seven years old. The Moors, indeed, marry so extremely young, that the mother and her first born are often seen together as playmates, equally anxious and angry in an infantine game. The women here are often grandmothers at twenty-six or twenty-seven years of age ; and it is therefore no wonder they live frequently to see the children of many of their generation. From the melancholy turn of Lilla Halluma's mind at present, she has always some article of her dress in a state to denote deep mourning.

The Moorish habit for mourning consists only in the clothes being entirely deprived of their new appearance, and the deeper the mourning is meant to be the more indifferent and even shabby the clothes : therefore, when she orders a new cap, which is so richly embroidered that it is like a solid plate of gold, she never puts it on till it has passed through water before her, and all the beauty of it destroyed. She weeps over the operation, and her tirewomen make extempore verses

[1] The left hand being that always used by Moslems to perform the unclean offices of the body.

on the cause of her distress. The rest of her clothes were grand, and she wore costly jewels ; a transparent veil of many yards, flowing carelessly about her in graceful drapery, displayed through it the whole of her rich dress ; and her figure was altogether majestic, with the sweetest countenance. The apartment she was in was hung with dark green velvet tapestry ornamented with coloured silk damask flowers ; and sentences out of the Koran were cut in silk letters and neatly sewed on, forming a deep border at the top and bottom : below this, the apartment was finished with tiles forming landscapes. The sides of the doorway, and the entrance into the room, were marble ; and according to the custom of furnishing here, choice china and chrystal encircled the room on a moulding near the ceiling. Close beneath these ornaments were placed large looking-glasses with frames of gold and silver ; the floor was covered with curious matting and rich carpetting over it ; loose mattrasses and cushions placed on the ground, made up in the form of sophas, covered with velvet, and embroidered with gold and silver, served for seats, with Turkey carpets laid before them. The coffee was served in very small cups of china, placed in gold fillagree cups without saucers, on a solid gold salver, of an uncommon size, richly embossed : this massive waiter was brought in by two slaves, who bore it between them round to each of the company ; and these two eunuchs were the most richly habited slaves we had yet seen in the castle : they were entirely covered with gold and silver. Refreshments were afterwards served up on low and beautifully inlaid tables, not higher than a foot from the ground ; and amongst the sherbets was fresh pomegranate juice, passed through the rind of the fruit which gave it an excellent flavour. After the repast, slaves attended with silver fillagree censers, offering, at the same time, towels with gold ends wove in them near half a yard deep.

The two youngest princes, Sidy Hamet and Sidy Useph, being returned from racing on the sands, a diversion they frequently take, entered the apartments to visit their mother. Their sisters veiled themselves while they staid, which was but a few minutes, as they were hastening to the Bashaw before his levee finished ; for when he gives audience, which, owing to ill health, is not daily, every one entitled to approach is expected to be present, particularly his family.

We attended Lilla Halluma and her daughter to the Bey's house to visit Lilla Aisha, his wife. We saw in our way a new grand golphor building for the Bey, of variegated marble, brought from Genoa, and Chinese tiles from Malta. Maltese are come over to lay the terraces, which they do with an art peculiar to themselves. Lilla Aisha, the Bey's wife, is thought to be very sensible, though rather haughty. Her apartments were grand ; and she herself was superbly habited. Her chemise was covered with gold embroidery at the neck : over it she wore a gold and silver tissue jileck, or jacket, without sleeves ; and over that another of purple velvet, richly laced with gold, with coral and pearl buttons, set quite close together down the front : it had short sleeves finished with a gold band not far below the shoulder ; and it discovered a wide loose chemise of transparent gauze, ornamented with gold, silver, and ribband stripes. The drapery or baracan she wore over her dress was of the finest crimson transparent gauzes, between rich silk stripes of the same colour. She wore round her ancles, as did all the ladies of the Bashaw's family, a sort of fetter made of a thick bar of gold,[1] so fine that they bind it round the leg with one hand ; it is an inch and a half wide, and as much in thickness : each of these weighs four pounds. None but the Bashaw's daughters and grand-daughters are permitted to wear this ornament in gold ; and ladies who are not of the blood royal are obliged to confine themselves in this article of dress to silver. Just above this a band, three inches wide, of gold thread, finished the ends of a pair of trousers, made of pale yellow and white silk. She had five rings in each ear, two were put through the bottom of the ear, and three through the top, all set with precious stones. She was extremely stately, and has infinitely more influence with the Bashaw and Bey than the rest of the princesses. She is thought to meddle much in politics, but keeps up an appearance of paying a deference to the opinion of Lilla Kebbiera, who is very much attached to her. We quitted the castle about seven o'clock, when the marabut's call, or the Moor's fifth time of praying, was announced. We were conducted through the harem, and though day-light, we were obliged to have torches, on account of some long dark passages we had to go through. Could the subterranean ways and hidden corners of this castle tell the secret plots and strange events that happen daily within its walls, they would be most extraordinary to hear. When we came near the bagnio of the Christian slaves, our guide from the harem quitted us, and the guards or hampers conducted us, with the gentlemen who had waited for us, through the outer fortifications.

---

[1] Most Bedouin women wear an anklet of silver even to-day. The custom among Semitic women is certainly as old as the time of the biblical prophets. (See Isaiah 3 : 16.)

November 3, 1783

I shall continue in this letter to give you some further account of the Bashaw, Alli Corromalli. He is short in stature, and by no means equal to his sons in figure, but he looks both consequential and venerable, though he is not fifty.[1] He is the second Moorish Bashaw who has reigned since his grandfather, named by the Moors, Hamet the Great, for having made himself sovereign of Tripoli in 1714,[2] after it had been for several hundred years under the tyranny of Turkish Bashaws, and a standing rapacious army of Turks, who kept the Moors in the utmost state of subjection. The whole country was tributary to the Porte. A Turkish garrison had been maintained here for many years by the people, to support the power and consequence of Bashaws sent from the Grand Signior, who were stationed in this place for three years. Hamet, the grandfather of the present Bashaw, was Bey or prince of Tripoli during the reign of the last Turkish Bashaw, whose son he adopted when the Turk returned to Constantinople, by passing the child through a chemise of his wife's, a ceremony necessary to the adopting him for his own. This infant lived to grow up, and is now the Great Chiah ; a most venerable figure with a beard as white as silver. When the Turkish Bashaw returned to Constantinople, he left a standing army for the security of the place, or rather to collect the revenues for the Grand Signior. During this period, Hamet-Bey, applying to the Porte, was made Bashaw. He soon found means of making a total alteration in the government ; and the sudden manner in which he effected this change was truly singular. He contrived, without any disturbance, to clear Tripoli, in the space of twenty-four hours, of all the Turkish soldiers, amounting to several hundreds of disciplined troops. At his palace, not far from the town, he gave a superb entertainment, and invited all the chiefs of the Turks to partake of it. Three hundred of these unfortunate victims were strangled, one by one, as they entered the skiffer, or hall. This skiffer is very long, with small dark rooms or deep recesses on each side, in which a hidden guard was placed. These guards assassinated the Turks as they passed, quickly conveying the bodies into those recesses out of sight, so that the next Turk saw nothing extraordinary going on when he entered the fatal skiffer, but, quitting his horse and servants, met his fate unsuspectingly.

---

[1] Lucas, the traveller, describes him as " a short, robust old man of a fair complexion, a pleasing countenance, and an affable, joyous disposition. . . ." (*Proceedings of the Africa Association*, vol. III).   [2] Ali Karamanli's accession was actually in 1711.

Next day, the Turks who remained in this city, were (no doubt by order) found murdered in all parts, and little or no inquiries were made after those who had perpetrated such horrid deeds. Only a few straggling Turks remained to tell the dreadful tale. Great presents were sent by the Bashaw to Constantinople to appease the Grand Signior, and in a day or two no one dared to talk of the Turkish garrison, which, in a few hours, had been totally annihilated. Having in this dreadful manner freed himself and his family from the Turkish yoke, and having succeeded in keeping the Grand Signior in humour, he caused Tripoli to remain entirely under a Moorish government, for which the Moors still call his reign glorious. If Bey Abdallah, the son of the Turkish Bashaw, whom Hamet the Great had adopted for his own, had been intended by him, and the Turkish Bashaw, to have had any share in the throne, it was a circumstance that escaped his memory. He named his own son Mohammed, while an infant, Bey of Tripoli ; and he accordingly succeeded him, and was the father of the present Bashaw.

Bey Abdallah was, however, honoured by having a high post assigned to him. This prince is now Great Chiah of the castle, commanding it in the Bashaw's absence, and guarding it while the Bashaw resides there. This officer never quits his post day or night : he sits always in the skiffer, and has a deputy under him, called the Little Chiah. Though the town is governed by a Chiah, yet the keys of the town-gate are at night delivered to the Great Chiah. The keys of the castle, however, are every evening carried to the Bashaw, who keeps them in his own apartment, and no farther access can be had to the palace till the morning, but by ascending the walls with ropes, which, from their height, is both dangerous and difficult, and never attempted but on some great emergency, and then not without leave of the Great Chiah.

The Bashaw, though not fifty, appears an old man from the whiteness of his beard. The Bey,[1] his eldest son, is not thirty, a fine majestic figure, much beloved, being extremely mild and just to his people. His guards and his power are nearly equal to the Bashaw's, a circumstance which raises a jealousy in his two younger brothers, which is cruelly heightened by disaffected persons round them, and renders both of them exceedingly troublesome to him. Though the Moors and Turks are allowed to marry four wives, the Bashaw has married

---

[1] Lucas describes the Bey as " tall and well shaped, but dark complexioned " and with " an engaging politeness."

only Lilla Halluma, who speaks with a great deal of satisfaction of the Grecian and black beauties, brought to the castle, having occasioned her no other inconvenience than the expense of keeping them. She therefore considers herself to have been, in this respect, far happier, as she says, than even the Great Sultaness of Constantinople, who, in the midst of brilliancy, finds no domestic comforts within the walls of the Seraglio. The customs of the Seraglio, singular as they are and inimical to social happiness, either render the heart a stranger to its enjoyments, or oblige it to seek them in vain. But of a sultan's life at the Ottoman Porte, you will better judge by the following description of the Seraglio, or rather of the Harem belonging to the Grand Signior ; for the Seraglio means the enclosure of the whole Ottoman palace, which is not less than a moderate town. The wall surrounding it is thirty feet high. The Seraglio has nine gates, two of which are magnificent. From one of these the Ottoman Porte takes the name of Sublime Porte ; but the place where the ladies live, who belong to the Grand Signior, is called, as it is here, the Harem ; and no persons, but those officially belonging to it, can enter the first gate. The Harem looks upon the sea of Marmora. The Grand Signior and his eunuchs are the only persons that come within sight of these ladies. When any of them leave the Seraglio to go upon the water, or into the country, the boat or the carriage they go in is closely covered up. A passage enclosed with linen is prepared all the way from the door of their apartment to the place of their embarking, or getting into their carriages. The number of the ladies, always numerous, is regulated by the order of the Sultan ; and among them all, owing to a singular regulation, there is but one servant. They wait upon one another in rotation : the last who enters serves her who entered before her, and serves herself also ; so that the first entered is served without serving, and the last that enters serves without being served. They all sleep in separate apartments, and between every fifth there is a preceptress, who minutely inspects their conduct. Their chief governess is called Caton-Ciaha,[1] which means governess of the noble young ladies. When there is a Sultaness-mother, she forms her court from amongst the ladies of the Harem, having the liberty allowed of taking as many young ladies as she chooses and those she likes the best. When the Grand Signior's intention to allow the ladies to walk in the gardens of the Seraglio is made known to the Caton-Ciaha, or governess of the Harem, all persons are ordered to

[1] The *Khatun Kehya*.

retire. A guard of black eunuchs are then commanded to place themselves along the walls of the gardens with their sabres drawn, while
another party of them guard the walks. If unfortunately any one is
found in the gardens, even through ignorance or inadvertency, he is
instantly killed, and his head is brought to the Grand Signior.

The mother of the eldest son of the Grand Signior is called Asaki,
that is Sultaness-mother. For the first son she is crowned with flowers,
and she has the liberty of forming her court as above-mentioned, and
takes upon her the prerogatives of a wife. Eunuchs are assigned for
her particular service. No other ladies, though they have sons, are
crowned, or maintained with such costly distinction as the first, or
Sultaness-mother ; but they are served apart, have grand apartments
assigned to themselves, and are exempt from serving. After the death
of the Grand Signior, all the mothers of the male children, who are
considered as queens, are shut up in the old Seraglio, whence they
can never come out unless any of their sons ascend the throne. From
this account it may be easily imagined that, at Tripoli, Lilla Halluma
puts a right value on her own condition.

An immense number of horses are kept for the Grand Signior's
use, which can neither be augmented or diminished, and which no
person but himself must mount. All the pages of the Seraglio are
sons of renegados, or Christians who have become Turks.

To return to Lilla Halluma : she speaks with her usual compassion
of the surviving widows of the late Mohammed Bashaw, who by her
orders are treated with as much indulgence as possible. She tells us
there are three of these queens yet living in these castles in the Harem,
that belonged to the late Bashaw. They are very cheerful and agree
perfectly together, free, as she says, from apprehension that every day
terrify herself for the fate of her three sons, all equally dear to her,
and all equally jealous of each other.

December 29, 1783

The great mosque, in which is a grand mausoleum for the reigning
family, is by far the handsomest in this city : the rest are neat, but
very inferior to it. The Moors oblige everybody, women as well
as men, to go over it barefooted. They take their shoes off at the
entrance and deliver them to their servants. This custom of taking
off their shoes at the door is of less consequence, as the floor of the

mosque is entirely covered with beautiful mats, over which are laid rich Turkey carpets. The building of which I am speaking, is large, lofty, and almost square. The walls, to within three feet of the ceiling, are lined with handsome figured china tiles placed uniformly : the ceiling is ornamented in the same manner. The sixteen marble columns have thin iron rods, painted blue and gilt, reaching from one to the other, and forming a large checkwork through the whole edifice, about six feet below the roof, from which are suspended in festoons antique lamps with long silver chains, some of them very large, with silver filagree vessels for incense, and painted eggs hung on silken cords. On three sides of the mosque are square bow windows grated with iron without glass. On the side toward Mecca is a pulpit of marble resembling alabaster, with a flight of fourteen steps, enclosed with a marble balustrade : this pulpit is covered with Chinese tiles. Over it is a small alabaster dome supported by four white marble pillars which rest on the pulpit ; and the outside of this dome is entirely covered with gold. Near to this pulpit is a small arched recess or niche in the wall, to which the Imam descends from the pulpit to pray, with the Shiak [1] on one side of him and the Chiah on the other. The Imam always prays with his face towards Mecca, as other altars are opposite to the east. There is no seat, bench, or resting place in the mosque.

The windows on two sides look into a cloister which surrounds the mosque : on the third side they open into a neat white stone building resembling a mosque in appearance, but which is the mausoleum called the Turbar. It is filled with handsome tombs of all the relations of the royal family, excepting those who have died out of town, as it is against the laws here for a corpse to be brought in through the gates of the city, though all are carried out of the gates of the city that die in town. The Christians' burial ground is close by the seaside without the marine gate : there is no way to it from the country but through the town, and the corpse consequently cannot be carried there, but by crossing the sea before the harbour's mouth. If a Christian die in the country, fond of money as the Moors are, there is no sum that would prevail on them to let the body pass the gates ; no resource remains but a sea voyage to procure its interment.

To return to the Turbar : it is throughout of the purest white marble, and is filled with an immense quantity of fresh flowers, most of the tombs being dressed with festoons of Arabian jasmine, and

1 The *Sheikh el beled* : see Introduction.

large bunches of variegated flowers, consisting of orange, myrtle, red and white roses, etc. They afford a fragrancy which those who are not habituated to such choice flowers can scarcely conceive.

The tombs are mostly of white marble ; a few being inlaid with coloured marble. Those of the men are distinguished from the women's only by a turban carved in marble, placed at the top.

As the windows of the great mosque are very low, and made deep, the light is everywhere faint, which adds much to the solemnity of the place, and affords a most pleasing relief from the strong glare of light without. Owing to the perfumes of orange-flower water, incense, and musk, added to the great quantities of fresh flowers I have mentioned, and the agreeable coolness of the place, on our entering it from the burning dusty street, it seemed to us a sort of paradise. Its extraordinary neatness, solemnity, and delicious odour, struck forcibly on the imagination. This mosque was rebuilt forty-two years ago by the Bashaw's father, Mohammed.

The Moors are well paid for the trouble the Christians give them when they visit any of their buildings ; but it must be allowed, that, in general, nothing can exceed their attention and civility : a merit which it is extraordinary to find in the common people, when we consider how diametrically opposite their manners are to ours. But no part of Barbary is like this place for the respect paid to Christians.

The Moors, we know, have varied little in their customs for many centuries ; it is therefore no wonder that all their buildings impress the imagination so powerfully with an exact similitude to what we read of in Scripture, or see represented in scriptural paintings. The people, as well as the priest, when in the mosque, direct the whole course of their devotions to that part of it which is supposed to stand towards Mecca, in the same manner as they turn their face to Mecca, whenever they kneel to pray in the street or elsewhere. All the mosques are adorned with minarets or spires, whence a man on the outside, with a small flag in his hand and by loud cries, which they term singing, announces the hour of prayer.

The Bashaw, the Bey, and his second son Sidy Hamet, went to-day to attend the mosque. None but the royal family ride in town. Their suite follows on foot, excepting the head Chaoux, who is first in the procession, richly drest and mounted on a stately horse : he has a large kettle-drum before him on which he strikes minute strokes, going before in the manner of a herald, proclaiming the Bashaw at the entrance of every street. He rides before the Bey in the same manner when the Bashaw is not present, but does not accompany any of the other sons. His dress is nearly the same with that of the other Chaouxes, with the difference of a large gold claw on the left side of his turban, and the front of his under jileck, or waistcoat, being almost an entire breastplate of silver. Six Chaouxes followed him on foot, dressed uniformly in scarlet cloth close dresses, quite plain, not very long, and fastened round the waist with a leather belt. They had all of them plain white stiff high caps, made exactly in the shape of a cornucopia. The insignia of the tails were carried next (the sovereign of Tripoli being a Bashaw of three tails) : [1] then followed the hampers, or the Bashaw's body-guard, very richly drest, who carried short silver sticks in their hands. After these followed the attendants and suite of the Bashaw : round him were the officers of state, those highest in rank, of course, nearest his person. The swordbearer was on one side of him, and his first minister of state on the other, to whom he seemed talking very earnestly. He was drest in a yellow satin caftan, lined with rich fur. His turban was very large with gold ends. He was without jewels to-day, though usually adorned with very fine ones. This omission of precious stones is to indicate to his subjects, that the Bashaw's mind is oppressed. The horses of the Bashaw and Bey were particularly beautiful and were buried in their trappings. Both their saddles were embossed gold, and had gold stirrups weighing more than thirteen pounds each pair. The Bashaw's horse had on five solid gold necklaces ; the Bey's horse, three. The Bey wore a pale green and silver caftan, and a crimson shawl with rich gold ends twisted over his turban. One of his officers of state had on a caftan of gold tissue, with a fine purple cloth bernuse over it. You may perceive, that in few places the costume can be grander than it is here.

The Bashaw looks venerable ; but the Bey seems much more like a sovereign. He is a noble figure and remarkably handsome. An immense number of black slaves and servants encircled the whole procession and kept off the crowd. The Bashaw visits the mosque on every particular event, good or bad, that concerns himself or his state. He sometimes, though not often, pays a visit to the Rais of the marine, who cannot wish much for the honour, as it costs him two of his blacks, whom he is obliged to present to the Bashaw for his gracious condescension. While the Bashaw was passing, a man who was in

---

[1] See Introduction. The Ottoman insignia of horse tails must derive from Magyar origins. This habit was clearly acquired by the Crusaders, since Richard III had fox tails carried before him in processions.

our house for protection (all the consulary houses being sanctuaries) [1] ran out and touched his horse, and was on that account pardoned. This privilege [2] extends to the touching any part, not only of the Bashaw's but of the Prince's garments or horses when they are out ; but the Bashaw's horse protects at all times, even in his stable : if a criminal can get under him or cling round him, his life is safe. When the Bashaw goes to any of his gardens, which he always does on horse-back, he has three relay horses, richly caparisoned, led before him by slaves, and all his suite then ride. Almost all the chief officers of state were with the Bashaw, except the Grand Chiah, who, as I have before observed, cannot leave the castle when the Bashaw is out.

All affairs of moment are laid before the Chiah ; but with regard to the distribution of justice, the Cadi, who is considered the head of the law, is the judge.

The Dugganeer was in the Bashaw's suite. He is of great conse-quence here, and has the management of the customs, which forms in Tripoli, as in all parts of Barbary and Turkey, one of the principal employments under government. He is at once comptroller and farmer general : all the taxes on exports, imports, and home con-sumption, depend on him ; in short, he has the regulation of every thing. He is subject to large sums of money being demanded of him by the Bashaw at a moment's warning, for which he lays on additional taxes. A refusal to pay these sums would certainly cost him his place, and very likely his life. All the goods which a Consul imports for his own consumption pass entirely free. The Dugganeer furnishes the castle with everything that is wanted, as bread in loaves, meat, charcoal, oil, and soap ; all of which are sent from the custom-house every day to the Bashaw's and to the houses of all the different branches of the royal family within the castle. The distinct allowances of the separate articles for each family are fixed by the Bashaw. The Dugganeer is a Neapolitan by birth, of very low extraction, though married, as I have said, to the Bashaw's eldest daughter, and was brought a slave here many years ago. He is now extremely rich, has great influence, and is liked by the people. It is expected that a nephew of his will likewise marry into the Bashaw's family, with a good portion of the wealth his uncle has made in the Bashaw's service.

The government is at present extremely mild ; so much so, that

---

[1] See Introduction.

[2] A similar habit obtains among the Bedouin. To touch the headdress of a tribal sheikh is to be provided with instant sanctuary.

the Bashaw endangers his throne by it, as he leaves the Moors too much to themselves. It is not so at Morocco, where a despotic tyrant reigns. A singular circumstance happened there not long since, relative to a fortunate Moorish merchant, who is just arrived here. While at Morocco, he imported a great quantity of wearing apparel which a rich Jew had given him a commission for, when the Jew not approving of them declined his bargain. The merchant went himself and laid his cause before his sovereign praying for redress : the sentence pronounced was, that the Emperor would not suffer the Jew to be obliged to take the goods if he did not approve them. The Moor returned to his home inconsolable ; he had laid out his all, and saw himself ruined : but in a few hours after, he heard proclaimed through all the streets of Morocco, a royal edict, that any Jew who appeared in the city after that notice from the Emperor without yellow stockings, a black hat, and some other articles which the commission consisted of, should die under the baston immediately. The Moor then found his house too small to admit the buyers of his merchandize, and in a few hours made a little fortune of what he had before thought such an unlucky purchase.

February 11, 1784

During the absence, at Morocco, of the ambassador from Tripoli, his son, who is about twenty-five years of age, invited a party of Christians to his father's country residence, the grounds of which, owing to the taste of its owner, who has visited most of the courts in Europe, are in much better order than any of the plantations near it. It is a wilderness of sweets, beneath thick orange groves, through which the sun's beams but faintly shine. White marble channels with rapid clear streams of water cross the gardens in many directions ; and the air in them is fraught with the scent of oranges, roses, and Arabian jasmine, whose thick shade forms an agreeable contrast with the burning atmosphere surrounding them. In the centre of the largest garden, nearest the house, is a most pleasant golphor built a considerable height from the ground. The floor, walls, and window-seats are lined with Chinese tiles of lively colours : the windows are placed round it, through which honeysuckles, orange flowers and jasmine, make their way. The shrubs reflect through them everywhere the most lively green, and fill the whole with the richest perfume.

C.T.—3*

These golphors are for the use of the master of the mansion and his friends, as they cannot visit him in the dwelling-house on account of the female part of the family, who are, therefore, never expected ; but the ladies of this family do not confine themselves to that rule, and it is feared that some fatal consequence will result to them for trespassing, in so many instances, the narrow limits of indulgence allowed to Moorish ladies. The ambassador's son spoke English, talked much of his sister, but in a manner that spoke his fears for her, and his disapprobation of her conduct. It has been already observed, that it was apprehended her uncle would put her to death. An event which appears to us of such enormity, takes place here without hesitation or inquiry. The head of a house, whether father, brother, or husband, having the power of life and death relative to the female part of his family, has only to get a teskerar of the Bashaw, which is a small bit of paper with his signature, giving leave to the person who requires it, to put to death the object of his anger ; and this fatal paper is procured with the greatest facility.

This ambassador, a few years since, possessed a favourite Circassian slave, who lived at a garden a little distance from the family residence. He thought her conduct reprehensible, and after having often threatened and as often pardoned her, she at length fell a victim to the rage of a Mameluke belonging to her lord.

This wretch was an enemy to his master, and an unsuccessful admirer of the fair Circassian. Hearing that his master was engaged at an entertainment given by the Christians, he came to him late in the evening, and worked on his imagination till the fatal teskerar was obtained. The Mameluke immediately rode off full speed to the garden where she resided, and had departed on the wretched errand but a few moments, when the visible alteration and the agony in the countenance of the ambassador, led his friends soon to the supposition of the cruel orders he had issued, and he was easily persuaded to countermand them. He sent horsemen with every inducement given them to overtake the sanguinary Mameluke, and arrest his hand from the murder he was so eager to perpetrate. They reached the garden a few seconds after him ; but he knowing of a breach in the garden wall, had, assassin-like, entered that way to prevent alarm, and found the fair Circassian walking solitarily in the garden at that late hour. At the sight of him she fled, having long considered him as her destined murderer. She, in her terror, climbed up the garden walls, and ran round the top of them. Those who were sent to save her saw her run in vain. They forced the gates and entered them ; in the mean while, twice they heard a pistol fired, and soon after the dying groans of the unfortunate female, whom the Mameluke, to prevent explanations, had stabbed to death, after having discharged two pistols at her.

The ambassador having given orders for her death in a moment of despair, and from accusations against her which he probably thought exaggerated, seems never to have been happy since, and from the accumulated anguish he suffers through the conduct of the ladies of his own family, it is generally supposed that he will not return to this country. He is considered as extremely tenacious of his honour, free from bigotry, and possesses an enlightened understanding. The two latter qualities disqualify him for comforts in his own country.

Not far from this ambassador's gardens are the remains of an old building, called the castle of Lilla Zenobia, it having remained in her possession after the death of her father, Hamet the Great. It was within this century a very grand palace where the court of that sovereign was kept ; in one corner of the gardens belonging to it is a very large mound of earth, covering the bodies of several hundred massacred Turks, who were buried in that spot at the time her father subdued the Turkish garrison. This is the palace the Turks were invited to by Hamet the Great and murdered, as I have described to you in a former letter. The fatal recesses in the skiffer, which were the receptacles of the murdered Turks, are still entire, as is the skiffer through which the Turks passed in their way to the interior of the palace. Lilla Zenobia has been dead many years, and the building has been neglected and suffered to go to ruin. It is said that Turkish ghosts hold here their midnight haunt and revels. The Moors say it is so full of such company, that there is no room for any other. There are but a few of the inferior apartments, and one grand room (said to be that where the Bashaw gave audience) still standing. It is without floor or roof ; the walls have some remains of painting still fresh in colour, and many ornaments are yet visible ; and part of the ceiling lies in the middle of this spacious room grown over with grass : the gates are immensely large and formidable. Having explored every part of this ruined castle that was passable, we returned to the ambassador's gardens to take refreshments : thither the Christians' servants had arrived with the remnant of such provisions as they had saved from the eager grasp of the famished Moors. The city had been long distressed for corn, and a considerable crowd had gathered round the servants imperceptibly, and attacked the loaded mules as they were passing through the town gate. In a few moments no eatables were left, except some few dishes of pork, a food which the true Mussulman looks on with horror : the rest was seized by a number of hungry wretches, who tore it with a savage fury from each other. Not an article was lost but eatables—food was all they contended for. They fought together for the crumbs that fell on the ground ; to such an extremity had hunger brought them.

The starved objects we passed this morning in the streets were shocking to behold. A total want of rain occasions this dreadful distress for the present, and makes us fear a famine will soon be at the height here, which surely, of all calamities, is the most horrid : the great must pay for it, but what the poor will suffer must agonize every feeling heart.

ᗰ

April 20, 1784

During our ride yesterday, we were struck with the singular appearance of the country at a small distance from town. In Barbary, the burying places are out of the cities, in the manner of the ancients ; and the numerous burying-grounds, from the shape of the tombs, resemble roofs of houses, and appear like towns in miniature. The large mausoleums, belonging to people of distinction, represent capital buildings, proportionate in size to the little towns by which they are surrounded. In some of them lights are kept constantly burning, with the choicest flowers, the fragrancy of which strikes you on approaching the tombs. The numerous Moorish gardens appeared to be so many woods of oranges ; and these, added to detached plantations of olives and dates, formed a scene totally different to what is met with near the capitals of Europe. We alighted at a farm : the ladies were admitted into the house, where we had fresh and sour milk, and dates just gathered from the tree of the most beautiful transparent brown, and having the appearance and taste of fruit preserved in the highest manner. Some of the same refreshments were procured to be sent to the gentlemen in the garden. The Moors were obliged to secure a camel, which with much difficulty was prevented attacking our horses while they stood in the yard ; though the camel is, with very few exceptions, perfectly mild, this having a young one unable to feed itself was the cause of its ferocity. The camels' milk is drank here by consumptive people : it is extremely salt and ill-flavoured, richer than cows' milk, and of a red colour. The young camel, when a few weeks old, is remarkably handsome. Nothing can be more distressing than to hear its cry at that age, as its voice then so exactly resembles the cries of a young child, that it is impossible to be distinguished from them. When they are grown up, their voice is very loud and rough, and when angry, they make a particular rattling in the throat that cannot be mistaken, which is a lucky circumstance, as it is a warning of their intention to bite ; for, from the size of their mouths, and their never wearing a muzzle, a bite is nearly fatal. Fortunately, they are in general so inoffensive and tractable, that they commonly go without bridle or halter, and a single straw in the hand is often the only weapon used to drive them along with a burden of nine hundredweight.

The dromedary seems to be used in this country only for the courier or post. The Moors never dress their camels with bells, as we do horses in England ; and though these animals shew no emulation for dress, they are evidently pleased, and hasten their steps when accompanied by their masters' song ; they, therefore, sing to them while they drive them. This useful patient animal will sustain many days' thirst when traversing, heavy laden, the burning sands ; but in town, where it is cooler, and during the winter, he can remain some weeks without drinking, living on the water he has within him, preserved in a reservoir, whence he conveys it into the stomach at pleasure. The last time the Bey was encamped, a camel was opened for the water it contained, when several gallons were found in a perfect state. The camp was at that time in want of water ; the people having a very short allowance of it, and dying daily, when the Bey made use of this costly expedient, as a camel is very valuable. The flesh is eaten by the Moors, and they say it is exceedingly good.

Continuing our ride to the sands, we had a distant view of two of the most capital mosques[1] in this kingdom, situated at some distance in the desert, where criminals take shelter, and are safe as long as they can stay in a certain district round them. This district extends to a quarter of a mile, and sometimes to two or three miles, according to the mosque it belongs to, and cannot be violated even by the Bashaw. All persons may be apprehended if seen in the act of procuring food for the culprit, in which case he is either starved to death, or forced

---

[1] The author means not a mosque but the tomb of a holy man, or *marabut*, often built on the site where he lived.

by hunger to surrender. One of the marabuts we saw to-day is called the Seide,[1] the history of which is related by the Moors with a number of fictitious circumstances. The word *seide*, which in Arabic means lion, was given to a Moor, who, with little more assistance than his own courage and strength, drove all the lions from that part of the country, and his son was the marabut of this place. The name of marabut is given both to the mosque and to the saint, or holy man, who resides at it ; and the simple story of the Seide, related as a fact, is as follows :

Hamet Bashaw, grandfather to the present, went, as customary, on particular occasions, to visit this mosque or marabut. In the hurry and confusion of the family of the Seide, during the visit the Bashaw honoured them with, and in bringing him all the refreshments in their power to procure, he got a momentary sight of the marabut's eldest daughter, said to be one of the most beautiful women at that time. He was so much struck with her appearance, that he directly told the marabut his fortune from that hour was made by sending his daughter immediately to Tripoli, as he was determined she should be the first lady of his seraglio. The aged and religious marabut, far from being pleased at the honours offered him on such terms by his sovereign, expostulated, and made great objections to his orders, when the enraged Bashaw told him, that if he did not send his daughter richly drest and perfumed to the seraglio that very night, by morning there should not remain a vestige of himself, or any part of his family. Saying this, he departed and left guards to see his orders executed.

The unfortunate marabut, unable to extricate himself or his lost child, loaded her with gold and jewels, and drest her in the richest clothes she had ; she having acquiesced in his wishes of taking a deadly potion to save her from the violence of Hamet Bashaw's passion. He wept over her and led her to the door of his house, where he ordered the bridal song to be sung over her before she quitted her home.[2] He then placed her in a linen couch on the back of a camel handsomely ornamented, such as the ladies of this country travel in, and gave her up, with tears and heavy imprecations on the Bashaw's head, to his officers.

A numerous suite of attendants, in addition to those the Bashaw

---

[1] See above, p. 30.
[2] Moorish women who die before they are married are buried in wedding clothes, and the bridal song is sung over the corpse before it leaves the house.

had left, arrived to conduct her to the castle. On her arrival there, she was immediately carried to the royal apartments, where not long after the Bashaw hastened to receive her. But on entering the room he was struck with horror and surprise on perceiving a beautiful corpse stretched on the floor, stiff and cold. He found not the least mark of violence upon her, and he knew no one had been suffered to enter the apartment after her arrival but himself. He had probably heard of the curses her father sent him, by the attendants, who came with her, which did not fail, with the reproach of his own conscience and the superstitious ideas of the Moors, to throw him into the greatest agitation, and he seemed to be nearly in the same state as the sacrificed victim laying before him.

At the dawn of day, Hamet Bashaw set off to the Seide, and asked the marabut if he could any way account for the suddenness of his daughter's death ? The marabut returned for answer, that his daughter had honour enough to receive a deadly poison from his hand, before her departure from his house, and that now he had but one favour more to entreat of the Prophet Mahomet, who had so mercifully saved his child in the moment of distress, which was, that he would strike him, Hamet Bashaw, blind. This misfortune actually happened to the Bashaw four or five years before his death ; but, in the fable, the Moors say it happened at the instant the marabut implored Mahomet, and call it, of course, the vengeance of the Seide. But Hamet the Great was advanced in years when he lost his sight, and finding from this unhappy circumstance his power decreasing rapidly, he determined not to outlive his consequence, and the great name he had acquired amongst his subjects. He employed himself in regulating all he wished to have done before his death, naming his own son Mohammed for his successor, and immediately afterwards he ordered one of the youngest pages of his golphor to attend him thither, where he frequently spent many hours in close retirement. As soon as they entered the apartment, the Bashaw desired the page to give him his pistols. He bid the youth stand close by his side, and if one pistol missed fire, to be ready instantly to deliver the other to him, at the peril of his life. The Bashaw shot himself dead with the first pistol, in the presence of his adopted son, Bey Abdallah, the present Great Chiah, before either of them were collected enough to prevent the catastrophe. Bey Abdallah was at that time a child about eleven years old. Thus fell Hamet the Great, after a successful reign of thirty-two years.

The country round where the marabut of the Seide is built is entirely a desert, without any object in view but the city of Tripoli at a distance.

We remained on the sands some time, as the two youngest princes, Sidy Hamet and Sidy Useph, were there with a number of cavalry. This is a sight quite new to an European eye, and not less superb than strange. Their movements consist chiefly in sham fights. Sidy Hamet, to shew us the manner of laying in ambush, got off his horse : they almost bury themselves in the sands, firing from thence on the enemy. One of the most surprising feats in these kind of reviews is the great swiftness with which they ride, and the wonderfully sudden manner they stop and turn their horses, the animal appearing almost flat on his side at that instant. Sidy Hamet and Sidy Useph more than once rode up full speed to the Christians, and stopping their horses just at their feet, fired their pieces so extremely close to them that it was not very pleasant ; but this they meant quite as a compliment. They fire at each other in this manner so frequently that it is wonderful accidents do not often happen.

Sidy Hamet was very richly dressed in a purple flowered gold and silver brocade caftan ; and had a crimson velvet and gold jileck, or short jacket, over it without sleeves. The two dresses were tightened at the waist with a rich broad girdle. His turban was white, with a crimson shawl wound over it. His arms were beautiful ; the handle of his sabre was gold and silver, set with precious stones; the scabbard of it chased. His pistols were set in gold and silver, curiously wrought. The front and back of his saddle was covered with plates of gold embossed. The Moorish saddles are made to come up very high before and behind.

The first housings of Sidy Hamet's horse were of crimson velvet with gold embroidery ; the second, purple with a broad silver lace, and a very rich gold fringe ; and the third was of dark plain velvet with a broad dead gold lace. His brother Sidy Useph was equally well dressed, as were all the principal officers and their chief blacks, and they made, as may be imagined, a very grand appearance.

They remained on the sands a long time : indeed many of the inferior horses seemed quite exhausted, and I heartily rejoiced to see the poor tired animals return home. The Moorish stirrups make a very singular appearance. Those belonging to the princes were of silver richly gilt. They weigh from ten to thirteen pounds, and measure more than half a yard from the toe to the heel : they are a flat plate under the foot with high edges at the sides, widening considerably at the toe and heel in the shape of a fire-shovel. They cut at both edges like a razor, and make one shudder on the poor animals' account ; for when they arrive at their stables they are often obliged to have their sides dressed, and to be carefully attended.

This, my dear friend, is among the many things I cannot account for : to me it is the greatest paradox, why any creature has life given it to suffer unmerited torture, or why life is given to a being who can wantonly inflict pain.

When the two princes passed us they stopped some time to converse, explained the meaning of some of their particular feats, and behaved very affably. On taking a polite leave they went off, racing backwards and forwards, and firing all the way to town. Gunpowder costs the Bey but little ; immense quantities being sent him as presents from the Emperor of Morocco by the Tripolitan ambassadors.

In our way home we passed through a street noted for its corn wells, or rather caverns, dug very deep into the earth. They are situated on each side of the street, at about thirty yards distance. They were designed for magazines to lay up corn in ; and they say it will keep in them perfectly good a hundred years. Happy were it for the inhabitants of this country if these caverns were filled now as they were formerly, when the country was so rich in the produce of corn that it was hence exported to many parts of the world, and prized almost above any other. The barley when sown here yields twice as much as it does in Europe. When it grows properly, they reckon twenty-five and thirty ears for one an ordinary produce, while in Europe fourteen or fifteen is considered as a good return. The times are so much altered now that corn is imported at an immense expense. This melancholy change is attributed to the want of rains, which have failed for several years past. There have not been more than one or two good harvests for thirty years. If cargoes of wheat do not soon arrive from Tunis, the state of this place will be dreadful beyond description. Corn is expected from the Emperor of Morocco, who has been grateful enough never to forget the civilities he received from the Bashaw, when passing many years since through this place in his pilgrimage to Mecca. His son, Muley Yesied, who is by all accounts a most depraved character, is expected here soon on his return from Mecca. His mother and sister are with him ; and the latter is expected to marry a shrieff of Mecca before she returns.

May 24, 1784

The Bashaw has not given his consent for some time past to the Christians to reside in the country, at a greater distance than four or five miles from the city of Tripoli, as he cannot answer for their safety, on account of the incursions of the Arabs, and even of the Moors, many of the cyderies being at present nearly in a state of revolt. We have the use of a large Moorish country-house on the skirts of the sands ; and though the grounds belonging to it are not in the best order, yet they are in the stile of all African gardens—a mixture of beauty and desolation. The orange, citron, and lime trees are in their fullest bloom : their branches, covered with flowers, are at the same time bending down with the weight of fruit ready for gathering. The Arabian jasmines and violets cover the ground ; yet in various parts of the garden, wheat, barley, water-melons, and other still coarser plants, are indiscriminately found growing. The high date tree, with its immense spreading branches, is planted round the gardens near the walls. The branches of this tree, which extend fourteen feet, grow from the top of it, furnished with close leaves from two to three feet long. Each bunch of dates, which resemble colossean bunches of grapes, weighs from twenty to thirty pounds. The tree grows nearly a hundred feet high. From this tree the Arab gathers the richest nourishment for his family, and from its juices allays fevers with the freshest lakaby, and cheers his spirits with that which has been longer drawn. They extract the juice from the tree by making three or four incisions at the top of it. A stone jar which will contain a quart is put up to each notch : the jars put up at night are filled by the morning with the mildest and most pleasant beverage, and, on the contrary, the contents of those jars which are put up in the morning and left till late in the day, become a spirituous strong drink, which the Moors render more perniciously strong by adding leaven to it. The tree will yield this juice for six weeks or two months every day ; and after the season, if taken care of, it recovers in three years, and bears better fruit than before it was bled, as the Moors term it. It is customary in noble families to have the heart of the date tree at great feasts, such as weddings, the first time a boy mounts a horse, the birth of a son, or the return of an ambassador to his family ; thus condemning this valuable tree from yielding further profit, for as timber it is of very little value. The heart lays at the top of the tree between the branches of its fruit, and weighs when cut out from ten to twenty pounds : it is not fit to be taken out before the tree has arrived at the height of its perfection. When brought to table its taste is delicious, and its appearance singular and beautiful. In colour it is composed of every shade, from the deepest orange and bright green (which latter encompasses it round) to the purest white ; these shades are delicately inlaid in veins and knots, in the manner of the most curious wood. Its flavour is that of the bannan and pine ; except the white part, which resembles more a green almond in consistence, but combines a variety of exquisite flavours that cannot be described.

The best dates, called by the Moors and Arabs taponis, when fresh gathered have a candied transparent appearance, far surpassing in richness any other fruit. In these gardens the Moors form no walks, only an irregular path is left, which you trace by the side of the numerous white marble channels that cross it with rivulets of water, as I have before described to you, through an almost impenetrable wood of aromatic trees and shrubs. The sweet orange of Barbary is reckoned finer than those of China, both in flavour and beauty ; and the next best is a small red orange which grows at Malta, almost crimson within. Cherries are not known here ; and pease and potatoes only when cultivated by the Christians. Water melons, as if ordered by Providence, are particularly excellent and plentiful. Many owe their lives to this cooling and grateful fruit, when nearly expiring through insupportable heat. The pomegranate is another luxurious fruit of this country. The Moors, by pressing the juice through the rind of it, procure an exquisite drink. The Indian and Turkey figs are acknowledged to be extremely good here. There are two sorts of apricots ; one which is remarkable for its large size and excellence, while the other, with the musk melons and peaches, is very indifferent. There are several sorts of fine plums and some very high flavoured sweet grapes, which, if cultivated in quantities for wine, would render this country rich in vineyards, from the ease and excellence of their production ; but Mahomet has too expressly forbidden wine to Mussulmans to admit of its being made in their presence, for even the sight of it is repugnant to the laws of the Koran. There are delightful olive woods near us, but when the olives are ripe it is inconvenient to walk under the trees on account of the olives continually falling loaded with oil. Near to these woods are marble reservoirs to receive the oil the Moors extract from the olives, and from these reservoirs they collect it into earthen jars : it is as clear as spring water, and very rich. The natives who can afford it are so delicate in their taste of oil, that they allot it to their servants when it has been made eight or nine months, and yet when a year old it often surpasses the finest Florence oil. The walls which surround the houses and gardens of the principal people divide this part into a number of narrow roads in all directions : beyond them are date-trees interspersed with fields of barley and high Indian corn. If to spaces of sand separated by olive plantations, sun-burnt peasants, and camels without number, are added a burning sun and the clearest azure sky, a just picture may be formed of this place. The deserts adjoining, though singular in appearance, seem frightful from the frequent and recent examples we have had of their victims. A party arrived from them yesterday so exhausted that they would have died on the road if they had not been instantly relieved by the Moors. Four of their companions had perished the day before for want of water and from the excessive heat. Hadgi Abderrahman, who is just named ambassador to England, often speaks of the death of his favourite daughter, who died in great anguish two days after crossing these deserts with him in his last return from Mecca. Being extremely delicate in her constitution, from the scorching heat of the ground at the different places they stopped with the tents, her feet became blistered and mortified.

An author, writing on the deserts near Suez, describes them in the following manner. " On the adjacent sandy desert, if reflection dwells, it is shocking to think how the tired traveller is discouraged ; his heart fails him at the immense space that separates him from the world, a space where neither tree nor herb is to be found to rest the searching sight on, no object between heaven and earth. A sandy ocean, boundless as the sea, and like that restless element blown by the winds into agitated waves. Destitute and alone in the wilderness, he sighs in vain for one drop of water ; fainting with thirst and heat, he groans and dies unpitied by any human heart." And the following lines from Addison can never be quoted too often for what they so well describe.

> " So where our wide Numidian wastes extend,
> Sudden th' impetuous hurricanes descend ;
> Wheel through the air, in circling eddies play,
> Tear up the sands and sweep whole plains away.
> The helpless traveller, with wild surprize,
> Sees the dry desert all around him rise,
> And, smothered in the dusty whirlwind, dies."
>
> *Cato*, act ii, scene vi.

The heat is so intense at present, that even the hardy Arab, inured to the climate, at ten in the morning retires from his work, and all his animals for labour are put up under shade.   At this time of the day, the Christian families seeking shelter in their gardens, enjoy their luxurious coolness and relief from the heat of the sun.   The warm air abates nothing of its oppression till a sudden cool breeze arises from the sea,[1] which during these intense heats happens regularly every afternoon ; but this sea air rusts all sort of steel work even in the pocket, and will wet a person's dress entirely through in a very few minutes. The gasping Moors regale themselves as soon as they feel it, by retiring to the terraces on the tops of their houses, and sleeping there for hours, which circumstance is deemed the cause of so many people being blind in most parts of Barbary.

The golphors and best rooms in the country houses are sometimes delightfully relieved by a considerable stream of clear flowing water, conducted in a marble channel through the middle of them.   The floors and sides of the apartment are finished with coloured tiles, and the ceilings carved and painted in Mosaic.   In the inner court belonging to the house is a gebbia, or reservoir, continually filled with fresh water from the wells near it, and which flows through it into the gardens ; it is surrounded with a parapet of marble, and a flight of marble steps leads into it.   There is only a broad walk left round it, which is paved or terraced, and into which the best apartments belonging to the house open.   This circumstance affords a refreshing coolness to the house, and is most delightful during the extreme heat.

July 24, 1784
I think it probable that the life of a Grecian beauty, related by herself, may gain additional interest with you, from the circumstance of her being wife of the ambassador, Haggi Abderrahman, whom you will soon see in England.   He is a most enlightened man, having been repeatedly at the chief courts of Europe.   Through the distinguished manner of conducting himself, he has been honoured by different sovereigns with many very valuable tokens of favour, which the Greek exultingly shews to all her visitors.   He bears here so excellent a character, that he is universally beloved by Christians as well as Moors, and is adored in his family.

This Grecian lady related the events of her life in the most interesting manner.   We saw her by appointment : she was evidently dressed

1 The *inbat*.

with studied attention, and looked particularly beautiful. She wears the Moorish dress, not by choice but compulsion, as she observed with a sigh, that she was compelled to lay aside the Grecian habit when she embraced the Mahometan faith, on the day she was married. She had dispensed with as many of the Moorish artificial additions to her dress as she could. Her jewels were brilliant from being all polished (the Moorish ladies often wearing them in a rough state), and what other arts she had used were not in opposition to nature, but successfully employed to improve her appearance ; but any compliment paid to her person seemed much to distress her with the unhappy recollection, as she termed it, of her beauty, at the time Abderrahman purchased her. Her expressions of regret on this occasion, puerile in another, proceeded entirely from her education. She is sensible and amiable, of a very fine figure, tall, with blue eyes and beautiful small white teeth. Her countenance, though lively and spirited, is the picture of innocence itself. She was as superbly drest as the Moorish costume would permit, and had for the outer covering a blue transparent baracan, fastened at the shoulders with a large cluster of brilliants, with several rows of very large pearls hanging from it. She had double gold bracelets on her arms ; her cap was entirely of gold, with a binding of black over the forehead set with jewels hanging over the face ; and she had six large rings in each ear, set with diamonds, pearls, and other precious stones. Two black slaves remained at her feet the whole time we were with her : when she removed from one place to another they rose up and followed her, and laid down at her feet again when she sat down : two other blacks constantly stood behind her. No Moorish lady keeps up near so much state as the Grecians and Circassians. Abderrahman remained a widower a few years with several children, and, rather than take a wife amongst the Moorish ladies, preferred looking out for a Grecian or Circassian slave, thinking she would behave with more attention to his children, through the fear of being sold again, or put to death : he therefore determined to go himself to the Levant to choose one for himself, and bring another with him for his nephew.

In his researches he met with two sisters equally handsome. Their being so nearly related would have deterred many Moors from taking them, from being both intended for one family ; but Abderrahman, ever benevolent and kind, and unlike the jealous Moor, hoped to excite affection by becoming the constant theme of two so nearly related, if fortunate in his purchase ; and he determined to wait for a proof of this before marrying the Greek he intended for himself, or persuading his nephew to marry the other. Strange to relate, the bargain was made for both, in her own hearing, with her father ; and her price was greater than her sister's, by possessing the acquirements of drawing, singing, and music. Equal care had been bestowed on their accomplishments, for on these is placed a Georgian's hope on the birth of a female infant. He views her only with the idea of future gain, and beauty without accomplishments would raise her no higher in the market than a common slave. Every nerve is therefore strained to excite natural and artificial graces, to make her excel in vocal and instrumental music, in all elegant works, and every thing which can add to the fascination of her person.

She spoke with enthusiasm of her country, as a garden in the richest quarter of the world, where the choicest fruits and flowers grow spontaneously. The inhabitants make the finest wines and as much as they please, without consuming half the grapes that grow without cultivation, and overrun their hills. But it was not without some emotion she described to us the hard lot of her handsome country-women : born to a life of slavery, chains await them in the cradle. In this first affecting state, the unnatural parent with impatience views the rising beauties of her infant. Every growing charm fills her with rapture, not excited by that maternal affection which should character-ize the mother, but, inconceivable to believe, by the sordid idea of how much gold every heightened charm will bring her, when her child is put up to be bought by the best bidder. She expects offers from a number of different Turks who come to purchase these un-happy beauties, not for themselves, in which case the mother having seen the man but for hours, might still recommend to him the fate of her offspring ; but, no, the Turk purchases for the merchant he deals with, or worse, to carry her to the next market, where he expects a handsome profit on his fair prize, by putting her up to sale to a crowd of crafty traders. Those fair creatures whose parents may cherish feelings uncommon to the generality of people there, or whose vast riches may make them decline, or not think of selling their children, even those few are exposed to a lot as bad or worse, as they are frequently carried off by parties of Turkish robbers, who make incursions into their country, to seize on such unhappy people as fall in their way, and by that means procure beautiful women at a cheaper rate. These sons of rapine watch for those who incautiously stroll too far in their walks accompanied only by a few female attendants.

They ride up to them in full speed, seize on their wretched prey, and placing them behind them like a bale of goods, ride off with the same celerity ; all which they do too quickly to admit of a discovery in time to redeem the unhappy captive, who has frequently many days' hard travelling to undergo in this manner, over barren deserts, before they reach any habitation.

These ruffians shew their unfortunate victims no other indulgence than that of keeping them free from bruises and hunger, and that from the motive of a cattle driver, who considers that a broken limb or a meagre appearance would spoil the price of his beasts at market.   But the hardship and fatigue these fair creatures endure in this first part of their journey often prove fatal to a frame too delicate to bear it, and rob the plunderer of his prize.

The first moment he thinks himself safe from pursuit, he encloses his wretched victim in a sack, which he carries with him for that purpose, to preserve her from the rays of the sun and other injuries. Incredible as these sufferings may appear, I shall transcribe for your perusal, in addition to the story of Lilla Amnani the Greek, the events of another Grecian lady, at present residing here, who herself endured the hardships Lilla Amnani has described.

Amnani [1] is the Moorish name the Greek received on her marriage with Abderrahman.   She was about seventeen, and her sister younger, when they embarked with him from Alexandria.   His attention at first was paid to her sister, and she herself was neglected.   On their arrival at Tripoli, her sister beheld with perfect indifference the preparations making at Abderrahman's for her reception, while Amnani could not conceal her tears when the day was named for her removal to the house of Sidy Mustapha, Abderrahman's nephew.   The first stern look, she said, she had ever received from Abderrahman, was on this occasion, when he bid them both withdraw, and for several days they heard no more of him.   They talked over their misfortunes, and shuddered with the fear of being sold again, particularly Amnani, who had regarded Abderrahman with partiality.

At their next meeting, he presented her sister to his nephew, and desired Amnani to consider herself as the mother of his children, and to prove her regard for him by her attention to them.   At this most happy period of her life, as she termed it, her courage almost forsook her : she fancied herself altered in her person, which seemed not yet to have recovered from the ravages of a sea voyage : she feared also

---

[1] Literally : " the desired one."

a greater change from suddenly quitting a life of luxurious ease, where every indulgence and attention had been most profusely allowed her. To keep herself cheerful, and improve her looks, required now her utmost exertions, in order to convince the friends of Abderrahman, who were her enemies, that she was wholly taken up with the charge of the family. All of them were very young, except the eldest daughter, who was near her own age and a great favourite with her father. The Greek could not speak a word of Moorish, and was besides a Christian brought into a Barbarian family, where the only enlightened person she could talk with was Abderrahman. Her first days were spent in endeavouring to divert Abderrahman's vigilance from perceiving the many malicious traits she suffered from the female part of his family, as she thought his displeasure, however excited, might only serve to irritate them, and consequently increase her own difficulties. Their continual visits, or rather examinations, she would gladly have dispensed with ; and though she was treated, by Abderrahman's order, with every mark of attention, yet in her precarious situation, as his slave, she was obliged to pay the greatest deference to their counsels, though often against her interest, till she gained sufficient confidence with him and Lilla Uducia, his daughter, to become more the mistress of her own proceedings. Abderrahman soon afforded her this advantage : he seemed to think all he could purchase for her was inadequate to her merit, and insufficient to shew his attachment to her ; and as a proof of the unbounded confidence he placed in her, he allowed her an indulgence quite novel to the Moors, that of writing to her friends, and receiving letters from them ; but this was not granted her till after her marriage, which took place, with great pomp, in twelve months after her arrival at Tripoli, on the birth of a son, who is now living, and for whom she confesses a distinguished fondness, by the circumstance of his birth having so soon terminated her captivity, made her Abderrahman's wife, and placed her on a level with the first ladies in Tripoli near the sovereign's family. Abderrahman introduced her to his relations as a person to be respected as himself, and had her presented to Lilla Kebbiera, who, from Abderrahman's long and faithful services to the Bashaw, gave her a most flattering reception. Finding herself perfectly happy at home, a favourite at the castle, above the power of those who might wish to annoy her, and respected by the country, she appeared now at the zenith of her happiness, when she received news from Georgia that her parents, by some unexpected losses, were reduced to the greatest distress. Amnani regarded her father with the strongest affection for the education he had given her, and almost lost sight of his cruelty in selling her. At this time Abderrahman, owing to a commencing scarcity in Tripoli, which has prevailed ever since, felt, in common with others, a great deduction in his revenues, and his increasing family made him very anxious to lessen his expenses.

Amnani was generous and timid, she brooded, therefore, over her family misfortunes in silence : her lyre was laid by, her songs were cheerless and her looks grave, and often an involuntary tear spoke her unhappy. She was not aware of the danger of her silence till she perceived it from Abderrahman's looks. He lamented the change in her manners, without inquiring into the cause of it : this alarmed her, and she determined to acquaint him immediately with the source of her grief, without seeming to impose on his liberality, which to her was unbounded, nor to give up easily her parents, whose sufferings she could not bear to think on without agony. While making up her mind to this explanation, Abderrahman was unexpectedly nominated, for the third time, ambassador to Sweden. So sudden was this embassy, that the day he received the proposal from the Bashaw, before his return to this house, the news of his appointment had already reached the unhappy Greek, and then an ambassador's flag was hoisted in the harbour for his departure. He found her more dead than alive. She told him the cause of her first distress, light in comparison to the present, in too short a time to explain it. He cautioned her to be aware of offending him a second time, by not making him her only confidential friend. The few hours that remained were obliged to be spent in audiences with the Bashaw and transacting business, leaving a very short space of time to take leave of his family. To console Amnani for the distress she had brought herself into, on parting with her, he left her in his absence an unlimited power over all that belonged to him, and entrusted her to his brother, only to demand protection if wanted, but to be under no subjection —a circumstance most uncommon, as Moorish ladies are generally exposed to the vigilance of the husband's family in his absence.

Not long after his departure, one of his favourite children, by the first wife, died. The Greek dreaded, and with reason, that the different branches of the family would attempt to injure her in the ambassador's opinion, with respect to the management of the child ; but, as she expressed it, their malice blunted its point against Abderrahman's heart, without piercing it. She neglected (as is the custom here) to break and destroy the choicest of the furniture or looking-glasses in her house at the death of this child, for which she was much blamed, and said to have shewn great disrespect to the family. All her enemies had persuaded themselves that she had, upon the whole, behaved so ill in his absence, that her destruction was inevitable at his return. Contrary to their expectations, however, when he arrived, Lilla Amnani was loaded with fresh presents, her brother sent for from the Levant, and her father and mother provided for. Abderrahman's attentions to her have never in the least diminished, and she often expresses her gratitude that her former wishes were not realized of being disposed of to a sovereign ; and with reason, when she compares her situation with that of the three queens or wives of the last Bashaw at Tripoli, who are imprisoned, or obliged to live in the castle for the rest of their days.

July 1, 1784

In the following events related by the Greek lady whom I mentioned in my last, you will find one of the few instances of a beautiful and delicate being having surmounted such sufferings as she experienced in the savage hands of Turkish robbers. Signora S——, who is still handsome, was born in Dalmatia ; her Christian name was Juliana : her father was an officer of distinction in the Venetian service. Her family was disliked by the Turks, on account of the skill and courage her grandfather displayed in endeavouring to defend the Morea from the Turkish arms when they last gained possession of it. Her mother, herself, and two sisters were living on an extensive estate, beautifully situated on the borders of Macedonia. Rich villages, though belonging to Turks and Tartars, surrounded them, and that part of the country was interspersed with aromatic heaths, impenetrable woods, and thick vineyards, but they were remote from any capital ; Salonica, the ancient Thessalonica, being the nearest to them, and they were not far from the village of Contessa. This lady thinks, if her mother had caused alms to be sent to the Holy Mountain of Athos, they might have averted all the troubles she experienced. This mountain is inhabited by friars, of whom there are no less than three thousand living in thirty monasteries : many of the Greeks visit it, and purchase separate blessings from the different convents at a very great expense. As the inhabitants of the surrounding villages were mostly Turks and Tartars, their society consisted only of a few families of Armenians, Dalmatians, and Sclavonians, who, like themselves, had retired to that part of Macedonia, while the heads of their families were fighting under the Venetian banners against the Turks in Venetian Dalmatia. Buried in the woods of Turkey, they remained often a long while without intelligence from the more civilized part of Europe, which this lady's mother seemed to regret infinitely more than the other Grecian ladies. She had passed the chief part of her life at Venice, and from being better informed, felt greater fears. She seemed to foresee the catastrophe which happened, and daily forbad her attendants to walk far from their dwelling with her children, fearing, as she said, the incursions of the Turks and Tartars, who, after every victory, usually scour the country, enriching themselves by plunder all the way on their return to Constantinople, or to their different Beys or Chiefs near the Black Sea ; yet, as they abstain from breaking into palaces and principal houses in their route, there is a possibility of being safe by keeping within doors.

At length some vague reports of the success of the Venetian arms lulled her into an idea of security, and she fatally acceded to the entreaties of her friends to spend the day at an Armenian's, whose residence nearly joined her own estates. She was accompanied by her two beautiful daughters, Juliana, then about thirteen, and her sister, about eleven years old ; and she confided her youngest child, an infant of two years, to the care of its nurse, a young Circassian slave, who had been with her some years.

She set out on this journey with nearly all the attendants she had, for greater security, though without the least apprehension. Within sight of her own domains, at the angle of an immense forest, of which they had a few paces to pass, as a tiger rushes on his prey, so sprang upon them from this wood a party of Turks.

The affrighted mother dropped instantly at the sight of them. Each ruffian seized a surprised and helpless victim, and it was the work but of a few moments for this banditti, in so unequal a combat, to cut to pieces the attendants that opposed them. Covering their wretched captives with large canvas bags which they tied over them, and fastening their prey on different horses, they took with them Juliana, her sister, and the Circassian, who, from affection, struggled to keep in her arms the infant she had with her ; and, unfortunately (as it afterwards proved) succeeded, though the Turks repeatedly commanded her to leave it on the ground at their first setting off : but, as the mother lay senseless and apparently dead, the Circassian could not think of abandoning the infant to himself. With incredible swiftness they continued pushing their horses up the steepest hills for several hours, till a tremendous storm of thunder and lightning obliged them to stop. They spread bags on the ground by the side of a woody mountain, and pitched some wretched tents which ill-sheltered them from the rain, in one of which they placed their miserable burthens, more dead than alive.

After the storm subsided, they brought them dried salt meat, called by the Moors kadeed, which they had toasted, with black bread and water, and threatened them with death if they did not eat. The Circassian endeavoured to stifle the cries of the unhappy child in her bosom, frightened at the rage with which the Turks had complained of its screams ; nor did her fears suggest to her the horrors they had yet to witness, for at sunrise these savages committed the infant to the flames, to ease themselves of its cries and the inconvenience of its being attended to, and then travelled with increased celerity across sandy deserts, through thick woods, and over rugged and steep mountains, till within a short distance of Constantinople, where they sold the unhappy Juliana and her sister to an Aleppo merchant who, for their farther misfortune, rejected purchasing the Circassian ; and thus parting them from their faithful domestic and fellow sufferer, carried them on towards Constantinople.

Their disconsolate and wretched mother, soon after they were torn from her, was sought for and recovered by her friends. When able to rouse herself from the lethargy which this dreadful catastrophe had thrown her into, by her unremitted inquiries she learnt the cruel news of her husband having been massacred with a party of Venetians by the Turks, and that the banditti, or Turkish soldiers, who had carried off her daughters, had taken them to Constantinople. In a distracted state, she immediately collected all she could of her property, and determined to follow them. She applied to an Armenian merchant at Constantinople, under whose protection she meant to place herself while she remained at the Porte, and employed him to make every possible search for her lost children. When she had informed him of her wretched story, he told her that he was at the same time lamenting the fate of a Venetian youth of family, with whom he had spoken that morning, and despaired of getting him ransomed. He had been taken prisoner, and was become the property of a Turkish Bashaw, who had been recalled by the Porte to be appointed to a new government, and who every day increased the sum he demanded for this unfortunate gentleman's liberty. As Juliana's grandfather had fought in several campaigns for the Venetians, and her father had now fallen in their service, the moment the wretched event of her's and her sister's capture was known at Venice, an order was sent from the States to ransom the children as soon as they could be found. The order reached Constantinople a few days after their mother had arrived there. This public tribute paid to the memory of those so dear to her, was truly consoling ; but no one knew where to find the unhappy captives. The Armenian merchant she was with, though very young, was extremely opulent and universally beloved as a most amiable character. He felt sincerely for her distress, and his age and temper led him to be highly interested from the picture she gave him of the two beautiful sufferers.

He had nearly abandoned the hope of finding them, when the young Venetian noble, whose chains he was endeavouring to remove, surprised him by a visit. He came accompanied by a Mameluke of the Bashaw's, to bring him a proposal from that prince, for selling a great number of black slaves before his departure for his new government, to which as he was already named and his retinue and equipage ordered to attend him in eight days, he could give but a short time for this commission. The merchant could only feel for the distress of his friend, whom he saw on the point of being hurried off to Persia before their last letters to his family had been answered for increasing the ransom offered for him, which the Bashaw had refused. He was shocked with the visible despair in his friend's countenance, and was encouraging him to hope that letters might yet reach Constantinople before his departure, when he was surprised to hear him declare that the arrival of such letters could not relieve his present sufferings. He told the merchant, that some time since the Bashaw got into his possession two of the most beautiful Grecians he had ever beheld, whom he purchased of Turkish robbers near Adrianople. It was at first thought the officer who bought them would have fallen into disgrace, as from their sufferings they were in a most emaciated state. He had paid many purses of gold for them, and on their arrival it was feared they would not recover from the excessive hardships they had endured in the first part of their journey ; but as they now became every hour more beautiful and displayed the highest accomplishments, the Bashaw had destined one of them for himself, and he meant to send her sister to his brother, a prince of Evrivan. They were at present, he said, confided to Zeleuca, a confidential Greek woman of the Bashaw's in the palace, to remain with her till the Bashaw's arrival in Persia. Zeleuca was a Grecian slave, who had been a long time in the Bashaw's family and had great influence with him. The Venetian told the merchant, that previous to the Bashaw's avowed partiality for the eldest, he had resolved to pay his own ransom for their liberty, and purchase his freedom some other way, but as he was now certain the Turk would not part with them, freedom, he said, was become indifferent to him. The Armenian endeavoured to conceal his own strong emotions from the Venetian youth, as he instantly conceived these were the two beautiful sufferers he was so earnestly in search of. He soothed the unhappy youth, entreating him to be patient and secret, and above all to profit no more of any opportunity accident might furnish him with of seeing or speaking to the Dalmatians, till he himself should meet with him again at the Bashaw's. The youth informed him, that owing to public business, the Bashaw would not take his family with him, and a Mameluke was appointed to superintend their journey, and they were to set out four days after the prince. The young Venetian then parted with his friend the merchant, and reflected with surprise on the uncommon agitation that he seemed to suffer, and his earnestness in enjoining him to avoid seeing more of the fair slaves ; but he had witnessed so many instances of generous and kind actions in the merchant during his frequent interviews with the Bashaw, that he had conceived the highest esteem for him, and therefore determined with confidence to put himself under his guidance.

The Armenian having communicated his suspicions to his afflicted guest, she was so transported, that she would instantly have gone to embrace her children, and claim them with prayers and tears, at the feet of their Turkish master, had not her friend prevented her from so rash a step. He reminded her that, with every reason to hope that the young slaves were her children, yet it was not fully ascertained, and it would be necessary to deliberate on the most cautious and practicable means of redeeming them should they prove so. He persuaded her to leave their fate in his hands for a few days, and trust to his endeavours to work out their deliverance. He knew that the Bashaw, fond of popularity, yet feared to appear severe or unjust. He was, however, ferocious, violent in his passions, and prone to secret revenge, and was one amongst the most powerful officers of his rank belonging to the Porte ; but as avarice was the leading feature in his character, the merchant nourished a faint hope of placing the children in their mother's arms again. He desired her to give him an open letter for her daughter, which he would endeavour to convey to her himself, and by that means discover if the children were hers or not. The account he had received from the Venetian left him no room to doubt it ; but to gain their confidence, and make them alone acquainted with a plan for their escape, seemed almost too difficult to accomplish.

He went as usual to the Bashaw's on business, and took with him bunches of pearls and an embroidered Persian web of gold and silver silk. He was admitted to the preceptress Zeleuca, as soon as she was told he knew of some great purchases to be made from the Turks, who were preparing for their pilgrimage to Mecca. He laid before her the pearls and silks, which were worth many hundred pataques, and when he had explained to her at what price she might obtain them, namely, by making immediate intercession with the Bashaw for the freedom of the Venetian youth, she lost no time in endeavouring to possess them. He required of her, that while he waited, she should inform the Bashaw, a ransom, equal to what he had last demanded for the Venetian, was ready to be paid. He told her he had not the courage to apply to the Bashaw himself, having been so often put off. The Greek, overjoyed and eager to obtain the riches that lay waiting for her, instantly disappeared to return in a few moments. The Armenian, by sacrificing a sum sufficient to make up the money demanded for the Venetian, was sufficiently sure of his enlargement without the help of Zeleuca ; it was not her interest with the Bashaw, but her absence from the apartment they were in, he was now so dearly purchasing. The Grecian ladies were seated at their embroidery frame. The Armenian availed himself of this moment to shew to the younger of the two her mother's letter open. Her agitation, her tears, her screams of joy, confirmed him he was right. He comforted her : he assured her he should soon be able to deliver her and her sister into their mother's arms, if the unfortunate agitation he had thrown her into did not prevent it. He told her, that on her prudence and dissimulation all depended, for if the least hint was given that she had been shewn a letter, the hope of liberty would be over. He had but just time to say that a woman from his sister would be the next person she would see, when Zeleuca returned with an order from the Bashaw for the Venetian's freedom on the payment of the ransom.

The Armenian now opened the silk for Zeleuca to inspect it more narrowly. He noted to her a considerable damage in it, apparently, as he said, from the circumstance of packing (a gold flower was entirely defaced), but he would send her a Greek, an adept in the Persian work, who would completely replace it : Zeleuca was delighted. Two days after the Bashaw had set out on his journey, the Armenian's sister, as eager as himself to restore the peace of this unhappy family, engaged one of her women, a faithful domestic who had been with her many years, to go as a sempstress to Zeleuca. This commission was received with joy by Acassia from her mistress, for the events of her own life had been such as to make her anxious on all occasions to shew her gratitude and love to the family with which she lived.

Acassia now went to Zeleuca, and conveyed to the Grecians sufficient attire for their disguise. She took the advantage of the time of day during which, in that part of the world, chiefs and servants universally retire and indulge themselves in repose ; and while Zeleuca was sleeping, Acassia conducted the trembling Grecians through a private door into the street. On their arrival at the Armenian's house, he immediately left it, and went to the Bashaw's palace, before Zeleuca or the Mameluke had time to cause a public alarm to be made for their master's loss. He found Zeleuca, as he expected, in the greatest consternation, but he easily prevailed on her and the Mameluke to be pacified, by his professions to serve them and his ability to do so. He wrote in their presence to their master, pleading their excuse for having been so unfortunate in their duty, and informed the Bashaw of (what he termed) the unexpected circumstance of the Grecians having escaped to his house. He told him of the sums lately remitted from the States of Venice for their redemption, and to what amount he would assist their afflicted mother in further augmenting those sums. He entreated the Bashaw to accept the gold for the two slaves, who were never likely to make him a better return. The Armenian, from long experience, had formed so just an idea of this Turk's predilection for riches, that if the Bashaw doubted the truth of any part of the account given him, he reconciled the loss of his fair slaves, by the unexpected wealth that loss produced him.

The Armenian, during the short period of these events, had sacrificed one-quarter of his whole fortune, for which he thought himself repaid with the hand and affections of the younger of the two beauties, and the extreme satisfaction of bestowing the elder on his Venetian friend. He pictured to himself, also, the chearful acquiescence of their mother in his plan for happiness ; nor was he mistaken : with grateful joy she saw him dispose of her children, in a manner so consonant to their wishes and her own.

The Venetian, by the consequence of his family, had the interest to obtain a diplomatic appointment very soon after his marriage with the fair Juliana. Many years after they were married, on account of the ravages of the plague in Africa, he overruled the affectionate scruples of his wife, and persuaded her to leave him for a time with their only daughter, a most beautiful girl, whose talents in Europe acquired all possible lustre from the first stile of education. She was married with every advantage her affectionate mother could wish, and they both at present make an invaluable part of our society.

The mother of Signora S—— was spared the horrid account of her little infant's fate. She was always humanely deceived with the assertion of its having died a natural death, owing to the hardships of the journey in the first day after her family was torn from her.

August 2, 1784

The serious intelligence received in the last few days has caused an unpleasant agitation in this place, and obliges all the Christians to return immediately to town. A courier has arrived at the castle by land with an account of their apprehension of the plague appearing at Tunis, and the preparation of the Spaniards to attack this place if they are successful against the Algerines, with whom they are now at war. The latter circumstances would make it necessary for the female part of the Christian families to go to Malta for a time ; but that will be impracticable, as the plague having appeared in these parts they cannot expect to be received any where in the Mediterranean.

It has been ascertained by the Bashaw to-day, that there is only barley for sale at two bazars, or market days, left in the place. A few years since the barley here grew so favourably, that it produced in return three times as much as in any part of Europe. Such quantities of it were exported, that Tripoli was much enriched by its sale ; but the failure of rain has left the country for several years without one good harvest. At present, they are grinding down the bark of the date-tree to support the cattle, asses, camels, and mules ; the horses, however, will not touch it.

Wheat has been sent for to Malta and Tunis, but it is so long in coming, that it is necessary to purchase what biscuits can be had from the few merchant vessels which touch here.

The place is, at present, in so dreadful a state of famine, that it is become horrid to walk or ride out, on account of the starved objects that continually die in the streets. The Christians have lessened, as much as possible, the consumption of provisions for their tables, in order to have a portion of meat dressed, which is given daily at the door to a certain number of hungry supplicants, and the greatest precaution is necessary to prevent giving them bread baked the same day, as some of these starved beings were in so famished a state, that their eating a small hot loaf occasioned their instant death.

Every article, even the most trivial, is at an enormous price. A very great number of Jews have emigrated from this distressed place to Leghorn, which renders the purchase of every thing more difficult and exorbitant, as trade here is chiefly carried on by the Jews. Money is now furnished at the dreadful sacrifice of from thirty to forty per cent. and the deduction paid on the delivery of the cash. I think, on the whole, you will agree with me, that it is easier to feel than describe the present state of this place, which, at this moment, only affords a prospect of increasing distress.

The communications from Tunis are continued by sea and land. The Venetians being at war with the Tunisians, the admirals Emmo, Priuli, and Querine, are in these seas with a very large fleet, and send their ships frequently into this port after their engagements on the coast of Tunis.

A deplorable French vessel with the plague on board lays in the harbour. She has been driven about at sea for a long time, and being refused entrance at Malta and several other ports, she went to Lampedoza, an island between Malta and Susa, where some friars and a few happy people had lived in a state of calmness for many years, in the cultivation and enjoyment of the produce of the island, and hardly holding converse with the rest of mankind. Here the captain attempted to air his cargo ; but as the opening of it proved instant death to those who did it, he was obliged to desist. During the seven days he remained there, the superior of the convent and nearly all the inhabitants of this little island died, and two Tripolitan corsairs who had put in there for water were burnt. He is arrived here with the same cargo, which consists of bales of cotton. There are a great many Turks on board, who offer to shave themselves and swim on shore : the rest

of the crew are constantly applying round the harbour for leave to
land and burn the vessel, which the Moors have not yet agreed to.

Though the people die of famine here daily, there is no other
appearance of sickness or fever.

A Caffagee [1] arrived to-day from Constantinople with a caftan
from the Grand Signior, which he presented to the Bashaw in public,
informing him of the birth of the Grand Signior's son. The guns
fired while the Bashaw put the caftan on to-day, and to-morrow they
will fire for the birth of this Turkish prince. These caftans are worth
so little, that after the Bashaw has gone through the ceremony of
putting them on, he gives them away to his attendants.

As the description of a Moorish lady of quality laying in state
presents itself in consequence of a recent event, I shall give you the
following account of one.

The mother of Lilla Kebbiera died yesterday at lazero, that is at
four o'clock in the afternoon, and was buried at the Moors' high mass
or namuz of noon to-day. The account of her demise affected her
daughter so much, that the death of this afflicted sovereign was reported for a short time ; a report which evidently displayed the high
place she possesses in the affections of her subjects.

She was this morning escorted from the castle with three of the
princesses, and Lilla Aisher the wife of the Bey, to mourn over the
body, till it is carried to the grave. It lay in state at the residence
where she died. The court-yard, stairs, and galleries, were filled with
such a concourse of people, that the way to the apartments was almost
impassable early in the day.

An immense number of women were assembled to shew their
loyalty by screaming for her death, and this scream was repeated at
different periods through the whole of the city, with such violence,
as to be heard distinctly a mile distant. Every place was filled with
fresh flowers and burning perfumes. The whole of the incense in
the apartment where the body lay was of amber and cloves, which a
number of black women carried about in silver censors.

The room was darkened, and hung with very rich drapery. The
body was raised on a bier, about three feet from the ground, which
was covered with velvets and silks, edged with gold and silver embroidery and very deep fringes. There were several coverings over

---

[1] A Caffagee differs from a Chaoux only from being higher in rank ; both acting as
messengers from one Turkish court to another. A *Khaffaji* would be a specially speedy
messenger. I assume the origin of the word to be from the Arabic *Khafa*, to speed up.

the bier : the two undermost being worked in stripes and borders representing sentences of the Koran. They were put on previous to the coffin (the lid of which was raised in a triangular shape) being placed on it.

As none but the royal family and the nobility use coffins of this shape, it is easy to distinguish the funerals of the great. All other coffins are quite open at top, and the body simply guarded by a drapery of cloth or silk, according to the circumstances of the family ; but over the poorest person, man or woman, who has lived so holy as to obtain the great title of *shrief of Mecca*, they put a Mecca cloth, round which is a deep border of chosen sentences from the Koran ; and if the deceased be a man, a green turban, which a shrief is entitled to wear, is laid on the top of the coffin. In the present case, the coffin was covered with a number of gold and silver habits belonging to the deceased. At the head was a very large bouquet of fresh and artificial flowers mixed, and richly ornamented with silver ; and to this bouquet they were continually adding fresh flowers. Mats and Turkey carpets were spread on the ground round the bier, at each end of which were embroidered cushions.

Lilla Kebbiera was sitting on one of these cushions at the head of the coffin, with her hand and arm resting upon it : she seemed much affected, and spoke very little. She was richly dressed, but wore no jewels nor any thing new, which denoted her being in mourning. When they came to take the body to the grave she retired, her ladies and black slaves encircling her with agonizing screams. When the coffin was carried out of the house it was covered with a party-coloured pall of black and coloured silk, richly ornamented with gold and silver : a massy gold work, with a black silk fringe, formed a very deep border round it.

It was met at the threshold of the door by the Mufti, or bishop, who walked close before it, preceded by the Bashaw's sons ; then followed the chief officers of state ; and next all the people of consequence in Tripoli. Immediately after it followed a great number of black men and women, each carrying a wand in their hand with a label at the top of it, declaring them freed from slavery by their late mistress, and by her daughter Lilla Kebbiera. All these wore their caps turned inside out, their clothes in a neglected state, and divested of every thing like ornament, such as silver or beads. The body was buried in a profusion of costly clothes and jewels.

September 24, 1784

To-day the colours were hoisted and the guns fired, much to the satisfaction of all here, for the Neapolitan and Spanish peace concluded with the Bashaw. All the Spanish and Neapolitan slaves are freed on this occasion, and this circumstance relieves the country from the fear of being attacked by the Spaniards. This agreeable event has been succeeded by another within the last few days, which is that of an unexpected supply of corn from the Emperor of Morocco.

The following account will afford you an example of how far gratitude and hospitality prevail among Moorish sovereigns. The Emperor of Morocco contracted a very sincere friendship with the Bashaw of Tripoli many years since, when passing through this kingdom on his way to Mahomet's tomb ; and the Bashaw has since always given a patient and kind reception to the emperor's eldest son, Muley Yesied, whose unexampled ferocity obliges his father to order him frequently to Mecca, keeping him by this means from Morocco three years at a time (as the pilgrimage takes him that time to complete it), during which journey he carries terror and dismay through every place he passes, and is tolerated here only from the friendship the Bashaw bears his father. The Emperor of Morocco considers the Bashaw's conduct to his son so great an obligation, that, on being informed of the distress of this kingdom, he has sent a present to the Bashaw of three cargos of wheat, to the amount of sixteen thousand potaques, and a saddle set with jewels and gold stirrups, worth ten thousand potaques more (about seven thousand pounds).

Muley Yesied is expected soon to pass this way on another pilgrimage to Mecca. The first of the cargoes of wheat sent from Morocco arrived here some days since, with which were letters to say the ship that brought it had taken the plague at Tunis, where it raged with uncommon violence when the vessel sailed for Tripoli. There are no lazarettos here, consequently no quarantine can be made to any effect, and therefore this circumstance occasioned the greatest consternation.

The Bashaw called a divan, and as the ship belonged to Christendom,[1] they assembled accordingly, when it was agreed on to receive the wheat, the country being in so famished a state, and to oblige the vessel to depart for Europe to perform quarantine.

The vessel is so infected it is expected the whole crew will die

---

[1] Then when any occurrence happens that jointly concerns the Christians and the Moors, the Bashaw calls a divan (a privy council), at which are assembled his chief officers of state and the Consuls from the different courts of Europe. (T.)

before they can reach a quarantine port, Leghorn being the nearest that will, or is fit (from the excellency of the Grand Duke's well-conducted lazarettos), to admit them in so bad a state.

📖

November 10, 1784

Admiral Emmo, with a large part of the Venetian fleet under his command, sailed from this port a few days since. It is the first visit he has paid to this part of Barbary during his expedition against the Tunisians. From the custom he has adopted of distinguishing himself on these occasions, he has entertained on board his ship the sovereigns of most of the courts in Europe. He has been lately at Leghorn, where he gave a dinner, and was honoured with four crowned heads at his table—the King and Queen of Naples, and the Grand Duke and Duchess of Tuscany. He has given a splendid entertainment during his stay here. The immense quantity of plate and valuable ornaments he has on board is owing to a singular custom, not unusual at Venice, to display the extreme grandeur of their richest houses. From the different branches of his family he has received for this expedition the most costly plate and valuable decorations they possess, which added to his own, and what the States of Venice afford him, enable him to display a sideboard which, for elegance and value, is allowed to be equalled or surpassed only by that of a sovereign. Piles of silver plates were placed on it, each amounting to many dozens, to supply the guests, who partook of three courses served in gold and silver only. The dessert exhibited a service of the finest porcelain, presented to Admiral Emmo by the Queen of Portugal, representing the history of the heathen gods, executed by the first artists. The Venetian men of war, by the sumptuousness of their decoration, the general richness of their arms, their shining military uniforms, and the showy habits of the private attendants, surpass all other ships in brilliancy of effect.

The famine continues to increase here, and, except from partial supplies, the place is in general distress. We yet escape the plague, though it is at Tunis.

📖

December 20, 1784

The Christians were invited to be present yesterday at the launching of one of the Bey's cruisers; when there was little to notice except one or two singular circumstances.

Just at the moment of its quitting the stocks, a black slave of the Bey's was led forward and fastened at the prow of the vessel to influence a happy reception of it in the ocean. Some embarrassment happened at the time of its going off, and Mustaphar (the first minister) not having seen the black attached, said it was no wonder the vessel did not go easily off the stocks, for they had neglected to bind a black on board and send off with it. A beautiful lamb fitted for the purpose, washed white as snow, and decorated with flowers and ribbands, stood on the deck, and at the instant the vessel plunged into the water received the fatal knife, being devoutly offered as a sacrifice to Mahomet for the future prosperity of the cruiser. It was saluted by the colours and guns on shore, and by those of all the different ships in the harbour.

The Bey's chief revenues are produced from his own navy, which his father allows him. His dock-yard, the only one here, is regulated by himself entirely ; the two young princes never interfering concerning it, though they often wish to do so. This establishment costs the Bey so much, that when the cruisers fail for a time in making adequate returns it is a serious loss to him. Though fond of state, and princely in his manners, he is mild in his measures, and suffers many checks on his grandeur from the fluctuating state of his cruisers without availing himself of imposition on his subjects, a practice too commonly followed by the Barbary and Turkish princes.

The Bey's Rais, or captains, are much displeased at the Bashaw having made peace with Spain, as it deprives them of the treasures they were used to make by Spanish prizes and Christian slaves ; but this peace raises a particular sensation of joy in the mind of those acquainted with the sufferings of the Christians at Algiers. The captains of the Algerine cruisers, if they are not the sole owners, have always a share in the vessels they command ; they cruise where they please, but are obliged, when summoned, to attend the service of the state, in transporting men and provisions at their own expense. They always have on board an experienced officer, appointed by the Dey, without whose consent they can neither give chace, return to Algiers, nor punish the sailors.

On their return, this officer reports to the Dey the conduct of the captain of the cruiser and his crew, and the captain must deliver immediately an account of his success to the government, which claims an eighth part of the prizes, slaves or merchandise, he has taken.

The Christian prisoners are brought to the Dey's palace, where the European consuls repair, in order to examine whether any of them belong to their respective nations : if they do, and are only passengers, they can reclaim them ; but if it is proved they have served for pay any nation which is at war with Algiers, they cannot be released without paying such ranson as the government may set on them.[1] The Dey has his choice of every eighth, and generally prefers those who are good mechanics to others. The rest, who are left to the owners and captors, are directly led to the besistan, or slave market, where they are appraised and a price is fixed upon each person, from whence they are brought back to the court before the Dey's palace, where they are sold by auction, and whatever is bid above the price set upon them belongs to the government. On the spot where they are sold, these unhappy people have an iron ring fastened on their ankle, with a long or short chain, according as they are supposed to be more or less inclined to escape. Instances do happen of their voluntarily after a time becoming renegados. If any of them can procure money they are allowed to trade, by paying a high tribute to the Dey, and some in this way subsist and yet remain in slavery. Those who cannot do this and know no trade, are used with great severity : they fare ill and work hard all day, and at night are locked up in public prisons without roofs, where they sleep on the bare ground exposed to the inclemency of the weather, and they are sometimes almost stifled in mud and water. All slaves must go to the public bagnio at night to sleep, unless permitted by favour of the Dey to do otherwise. In town the slaves are seen at the lowest and hardest kind of work, while in the country they are sometimes obliged to draw the plough instead of horses, and are in all other respects treated with such inhumanity as would, even there, be severely punished if exercised on brutes. The Christians at Algiers are permitted to apply for slaves and hire them as servants ; but then they must be answerable for returning them to the government when called for, or pay such a ransom as the Dey may choose to demand for them. Leave is sometimes obtained for the slaves to sleep at the house of their employers, if the Algerines have not been too much exasperated against the nation to which the slave belongs.

The mode of treating the Christian slaves is pourtrayed in the following instance of a Spanish family, just ransomed by the peace concluded this year between Spain and Barbary. They owe their

[1] See Introduction.

lives to a lady, who afforded them such protection in her own house as preserved them all from falling a sacrifice to their chains.

A Spanish lady, the wife of an officer, with her son, a youth of fourteen, and her daughter, six years old, were taken in a Spanish vessel by the Algerines. The Barbarians treated her and her children with the greatest inhumanity. The eldest they kept in chains, and the defenceless little one they wantonly treated so ill, that the unhappy mother was often nearly deprived of her reason, at the blows her infant received from these wretches, who plundered them of every thing. They kept them many days at sea on hard and scanty fare, covered only with a few soiled rags, and in this state brought them to Algiers. They had been a long time confined in a dreadful dungeon in the bagnio where the slaves are kept, when a messenger was sent to the Aga, or captain of the bagnio for a female slave. It fortunately fell to the lot of the Spanish lady, at the instant she was embracing her son, who was tearing himself from his mother with haggard and disordered looks to go to his imperious drivers, and while in despair she gazed on her little worn-out infant, to hear herself summoned to attend the guard of the prison to a family that had sent for a female slave. She obtained permission to take her little daughter with her. The state of the Spanish slaves at this time at Algiers was very shocking, not the least indulgence being allowed them. The Algerines were so much exasperated against the Spaniards, owing to the war, that they made it a point to treat the slaves with the greatest severity : it appeared therefore to this lady a happiness to be sent for to any place which had the name of a Christian house. Considering herself burdened with a child and apparently in bad health, she went with her little fellow slave in all the horrors of despair and anxiety. She dreaded being refused and sent back to the horrid dungeon she was leaving, where no deference was paid to rank, and slaves of all conditions were huddled together. At one moment her ears were shocked with indecencies, and at others with the sighs and groans of those as wretched as herself. Her son could do nothing to assist her, and the filth and stench of the prison were rapidly undermining her health. She went therefore prepared to accept of any thing short of these sufferings, but was, as she expected, at first refused, being every way so opposite to the description of person sent for. At length compassion overruling every obstacle, she was with her little girl accepted. But there remained another difficulty : she had left her son chained in the midst of that wretched filthy dungeon she herself had escaped from. To be at peace in this case without him, and eat the morsel she knew his hunger craved, was not in nature. Her truly kind patrons, observing that the singular favour they had bestowed was by some means wanting in effect, soon discovered her farther cause of distress ; but to send for this young man and treat him kindly, or in any way above that of a common slave, must hazard the demand of so high a ransom for him and his mother, as would preclude for ever the hope of their liberty. He was however sent for, and the menial offices they were both engaged to perform were only nominal. With circumspection the whole family were sheltered in this manner for three years, when the war with the Spaniards growing more inveterate, the Algerines demanded the youth back to the bagnio, to work in common with the other slaves at repairing the damages done to the fortresses by the Spanish cannon. He was now obliged to go loaded with heavy stones through the whole of the town to the walls, and at almost every step received dreadful blows, being unable to hasten his pace from the great weight.

Overcome at last with ill usage, the delicacy of his form and constitution being such as to make it impossible for him to support the labour, and finding himself at the point of death, he one morning refused the orders of his master or driver to arise from the straw he had laid down on, declaring if they chose to kill him they were at liberty to do it, for he would not even try to carry another load of stones. Repeated messages had been sent from the Venetian consul's, where his mother and sister were sheltered, to the Aga of the bagnio to return him, and when the Algerines found they had absolutely reduced him so near death, they thought it best to spare his life, in the hope that a Spanish peace, which was every day expected, might produce something for his ransom, and it being less trouble to them to send him away than to nurse him at the bagnio, they agreed to let him return to the Christians. His life was for some time despaired of, but his wounds were carefully dressed, and the attentions of his patroness, his mother, and sister, rescued him from the threatened dissolution. His recovery was concealed for fear of his being demanded back to work ; and a few months after, the Spanish peace being concluded, a ransom was accepted by the Algerines for this suffering family, and they were set at liberty.

Through the farther kindness and interest of their friendly patroness, they soon after obtained their passage, with every accommodation, and embarked for Spain, whence this now happy family greet their never-to-be-forgotten benefactress with every mark of gratitude and affection.

January 8, 1785

We have hardly a hope of escaping the plague : it increases daily at Tunis ; and to add to the misfortune of its reaching us, this kingdom is already in so unhealthy a state from famine that it is thought it will considerably add to its ravages. The cattle are all so curtailed of their food, that the horror of seeing them would be insupportable, were it not entirely done away by our still continuing to meet with human beings in the same emaciated and wretched state. The present lamentable situation of the kingdom renders it difficult for the different beys to gather in the Bashaw's tributes from the Arabs, who are so discontented that they are nearly in a state of insurrection. The Bey, the Bashaw's eldest son, has been obliged to go out with a camp to endeavour to bring them to order, and there are continual skirmishes in the deserts between the Arabs and the Bashaw's troops. Of the honour, courage, and hospitality of these warriors, there are some striking anecdotes.

A chief of a party of the Bey's troops, pursued by the Arabs, lost his way, and was benighted near the enemy's camp. Passing the door of a tent which was open, he stopped his horse and implored assistance, being almost overcome and exhausted with fatigue and thirst. The warlike Arab bid his enemy enter his tent with confidence, and treated him with all the hospitality and respect for which his people are so famous. The highest among them, like the heroes of old, wait on their guest. A man of rank, when visited by a stranger, quickly fetches a lamb from his flock and kills it, and his wife superintends her women in dressing it in the best manner. With some of the Arabs the primitive custom of washing the feet is yet adopted, and this compliment is performed by the head of the family. Their supper was the best of the fatted lamb roasted ; their dessert, dates and dried fruit ; and the lady of the tent, to honour more particularly her husband's guest, sat before him a dish of boseen [1] of her own making. It was of flour and water, kneaded into a paste, and left on a cloth to rise while the fire was lighted, then throwing it on the embers, and turning it often,

---

[1] *Bazeen*, still a popular dish among Libyan Arabs ; so much so that they call themselves *ahl el bazeen* or *bazeen* eaters.

it was taken off half-baked, broke into pieces, and kneaded again with new milk, oil, and salt, made into the shape of a pudding and garnished with kadeed, which is small bits of mutton dried and salted in the highest manner.

Though these two chiefs were opposed in war they talked with candour and friendship to each other, recounting the achievements of themselves and their ancestors, when a sudden paleness overspread the countenance of the host. He started from his seat and retired, and in a few moments afterwards sent word to his guest that his bed was prepared and all things ready for his repose ; that he was not well himself and could not attend to finish his repast ; that he had examined the Moor's horse and found it too much exhausted to bear him through a hard journey the next day, but that before sunrise an able horse, with every accommodation, would be ready at the door of the tent, where he would meet him and expect him to depart with all expedition. The stranger, not able to account farther for the conduct of his host, retired to rest.

An Arab waked him in time to take refreshment before his departure, which was ready prepared for him ; but he saw none of the family till he perceived, on reaching the door of the tent, the master of it holding the bridle of his horse, and supporting his stirrups for him to mount, which is done among the Arabs as the last office of friendship. No sooner was the stranger mounted than his host announced to him, that through the whole of the enemy's camp he had not so great an enemy to dread as himself. " Last night," said he, " in the exploits of your ancestors you discovered to me the murderer of my father. There lie all the habits he was slain in (which were at that moment brought to the door of the tent), over which, in the presence of my family, I have many times sworn to revenge his death, and to seek the blood of his murderer from sunrise to sunset. The sun has not yet risen ; the sun will be no more than risen when I pursue you, after you have in safety quitted my tent, where fortunately for you it is against our religion to molest you after your having sought my protection, and found a refuge there ; but all my obligations cease as soon as we part, and from that moment you must consider me as one determined on your destruction, in whatever part or at whatever distance we may meet again. You have not mounted a horse inferior to the one that stands ready for myself ; on its swiftness surpassing that of mine depends one of our lives or both." After saying this he shook his adversary by the hand and parted from him.

The Moor, profiting by the few moments he had in advance, reached the Bey's army in time to escape his pursuer, who followed him closely, as near the enemy's camp as he could with safety. This was certainly a striking trait of hospitality, but it was no more than every Arab and every Moor in the same circumstances would do.

This fortunate chief, whose name is Hadgi Ben Hassunna, in consequence of his returning from the camp—a circumstance which led all his friends to congratulate and entertain him—dined with us but a few days after the above mentioned event. He is thought one of the Bashaw's best generals ; but he is so much attached to the Bey and noticed by him, that he has on this account very formidable enemies in the Bashaw's suite, among those leaders of faction who abound here.

ՒՒ

March 5, 1785

As it is contrary to the Mahometan religion to endeavour to avoid contagion, the Moors expose themselves so much to the attacks of the plague, that we have been obliged to defer our visits to the castle and to Moorish families for some months past. The plague is not said to be yet in Tripoli, but evil spirits (according to the Moors) have been so very busy lately, in seizing on people and occasioning their death in an extraordinary manner, that all who do not believe in supernatural causes, think the infection is in the country, and even in town, which is worse. By the last accounts from Tunis, which is not three hundred miles from us, seven hundred die daily of this dreadful malady.

A Moorish family of consequence here, who had adopted the advice given them of using some precautions against the plague, began a sort of quarantine ; but yesterday the eldest daughter was married to her cousin, who lives with his uncle, the bride's father ; and the public ceremony of sending the presents from the bridegroom to the bride's family, and the bride's dowry from her father to the bridegroom, could not be dispensed with. Accordingly camels, mules, and guides attended at the doors of the bride's father, and an immense concourse of people crouded into the court-yard and the entries of the mansion, whence many deal boxes of the same shape and size, containing treasures and rich apparel, were placed on the different animals. Numerous bundles in costly silk handkerchiefs of gold embroidery, and a number of neat white baskets made of the palm-leaf, filled with refreshments and sweetmeats, and covered with choice flowers (a certain means of communicating the plague), were carried by black men and women. The whole moved in procession through the town and returned to the house, where they were admitted through a different entrance from that they came out at.

The family, to guard themselves from the effect of so dreadful a guest as the plague, very likely to be introduced by this indispensable ceremony, have armed themselves with what they deem an invulnerable shield, prepared according to the Moorish custom, of writings from the Koran.[1] These ceremonies, with many days spent in sacrificing to Mahomet through the Imams, have cost the family great sums of money, and large quantities of oil and other provisions sent to the marabuts or saints.

When we saw the bride's mother, a few months ago, one of her favourite children had been ill some days ; a marabut then attended, and writing sentences applicable to her situation out of the Koran, they were directly consumed on a china plate, and the embers being carefully gathered into a glass of water, she drank it off. Relics of every description from Mecca covered the infant from head to foot : its nurse held it aloof from the Christians, as she feared, more than its mother did, the effect of their embracing or looking on it. A priest had attended the sacrifice of a lamb, to see that no bone was ill-formed, or injured in the least, in dividing the animal, and likewise to see that the blood was all carefully buried. The meat was dressed and eaten by the family, and all the bones were collected and buried with the same care and ceremony as the blood.

The writings of no prophet excite a more fervent zeal than that with which the true Mussulman at this day beholds the Koran. They say of it, " that the Koran, their prophet's celestial present to all true Mussulmans, was delivered to Mahomet, verse by verse, by the angel Gabriel, in the night of Al-Kadir."

A verse in the chapter of Al-Kadir[2] says, " Verily, verily, we sent down the Koran in the night of Al-Kadir.

" The night of Al-Kadir is better than a thousand months ; therein do the Angels descend, and the spirit of Gabriel also, by permission of their Lord, with his decrees concerning all things. Through the night of Al-Kadir is peace, until the arrival of the adan " (morning).

[1] The more ignorant Moslems still resort to this kind of sympathetic magic. The *Ayat el Kursi,* or 255th verse of the Surah, " The Cow," in the Quran, is that usually employed.

[2] *I.e. el Qadr :* the 97th Surah of the Quran.

To prove that the Koran is of celestial origin, and conducted to earth by heavenly messengers, the Moors quote to themselves the above verse of Al-Kadir, place it over the doors of their mosques, and write it on the walls of their apartments.

It is not lawful for Mahometans to print the Koran ; but their manuscripts are preserved with the greatest care and jealousy, and the most minute alteration in them is impossible, as the Moors recede, with horror, from the thought of any one point being altered in this sacred book. They believe a chapter or verse of this book will relieve them in dangerous sickness, guard them from accidents or approaching evils, and lengthen life and render it prosperous. In short, they have recourse to quotations from the Koran in all their troubles ; which quotations are procured from the imams or marabuts, at a very great expense. A Moorish ablution is necessary before they presume to touch the sacred book, and Mahomet pronounces it contaminated when any but a Mussulman looks upon it.

෴

April 29, 1785

In the last few weeks several couriers have crossed the deserts from Tunis to this city, disseminating the plague in their way ; and consequently the country round us is every where infected. Even the Moors now allow it ; but their precautions are rendered useless by not continuing them ; for though from circumstances they are induced at one moment to check an indiscriminate intercourse between the sick and healthy, they give way to it the next.

Last night, a little before midnight, the wife of the Bey, Lilla Aisha, with the three eldest princesses, Lilla Udacia, Lilla Howisha, and Lilla Fatima, walked through the streets by torch-light, from the castle to a mosque, to make offerings and worship at the shrine of one of their great marabuts. They were completely surrounded by their ladies, who were again encircled by black slaves, round whom proceeded the eunuchs and mamelukes of the castle, while the hampers, or Bashaw's body guards, followed. The princesses were accompanied by their brothers, the two youngest princes, Sidy Hamet and Sidy Useph, with their suite. It was one of those fine calm nights, with a clear brilliant sky, peculiar to the Mediterranean. Not a breath of air disturbed the cloud arising from the aromatic vapour that enveloped this body, as it moved slowly along. Some minutes before it approached, a warning cry was heard from the chaoux (herald), who carried a decisive denunciation of death to all who might attempt to view this sacred procession. Guards hurried through the streets to clear the way, and the loud cheers or song of Loo, loo, loo, sung by a great number of their best female voices selected for that purpose, were heard at a great distance. The princes, their suite, and all the male attendants, waited at the gates of the mosque till the princesses had completed their oblations, which lasted about half an hour, when they all returned to the castle in the same order in which they had left it.

The present state of the castle, menacing all its inhabitants in so dreadful a manner, is the cause of this royal nocturnal visit to the shrine of the marabut.

May 27, 1785

The prime minister Mustapha Scriven's house is at present as much in a state of quarantine as he can put it, consistent with the ideas of the Moors ; yet he will not admit to any one, nor to the Bashaw, the necessity of taking precautions at the castle, where he alleges sovereignty is the greatest shield, and whence he says it is necessary to give the Moors an example, not to try to resist the hand of fate.

It is against the Mussulmans' faith to number the dead ; they are not, therefore, exactly aware of the increasing mortality : but the castle is much infected ; one of the princesses, a child of six years old, died two days since, and one of the three remaining queens of the last sovereign was buried to-day. By the Bashaw's orders, her funeral was attended by several of the officers of state, and by four black slaves, freed by him in compliment to this relict of his father ; she was buried in very rich clothes, and with all the jewels found in her possession. The four enfranchised slaves who followed her were about four hundred pounds ; they cost from about two to three hundred maboobs each.

A long succession of coffins, purposely kept back for some hours, were carried close after this queen's funeral, to profit by the mass (much grander than usual) that was to be performed for her. From the richness of most of these coffins, they appeared, in the bright glare of the sun, a line of burnished gold, too dazzling for the sight. The castle gates were for the first time closed to-day, allowing only a partial admittance. Four people who were perfectly well in the morning were taken ill there yesterday afternoon ; they were brought out of the castle last night at ten, and died at midnight. Two of them went raving mad, and they were all afflicted with large swellings on different parts of the body when they died.

The symptoms of the plague at present are, that of the person being seized with a sort of stupor, which immediately increases to madness, and violent swellings and excruciating pains in a few hours terminate in death.

The Bashaw expresses great regret at the thought of the Christians shutting their houses so soon, as the country is in so famished a state ; for he says that will declare it in a state of infection, and prevent the arrival of grain. The Christians' houses will, however, all be closed in about a week, each one hiring a set of servants to remain with them imprisoned till the plague is over. Halls, windows, and terraces are undergoing a scrutiny for a strict, and we fear a long quarantine. The terraces and windows fronting the street are to be secured from the servants, and the halls prepared for a mode of receiving what is wanted with safety to the family. Should it be necessary to change servants, or to take in additional ones, it can be done only on condition that they relinquish the cloaths they have on ; go into a bath prepared for them in the skiffer or hall of the consular house, and submit to remain in one room a fortnight to ascertain their not having the plague. Many jars, containing several pounds each, are prepared with ingredients for fumigating the apartments, two-thirds of which are bran, and the rest equal parts of camphire, myrrh, and aloes. This perfume, and small quantities of gunpowder, are burnt daily throughout the houses. All animals and fowls whatever are sent out of the Christian houses, for fear of the infection being communicated by their hair or feathers.

The present moment is the most dangerous period of the disorder for the Christians. When once the houses are shut, their safety will depend greatly on the strictness of the quarantine they keep. No business is now transacted but with a blaze of straw kept burning between the person admitted into the house and the one he is speaking to. A friend is admitted only into a matted apartment, where he retires to the farther end of the room to a straw seat, which is not touched after his departure till it is fumigated. The keys of all the ways into the house are kept by the master of the family only. If any of the Christian gentlemen are obliged to go out on business during this interval, before the houses are closed, a guard walks before and one behind, to prevent any person approaching too near ; and, on returning, the guards are put into quarantine for some days. Without these precautions, it would be impossible to escape this dreadful disorder, the rage of which increases every hour.

June 28, 1785

It is impossible to give you a just description of this place at present ; the general horror that prevails cannot be described. Hadgi Abderrahman sailed from the harbour of Tripoli on the 20th of this month, as ambassador to Sweden and England. From the state Tripoli is in, sinking under plague and famine, the departure of the ambassador from his handsome Greek, Amnani, and her children was dreadful. He made up his mind to see but few of them again, and with reason : the dire infection had entered his walls, nor was it to be imagined that even his own suite could embark untainted with the same. If he is so fortunate as not to fall a victim to the plague before he reaches Malta, he will perform there a heavy quarantine of ninety days at least. They perceived before they quitted the harbour, one of his people, a Jew broker, severely attacked with the plague ; and they put him on shore before they sailed. Abderrahman is so much be-loved, that the people in general participate in his sufferings, and the screams for the calamity of his family, which began before he sailed from the harbour of Tripoli, have continued to the present moment, and are still augmenting from increasing deaths. At this awful period, the care of Lilla Amnani, his wife, and his favourite eldest daughter, devolves on his brother Hadgi Mahmute, who is dying in torments unheard of, from the singular instance of the plague having at first seized him in his mouth, producing violent tumours, by which he is now starving : he is at times so raving that many people are required to secure him. Though none of his family were ill when his brother sailed for Europe, his wife and children (one already buried), with many more relations of Abderrahman's family, are dying very fast. Lilla Amnani, Abderrahman's daughter, and his niece, are all the ladies that remain of his family. Of his slaves and attendants only an old black eunuch lives, who is confined with the plague for the third time. In the short space that has elapsed since the ambassador left Tripoli, only eight days, nearly one hundred persons have died belonging to him ; and consequently, it is thought, not one will remain of his family to give him an account of these sad times.

The plague now depopulating this place is said to be more severe than has been known at Constantinople for centuries past, and is proved by calculation to destroy twice the number of people in proportion to those who died of the same disorder lately at Tunis, when five hundred a day were carried out of that city. To-day upwards of two hundred have passed the town gate. The city of Tripoli contains 14,000 [1] inhabitants, and the city of Tunis 30,000.

Our house, the last of the Christian houses that remained in part open, on the 14th of this month commenced a complete quarantine. The hall on entering the house is parted into three divisions, and the door leading to the street is never unlocked but in the presence of the master of the house, who keeps the key in his own possession. It is opened but once in the day, when he goes himself as far as the first hall, and sends a servant to unlock and unbolt the door. The servant returns, and the person in the street waits till he is desired to enter with the provisions he has been commissioned to buy. He finds ready placed for him a vessel with vinegar and water to receive the meat, and another with water for the vegetables.

Among the very few articles which may be brought in without this precaution is cold bread, salt in bars, straw ropes, straw baskets, oil poured out of the jar to prevent contagion from the hemp with which it is covered, sugar without paper or box. When this person has brought in all the articles he has, he leaves by them the account, and the change out of the money given him, and retiring shuts the door. Straw previously placed in the hall is lighted at a considerable distance, by means of a light at the end of a stick, and no person suffered to enter the hall till it is thought sufficiently purified by the fire ; after which a servant with a long stick picks up the account and smokes it thoroughly over the straw still burning, and locking the door returns the key to his master, who has been present during the whole of these proceedings, lest any part of them should be neglected, as on the observance of them it may safely be said the life of every individual in the house depends.[2]

Eight people in the last seven days, who were employed as providers for the house, have taken the plague and died. He who was

---

[1] According to consular estimates the population of Tripoli in 1790 was about 25,000.
[2] Although in the eighteenth century it was not known that the carrier of bubonic plague was the flea, these precautions seem eminently sensible.

too ill to return with what he had brought, consigned the articles to his next neighbour, who faithfully finishing his commission, as has always been done, of course succeeded his unfortunate friend in the same employment, if he wished it or recommended another : it has happened that Moors, quite above such employment, have with an earnest charity delivered the provisions to the Christians who had sent for them. The Moors perform acts of kindness at present, which if attended by such dreadful circumstances, would be very rarely met with in most parts of Christendom. An instance very lately occurred of their philanthropy. A Christian lay an object of misery, neglected and forsaken ; self-preservation having taught every friend to fly from her pestilential bed, even her mother ! But she found in the barbarian a paternal hand : passing by he heard her moans, and concluded she was the last of her family ; and finding that not the case he beheld her with sentiments of compassion mixed with horror. He sought for assistance, and, till the plague had completed its ravages and put an end to her sufferings, he did not lose sight of her, disdaining her Christian friends, who left her to his benevolent care.

The expense and the danger of burying the dead has become so great, and the boards to make the coffins so very scarce, that the body is brought out of the house by friends to the door, and the first man they can prevail on carries it over his shoulder, or in his arms to the grave, endeavouring to keep pace with the long range of coffins that go to the burying ground at noon, to take the advantage of the great mass. To-day the dead amounted to two hundred and ninety.

A Genoese doctor, who has been here some years receiving a fixed salary from the court of Tripoli, and from all the Consuls residing here, had orders from the Bashaw to repair to the castle. On his not immediately obeying the summons, a guard was appointed to bring him there by force ; but the doctor being conscious he must immediately fall a victim to the plague, without a chance of mitigating its horrors in the castle, it being unfortunately a malady which rarely yields to medicine, determined to elude their search, and embarked without being discovered on board the vessel in which Hadgi Abderrahman sailed for Europe.

July 1, 1785
The cries of the people for the loss of their friends are still as frequent as ever ; not a quarter of an hour passing without the lamentations

of some new afflicted mourner. No more masses are said in town at present for the dead ; but the coffins are collected together and pass through the town-gate exactly at noon, when the great mass is performed over all at once, at a mosque out of the town, in their way to the burying ground. The horrors of the melancholy procession increase daily. A Moor of consequence passed to-day, who has not missed this melancholy walk for the last fifteen days, in accompanying regularly some relic of his family. He is himself considered in the last stage of the plague, yet supported by his blacks he limped before his wife and eldest son, himself the last of his race. The riches of his family become the property of the Bashaw, no one remaining to claim them, as does all other property except what returns to the church ; lands or houses of this description annexed to the church, in possession or reversion, being deemed sacred both by prince and people in all Mahomedan states : therefore, by whatever means the property is acquired by those who give the reversion of it to religious foundations, those riches are transmitted unmolested to their direct male issue. Mecca and Medina are the places generally preferred for such dotation ; the cave at Mecca, in which the angel Gabriel delivered the Koran to Mahomet, and the tomb of Mahomet at Medina, rendering these places sacred above all others. They give the name of vacaf [1] to this settlement, for which they pay a very small acknowledgment yearly till the extinction of the issue that holds it, when it all devolves to the religious foundation on which it was settled.

Women, whose persons have hitherto been veiled, are wandering about complete images of despair, with their hair loose and their baracans open, crying and wringing their hands and following their families. Though a great deal of their grief here by custom is expressed by action, yet it is dreadful when it proceeds so truly from the heart as it does now, while all those we see are friends of the departed. No strangers are called in to add force to the funeral cries : the father who bears his son to-day, carried his daughter yesterday, and his wife the day before : the rest of his family are at home languishing with the plague, while his own mother, spared for the cruel satisfaction of following her offspring, still continues with her son her wretched daily walk.

Since the beginning of this dreadful infection, which is only two months, three thousand persons have died in this town (nearly one-fourth of its inhabitants),[2] and its victims are daily increasing. It must

---

[1] Literally *waqf*.
[2] This figure is clearly incorrect. See note on p. 116.

be observed, that the Moors, in all maladies, have great disadvantages, arising from the manner the people here treat their sick. I believe it to be often a doubt, whether the patient dies of the malady he labours under, or by the hand of those attending on him. They seem to have but a slender knowledge of physic : fire is one of their chief remedies ; they use it for almost every thing ; for wounds, sickness, colds, and even for headaches, they have recourse to a red-hot iron with which they burn the part affected.[1] They perform amputations safely, though in a rough manner ; but in all kinds of diseases, such as fevers, etc., it is thought one-fourth die of the disorder, and three of the remedies made use of. They will give fat boiled up with coffee-grounds to a child of three months old for a cough ; and to a man in a high fever, a dish called tarshia, made of red pepper, onion, oil, and greens ; or a dish called bazzeen, a kind of stiff batter pudding, dressed with a quantity of oil, and garnished with dried salt meat fried, known by the name of kadeed. When a person is thought to be dying, he is immediately surrounded by his friends, who begin to scream in the most hideous manner, to convince him there is no more hope, and that he is already reckoned amongst the dead ! The noise and horror of this scene cannot surely but serve to hurry the patient, worn down already by sickness, to his last state. If the dying person be in too much pain (perhaps in a fit) they put a spoonful of honey in his mouth, which in general puts him out of his misery (that is to say, he is literally choaked) ; whereas, by being treated differently, or even left to himself, he might, perhaps, have recovered. Then, as according to their religion they cannot think the departed happy till they are under ground, they are washed instantly while yet warm, and the greatest consolation the sick man's friends can have is to see him smile while this operation is performing, as they look on that as a sign of approbation in the deceased of what is doing ; not supposing such an appearance to be a convulsion, occasioned by washing and exposing to the cold air the unfortunate person before life has taken its final departure. This accounts for the frequent instances which happen here of people being buried alive : many of the Moors say a third of the people are lost in this manner.

A merchant, who died here a little while ago, was buried in less than two hours after they thought he was dead. In the evening of

---

[1] The Traditions of the Prophet Mohammed, which formed the basis for much Moslem medical practice, gave three basic cures for illness. These were cautery, honey, and cupping. All three are still employed in the remote areas of Libya.

the same day, some people passing by the burying ground heard dreadful cries, and when they came into the town, they reported what had happened. As this man, whose name was Bio, was the last buried there that day, his friends went in the morning early to look at his grave, which they opened, and saw him sitting upright : he had torn off all his clothing, but was suffocated.

When they prepare a body for the grave, those who can afford it fill the ears, nostrils, and under the eyelids with a quantity of camphor, and the richest spices they can procure, and burn a great quantity of aromatic herbs under the boards the body is washed on. They then dress it in the best clothes they have, and put on it all the gold and jewels they can spare. An unmarried woman is dressed as a bride, with bracelets on her hands and feet ; her eyebrows painted, and the hairs plucked out that they may look even. When dressed, the body is wrapped up in a fine new piece of white linen, brought from Mecca where it has been blessed. The poorer Jewesses will work night and day till they have amassed money enough to purchase a piece of linen, which remains by them till wanted to bury them.

The coffin is covered, if a woman's, with the richest laced jilecks or jackets they have ; if a man's, with short caftans of gold and silver tissue. At the head of a man's coffin is placed his turban, made up as handsome as possible, and as large as his rank will allow. The turbans, to those who are versed in them, clearly point out the description of the persons who wear them. By their fold, size, and shape, are known the ranks of military and naval characters, the different degrees of the church, and the princes from the sovereign. A turban worn by a Hadgi is different from others, and a green one can be worn only by a shrief of Mecca. The size then of the turban is increased according to the rank of its wearer, and whether he belongs to the military, the navy, or the church, is known by the folds of his turban. At the head of a woman's coffin is fastened, instead of a turban, a very large bouquet of fresh flowers, if they are to be procured ; if not, artificial ones. The body is carried often by its nearest relations, who in their way to the grave are relieved every moment by some friend or acquaintance of the deceased, or some dependent on the family ; all of whom are so very anxious to pay this last respect in their power to the remains of the departed, that the coffin is continually balancing from one shoulder to another till it reaches the burying ground, at the risk of being thrown down every moment.

When an unmarried woman is brought out of the house to be

buried, they sing a song, which they call making Loo, loo, loo, over her. A number of women are hired to sing this song (which is but a succession of the above words) at all feasts and weddings ; and they look on it as a bad omen to bury any woman without it who has not lived to have it sung at her wedding, that being the first time she can hear it for herself. A space is dug very little more than big enough to hold the body, and plastered with a composition of lime on the inside, which they make in a very little time as neat as china-ware. The body is taken out of the shell, and laid in this place, where prayers are said over it. The imam of the parish accompanies it from the house to the grave. If the corpse is buried at noonday, they stop at the most capital mosque in their way to attend the great mass. When the body is laid in the earth, the pit is covered with broad deal boards, to prevent the sand from falling in. These boards form a very considerable trade to this place from Venice, whence they always procure them. They bury very near the surface of the earth ; which is the more extraordinary, as they know that an immense number of dogs from the country come in droves every night to the graves of their departed friends ; and yet there is not any people who hold their own dead, or those of any other religion, more sacred.

Inscriptions are found only on tombs belonging to people of consequence. It is the custom here to visit often the spot where the remains of a friend are deposited. The women mostly pay these visits, and generally on a Friday,[1] the eve of the Mahommedan sabbath, when they believe the dead to be in general commotion, every one awakened up, visiting his relations or friends that lay near him ; and this extraordinary idea is one of the reasons why they attach so much consequence to the dressing of the dead, as they say (justly, while they harbour this idea), what could equal the indignation of a deceased friend, to find himself at so great an assembly indifferently dressed, through the neglect of those nearest related to him when he died ?— The tombs are whitewashed, and kept in constant repair. The most miserable women here observe these customs, even at the expense of their daily bread. A poor Jewess will buy a basket (called here a cuffa) [2] of lime, and go herself to decorate and whitewash the grave of any near relation she has lost, and plant fresh flowers round it, clearing the ground carefully of every thing she thinks ought not to grow there. The tombs of the great are distinguished by a marabut or

---

[1] The author is incorrect : the " Moslem Sabbath " is a Friday.
[2] Literally *quffa* (Arabic).

small chapel being built over them, which is kept in the nicest repair imaginable, and supplied daily with the most expensive flowers placed in china vases during the life of any near relation.

There is here, belonging to the family of a Bey, a tomb kept in the highest preservation ; it is in a burying ground not far from town. Lights are always kept burning in it, and a great number of fine fresh bouquets and Arabian jasmines, threaded on a thin slip of the date leaf, are hung in festoons and tassels all over the grave. This little chapel is open on the four sides : it has arches from the top to the ground, closed with iron rails, handsomely wrought and gilt.

The appearance of the variegated fresh flowers arranged with taste, and their delicious fragrance, added to the clean, pleasant, and solemn place they are in, has for the moment a forcible effect on the imagination. This is the only tomb (except those of the royal family in the great mosque in town) that is so well preserved.

The moment a death happens in a family, the alarm is given by the shrill screaming of the words *woolliah-woo* repeated incessantly by the relations and every body in the house. These cries, heard at a great distance, bring every female acquainted with, or dependent on the family, to scream over the dead, and mourn with the nearest relations of the deceased ; and it strikes one with the greatest horror to see the afflicted widow, or mother, half dead with grief for her loss, obliged (according to the custom of her country) to receive the visits of not less than a hundred different women who come to condole with her. They each take her in their arms, they lay her head on their shoulder, and scream without intermission for several minutes, till the afflicted object, stunned with the constant howling and a repetition of her misfortunes, sinks senseless from their arms on the floor ! They likewise hire a number of women who make this horrid noise round the bier, placed in the middle of the court-yard of the mansion, over which the women scratch their faces to such a degree, that they appear to have been bled with a lancet at the temples ; and after the ceremony is over, they lay on a sort of white chalk to heal the wounds and stop the blood. These women are hired indifferently, at burials, wddings, and feasts : at the two latter, however, they sing the song *loo, loo, loo*, and extempore verses. Their voices are heard at the distance of half a mile. The Bedouins differ from the Tripolitans in this ceremony of the bier : they do not scream so much over it ; but only sing extempore verses on the departed, their relations dancing slowly in a circle round it.

It is the custom here for those that can afford it, to give on the evening of the day the corpse is buried, a quantity of hot dressed victuals to the poor, who come to fetch each their portion, and form sometimes immense crowds and confusion at the doors : this they call the supper of the grave.

The singularity of these customs, which I have witnessed myself, will, I hope, recompense you for the length of my letter.

July 20, 1785

In the beginning of this month, owing to the increased ravages of the plague, the events connected with it assumed a more horrid character, and instead of shining coffins, imams and friends, to make up the sad procession, five or six corpses were bound together, all of them fastened on one animal, and hurried away to the grave ! Collogees [1] (soldiers) were appointed to go through the town, and clear it of objects who had died in the streets and were laying about. A female in the agonies of death they would have seized upon, while the spark of life was still lingering, had not the frighted victim with great exertion extended a feeble arm, and resisted the disturbers of her last moments, imploring the patience of the collogees till they came their next round.

A circumstance has just been fortunately discovered which was adding dreadfully to the increase of the plague and the foulness of the air. The Cyde, or governor of the Jews, had laid a tax of twenty pataques (or five pounds) additional on all burials, to defray the expenses of interring the poorer people ; and in consequence of this, in order to avoid the tax, a very great number of bodies were buried in the Jews' premises. These people dug graves in the yards belonging to their houses, and from the necessity of making them only at night, for fear of discovery, the bodies became so offensive, as to betray them during their operations, and occasion the death of numbers by this dreadful proceeding. Many poor wretches, who had no friends to lament or bury them, flocked round the consular houses and died under their walls, and many bodies were laid there by their surviving friends, whence they were removed with great inconvenience and expense. Madness continued till lately to prevail in those attacked with the plague. A slave in a state of delirium escaped from the castle, and the poor wretch running through the town before the

[1] More correctly Cologhlis. See Introduction.

people could prevent him, jumped over the battlements and was dashed to pieces : many people, in the same deranged state, were met in different parts of the town. The castle has exhibited a much more melancholy scene of destruction than any other part of the city, which was accounted for by the immense number of people it contained. Almost all the chief officers of state are dead. The Bey has lost two fine boys. For the eldest all the flags of the consular houses were half-masted, and the vessels in the harbour fired minute guns till lazero (or afternoon), when the body being buried, the flags were all hoisted, and the ships fired twenty-one guns each.

In the last six weeks, this dreadful pestilence has carried off two-fifths of the Moors, half the Jews, and nine-tenths of the Christians, who could not procure the conveniences necessary for a quarantine ; but the violence of the contagion has decreased so much, that for some time past not more than seven or eight have died in a day, and we therefore flatter ourselves it is nearly over. Notwithstanding this happy change, the consular houses are not yet all opened, and those who have relaxed their quarantine have paid severely for doing so, by the alarm occasioned in the family from infection and death among the servants.[1]

August 10, 1785

To keep up our agitation, which had abated a little with the decrease of the illness, a part of the Captain Pacha's [2] fleet has been here and caused a general alarm. His gallies and cruizers are chiefly manned with the most desperate crews, and their commanders differ little from captains of banditti. The Captain Pacha is a professed enemy to the Bashaw of Tripoli, and from the dreadful state of the place at present, it laid entirely at his mercy, had he been inclined, under any false pretence, to have annoyed the Bashaw and distressed the town. A boat with a chaoux from the castle was sent to the Turkish commander ; but he would not speak with him, further than by saying he expected several Turkish frigates every hour to join him. All the Christian flags were hoisted as well as the Moorish in compliment to the Grand Signior ; but the Bashaw gave orders for

---

[1] Feraud records that in three successive days in June 1785 the entire Catholic mission in Tripoli died of plague. He estimates about 27,000 persons died of plague in the whole area.

[2] The Captain Pasha was commander of the Ottoman Sultan's fleet.

them not to be saluted with guns. The day after they anchored the Turks sent a chaoux on shore with a letter to the Bashaw, informing him they were come in quest of a pirate who was in the harbour : upon this message the Bashaw ordered that the batteries should salute them, and begged of the Consuls that the Christian vessels might do the same. After this general salute, the Turks only returned four guns. The Turks always fire an even number. The cruizer that entered the harbour before them proved to be commanded by one of the most atrocious pirates that infest these seas, with two hundred banditti of Arnauts. Amongst other acts of atrocity, they had lately murdered the greatest part of the passengers and sailors of a Venetian ship ; and they had the remainder of the unhappy people still on board. Only four Venetians remained alive, who were returned to the Consul of that nation. The commander of the corsair was said to have died of his wounds from the resistance of the Venetians ; but this report was only raised to screen him : he eluded the search of both the Turks and the Bashaw's people, and reached the mosque on the sands about two miles from this city, where he now is.[1] The Captain Pacha intends to complain of the Bashaw to the Grand Signior for giving, as he calls it, refuge to this wretch. The Consuls have all sent certificates in favour of the Bashaw to the Grand Signior concerning this event ; and, notwithstanding the plague, the sheik [2] has been admitted into the Christian houses for the purpose of procuring these declarations. When the Turks sailed, they were saluted by thirty-three guns from the town, and they returned only six. There were no English in the harbour at this time.

The Venetians are still at war with Tunis. They have been offered forty thousand pataques (about ten thousand pounds) from that kingdom to make peace, but they will not accept the offer.

August 30, 1785

Some extraordinary instances have lately happened of several people who had taken the plague, recovering from it and taking it again, successively for seven or eight times, and dying of it at last. Many people affected in this way were saved by the assistance of a Moorish woman, who has for a long time persisted in opening the tumours, after which her patients have recovered ; but it is not thought that

---

[1] *I.e.* the sanctuary of the Seide.
[2] The *Sheikh el beled.*

this expedient, though successful of late, would have had any effect in the height of the disorder. This woman lost all her own family and connections in the first ravages of the plague.

We have received letters from Hadgi Abderrahman, the Moorish ambassador, on his way to England. He has, as was expected, performed a long quarantine off Malta of a hundred and four days, as one of his secretaries had the plague. The doctor who fled hence on account of the infection, and whose departure I told you of in my letter, dated June 28, has rendered such assistance at the Maltese lazaretto, that it will probably stamp his fame and make his fortune. He has, among other singular operations, followed the Moorish doctress in her practice, and opened the tumours of the plague, at the distance of eight or ten feet from the patient, by fixing a lancet at the end of a stick and using a magnifying glass. This operation has gained him great popularity at Malta.

﷽

October 28, 1785

Several periods have been fixed on to open the consular houses ; but a circumstance so desirable would have been most unfortunate at the present moment, as the plague still rages in and out of town, and the cause as yet is undiscovered. A Christian rode out some days ago to the Friday bazar, which is about two miles [1] from the town, since which his horse has had three swellings resembling the plague, and is expected to die.

In the beginning of this dreadful infection, the cattle appear to be seized before the human species.

A shocking instance of the effect of interest and fear occured yesterday, in the case of a poor black woman, who was bought by a Jew merchant. After the bargain was finished, the poor wretch was brought in the evening, and left at the house of her last purchaser, who perceiving she had taken the plague, immediately sent her back to her former master, from whose door for the same reason she was as quickly driven. Both these merchants fearing to lose their money by her death, denied her admittance into their houses. In this wretched state, she ran distracted through the streets, and every one knowing she had the plague, drove her from door to door, till Providence put

---

[1] Suk el Jum'aa, now a suburb of Tripoli.

an end to her misery by suffering her to drop near the house of a Moor, who did not attempt to disturb her last moments, though he himself had been terribly alarmed, having already met her several times while he was swiftly passing through the streets to his home, to prevent her dying in his own house, as the poor unfortunate endeavoured to get in every where.

Some most extraordinary circumstances which befel the above Moor in his last hours, under my own eyes, will serve further to delineate to you the manners of this part of the world. I am sorry they must show that the name of Barbarians is sometimes applicable to the actions of the natives. This man, who was a Hadgi, and named Hamet, was a Dragoman (an officer of the guard belonging to the English Consul), and declined being in quarantine in the consular house during the plague, on account of his family. He was married to a beautiful woman, named Mariuma, and had not been many days at home before he caught the fatal distemper. During the last stage of it, his disconsolate wife was sitting by his bedside : she had been cherishing a faint hope of his recovery, and had been watching him into a soft sleep. Worn out herself with fatigue, her mind soothed by the delusive prospect she had formed of seeing Hadgi Hamet awake recovered, Mariuma was sinking in repose, when she was disturbed by the hand of a man opening her baracan, and advancing a poignard to her heart, while with the other he was endeavouring to obtain some keys and papers belonging to her husband, which she wore in her bosom. She eluded his grasp, and beheld in her intended murderer her husband's brother, whose emissaries having informed him that Hadgi Hamet had just expired, imagined that it was a fair opportunity to favour his plot of destroying the whole family together, while the horrors of the plague drove far from the habitation of the sick all those who would otherwise approach it ; for Hadgi Hamet's only child, a fine girl of seven years old, had died that morning, and was yet unburied. When he entered his brother's apartment, he considered him dead, and seeing Mariuma sunk on the bed, supposed she had fainted over the body. At his rough approach, Mariuma awakened Hadgi Hamet by her screams, who, on seeing her distress, instantly sprung from his bed. The disappointed wretch finding his brother not dead, but rising from his couch with tenfold strength for the moment, retired affrighted to the skiffer, where his mother and sister were waiting, to whom, for the sake of humanity, it is to be hoped, he had not yet imparted his worst intentions. They had accompanied this assassin to town from the country-house where they lived, but which belonged to Hadgi Hamet.

The effect of this horrid event, joined to that of the plague, at once bereft Hadgi Hamet of his senses. He broke loose from them all, and rushed from his apartment into the street. The scene at that moment was truly awful. Hadgi Hamet, in his night-clothes, stood opposing himself to those around him, with all the wild fury of an enraged Moor, with his attagan or knife drawn, to keep those who would approach him at a distance. Prostrate at his feet was his wife, with her baracan loose, tearing off the few ornaments she had on, and wiping away her tears with her hair, whilst she implored her husband with every soft endearment to return to his bed, and live to protect her from his wretched brother. Insensible and deaf to her intreaties, he set off towards his house out of the town, whence his mother, brother, and sister had just arrived. His wife, shocked at any one's attempting to lay hands on him for fear of increasing his pain, insisted that no one should touch him, but followed him in silent anguish with those who would accompany her. After they had walked some distance, Hadgi Hamet returned quietly with Mariuma to his house, where he died soon after, leaving his effects in the hands of the English Consul, by which means his unhappy widow was saved from the avarice of his brutal family.

October 31, 1785

A Spanish fleet has just left this place ; they have been here with presents for the peace which they have newly concluded with the Barbary states, Tripoli, Tunis, and Algiers ; and it is the first peace they have had with this part of the world. Of the jewels which were sent, I saw two of the rings to-day ; one a topaz set with brilliants, for the youngest prince, worth about two hundred pounds, and the other a single diamond for the Bashaw, worth five hundred pounds. The Spaniards are said to have paid very high for the peace ; as much as three millions of hard dollars, or about £60,000. The Venetians still continue at war with Tunis, as they will not give what that state demands for a cessation of hostilities.

This paragraph will appear extraordinary, after having declared to you that we are close prisoners, secluded from the rest of our species ; but the Venetian Consul goes out often, by which he risks a great deal, though he takes every possible care, having always a guard with him to clear the way and hinder any person coming too near him— a proof of the attention paid to Christians here : but of the three Barbary states, Tripoli, Tunis, and Algiers, Tripoli is acknowledged to be by far the most civilized. At either of the other two states, particularly Algiers, they are not enough attached to the Christians to allow them such an indulgence. I am happy to think that you must be a stranger to the satisfaction which the sight of a friend now affords us, unless you were shut up, as we are, in the midst of pestilence, and in a place where the state of the government and country are equally alarming, and render every one painfully anxious for such accounts as can be depended on, while false ones are continually issuing from chimerical minds.

Tremendous as it may seem, to be in the same room with one who has just passed through a multitude of martyrs to the plague, many of whom were expiring in his sight, yet with proper care danger may be avoided. When any person visits us, the greatest precautions are mutually observed. The drawing-room has neither linen, silk, nor carpets ; no other furniture than tables and matted chairs : the floor is also matted. Every visitor is his own valet ; he is not admitted but in the presence of the master of the house ; no servant is permitted to attend him or hand him a chair ; and he helps himself to refreshments, which are brought to a corridor, or anti-chamber. This is done to prevent a servant, by inattention, going too near his person ; and whatever he has handled, or the chair he has occupied, is not touched for hours after his departure. Such purity in quarantines is taught, and only to be found complete in the singular lazarettos at Leghorn, built by the present Grand Duke Leopold, whose protection of the commerce and comforts of the inhabitants of Tuscany is unequalled. The alterations and additions he has made in the lazarettos have been the salvation of Europe.

To return to the dangers of the plague. To be secure in the midst of this dire contagion, requires a thorough knowledge of its effects. Many who have seen its ravages lull themselves into a false security, while many who are strangers to it cannot believe there is any safety in the country where it exists. It is certainly necessary to become perfectly acquainted with the differente articles which will imbibe the particles of this fatal disorder in order to be safe from its effects.

Most of them are well known, as cotton, woollens, linen, hides with the hair on, hemp, hops, etc., while corn, barley, fruit, vegetables, and meat are deemed incapable of taking or communicating the infection. But to these articles there are both additions and exceptions : bread, though perfectly safe after having been baked some hours, is fatally dangerous if handled while it is hot or warm. A peach, or any downy fruit or vegetable, such as unshelled filberts or almonds, have been known to communicate the plague. This disorder has been conveyed from friend to friend in a high scented bouquet of flowers ; and most perfumes are considered as propagators of this infectious disorder. Whenever it is requisite to commence a quarantine, it cannot be secure, whatever precautions may be taken, unless all animals are made away with that can possibly wander unnoticed from the house, and return again, such as pigeons, cats, etc.

December 8, 1785

In vain the Christians wish to finish their long quarantine, for notwithstanding their houses have been shut six months, they are likely to continue so much longer. A short time since, few deaths were heard of, but in the last five days they have increased from four a day to fifteen. Though the plague is so continual at Constantinople, and is frequently carried from thence to the Levant, yet this place has escaped it till now for the last seventy years.

In 1783, the plague raged at Cairo, being communicated to that place from Constantinople, and they daily took out of its gates fifteen hundred corpses. The severity of it so often occasioned the people to drop while walking in the streets, that an order was issued, that neither man, woman, or child, should attempt to go out of their houses, without having their name and place of residence written on paper and sewed to their caps.

A great many of the unfortunate inhabitants to escape death fled to the neighbouring countries ; notwithstanding which, and although the plague advanced and raged with equal violence at Alexandria, between which and this place there is a constant communication, Tripoli remained unassailed by it. We must therefore consider ourselves singularly unfortunate to have witnessed its horrors in the short time (not two years) that we have been here.

The burning deserts which surround this country defend it in general from the plague. Infected caravans which set off for this city are completely cleansed by the dry parching heat of a hot land wind, which generally occurs during the length of sands they pass before they reach Tripoli.

The winter here being very mild maintains the plague, which equally disappears under extreme cold, and under the force of a burning atmosphere. At Constantinople, on the contrary, the winter is cold enough to repel it in some measure ; though it blazes afresh from the damp unwholesome heats collected from the neighbouring woods and mountains during the summer.

***

December 10, 1785

To-day we have witnessed an extraordinary scene at a Moorish house in which one of their holy saints was concerned.[1] The Mahomedans have several distinct orders of shrieffs, or holy men. Owing to the depression of the Moors at this second attack of the plague, these sort of marabuts are frequently consulted, and are oftener to be met with than at any time since we have been here. One of them was solicited a few days since to attend a Moorish family ; and he came from a distance of many miles on horseback, accompanied by his follower. The dress of this marabut consisted only of a blue shirt and trousers without turban or shoes. On his arrival, he called for drink, and immediately broke the vessel he drank out of. They accounted for this extraordinary conduct, by saying it was become too sanctified by his touch for other less worthy to approach it. They brought him out the garments, one by one, of the master of the house, of whom, being absent, they implored the marabut to give an account. The marabut retired to a room where another shrieff was said to have been buried, and returning with each separate piece, gave the answers. He for a length of time, in an act of devotion, turned round with such velocity that his features were not discernible, and continued to do so till he sunk on the ground through fatigue. At other times, he sang and played on the tambourin extremely well, and in the end, according to the duties of his order, washed the feet of those who employed him before he went away.

The devotion of another order of marabuts frequent here, consists in wounding themselves, affecting madness, and walking the streets almost naked, or dancing religious dances for many hours, during which they incessantly scream out one of their names of the Deity. They at last throw themselves on the ground, foaming at the mouth,

[1] Probably witnessed from the roof-top of the Consulate.

appearing in a state of madness and in the agonies of death. This order is named the Kadri :[1] they have a convent near Pera.

A third order of marabuts, often met with here, is the Seyah.[2] One of these people went to the last Friday bazar out of town, where he was very troublesome, calling on the Bashaw of Tripoli, and on his subjects, for supplies, which were instantly brought him to the extent of what the people could afford. The communities of this order, when they get leave to quit their monasteries, engage themselves to their superiors to send back money and provision to their convent ; and they contract the habit of insolent beggars, taking advantage of the shield of their religion. On their first arrival at any town or market-place, they immediately proceed to the centre of it, and getting upon some conspicuous place, call out with violence for a sum of money, or a quantity of corn, barley, meat, or fruit, without ceasing, till the people come in numbers, bringing what they can collect.

One of these marabuts sent an insolent message to the castle, for which he was desired to quit the town, as a punishment for an offence which, perhaps, another man would have paid for with his life. On quitting the town the marabut prophecied, that the Bashaw would be stabbed in the messelees (the divan or council chamber) on his next appearance there. On this account the Bashaw has never entered that chamber since, but holds the divan in an apartment in the castle, fitted up for the purpose.

A short time since one of these saints had the audacity, in the Bashaw's presence, to give a violent blow on the face to a chief officer in waiting, for having ventured to disapprove of something he had said ; the only reproof the marabut received was, that if he repeated such an offence he would be forbidden the court.

▥

December 18, 1785

Yesterday, Baron de Haslien, a German nobleman, arrived here, to see if it were practicable to go from hence to Fezzan. He has left two brothers at Tunis, whose intentions are, if possible, to proceed this way to the coast of Guinea. Should they succeed, they will have

---

[1] The Sunni sect of Qadiriyeh, founded by Abdul Qadir el Qailani, whose shrine is in Baghdad.

[2] I cannot trace this sect, which is not among the thirty-two recognized : but *Seyah* in Arabic means " Shouter."

the merit of being the first Europeans ever remembered to have crossed in any direction over Africa. The additional circumstance of the plague, with other difficulties, renders the Baron's intention impracticable at present, and every body seems disappointed at the thought of his not being able to perform this perilous journey.

It is said, if Volney had penetrated as far into Africa as he has into Asia, we should have had a satisfactory account of the interior of this peninsula ; for those who are acquainted with the countries which Monsieur Volney passed through, say, he is the only writer who has given a correct description of that part of the world.

December 31, 1785

The plague does not finish with the year : it has been very severe this month, and nearly all the horrors of the last plague have been revived in the present. An imaginary security, which unfortunately led the principal Moors to neglect the few precautions they had taken in the beginning of the disease, has caused a greater number of the higher class to fall victims to it at present, than on the former occasion.

The Bey yesterday had two of his children seized with the infection ; and they are now at the point of death. They have taken the plague from a little female black slave, who has lately been admitted to play with them ; and the castle, having been tolerably clean for some weeks, is expected, from the great number of its inhabitants, to be thrown again into a dreadful state.

January 12, 1786

Imprisoned in the midst of increasing pestilence, your kind wishes for a happy new year can effect us but in a small degree. The plague seems likely to repeat all the horrors of the last year. Nobody is prepared to meet this second attack, though all were told, at the time the infection seemed to cease here, that a fresh and more severe disease was breeding within the mountains of Guerianno,[1] which can be seen hence with our glasses, and whence we have now received it. I have mentioned that the Arabs dig their dwellings within these mountains, and thus concealed in the bowels of the earth, they have for a long

1 Gharian, in the Jebel Nefusa.

time escaped the pestilence ; but it has now reached them, and in those airless tombs of the living, it finds every thing to accelerate its deadly strokes. The frighted Arabs, abandoning their retreats, crowd to the surrounding places, and carry new destruction with them. Owing to their hourly emigrating here, the plague increases from day to day ; and its devastation is greater, in consequence of the people considering the infection as being over.

The Bashaw's officers of state and all his best generals, have been twice swept off by the plague.

The re-appearance of this dreadful disorder has determined Baron de Haslien, who has been here for some time, to relinquish his intention of proceeding into the interior of the country : he will embark in a few days for Europe ; and the state of this place altogether seems to prevent his ever expecting to effect the researches he had planned. Independent of the plague, the Arab tribes render every place round impassable to strangers at present ; and by the distresses of the country, and the great want of unanimity in the royal family, they daily increase in power. There have been several skirmishes between the Moors and Arabs very near us, on account of the Bey, the Bashaw's eldest son, having sent out last week twelve hundred men to gather in tributes from them : the Bey's troops lost their chief, who was cut to pieces by the Arabs ; but they returned otherwise successful.

The Jews are at present loading vessels with the clothes of those who died of the plague, and are exporting them to Europe and Egypt : extraordinary precautions are, therefore, necessary in Europe, to prevent the effects of importing such cargoes.

To-morrow being the prophet's birth-day, the Moors call to-night the feast of Millute.[1] They make a general repast on basseen, a stiff paste made of their finest flour and dressed over the steam of meat, garnished with high salted mutton, dried in small pieces of an ounce or two in weight, and known all over Africa by the name of kadeed.

To-night the Moors make public rejoicings and bonfires, and walk in procession through the town, having collected all the little children of the place to precede the procession, who carry lighted wax candles in their hands and sing in praise of Mahomet.

The minarets are profusely lighted, and they seem to be making up to-night for the neglect of their two last feasts ; that is, the Ashura,[2]

---

[1] Literally *Maulud* or *maulud en nebi*. This falls on the twelfth day of Rabia' el Awal, the third month of the Moslem year.

[2] Yom el Ashura is the tenth day of the first month of the Moslem calendar, *Muharram*.

or new year's day, and the feast of Beiram,[1] both of which were hardly noticed owing to the horrors of the plague ; and it is expected that this general assemblage of persons will infallibly increase prodigiously the present desolation.

The following anecdote will serve to show you the force of religious principle in a Jew. The Cyde, or governor of the Jews, went hence to a distant part of the coast, where he remained some time, hoping to find this place clear of the plague when he returned. He was landed here yesterday in a dying state, and nearly starved, from not having tasted meat since he left this place some months ago, for want of having a rabbi, or priest, to kill the animals with which he was plentifully provided ; the rabbi he had taken with him having died on the way.

The Bey has gained to-day one thousand maboobs (rather more than three hundred pounds), on account of two Arab brothers, who parted some days ago at the Marine, or sea side. One of them embarked for Alexandria, and the other returned to the mountains. The former had taken the plague so severely that he died in a few hours after his brother parted from him. As he was a perfect stranger here, his property, with one thousand maboobs in cash, was delivered to the Bey, and the body buried at his expense. In such cases, all property belongs of right to the Bey and cannot be reclaimed.

The Bey feels very much the loss of one of his favourite and best Mamelukes, who died some days since of the plague : this Mameluke was much attached to him, entirely in his confidence, and a great warrior. Never could the Bey have experienced such a loss at a more critical moment, when the throne is every day expected to become vacant from the death of the Bashaw ; when his two brothers, the elder instigated by the younger with treacherous intentions, await his dissolution from one hour to another ; and when, owing to these circumstances, the Arabs are continually rising. The Bey had spent more on this Mameluke than he had on any other two. But all the Mamelukes cost their masters a little fortune : few therefore but princes are possessed of any. The Mamelukes are furnished with a succession of new habits and new horses, richly mounted pistols, and Damascus scimitars, peculiar for their lightness and beautiful workmanship, the blades being tempered with perfume : they cost from

---

[1] The feast of Bairam falls on the tenth day of *Dhu el Hijjah*, on twelfth month of the Moslem calendar.

one hundred and sixty to two hundred maboobs each (upwards of sixty pounds).

The dress of the Mamelukes, almost covered with gold and silver, and adapted to constant riding, is martial and graceful. It is in the Moorish style, but unaccompanied by long flowing coverings. Their heads are encircled with a rich embroidered shawl bound tight round their cap, leaving out a long end which hangs on the left side of the head, and which appears to be solid gold from the richness of the embroidery, as does the breast of their habit. They wear their trousers extremely ample, and of the finest muslin, quite down to the ankle, with bright yellow boots and slippers. They are frequently conceited and proud ; and where they find themselves of consequence to their masters, are sometimes so overbearing in the family that they are obliged to be admonished. Their origin is not always known ; but they are in general herdsmen's sons, purchased in Arabia, Georgia, and the places adjacent, which they no sooner quit and become used to dress and arms, than they imbibe a high taste for rebellion, seeking to promote themselves by any opportunity that may offer ; and their masters pay profusely for an apparent attachment, with which these Mamelukes often deceive them. The Mamelukes are all extremely fair, have light blue eyes, light eyebrows, and little or no beard, a very white skin, and a blooming complexion. Volney, speaking of them, says, " a fourth race of the inhabitants of Egypt are a people born at the foot of the Caucasus with white hair, found by our crusaders in the thirteenth century, and called Mamelukes, which means a military slave." There are but few of these people in Tripoli at present, and they are chiefly in the possession of the Bashaw and the different branches of his family.

January 18, 1786

We have at this time such a scarcity of wheat, that the Christians are glad to buy up all the biscuit from the ships in the harbour ; and if the plague had not swept off the chief part of the inhabitants, they must have perished by famine : indeed, the small quantity of grain we have, seems, for our misfortune, to be threatened by the locusts, which have been approaching from the deserts of Egypt. These destructive insects have seldom been known to annoy this place, though they are the almost yearly scourge of Egypt and part of Asia. They fly in compact bodies through the air, darkening the atmosphere, and occupying a space of many miles in their passage. They make a noise in the act of nipping off the corn and herbage that cannot be mistaken, and which is distinctly heard at a great distance. While these invaders pass along, as if by enchantment, the green disappears and the parched naked ground presents itself. The locusts are salted down in great quantities at Cairo and Alexandria, and carried to different parts of Africa : many are brought to this place and eaten by the inhabitants.

January 20, 1786

The circumstances which have occurred to a Moor who was taken ill of the plague, will add great strength to Mahomet's doctrine, which says, " fate is irrevocable, and to oppose destiny is sacrilege." This man, who was some months ago one of the richest merchants here, to escape the plague fled to a great distance on the coast, taking all his property with him. For further safety he left the coast, and went to a rock far off in the sea. Here the poor man thought himself out of danger, but without any extraordinary share of penetration, he might have anticipated what happened to him. In the first place, he became criminal in the eyes of all his countrymen for having, as they term it, flown in the face of his prophet, by attempting to run away from the plague and avoid his fate, which the Moors call mughtube : [1] the Arabs, therefore, with impunity, pursued this man to rob him, a few nights after he was settled on the rock. While the merchant was in his tent, he heard boats rowing towards his solitary island, and by the light of the moon he saw they were manned with Arabs, and soon discovered his perilous situation. He left all to their mercy, and by the greatest good fortune escaped being murdered. After their departure he returned to Tripoli, where he now faces all the danger of the plague without the least precaution, to expiate the sin he had committed in flying from his fate (mughtube). The Moors, thus struck with horror, seem sure he cannot recover.

The consolation and peace of mind the Moor procures himself, by thus placing his whole belief in predestination, is certainly inconceivable. In the heaviest hour of trial, they sooth themselves with the idea, that it is mughtube (decreed), and with that single word they pass from opulence to misery without a murmur. On their deathbed, nothing changes their security : the expiring Moor only calls out to

[1] Literally *maktub*, or " it is written." The Arabic word for fate is *bakht*.

C.T.—5*

have his face turned towards Mecca, and thus comforted he dies in peace. As an instance of their universal observation of this last custom, a boy not nine years old, who died a few days ago, screamed in agony to his disconsolate mother, and chid her for not turning his face towards Mecca, which when she had done, he recovered his tranquillity and calmly resigned his breath.

January 30, 1786

Every body has been seriously disappointed by the arrival of a vessel at this distressing moment without the provisions it was expected to bring : many of the articles ordered to be sent by it are not to be had here, or only of very bad quality, and at four times their original value. The ship is freighted by a Moor with an immense number of Venetian boards, to cover the graves and make boxes for the dead. The populace are ready to tear this speculating Moor to pieces for not letting the provisions, at least, come with the boards. They say, this inhuman wretch had certainly a wish that there might be as great a devastation from the plague this year as there was last, when some people would have paid for the boards nearly their weight in gold. The foresight of this Moor, who expected so great a demand for the boards, has made the man an object of horror to most of the people ; but should he outlive the selling of them at the rate this article was paid for before, he will make a considerable fortune. We hope, however, the plague is nearly over, though it is too bad yet to fix on the precise time for opening the Christians' houses. Three people died in town yesterday, and thirteen in the Messeah : among the former was the only remaining daughter of the Bey Abdallah, whom I have mentioned to you as son to the last Turkish Bashaw. His eldest daughter was to have married the present Bey of Tripoli ; and every thing had been got ready by Bey Abdallah's family for the most superb wedding, when by some unfortunate stratagem, certainly conducted by the female messengers of the castle, the Bey contrived in disguise to see her before the nuptials were celebrated, and to every body's astonishment, he suddenly declared his total aversion to her, and would not hear any more of marrying her. Added to this unfortunate young lady's disappointment in losing the next heir to the throne, it was thought she had seen and approved of the young prince, as she fell immediately into a state of grief which very soon after occasioned her death. Bey Abdallah's wife still mourns with the same attention she did when her daughter died, which is more than three years since : she keeps the fasts she first imposed upon herself, has all her embroidery and new habits defaced before she wears them, and regularly attends the tomb of her child, which she has made one of the grandest in Tripoli, excepting those of the great mosque. This tomb is in a burying ground not far from the town, and is distinguished by a small chapel, or marabut, being built over it, which is kept in the best repair imaginable : it has been supplied with the most expensive flowers in beautiful vases ever since her death, and, in addition to the flowers, great quantities of fresh Arabian jasmine threaded on a thin slip of the palm-leaf, ornament in festoons and tassels the revered tomb. The little chapel is open on the four sides, which are constructed in four neat arches, inclosed with iron rails handsomely wrought and gilt. The inside is finished with Chinese tiles and stucco-work, and within it lights are kept continually burning.

This great disappointment to Bey Abdallah's family was on the point of being, in some measure, compensated by Sidy Hamet, the Bashaw's second son, having lately determined to marry the youngest daughter. All was again prepared for a more costly wedding than the first.

A few days previous to this young lady being seized with the plague, her mother, in order to break through the mourning she had never interrupted for her eldest daughter, ordered a piece of perfume to be brought her, prepared of musk, ambergris, aloes, and other aromatics. This she broke in the presence of witnesses, and rubbing her own hands with it, she declared the mourning finished, of which this performance was an attestation, and left the family at liberty to celebrate the nuptials of Sidy Hamet and her daughter, which could not otherwise have been performed.

As the plague had greatly abated, and as the Moors advert so little to quarantines, this wedding was intended to have taken place immediately ; but it was the preparations for it which, by requiring a greater intercourse with people, communicated the pestilence to this young lady, and disappointed the expectations of herself and friends.

All the three princes attended her funeral—the Bey, Sidy Hamet, and Sidy Useph. The coffin, owing to her habits which covered it, appeared like massy gold. The head of it was adorned with a great profusion of natural and artificial flowers ; and according to the custom of the country, as she had not been married, she was buried as a bride, dressed in the richest clothes and jewels they could put on. Eight black slaves had their liberty granted them on this melancholy occasion, two from the Bey, in compliment to his brother, two from the intended bridegroom, Sidy Hamet, and four from the house of Bey Abdallah. These slaves accompanied the body, wearing their caps turned the wrong side outwards, and bearing each in their hand a long reed with a label at the top, declaring their names, and the occasion on which they were freed.

Bey Abdallah's wife had, for the accommodation of those persons assembled at her house to attend her daughter's funeral, a tent pitched in the court-yard, made entirely of crimson silk, and worked in gold and silver, sufficiently large to contain two hundred people. This costly tent was made for her own use, when she passed over the deserts, the last time she went in great pomp to worship at the shrine of Mahomet. Owing to the melancholy event of losing her second daughter, it is said she means to make a third pilgrimage to Mecca; and having now no family, it is supposed Mecca and Medina will be enriched by her property.

A prodigious quantity of rice, meat, and bread, is given away at Bey Abdallah's garden to-night, in separate portions to the poor, which is meant for the supper of the grave.

There being no lady of sufficient consequence left in this place for Sidy Hamet to marry, he will therefore be obliged to send to Georgia, or Circassia, for one of their beauties. The bride he has lost being a descendant of the last Turkish Bashaw, was what the Moors term a Coraglie [1] (a Turk). The Moorish princes, when they do not meet with Turkish ladies to form an alliance with, purchase Circassians, and usually marry the first by whom they have a son.

Most of the sacrificed beauties of this description, who have been brought here, have passed a life they could esteem only as a partial happiness, and mingled with great sufferings; as the story of one who died lately will further evince to you, and which shall be the subject of my next letter.

February 10, 1786

The name of the Circassian, whose history I promised you in my last, was Mariuma; she belonged to Mahmute Hogia, brother to

[1] Cologhli. See Introduction.

Hamet Hogia, now ambassador in Spain. Mahmute Hogia, on his return from Egypt to Tripoli, bought a Greek, intending her as a present for the Bashaw, but being particularly struck with her, he determined to purchase a Circassian for his sovereign, who not having seen either, he conceived, if she was as handsome as the first, would be equally, and perhaps, more acceptable to him : he remained some months in Egypt and then embarked with the two ladies for Tripoli.

Mariuma's companion in slavery, as handsome as herself, knowing she was purchased for the sovereign of the country they were going to, did not envy the daily increasing felicity of her friend, whose lot, she fancied, must fall far short of that luxury and grandeur which seemed to await herself as the favourite of royalty, while her companion had become the property of a subject. But still she trembled for the character of the man for whom she was destined : she hardly dared hope it could be their fate to meet with two men as amiable as Mahmute Hogia appeared ; and often from the deck of the ship, as she viewed the distant shores of Tripoli, her courage failed, her tears fell, and she envied Mariuma the confidence she perceived she drew from Mahmute Hogia's countenance, which evidently induced her to approach the coast, not only with calmness, but with heartfelt pleasure. The subsequent days of these two beauties proved neither of them to be free from acute sufferings.

Mahmute Hogia's first wife was much alarmed when her husband's return to Tripoli was announced, finding he had brought two females with him ; but she was in despair, when she was told that one of them had been delivered of a boy on board the ship in the harbour, where slaves and every indulgence and magnificence were allowed her, with all the respect and attention Mahmute Hogia could shew her ; nor could she form any hopes of his affections being divided between the two females, as on their arrival the other was immediately escorted to the castle.

Lilla Howisha was the name of Mahmute Hogia's first wife. She of course bore an inveterate hatred to the Greek he had chosen, and resisting all his entreaties, would not for a long while bear the sight of her. Notwithstanding the Greek was so ill received by Lilla Howisha, Mahmute Hogia, soon after their arrival, married her publicly. She had several children by him and lived for some years very happily, having prudently managed to conciliate so far the affections of Lilla Howisha, that this lady condescended to adopt the eldest son. For a long while the Greek spent her life comfortably, enjoying, in every respect, the same attentions and indulgences that the first wife received, with the advantage of being adored by her husband, which the former never had been. But the ravages of the plague had reached her, and all her support and comfort were lost with Mahmute Hogia, who died of this dire distemper but a few months ago.

The death of Mariuma's husband and protector changed the whole face of her affairs. Howisha, whose countenance through fear had smiled on her during her husband's life, now unmasked her hatred, to which she set no bounds. The Greek, when Mahmute Hogia's life was despaired of, carried to him her last infant, which he had not seen. This proceeding so much offended the first wife, that she made it a pretext for giving an order that the unhappy Greek should not see her husband at the moment of his death ; poisoning thus his last hour, to revenge herself on the unfortunate Mariuma, whose eldest son fell, also, a victim to the plague immediately after his father. This youth resented the behaviour of Lilla Howisha to his mother, and, though her adopted son, would not suffer her to be admitted into his presence afterwards notwithstanding she earnestly requested it. The afflicted Mariuma now remained friendless and alone with two small children, the eldest not five years old, deprived of all attendance, and without the means of procuring necessaries for herself and infants. Turned out of her house by Howisha, she must have starved, had she not found a patroness in the Bashaw's wife, who, with her accustomed liberality, soothed her, and immediately took her under her protection. Mariuma did not long survive her lamented lord : she was soon mingled in the dreadful heaps which the plague carried off daily ; and Mahmute Hogia's house is one of the many monuments of this fatal disorder. The family and servants in his house, a few months since, consisted of forty-five persons, besides thirty-five black slaves : there now remain of them only two individuals, Mahmute Hogia's first wife and a Russian renegado. Mariuma was very beautiful, with black eyes and brown hair : she was only fourteen years old when purchased by Mahmute Hogia, and was not more than twenty-nine years of age when she died.

Her companion in captivity lived but a short while after she came to Tripoli ; she had blue eyes and flaxen hair, and was very handsome, with a majestic figure. The Bashaw, however, was not struck with her, though he allowed her every indulgence. After she had remained some time unhappy and neglected at the castle, the Bashaw determined to marry her to one of his renegados by way of providing for her ; but she died of a broken heart before the wedding took place. Mrs. Tully had an opportunity of seeing her one day : she paid a visit at the castle to Lilla Halluma, who knowing how desirous all the Christians were to see this Circassian, ordered her women to shew her to the apartment of the handsome slave, as she called her, saying she knew she wished to see her. Mrs. Tully went, and found the Circassian richly and elegantly dressed, but quite alone, seated in a window which looked towards the sea, on which her fine eyes drowned in tears were fixed. She was so lost in thought that she hardly turned her head or spoke, but seemed buried in the vain wish of being again transported to her native country. She died soon afterwards, not having been two years at the castle.

April 10, 1786

Still imprisoned on account of the plague, a few Moorish domestic scenes are all I can at present give you ; but, in these family anecdotes, you will see more of the manners of the African and the Asiatic, than can possibly be learnt from the pen of the passing traveller. It is only through the medium of intimate acquaintance, that the genuine ideas and feelings can be truly delineated of a people, so entirely differing from Europeans in their minutest actions.

The plague has so completely desolated the house of Hadgi Abderrahman, the ambassador, since he left this place for England, that very few of his numerous family remain. His beautiful Greek, Amnani, whose history I have given you in my former letters, could no longer support her situation without changing her residence, where every thing reminded her hourly of past felicity and present losses : besides, she justly thought the air of her house so contaminated, that nothing could save the few that were living but the quitting it, at least for a time, as it has been infected with the plague for many months. Mr. Tully offered her a house of his adjoining the one we live in, which she most thankfully accepted, and came into it immediately, accompanied by her husband's eldest daughter and two of his nieces, with a sweet little girl of her own, whom she calls Fatima.

A few days after she arrived we spent some time in conversation with her from our terrace, at such a distance as not to endanger either party by imbibing the contagion. It was in the afternoon : we found all the ladies, except the Greek, already in the gallery before their rooms to receive us, but the Greek's apartment was still shut. She came out soon after we arrived, and went down to the square area of the house. This part of the building is secured from men or strangers : Lilla Amnani was followed by three of her blacks and two Moorish women. They tightened her baracan of white gauze round her, and assisted in washing her feet and hands, after which one of the blacks holding a large silver ewer of rose-water poured it slowly out while the Greek again washed herself. She then returned to her apartment, whence she talked to us, while the women plaited her hair and finished dressing her. Though she wears the Moorish habit (not by choice but compulsion), she puts it on with so much grace and simplicity, and there is such an ease and softness in her manner, that she does not appear like Moorish women ; and, although she was quite dejected from having lost so many of her family, and the greatest part of her attendants, yet the beauty of her figure, and the elegance of her dress and manners, rendered her strikingly agreeable. All the ladies of the family were with her, and were richly dressed ; but as I have already described to you the Moorish costume, I shall only mention the dress the Greek wore, which was very inferior to what it would have been, if the ambassador had been at home ; for on account of his absence, and the deaths that at present happen in his family, she lays aside the greatest part of her jewels and ornaments ; and yet she cannot wear what they consider here as full mourning during Hadgi Abderrahman's absence, as that would be accounted a bad omen to himself. There was a certain liveliness or brilliancy in her dress, which distinguished it from that usually worn by Moorish ladies. Her chemise was pale blue, pink, and white, in opposition to the heavier colours of dark green, red, blue, and orange, which are invariably used by them ; and the bosom and collar, instead of being bordered by gold threads, were finished with a broad bright gold lace from Venice. She wore two jelicks, or waistcoats, the under one a pale yellow satin, trimmed with silver lace in front, and over it a crimson velvet one with gold and coral buttons : she also wore yellow silk full trousers with broad gold bindings at the ankles, and a striped white gauze baracan or veil, formed a graceful transparent drapery round her. She had on each arm only one excessively large gold bracelet, nearly two inches wide and one thick ; if the ambassador had been at home she would have worn two. The bracelets were open, without lock or fastening, but so pliable from the pureness of the gold, as to be easily stretched and closed with the hand when put on or off. Her cap was of gold embroidery, and had a binding of black next the forehead, which, had she been dressed, would have been set with jewels to hang over the face. She wore several rings, four or five in each ear, of diamonds, pearls, and other gems : these were not rough as the Moors wear them, but polished and set in the European fashion. Her baracan was fastened under the left breast with a large gold bodkin set with diamonds, with several strings of pearls hanging from it, and over her bosom hung a string of massy gold ornaments of many relics and charms from Mecca, to preserve her from the infection of the plague, and from the dangerous effect of the malicious or too curious eye ; for nothing creates more alarm here, than the fixed gaze of a stranger : they hardly trust to these celestial charms, to do away the effect of a scrutinizing look, and often wet their finger and pass it over the object thus admired. Lilla Amnani had silver hall-halls,[1] or fetters, on her ankles, each weighing from two to three pounds.

She testified much gratitude for our coming up to see her. Her attendants placed a Turkey carpet and a crimson and gold cushion on the ground for her to sit down ; her blacks lay on the ground near her, and her two women stood by her, one on each side, with a silk handkerchief and a fan. She regretted much that she had not a lyre with her to play to us, and described the great care and expense that had been bestowed on her education. Speaking before the other ladies with exultation of having been early instructed to read and write, she observed (with truth) what comfort it now afforded her in reading the ambassador's letters from England, as she said, not curtailed by malice, nor altered by invention. After speaking of Hadgi Abderrahman, she ordered her women to sing, which they immediately did extempore, on the subject of the ambassador's absence, and Lilla Amnani's present sufferings. In these verses they recounted every anecdote of Abderrahman that could do him honour, and with enthusiasm pourtrayed the beauty, graces, and merits of Amnani. Though Abderrahman was many years older than herself, and had a family grown up when he brought her to Tripoli, yet she seemed to have lived always very happily, and to have complete dominion over

---

[1] Literally : *Khalkhal.*

her own house ; a circumstance very uncommon to Greeks here, when there are Moorish females in the family, who have it in their power to influence their masters or husbands.

☫

May 2, 1786

On the 20th of last month all the colours were half-masted for the death of the last of the Bey's sons : the Turkish vessels in the harbour fired minute guns ; and the Bey ordered all the prison doors to be opened, and every person set at liberty in his father's dominions.

We were very sorry, on this occasion, to find it was impossible for the ambassador's wife to avoid going to the castle, out of compliment to the family ; but as soon as her rank was announced, word was brought her from Lilla Kebbiera (the Bashaw's wife), desiring her to return home immediately, saying she considered the compliment fully paid, without Amnani's risking her life further by entering the apartments. As soon as Lilla Amnani returned to her house, Mrs. Tully had strong perfumes for fumigations, and vinegar prepared with camphire, conveyed to her, as antidotes to the dire disorder it was thought she might have taken, two of the Bashaw's family having been seized with the plague while Lilla Amnani was at the castle. She soon after determined to change her abode once more, and return to the family residence. I cannot give you a just description of the dejected state in which they took leave of us, finding themselves again surrounded with all the horrors of the plague. .

The evening before they went away, they performed for Uducia (Hadgi Abderrahman's eldest daughter) one of their extraordinary ceremonies, to protect her, in her removal to her father's house, from the effect of any ill-disposed persons looking on her with an unfriendly eye, which they call being taken with " bad eyes," and which might cause a disorder to prove fatal that would otherwise not be so. This charm consisted in having a writing from one of their Imams, which being burnt was mixed in wine and drank by Uducia, who was perfumed with musk and incense by her friends, they walking round her, repeating prayers for her while she drank it. When we heard how ill she was at the time she was obliged to go through this ceremony, we could not but consider her exertions, and her swallowing the sooty draft in such a state, a dangerous expedient.

These ladies having been for some time such near neighbours, afforded us an opportunity of seeing realized in part what writers say of the ladies in Mohammedan families. In the manner they are described by different authors, however, it is natural to imagine the day too long for their occupations, and their time oppressive for want of being filled up ; but, on the contrary, they are never unemployed.

The Moorish ladies are in general occupied in overlooking a numerous set of slaves, who make their sweetmeats and cakes, clean and grind their wheat, spin, and in short, are set about whatever seems necessary to be done. The ladies inspect by turns the dressing of the victuals, and during the time spent in this way, two sets of slaves are in attendance ; one set perform the culinary operations, while another station themselves round their mistress, removing instantly from her sight any thing that may annoy her, and using fans without intermission, to keep off flies or insects, while she leans on one or other of the slaves, walking about to direct and overlook what is doing.

One of the reasons given why even the ladies of the royal family must minutely attend to this part of their duty, is, to prevent the possibility of any treachery being practised in preparing their husbands' meals. The hours the Turkish or Moorish ladies have to spare for amusement is spent in singing and dancing. Abderrahman's eldest daughter and the pretty Greek tied up a swing the morning after they came to live near us, which constituted a great part of the day's amusement : their black slaves and servants served for playfellows. They seemed none of them, from the first, to want spirits ; except the Greek, in whose most cheerful moments there was a melancholy and care spread over her countenance, which reminded us of her losses, and of the anxious solicitude she felt that the ambassador might be convinced she had acted up to all his wishes in his absence. This painful, and sometimes dangerous diffidence of their husbands, must be the constant companion of the best female characters in this part of the world, where continual plots, the consequence of jealousy and interest, are working against them by all around.

June 1, 1786

We have been seriously alarmed by the Arabs ;[1] a body of five thousand of them advanced to Zavia, a village only one day's journey from Tripoli. Happily their hostilities proved only an incursion for

---

[1] The author means the Bedouins, who so call themselves.

plunder ; and it is the distressed and defenceless state of the Bashaw that at present encourages them to come so much nearer than usual. The Moors, aware of their intentions, blockaded the streets of Zavia with stones to impede their progress, and the Bashaw called in his auxiliaries (other tribes of Arabs in his pay). It was at first reported that they came with the connivance of the Bey of Tunis, and had with them a Tunisian army ; for at Tunis there is a Moor who went hence, called Mustapha the Pretender. This man is protected by the Bey of Tunis, and acknowledged by that prince to be an uncle of the Bashaw of Tripoli, who escaped when seven of his uncles were put to death on his accession to the throne. Owing to this circumstance, the Bashaw is always in dread of the court of Tunis. While this report prevailed, nothing was heard of but the names of Wield Maria and Mahmute Hogia, both of whom died of the plague, and both famous generals attached to the Bashaw. They drove back Mustapha the last time he approached Tripoli supported by a Tunisian army.

It is not easy to conceive the alarm the above circumstances occasioned throughout the kingdom. Several Arab tribes, which were sent for by the Bashaw, came to the city, and the greatest part of them are now stationed round the walls, for only their chiefs are permitted to enter the town. They waited for supplies of food, money, and clothing, before they would pursue the enemy. They had caps, shirts, trousers, and a large sum of money given them previous to their departure. The Nuolees [1] rank highest among the Arab tribes ; they are called the masters of the deserts. When their chief came into town a cannon was fired to salute him. Happily this matter has been adjusted without further mischief. The hostile Arabs have been driven off ; and the next desirable circumstance is to see the auxiliary Arabs depart in peace. As avarice is their passion, their demands are endless, and it often costs the Bashaw as much trouble to disperse them as to call them together.

There is a certain trait of honour in the Arabian character that keeps them faithful to their engagements ; and were it not for this tie, their strength in numbers, and their skill in war, would render them formidable enemies to the Moors. We were happy to see great numbers of them depart yesterday, and the rest are expected to leave us to-morrow.

[1] I can only think the author means here the Berber tribe, the Orfela from Beni Ulid ; they are sometimes referred to as the Beniolees.

June 18, 1786

Our house, the last that remained in quarantine, opened on the 16th ; but this happy event seems marked by a succession of alarms. The consternation lately excited at the approach of the Arabs, was trifling to that felt in the place at present. A courier from Tunis confirms the dreadful news, brought, it seems, through Moorish channels some time since, that the Captain Pacha had sailed from Constantinople with orders from the Grand Signior to depose the Bashaw of Tripoli. It is supposed that the dissentions in the Bashaw's family, and the total neglect of the kingdom (arising from that circumstance) makes the Grand Signior fear that Tripoli may at last fall into the hands of the Christians. He is otherwise well disposed to this government ; for although few or no tributes have been sent him during the reigns of the three last Bashaws, he has never sent to exact them.

Unfortunately the Grand Signior has promoted to the rank of Captain Pacha, a Turk named Hasseen, who has been an avowed enemy to the Bashaw of Tripoli for many years. This man, with a large fleet, is expected here from hour to hour. The Bashaw in the divan, this afternoon, declared his intention of quitting the town to-morrow, and of waiting at one of his palaces till the Turkish fleet arrives, and its destination is known. If it be necessary, he will attempt to escape over the deserts to Tunis, after placing the ladies of his family out of the town for the present ; as, according to the Turkish laws of war, they risk nothing from the enemy, who esteem the persons of the females belonging to the royal family sacred, with all the gold, silver, or jewels they may have on them. When the business of the state is over, the Bashaw at sunset returns to the harem, which to-night was in general commotion, and every one was on foot to listen and watch for the Bashaw's appearance. The consternation in the harem was indescribable when he confirmed to the females of his family the news, that he expected hourly to be driven from his throne, and that perhaps already a price was set upon his head, while the best fate his queen could expect, was to remain behind with her daughters, and see him depart a fugitive, after she has reigned with him nearly thirty years peaceably in the castle.

The whole town this evening partakes of the general confusion in preparing for the exile of the royal family, if necessary. Christians as well as Moors are much alarmed on this occasion, and I hope I shall have nothing seriously dangerous to relate to you concering ourselves.

June 24, 1786

Our apprehensions are for a time suspended. The Captain Pacha passed the harbour of Tripoli a few days since, and is for the present gone to Alexandria, with orders from the Grand Signior to punish the inhabitants for molesting the Christians, whose churches had been destroyed and several of whom had been murdered, owing to some disputes about a Moor, who had sought a sanctuary in one of the Christian churches. The Captain Pacha has gone to set them to rights, by making each party pay him handsomely for the blows they have given the other. But it is still affirmed he has a teskerra, or firman, with him for this unfortunate Bashaw. A teskerra is a written order from the Grand Signior, and is held so sacred that every Mussulman who receives it must obey its mandate, even to death.

June 30, 1786

Since writing the above, the death of the Grand Signior [1] has annulled the teskerra which the Captain Pacha has against our sovereign ; and Constantinople at present is in a state of insurrection, about placing the Grand Signior's nephew on the throne in preference to his son.

Extraordinary as it appears, the son of the Grand Signior loses his right to his father's throne, only by his cousin being a few months older than himself. The throne of Constantinople, though it remains in the same line, is filled by the eldest survivor, according to the Ottoman laws. This circumstance often causes a great deal of bloodshed, for it is not always that a son of the grand Signior's, or that the people will consent that the difference of a few years, or months, should cause the throne to be taken from the reigning family and be given to a distant branch—to one, perhaps, who finding but this one obstacle in the road to royalty, often unfairly removes the right heir, knowing that he himself will afterwards possess it.

The Venetian Consul, who has resided some years with the Venetian Ambassador at Constantinople, says, that among the remarkable circumstances which happened during his residence there, he saw a procession of the Grand Vizier and his officers, which was beyond description terrible, from the sensation it caused in the people. When it happened, an ague fit seemed at once to seize the whole populace ;

[1] Sultan Abdul Hamid I. He was succeeded by Sultan Selim III in 1789.

each individual as they passed along turned pale, hardly able to support himself, and appeared deprived of speech and motion, considering himself in the hands of death, whilst his ears resounded with the dreadful sentence of being immediately hung up at his own door, without any cause assigned or question asked. This happened, without any warning, to numbers during this procession, either on the account of their false weights, their tardiness in paying tribute, or any thing else the Vizier might, in his own mind, deem them guilty of; which charges the wretched culprit had scarcely time to hear before he paid the debt of nature for them. This most horrible procession is always made at a moment the people least expect it.

Those who suffer on this occasion, as well as criminals condemned by the laws, are left hanging in any part of the town, where they often remain long enough to be offensive, even to ambassador's houses; [1] and it is totally impossible to get them removed by any applications, if the Turks do not think fit themselves to take them away.

Ⴋ

July 30, 1786

Sidy Mahmoud, the Bashaw's grandson, has been the subject of so great a quarrel at the castle, that his mother, the Bashaw's eldest daughter, determined to quit the palace this morning and retire to her own garden in the country. All her property and jewels, gold, and furniture, are already conveying thither. Her son denies the charge alleged against him, of having secretly sent to solicit an interview with his uncle's bride, a very beautiful lady of Turkish extraction, married to Sidy Hamet, the Bashaw's second son.

This improper embassy from Sidy Mahmoud was effected through one of the female messengers, the common instruments of mischief in the castle. The bride feared to complain of Sidy Mahmoud to the female part of the royal family, who were but new acquaintances to her. Having been only three months married to Sidy Hamet, she dreaded so much the great influence Sidy Mahmoud's mother, Lilla Uducia, had over the Bashaw, that she dared not openly accuse the son of that princess; but conscious that the great attentions Sidy

---

[1] Until late in the nineteenth century it was a common practice for the public executioner in Constantinople to parade condemned criminals from door to door in the bazaars, collecting bribes to purchase immunity from having the felons hanged in front of shops.

Hamet paid to herself had already drawn the baneful eyes of jealousy and envy on her, and dreading, notwithstanding her innocence, some one might accuse her to her lord, she was impelled by her fears, when he entered the haram at sunset, to tell him of her distress. Sidy Hamet evinced the most violent agonies of passion ; nor could all her entreaties and prayers, delivered at his feet with streaming tears, undo what she had done. He determined on the death of his nephew Sidy Mahmoud, and arming his servants, he went immediately in search of him. Some one happily informed this young man just in time, of his uncle's approach, and he escaped to the Bey's wife's apartments, where he despaired of gaining admission, as it is not permitted for any man to pass the doors except the Bey, but where he fortunately found an asylum, and lay concealed some hours in a large chest in the Bey's wife's own room, while his enraged pursuer was exploring every secret avenue in the castle. By the help of a disguise he got over the castle walls during the darkness of the night, and escaped to the country house of his mother.

This princess took so ill her brother's sudden passion against her son, without his having first enquired further into the matter, that when she left the castle this morning she declared she would never again return to it.

This is the first instance of a Bashaw's daughter having lived out of its walls in the memory of any one here. Sidy Hamet, who is not friendly with his eldest brother the Bey, is terribly enraged against him for having screened Sidy Mahmoud from his vengeance.

August 8, 1786

The displeasure Sidy Mahmoud has so lately incurred at the castle has been much aggravated by the following circumstance, which has contributed not a little to incense him. A Tunisian woman of light character, of the name of Sulah, who has been for some years reputed as the first engaged in all the plots and secrets of the castle, became the favorite of Sidy Mahmoud, and had gained such an ascendancy over him, that he overlooked her troublesome behaviour to the Bashaw's family, though he repeatedly heard her accused. Sulah finding, in spite of her secret machinations to frustrate the Bashaw's intentions of marrying his daughter, Lilla Fatima, to Sidy Mahmoud, that the wedding was nearly taking place, has recently spoken so very ill of the princess, and has so publicly endeavoured to injure her in Sidy Mahmoud's opinion, that her imprudence was heard of at the castle. She reckoned so much on the power she had over Sidy Mahmoud, as not to reflect on the dangerous predicament she knew she stood in, being of that class of women which a single breath from the castle destroys at all times. Notwithstanding this, however, when Lilla Fatima yesterday paid the customary compliment of having prepared with her own hands a choice dish of viands, and sent it to her intended bridegroom, Sulah had the audacity, Sidy Mahmoud being from home, to send it back with a very impertinent message to the Bashaw's daughter. An order arrived instantly from the castle to Sidy Mahmoud to give her up, which he was obliged to do. The prayers of Lilla Fatima changed the woman's destiny from immediate death to the being banished to Tunis, whence she came ; and with this intent, she was put on board a vessel bound to that place, her clothes having been first changed for more ordinary apparel, and all her gold and jewels taken away.

After this woman had embarked, they reflected at the castle that she was well acquainted with all their political as well as their private secrets, and by that means had it in her power to injure them with the government of Tunis : three Hampers of the Bashaw's body guard was therefore sent on board, and with the welcome message of a pardon brought her willingly on shore. They carried her to the Rais' golphor, an apartment where the Rais of the Marine, the captain of the port, sits all day, but where he never is at night. Here the dreadful sash presented itself to Sulah's despairing eyes, and the Rais' chief blacks instantly put an end to her existence : so that, in less than a quarter of an hour, she was pardoned, deceived, and strangled, the usual fate of these unhappy wretches here.

Sidy Mahmoud has not quitted his apartment since this woman's death, and threatens vengeance on the perpetrators of what he terms the "horrid plot."

August 29, 1786

The appearance of a new moon, three nights ago, put an end to the Moors' great fast of Ramadan,[1] which had begun on the appearance of the new moon preceding.

[1] Ramadan, which lasts for a lunar month, falls on the ninth month of the Moslem calendar.

During these thirty days a number of circumstances having happened to create very alarming dissentions between the three sons of the Bashaw, Lilla Halluma, by exerting every effort, hoped during the feast of Beiram, which begins on the day after the fast, to put an end to these disputes and reconcile her sons ; for that feast is the time at which every good Mussulman endeavours to settle all quarrels which may have disturbed the peace of the family in the foregoing year.

On the first day of Beiram, which continues three days in town, the Bashaw usually has a numerous court, which he should receive in the chamber built for that purpose, called the messelees ; but owing to the prophecy I have mentioned to you before, of some years' standing, delivered by one of their most famous marabuts, that " the Bashaw shall end his reign in this chamber, by being stabbed on the throne by an unknown hand," he will not follow his inclination of resuming the custom of going there when dissentions happen at the castle ; and there having been such serious quarrels between his sons during this Ramadan, he still continues to receive his court in another part of the palace.

All his subjects are permitted to approach the throne to do homage to their sovereign on the first day of the feast. Two of the people in whom the Bashaw has the greatest confidence stand on each side of him : their office is to lay hold of the arm of the stranger that presents himself to kiss the Bashaw's hand, for fear of any hidden treachery, and people of consequence and trust are alone permitted to enter his presence armed ; others are obliged to leave their arms in the skiffar on entering the palace.

The drawing-room, in honour of the day, was uncommonly crowded ; when all the courtiers were, in a moment, struck with a sight which seemed to congeal their blood : they appeared to expect nothing less than the slaughter of their sovereign at the foot of his throne, and themselves to be sacrificed to the vengeance of his enemies. The three princes entered, with their chief officers, guards, and blacks, armed in an extraordinary manner, and with their sabres drawn. Each of the sons, surrounded by his own officers and guards, went separately up to kiss the Bashaw's hand. He received them with trembling ; his extreme surprise and agitation were visible to every eye ; and the doubtful issue of the moment appeared terrible to all present. The princes formed three divisions, keeping distinctly apart, and conversed with the Consuls and different people of the court as freely as usual, but did not suffer a glance to escape to each other.

They stayed but a short time in the drawing-room, each party retiring in the same order they had entered ; and it became apparent that their rage was levelled against each other, and not against their father, though the Bashaw seemed to recover breath only on their departure. The next morning, the second day of the feast, the Bey went to his mother's apartments to pay his compliments to her on the Beiram. She was very anxious to see him shake hands with his brother, Sidy Hamet, the second son ; at least to make up the last breach between them. She began by insisting, therefore, that the Bey should not touch her hand, till he consented to stay with her while she sent for Sidy Hamet's wife to come and kiss his hand, a token of respect never omitted by any of the women in the family to the Bey on this occasion, unless their husbands are at variance with him. Lilla Halluma hoped, by this mark of respect from Sidy Hamet's wife, to begin the work of a reconciliation between the Bey and his brother, as this would have been the means of disarming the anger of Sidy Useph, the youngest son. The Bey at length consented to his mother's intreaties, and a message was instantly sent to Sidy Hamet's wife, who most unfortunately was at that moment attending on her husband at dinner.[1] The message was delivered in his hearing, and it is thought with design, as there are so many intermeddlers at the castle. Sidy Hamet immediately ordered his wife to send a very severe answer back to the Bey. His wife was so alarmed and hurt at this new misfortune, which must occasion a further breach, that her women were obliged to support her. When she recovered, being willing to soften the matter as much as possible, she only sent word to the Bashaw's wife that she could not come because her husband was eating, and begged her to make as light of it as possible to the Bey ; but the answer was delivered in the worst words Sidy Hamet had delivered it, and the Bey left his mother's presence too much enraged for her to pacify him, while Lilla Halluma remained agonized, meditating on the scenes of blood that would, in all probability, be soon perpetrated in the castle.

On returning to his apartment, the Bey found that one of his servants had been laid down at his youngest brother, Sidy Useph's feet, and almost bastinadoed to death, for a dispute with one of Sidy Useph's servants. Had the brothers met at that moment it would have proved fatal to one or both of them. The next morning (the

___

[1] It is the Moorish custom for the princesses and ladies of high rank to attend their husband, standing by his chair whilst he eats ; they do not eat with him. Among the lower ranks, this ceremony is frequently dispensed with ; but even these women do not dine with their husbands. (T.)

third and last day of Beiram) the Bey went again to court, and in the presence of his father, Sidy Hamet, and Sidy Useph, and a very numerous assemblage of courtiers, he warned both his brothers of putting his prudence any further to the trial ; he said he scorned to take an unfair measure, though in his power to silence both of them ; but that if either of them wished to call him out he would condescend (for they had no right to demand it of him) to meet them on the Pianura, where he did not fear the zeal or numbers of his people, and where, if they irritated him too much, he would shortly summons them to feel his power. The Bey's suite seemed hardly able to abstain from confirming with their actions what their master had said, who, upon saluting his father, retired from the court.

Thus finished the great feast of Beiram, and with it all the hopes of the Bashaw's wife, who had reckoned so much on obliterating the dissentions of the castle. She is most sincerely to be pitied. When they speak of her they say she is an ornament to the throne, an affectionate mother, and a friend to the human race ; her actions, public and private, are constantly guided by humanity and benevolence.

September 10, 1786

Since our long quarantine (having been close prisoners for thirteen months, from the beginning of June 1785 to the end of July 1786) we have availed ourselves of every opportunity to enjoy our liberty ; though it was at first with great caution that we ventured to alight at any of the Moorish gardens, or to enter a Moorish house, particularly out of town.

In the country the villages are empty and those houses shut that have not been opened since the plague, and where whole families lay interred. The Moors carried a great number of their dead to the sea shore and laid them in one heap, which seriously affected the town, till the Christians suggested the idea of covering them with lime, which fortunately the Moors have adopted, but only from finding themselves dangerously annoyed, as they consider this expedient a sort of impiety, for which they express great sorrow.

The habitations in the mountains of Guerriana,[1] inaccessible except to the inhabitants, remain entirely deserted. The entrance to the dwellings are so completely covered up with sand as not to be

1 Gharian.

discovered by strangers; but they are now repeopling, and the remnant of those who fled thence are hastening back from Tunis, and the deserts around, to recover possession of these strange retreats.

The city of Tripoli, after the plague, exhibited an appearance awfully striking. In some of the houses were found the last victims that had perished in them, who having died alone, unpitied and unassisted, lay in a state too bad to be removed from the spot, and were obliged to be buried where they were ; while in others, children were wandering about deserted, without a friend belonging to them. The town was almost entirely depopulated, and rarely two people walked together. One solitary being paced slowly through the streets, his mind unoccupied by business, and lost in painful reflections : if he lifted his eyes, it was with mournful surprise to gaze on the empty habitations around him : whole streets he passed without a living creature in them ; for beside the desolation of the plague before it broke out in this city, many of the inhabitants, with the greatest inconvenience, left their houses and fled to Tunis (where the plague then raged), to avoid starving in the dreadful famine that preceded it here.

Amongst those left in this town, some have been spared to acknowledge the compassion and attention shewn them by the English Consul. In the distresses of the famine, and in the horrors of the plague, many a suffering wretch, whose days have been spun out by his timely assistance, has left his name on record in this place. Persons saved from perishing in the famine, who have remained sole possessors of property before divided among their friends (all now swept off by the plague), come forward to thank him with wild expressions of joy, calling him Boui (father), and praying to Mahomet to bless him. They say that besides giving them life he has preserved them to become little kings, and swear a faithful attachment to him, which there is no doubt they will shew, in their way, as long as he is in their country.[1]

⚏

October 12, 1786

The Bey having been out a month with his camp to Messurata, a sea-port belonging to the Bashaw, returned yesterday with four

---

[1] In the year 1793, when Ali Benzool invaded Tripoli, two hundred Gebbelins (or mountaineers) who lived in the town and suburbs of Tripoli, came voluntarily to guard the English Consul's house from being assaulted by the Arabs and the Turks, on a night when the town was expected to be demolished by the Turks or sacked by the Arabs. (T.)

hundred horse. He came off the deserts in the morning, and several
of the Consuls went out to meet him. His approach to Tripoli was
announced soon after the adan (or break of day) by the distant and
well-known sound of the royal nubar, the band of music that precedes
him, and from the voices of all the villagers round repeating their
festive song of *loo, loo, loo*. As he drew near to the town his horsemen
all passed to the front of his troops, and raced backwards and forwards
on the sands before him. The Bey and his chief officers were magnificent in their appearance. The Bey was resplendent with gold and
jewels. He wore a crescent chiefly of diamonds of great value in his
turban, which was very large and of the finest white muslin, and crossed
with a dark purple and gold shawl, the two ends of which were embroidered in gold nearly half a yard deep, and hung over the left
shoulder. His upper vest, or loose caftan, was pale yellow satin, lined
with ermine and ornamented with silver, and his under vest was of
green and gold tissue. Gold trappings, in the shape of drop necklaces, nearly covered his horse's chest. His saddle, which he received
not long since from the Emperor of Morocco, was gilt, highly embossed, and studded with rubies, emeralds, and other precious stones.
Two relay horses, with very rich housings, one of which was crimson
velvet almost covered with raised gold embroidery, were led by
blacks. The Bey slept at a village a few miles to the eastward of
Tripoli. He arrived there the night before so harassed and ill, it was
said from vexation, that it was thought he would not have accompanied the troops into the city ; but when he came into Tripoli he
had recovered all his usual good humour, and looked extremely well.
His two brothers, Sidy Hamet and Sidy Useph, went out to meet
him, and embraced him with every demonstration of joy, while their
suite repeated the song of *loo, loo, loo*,[1] in shouts that rent the air ; but
the Bey's friends watched his brothers' manœuvres with a jealous
eye, for while the Bey declares himself unconscious of danger, his
officers seem to tremble when they perceive him at any time surrounded by the people of either of his brothers.

Some of the Moors complain of the severity the Bey has shewn
in collecting his tributes, as they say, by putting many people to
death ; but as these tributes have been fixed for a number of years,
if the Arabs oblige the Bey to go out and levy them, they could not
suppose he would return unsatisfied, or that they would find him on
such an occasion a lenient visitor. Just as the Bey reached the city

---

[1] The cry of the women, called in Arabic *zagarit*.

gates, a courier from Egypt arrived : he was not detained by the Bey but ordered to pass on to the castle. The courier was on a dromedary, to which he was fastened, as is the custom here, with large ropes to prevent his being thrown off by the swiftness of his pace. He had been twenty-five days travelling on the same animal from Grand Cairo, upwards of nine hundred miles from hence. The length of time this journey was performed in, seems, to those unacquainted with these parts, not to agree with the extreme swift pace the dromedary is said to go at ; but want of water, the approach of savages, the rising hurricane in the deserts, and other similar delays which annoy the African traveller, often consume the major part of the time he is passing from one place to another.

This courier brings the account that the Captain Pacha and his fleet had exacted immense sums of money from the people at Alexandria, and made them promise to rebuild the Greek and Roman Catholic churches they have lately destroyed ; after which the Captain Pacha, hearing of the Grand Signior's death, sailed to Constantinople. His intention therefore of visiting this place, for the present, is entirely abandoned.

November 15, 1786

We are just returned from a visit to Lilla Amnani, Hadgi Abderrahman's Greek : she was not well, but we were admitted to her chamber, which was so full of visitors that it was with difficulty we could approach the bed on which she lay. Lilla Uducia, Abderrahman's daughter by his first wife, was seated close to Lilla Amnani's pillow, and seemed to pay her great attention ; and some of Lilla Amnani's blacks lay on the ground round the bed, while others stood waiting near her. She had sprained her hip and was in great pain, but had had a writing made for it by one of their Imams, and hoped for great relief from this charm. She was easier persuaded to add to the charm Tissot's simple remedy of vinegar and water, than many of the Moorish ladies would have been in such a case. Lilla Amnani looked extremely handsome, though indisposed. She was wrapped up in a crimson silk baracan, and was covered with a light counterpane made of fine linen and coloured ribbons, sewed together in numerous narrow stripes : her pillows were crimson silk embroidered with gold.

She rose to take coffee, which was served in very small china cups, placed in silver filigree cups; and gold filigree cups were put under those presented to the married ladies. They had introduced cloves, cinnamon, and saffron into the coffee, which was abundantly sweetened; but this mixture was very soon changed, and replaced by excellent simple coffee for the European ladies.

Amongst a number of Moorish ladies of the first rank, who had assembled to visit the Greek, was a beautiful woman, named Zenobia, wife to one of the Bashaw's chief officers of state. This lady has gained such power over the Bey, as to engross much of his attention. She exhausts her husband's treasures by the extraordinary extravagance of her dress: when her spies inform her of any article of attire ordered for the castle, she immediately obtains one similar to it; and, if it is not to be had in Tripoli, she sends for it at any expense, and generally succeeds in appearing the first in it at court, to the great mortification of the princess, who has sent for a similar article, and supposed no one could receive it before herself. This conduct occasions Zenobia so many enemies in the castle, that her life is endangered. She is a Moorish lady, born in Tripoli, was much painted, but with taste, and her dress was superb with a prodigious number of jewels.

When the Moorish ladies had all departed, Amnani, in addition to the history she had given us of herself, and which I have related to you, told us that one of her brothers came to Tripoli soon after her marriage. He had determined to propose the redeeming her from Abderrahman, expecting she was still a slave and not his wife; but she informed her brother it was too late, and told him the ceremony had passed, and that she had changed her religion; at which she says her brother shuddered, and agreed, that after such a circumstance it was not possible for him to see her again. He lamented, in the bitterest agony, the fate of his beloved sister, and left Tripoli a few days after. This unexpected visit of her brother, and his extraordinary affection for her, rendered Lilla Amnani for a time very unhappy, till she considered what she owed Abderrahman, how highly he thought of her, and with what profusion he provided for all her wishes, treating her with a tenderness and delicacy very uncommon among Moors or Turks: he still continues the same, giving her unlimited power when he is present or from home. As a proof of what she said, she informed us that, though the ambassador is at present absent, she has just expended large sums in purchasing for Lilla Fatima, her daughter, not six years old, articles towards her marriage portion, which it is the Moorish custom to begin to collect almost the moment a female is

born. She shewed us some very expensive curtains, curiously embroidered in narrow stripes, sewed together : each curtain had an
embroidery at bottom of gold and silver, full half a yard in depth ;
a broad fringe of gold and silver, mixed with the same colours which
were in the curtains, was round the edges of them. They dispose of
these curtains in the following way : before the alcove where the
bed stands they put up three of them, as much above one another as
will just shew the worked ends, which being put thus together make
about one yard and a half in depth of the richest gold embroidery ;
a crimson velvet curtain edged with a deep fringe of gold is then
thrown over the last curtain and drawn in folds to one side, discovering only the gold ends of the three curtains underneath. The Greek
then shewed us the gala furniture of her own room, which cannot
be used at present, as the house is considered in a state of mourning
for the ambassador's absence. The hangings of the room were of
tapestry, made in pannels of different coloured velvets, thickly inlaid
with flowers of silk damask : a yellow border, of about a foot in
depth, finished the tapestry at top and bottom, the upper border being
embroidered with Moorish sentences from the Koran in lilac letters.
The carpet was of crimson satin, with a deep border of pale blue
quilted ; this is laid over Indian mats and other carpets. In the best
part of the room the sofa is placed, which occupies three sides of an
alcove, the floor of which is raised. The sofa and the cushions that
lay around were of crimson velvet : the centre cushions being embroidered with a sun in gold of highly embossed work, the rest were
of gold and silver tissue. The curtains for the alcove were made to
match those before the bed. A number of looking-glasses and a profusion of fine china and chrystal completed the ornaments and furniture of the room, in which there were neither tables nor chairs. A
small table, about six inches high, is brought in when refreshments
are served ; it is of ebony inlaid with mother-o'-pearl, tortoiseshell,
ivory, gold, and silver, of choice woods, or of plain mahogany,
according to the circumstances of the proprietor.

Lilla Uducia had on to-day a sash of cloves strung in bunches,
nearly as thick round as one's wrist, and confined from space to space
with a large gold chased bead. Moorish ladies are never without this
sash : some shew it and some do not ; Uducia wore it over her dress,
across her left shoulder. She took us up to see what they termed
" the Black Rooms," or rooms of the dead, so called, from a dismal
custom they have of shutting up the apartments of any dear friend or

relation deceased. We saw five of these rooms shut up at Abderrahman's. The last was closed for one of his nephews who died in the plague ; and the other apartment had been shut up five years for the sister of the Greek, who, with herself, was sold to Abderrahman. The walls are painted black, and superstitious people among the dependants and servants, tremble when obliged to pass the doors of these melancholy rooms.

Lilla Uducia had eight black women slaves of her own when her father sailed for England, only one of whom has escaped the plague. Being herself attacked with a fever during the plague, and fearing the infection of every thing round her, she would not venture to go near any bed, but lay on the floor in the middle of her apartment, and would not make use of any thing but her wedding cloaths, which not having been touched since they were deposited in the chest many years since, she considered safe from infection. This circumstance will affect a considerable part of her marriage portion ; as the chest that contained them being opened in the height of the plague, the contents were subjected to be perfumed and smoked to purify them, which will destroy their freshness and brilliancy, as they were chiefly of gold and silver.

Moorish ladies seem conscious of their confinement when they see Christians, and express regret at their want of liberty. Not that they find the day too long on their hands, for those who are amiable and attend their families enter so much into domestic concerns that they have never time sufficient to complete the task they wish to perform ; and to those of a lighter turn, their intrigues, jealousies, and fears fully employ all their hours, which we may easily conceive, when we consider that the failure of their plots would often cost them their lives !

⊞

February 10, 1787

Three days ago we paid a visit to Lilla Uducia, the Bashaw's eldest daughter, for the first time since she quitted her father's palace, after the great quarrel at the castle on account of her son Sidy Mahmoud. She received us with all that engaging interest which so peculiarly marks her mother's manner ; but Lilla Uducia in her family is very haughty. She seems extremely hurt at having left the castle, and misses much the parade and state she enjoyed there ; where, as being the eldest of the princesses, great court was paid to her. She was so out of humour that her attendants hardly dared to speak to her, and her slaves were every moment in danger of being chastised for not executing her orders, which she gave and contradicted in the same breath. Her youngest children (two sweet boys and a fine little girl) were in the room ; and though the eldest of them was five years old, and the youngest not less than three, they were each attended by their wet nurses, who were blacks, very richly habited and entirely loaded with silver and bead ornaments.

Lilla Uducia is united to one of the Bashaw's chief officers, of the name of Hadgi Murat, a renegado ; for, according to the laws of the country, she could not marry a subject. Her husband was one of her father's Neapolitan slaves, and his origin unfortunately very obscure. The princesses who marry renegados are not considered as subject to their husbands ; they esteem them no higher than the meanest of their slaves ; and they often regret being allied to men, who from their manners are totally unfit to appear in their presence. In such cases, the father's birth does not affect the children : they, as the descendants of Lilla Uducia, and the grand-children of the Bashaw, lose none of their consequence. Lilla Uducia's eldest son is intended by the Bashaw to be sent ambassador to Naples very soon, and Hadgi Murat has amassed immense riches in the service of the Bashaw ; but in pecuniary matters Lilla Uducia need not consult her husband, as a word from the Bashaw is always sufficient to render her wishes complete. Her apartments were richly furnished, and her attendants very numerous ; and herself and her eldest daughter (by a former husband), a young lady about fifteen, were superbly dressed with a profusion of gold and jewels. She dwelt a great deal on the misfortune of her quitting the castle, attributing it entirely to the machinations of the underlings of the palace, who, as Lilla Uducia says, live only by selling the secrets of the family from one part of it to another. She remarked how much more fatally and easily plots were carried on against the peace of the royal family than against that of any other people in Tripoli, owing to the ladies being almost wholly excluded from all information but what is brought to them by a set of flattering interested dependants. Lilla Uducia expected her accouchement every day : she was not well, and therefore we staid with her but a short time. This morning we received another invitation from her to repeat our visit in the afternoon, as the Bashaw's wife and the princesses would be there to congratulate her on the birth of her son, which had taken place since we had left her. We went, and were much surprised to find the house crowded with several hundred visitors so soon after such an event, and a very grand repast, consisting of hot viands of every kind, prepared for all those who were of sufficient consequence to remain to partake of them.

The Bashaw's wife and the princesses were in the room with Lilla Uducia, all in full gala. The princesses changed their dresses several times for richer habits, and the Moorish ladies brought dresses with them to do the same during their visit. One of the princesses, Lilla Howisha, who is a bride, very lately married to the Rais of the marine, had her arms painted very curiously, similar to two bands of black lace round the thick part of the arm, and her fingers were deeply stained to near the first joint of the finest jet, to shew off the diamonds and jewels with which they were covered. All the princesses had bracelets round their ankles of an immense size, of solid gold, weighing from three to four pounds each. The infant was brought round in a new gold tissue mantle lined with satin : and it was laid in a quantity of fine white loose cotton in a neat basket.

Disapprobation was strongly displayed in the nurse's countenance while she by order shewed the infant to the Christians ; she covered it as much as she could with the charms which it wore, and, at every look the Christians bestowed upon it, she wetted her finger and passed it across the forehead of the baby, pronouncing at the same instant the words " Ali Barick " [1] (a prayer to Mahomet to preserve it from " bad eyes," or malicious observers). Before the apartment, in a covered gallery which surrounds the square area in the middle of the house, Indian mattings, Turkey carpets, and silk cushions were placed, and long tables raised a very few inches from the ground. On the tables were placed all sorts of refreshments, and thirty or forty dishes of meat and poultry dressed in different ways : there were no knives nor forks, and only a few spoons of gold, silver, ivory, or coral. When the ladies were seated, Lilla Halluma and the princesses, with their attendants, walked round the tables during the repast to attend upon their guests, according to the Arabian custom. The tables were completely filled with the different dishes : there was no room for plates, nor were they required ; for when a number of ladies had eaten what they chose out of one dish, it was changed for another. The beverage was various sherbets, some composed of the juice of boiled raisins, very sweet ; some of the juice of pomegranates squeezed

[1] Literally *Allah yubarick* or " God bless."

through the rind ; and others of the pure juice of oranges. These sherbets were copiously supplied in high glass ewers placed in great numbers on the ground, reminding one much of the ancient scriptural paintings. After the dishes of meat were removed, a dessert of Arabian fruits, confectionaries and sweetmeats was served : among the latter was the date bread. This sweetmeat is made in perfection only by the blacks at Fezzan, of the ripe date of that country, which is superior to all others. They make it in the shape of loaves weighing from twenty to thirty pounds : the stones of the fruit are taken out, and the dates simply pressed together with great weights : thus preserved, it keeps perfectly good for a year. When the dessert was finished, the blacks brought towels with gold embroidered ends, and soap and water, which were very acceptable to many of the ladies, who had used neither knife, fork nor spoon, during the whole repast.

According to a very singular custom here, when a lady is visited by her friends on the birth of an infant, the etiquette is for the visitors to put into her hand a piece, or a quantity of gold coin, as an offering. Lilla Halluma and the princesses made the largest offerings, and the rest of the ladies gave in proportion to their abilities. The remains of this feast were carefully gathered up and given to the poor.

When the three princesses departed in the evening, a great number of guards and lights were ready to attend them ; and the two youngest princes, Sidy Hamet and Sidy Useph, came to accompany their sisters back to the palace. All the ladies were wrapped up in white silk baracans, which concealed them entirely. I cannot help noticing to you the contrast which struck us between the costume of the infant of Lilla Uducia, and that of a Venetian lady whose christening we were at yesterday. While the one lay as I have described at its ease in its palm basket, encumbered only with an embroidered silk handkerchief thrown over it, the other had every limb confined, in the shape of an Egyptian mummy. It was tightly swaddled from head to foot with many yards of pink satin riband, on one edge of which was gathered very full the finest Brussels lace, which encircled the infant as many times as the riband was bound round it. According to the Turkish laws, Lilla Uducia's son cannot be seen by its father, Hadgi Murat, till eight days after its birth.

March 3, 1787

In consequence of having met Lilla Halluma and the princesses at Lilla Uducia's, as I informed you in my last, we went the next day to the castle. There being no carriages nor any sort of conveyance here, it requires some address and resolution on these occasions, to walk full dressed near three-quarters of a mile through the streets to the castle. It is only the ladies of a Consul's family who attempt to pass the streets in this manner. They are always accompanied by several gentlemen and guards ; but these precautions, though they might ensure safety, would not render the walking through the streets possible were the Moors inclined to be insolent : on the contrary, however, if the Moors are in the least troublesome, it is from their over kindness and civility.

As we were passing through a part of the castle, accompanied as usual by the Bashaw's hampers or guards, we met one of the noted Moorish saints, or holy men. I have already described these people to you ; but this man, contrary to the general appearance of these marabuts, was tolerably covered, with a long wide blue shirt reaching to the ground, and white trowsers underneath. He wore nothing on his head, which was shaved close, except a long lock of hair descending from the back part of it. The whole dress of many of these marabuts consists of a bit of crimson cloth, about four inches square, dexterously placed on the crown of their head. The marabut we met in the castle was returning from the Bashaw, with whom he had a long private audience. His appearance, from the furious and strange gestures he made, with an immense large living snake round his shoulders, was truly terrific, though we were all aware of the unfortunate reptile having been rendered harmless by the wearer's extracting its sting, before he attempted to impose on the credulous, in making them believe he alone was exempt from death by the power of the reptile. The Moors regarded him with great reverence. We had but just consoled ourselves with having passed this figure without his deigning to take notice of us, when a gentleman of the party perceived close to us a large tiger, just landed from the coast, as a present for the Bey : it was so insecurely fastened that they dreaded every moment it would get loose ; but still they kept it in this dangerous situation, to be shewn to the Bey when he returned from riding on the sands. These perils over, we entered those gloomy passages which always seem as if they led to some dreadful abode for the purposes of entombing the living. We were expected, and therefore relieved at the entrance of them by the appearance of Lilla Halluma's female slaves and eunuchs, who conducted us to her apartments. She was walking in the gallery with three of the princesses, the wife of the Rais of Marine, the widow of the Bey of Derne, and an unmarried princess. They were consoling her, as she was evidently in tears. Soon after we joined them, Lilla Halluma entered the sala, and having seated herself under the alcove, or place of honour, the princesses and the Christians were placed promiscuously on each side of her.

Their usual urbanity of manners was conspicuous. A number of the Moorish nobility had been invited ; but the entertainment was entirely damped by the uncommon melancholy visible in Lilla Halluma's countenance, and in those of Sidy Hamet's and the Bey's wives. These two ladies entered the apartment later, and seemed much agitated.

A serious dispute had that day occasioned a coolness between the Bey and Sidy Useph, his youngest brother, who though quite a youth is haughty and courageous, and, with the most insinuating address, bids fair to be a dangerous and severe character. The Bey, with a nobleness of mind peculiar to himself, overlooks this young man's assuming deportment, though shewn in the presence of his own people : he appears much attached to him ; till now, has admired his courage ; and to his accusers has pleaded the cause of, as he terms him, " the beautiful rash youth."

All the attendants at the castle were eager to relate the occurrences of the day, and each had a different tale to tell of these two princes. The circumstances of this quarrel had as yet only reached the ears of the ladies through the medium of the intriguing messengers of the castle. These designing women have not their abode in the castle, but live on the bounty of the different branches of the royal family, and having free access to them at all times, they stroll from one princess's apartment to another, mixing with the attendants and slaves, and learning from them all that has happened during the time they may have been absent from the castle : they then hasten to entertain their mistresses with the relation of what they have heard, turning it to their own advantage, or to the injury of those of whom they may be afraid. Their hearers, who may be truly styled prisoners, are thus entertained with all the news these women can collect in or out of the castle, true or false. When there is a dearth of intelligence, they continue to amuse the princesses by relating tales, or singing extempore verses on any subject proposed to them ; and they often give information and opinions in that manner which they would not dare to meddle with but under the mask of entertainment. Many of these people are clever, and therefore well calculated for messengers and spies, and are often in the pay of both parties, some of whom, as it may be expected, occasionally forfeit their lives by the treachery of these wretches.

Soon after we were in Lilla Halluma's apartment, we found that a message had been sent from her to Sidy Hamet and Sidy Useph, to inform them that the Christians were with her, and that she therefore begged they would call in and see her before they went to the Bashaw's levee ; but from the additional chagrin Lilla Halluma discovered when the messenger returned, and the displeasure imprinted on the Bey's wife's countenance, it was evident the princes were too agitated and angry to obey their mother's invitation. After the Bashaw's levee, the Bey came to Lilla Halluma, just before we quitted the apartment : he appeared in his usual manner, majestic, affable, calm, and cheerful, and seemed unconscious of what had happened. He mildly chid his wife, mother, and sisters for their fears, and told them never to alarm themselves for him, till they saw his people armed at an improper hour : " Till then," said the Bey, " while I live, depend upon it, not only you and I, but my father's subjects are safe." He made a longer stay than usual in the apartment, and Lilla Halluma seemed to have been greatly consoled before his departure.

She sent to make it known through the harem that the person who should bring her the first account of the Bashaw after his levee, should receive from her an extraordinary present in money, which is the custom here for any important news communicated. Lilla Halluma rewards so very liberally, that she is never in want of heralds. She came with us, accompanied by the princesses, to the Bey's wife's apartment, but soon returned, appearing very uneasy and dejected.

When we were leaving the palace, we met Sidy Useph's and Sidy Hamet's people, armed to the lowest black in their suite. The reason given for this hostile appearance to the Bey's friends was, that both the princes feared the Bey's intentions, and expected his people to rise against them, though the Bey's attendants, notwithstanding this assertion, appeared every where without any extraordinary addition of arms, and we were met by several of his chief officers before we left the castle, who blamed him much for not disharming his brother's people. The Bashaw's officers, whom we also met, did not agree in their opinion of this quarrel : some treated it very lightly ; and others spoke of it as if they did not consider the Bashaw safe on his throne an hour, but thought the country to be in a most alarming state for strangers as well as subjects, as they were sure, if any disturbance happened, the Arabs would take advantage of it, and plunder the town.

June 30, 1787

Captain Smith, who commanded the frigate dispatched from England with the Tripolitan ambassador, Hadgi Abderrahman, arrived here the 30th of last month. The captain had permitted a number of gentlemen from the Mediterranean to join the ship and come with him to Barbary : amongst these were Sir John Dyer, Sir Lionel Copley, Lord Garlies, a son of Sir John Collett Ross, and a son of Sir Charles Harding. Captain Smith did not disembark, being indisposed ; but the captain of a man of war, who was with him, appeared to take his place on shore.

On the day fixed for the officers to pay their first visit to the Bashaw, leave was obtained for them to see the great mosque, a favour seldom granted to Christians ; but, unfortunately, a dispute among the Moors about saluting the frigate prevented this circumstance from taking place, for as the captain could not come on shore, the Bashaw's officers had persuaded him not to salute the vessel. This occasioned a delay before the officers of the frigate could pay their visit to the castle. After a great deal of trouble taken to convince the Bashaw, that the captain's remaining on board made no difference, he agreed to give the salute which was waited for, and returned by the frigate, before the Consul could permit the officers to visit the Bashaw : the ceremony, therefore, being only completed by sunset, it was too late to see the mosque. These misunderstandings are not unfrequent here, owing to the particular etiquette of the Moors.

At a period when the English Consul returned to Barbary, after having been absent a short time, he found that the Bashaw expected the English ships to return upwards of thirty guns for a salute, and that this absurdity had arisen merely from the French having persuaded the Bashaw to give them always one or two guns more than the last ships belonging to other nations, which had come into the bay. It was necessary to put this extraordinary matter on a different footing before any English man of war arrived, as they would not have returned such an enormous salute, and could not, by the treaties, be saluted with an inferior number of guns to those given to other ships. On this occasion, it was proposed by the Consul to the Bashaw to salute the next flag that came into the bay with twenty-one guns only, of whatever nation it might be ; but, that if any other ship received one gun more than the last English ship which had arrived, the next should have ten guns for that one and return but twenty-one. This the Bashaw acceded to, and they have not been able to make him alter his decree. The Bashaw is much attached to the English ; and they have exclusive privileges here. By their treaties they trade free at Tripoli for every thing the place affords. On the other hand, the Venetians have just made an agreement with the Bashaw to pay him three thousand five hundred sequins (nearly two thousand pounds sterling) per annum, for the leave of loading two thousand five hundred measures of salt annually.

After the officers of the frigate had been received at the castle, a party was made to dine in the country the next day, for which the Bashaw allowed the Consul one of his gardens. It being now the season for oranges, the garden is in its greatest beauty. The want of order, neat walks, and regular alleys, might be much regretted, but that in the midst of these fragrant orange groves, the richest perfumes of Arabia freshly exhale from every surrounding plant, and the wonder excited by their costliness engages for the time every thought, and leaves no room for other reflections. The coffee, tea, and Indian banian trees grow in the Bashaw's garden, but only as exotics, and not cultivated in quantities. The palace in this garden is spacious ; it differs from other Moorish habitations only in its size and the materials it is built with, as the Moors have but one form of building from the palace to the cottage. It is chiefly of marble and beautiful Chinese tiles ; but, like Moorish buildings, it is unadorned by architectural ornaments. Lofty piazzas support four wide galleries round the square area in the middle of the palace. From each of the galleries, a large door opens into a suite of apartments unconnected with the rest. Each suite of apartments consists of one large hall, or sala, with an alcove on one side facing the door, where the distinguished part of the company is received. The sala is encircled with eight apartments, to which there is no communication but from this hall. Four of these rooms are called sedas and serve for bed-chambers, and the other four are called hozzannas[1] and serve for store-rooms, in which are kept sweetmeats, spices, and choice stores. Two of the hozzannas open

---

[1] An amusing rendering of *maghzan* (Arabic).

with low doors into the sala. These having no light, are but six feet in height, and full fourteen feet square, forming frightful places to the Moorish women and blacks, who relate stories of people murdered and secreted in them, and of the spirits of the departed keeping their nightly vigils there. They lock the doors of these dark recesses early in the evening, and from their dislike to enter them at night, they are seldom opened until the morning. The following anecdote will prove that a part of their fears are not without foundation. Not long ago a Christian, who had inhabited an apartment for some months in a Moorish-built house, was led to suppose there was hidden treasure buried in the hozzanna under the seda where his bed stood. He ordered his servants to dig there on some pretence ; and after they had broken up the terracing of the floor and laboured hard for two or three nights, they discovered a quantity of human hair and bones, which so alarmed them that they immediately closed it again, not daring to speak of it for fear of the Moors, who would have severely revenged their too prurient curiosity.

From the palace a covered way leads through the gardens to the harem, a much smaller building, with a square area in the middle, grated over the top with heavy bars of iron, as are all the windows. It is no wonder that those who see it at first suppose it a strong place of confinement, or state prison. This harem, which the ladies alone were permitted to enter, was empty, as the few favourites the Bashaw has at present are in town. One of the pleasantest apartments in this building had the walls nearly covered with fine china, and a great deal of alabaster and beautiful marble. This apartment was quite fresh, having been fitted up but a few years since for a favourite black woman of the Bashaw's, whom he has lately married to the Cyde of the Messea, with whom she lives and is highly respected. This is spoken of as a singular piece of good fortune for a black slave.

The ambassador, Hadgi Abderrahman, and three other Moors, joined the company at dinner, which was served in the galleries of the palace. Owing to the rank and religious turn of Hadgi Abderrahman, a Marabut unfortunately found his way to this repast ; and as it would have been too gross an affront to the Moors, on this occasion, to have insisted on his retiring, he was suffered to remain. His figure was disgusting, his whole attire being only a dirty woollen baracan, or blanket, wrapped round him. He kept close to the Moors, seating himself chiefly near Hadgi Abderrahman. He did not address himself to the Christians, but talked constantly of them ; and they seemed to

gain favour with him in proportion to the courtesies he saw pass
between the ambassador and them.   The Marabut ate heartily ; and
Abderrahman, well versed in the politest breeding, did not facilitate
his getting near the table, aware that his manner of eating would be
highly offensive to all present.

Before the company arose from table, information was brought
that the three princes were gone to the deserts for the diversion of
racing on the sands.   As this was known to be a compliment to the
English officers, every one hastened to be spectators of a scene so
singular and uncommon to Europeans.   The Bey and his brothers
appeared in their fullest splendour, each attended by the whole of his
officers and a great number of horse.   The nubar, or royal band,
attended the Bey.   When the Christians arrived on the sands, Sidy
Hamet and Sidy Useph performed many of their manœuvres over
again, which consisted in sham fights, etc. ; but having already
given you a description of a similar entertainment, I shall not now
repeat it.

When the three princes came off the sands, they joined us, and
stopped some time to converse, explaining the meaning of some of
their particular feats, and told us it was still the custom to fight over
their chiefs when slain in war, to prevent the enemy from insulting
their remains, and that numbers often fell in endeavouring to obtain
the mangled body, for which if they succeeded, their shouts or songs
of triumph were heard for miles.   While they were speaking the
Bey came up, and invited the Christians to stop at his garden in their
way to town.   The princes went off racing backwards and forwards,
at full speed, always firing at the feet of those they rode up to.

The Bey and Sidy Useph were equally rich in their apparel, as
were all their officers, mamelukes, and blacks, making on the whole
a very grand appearance.   When we arrived at the Bey's garden, he
had already dismounted, and with his chief officers around him, seemed
prepared to receive us.

The Bey's marked attention to the Christians was peculiarly striking
in a Moorish prince, who had never quitted his own dominions to
visit the polite courts of Europe.   It happened that, while he was entertaining the Christians, an orange from the unlucky hand of a young
midshipman struck the Bey's turban.   This very improper action
caused a sudden impulse on the blacks round the Bey, which seemed
to threaten a reprimand to the offender at the moment ; but the
unaltered countenance of the Bey not authorizing them to act, while

they only waited for his orders to resent the unmerited affront, it was happily passed over on apologies being instantly made to the Bey by the Consul and the English officers. This instance will elucidate to you the Bey's disposition, for the next day, when he was unavoidably again apologized to on this disagreeable event, he replied, he only feared his people's resentment at the moment, as they were unused to see a want of respect shewn towards his person in their presence ; and he desired a boat might be sent from the frigate for one of his best Arabian horses, which he should send as a present to the captain, and said he did not doubt that the young offender would be better taught by the time he was again admitted into the presence of royalty.

It is certain that had such a circumstance happened at Algiers, the officers might have been sacrificed to the rage of the Moors. The Consul would have been instantly dragged to the castle, and if not murdered there, he would not have been liberated before an immense sum had been paid by the English government for his ransom, which frequently happens at Algiers with much less provocation. This circumstance was more striking to the Moors, from its being so directly opposite to the manners of the rest of the English officers, who were noticed by the Bey then, as they have always been, for their liberal and unaffected politeness.

Sir John Dyer was very anxious to carry home a Damascus blade for the Prince of Wales ; and had the Hadgies been here on their return from Mecca, it is probable he might have succeeded in getting one.

These scimitars, besides being so famous for their beauty and lightness, have the steel so impregnated with perfume in the manufacturing of them, that their fragrance can never be destroyed while a piece of this extraordinary blade remains. Their price is from fifty to one hundred guineas, the blade only ; but imitations of them, which are superficially perfumed, are bought for a much less price.

Captain Smith sailed on the fifth day after his arrival at Tripoli, and the next day the ladies of Abderrahman's family invited us to a general rejoicing for the ambassador's return, of which I will give you some account in my next.

The solemn pace and gravity of a chamelion now climbing an orange branch at the window, leads me to introduce this curious animal to you. It was brought home with us this evening by one of the Moors, but shall regain its liberty if it lives till to-morrow. When it was taken off the ground, it was of the most beautiful green you can imagine, undiscernable from the grass, except by those used to search for these animals ; but by the time it was brought but a few paces, fright and anger had produced so vast a change in it, that it became perfectly black. It is now but a little lighter, with no tinge of green. Its eyes seem very curious, extremely prominent, bright as diamonds, and turning as if on a swivel : the one gazes at one object facing the animal, while the other is employed in observing a second exactly behind it. We have several times endeavoured to keep one of these creatures, but without success. So far from feeding on air, as is vulgarly said, they are voracious in their food, which consists of insects, caught by them with singular dexterity by darting their tongues at them. In none of the chamelions that we have seen, does there appear that great change of colour, described to be produced by laying them on bodies of various tint. The most visible change, which is indeed quite distinct, is the one I have mentioned from green to black. By placing this creature on the brightest coloured silk, the hue of the silk is only slightly perceptible in the small spots with which its body is speckled.

♏

July 2, 1787

The respect and affection the people of this country have for the ambassador and his family, is clearly evinced by the great number of Moorish ladies, all of the first distinction, who attended at the feast given by Lilla Amnani, on account of the ambassador's return.

The square area in the centre of the house was fitted up, as is the custom here, in the style of a sala, for the reception of the company. An awning was closely put over the top, which intercepted the light no more than to keep off the dazzling rays of the sun. The floor was covered with mats and Turkey carpets over them ; and sophas and cushions were placed round the four sides of the room for seats, which when filled, the rest of the company placed themselves without distinction on the ground, before the ladies already seated on the sophas. In the centre were a number of dancing women, and women who played the Moorish music, singing at the same time extempore verses on the return of the ambassador. It was expected of those present to give money to the musicians, which all the company did.

The festive song for this rejoicing we heard long before we reached the house, and it was not without difficulty and delay that we could be conducted through this crowded assembly to the ambassador's wife and family, who were seated with the most distinguished part of the company.

At sunset, about an hour after we arrived, Lilla Amnani rose and led the company to the galleries of the house, fitted up in the same manner as the area, covered with awnings and furnished with a profusion of mats, carpets and cushions. In these galleries were placed low Moorish tables, furnished with viands of every delicacy the place could afford. The chief beverage was a sherbet I have before described to you, made of boiled raisins mixed with sugar and the juice of lemon. Between two and three hundred weight of this fruit is made use of at one of these feasts. Lilla Amnani and the ambassador's eldest daughter walked round the tables while the guests were seated, to talk with them, and see they were properly served.

During the entertainment of the music, Lilla Zenobia, the wife of Sidy el Buny and favourite of the Bey, with a lady related to Hamet Hogia's family, and some other beauties of a gay description, unavoidably found entrance for a short time. Not long after they came in, a report spread through the apartments which caused a serious alarm : it was that Sidy Useph was present, having introduced himself disguised as a female, among the attendants. As such a discovery might have proved fatal to him, the thought of its happening at the ambassador's house was truly terrifying to Lilla Amnani. At the instant this report was spread, and every one in commotion, a number of women who had crowded into the avenues about the house, rushed into the street and disappeared ; and it was positively affirmed that Sidy Useph was amongst them. Lilla Zenobia, with her friend, departed the same instant. This circumstance led to some particulars being related of Hamet Hogia and his family since his absence. I wrote you word of the departure of this nobleman, who went ambassador to Spain two years ago. It appears that news have been received of his having embraced the Roman Catholic faith about six months since. This was done with the greatest pomp in Spain : he immediately received a Spanish title, and became one of the nobility.

A man more enlightened, more susceptible of the nicest feelings, or more truly unfortunate, is not often met with. Neglected by his wife, led by treachery to destroy his favourite, and dishonoured by his daughter's conduct, he left the country disgusted. In less than six months after his departure on his embassy to Morocco and Spain, his daughter, for her conduct, which was very reprehensible with

Christians as well as Moors, was (by order of her uncle) shot by her cousin in her bed. This young man, disguised in a baracan, contrived to enter her apartment as one of her women while she was asleep, and, levelling a pistol, shot her. The ball passed through the body without proving fatal. She was attended by the physician who visits the Christians, and soon got better of the wound ; but she was heedless of this most serious warning, though her brother, a youth of eighteen, who was very fond of her, continually informed her that a more certain attempt at her life was daily meditating, and begged her to be more cautious. Her doom, however, was sealed ; for a few months after her recovery, on going one evening to walk in the garden, she was missed ; and the attendants being sent in search of her, found her laying on the ground in a corner of the garden strangled. All present were interrogated about the dreadful deed, which every one denied. It was then declared, and readily admitted by her uncle, who was present at this examination, that evil spirits only had murdered this young beauty.

We saw her brother often at the time of her death, when he appeared inconsolable ; but according to the Moorish manner of thinking, as the honour of his family required this dreadful sacrifice, he dared not openly complain.

The company retired from Lilla Amnani's house at sunset. This rejoicing lasted three days, and was as numerously attended on the last as on the first day.

August 20, 1787

The Emperor of Morocco's son has been here some weeks, and will remain some days longer before he sets off for Mecca. He was expected here last year, and the year before, but his pilgrimage was put off on account of the plague. To talk of such a wretch making a pilgrimage seems sacrilege ; for the havock he makes of the unfortunate human beings in his power, marks every step of his sanguinary way, while he is on his journey to the Holy Land. He has seven wives with him, five Grecian beauties and two black women, and several of his children. One of his wives had a son born a few days ago, for which Muley Yesied [1] made a very great feast, as the boy is a Shrief, being born during a pilgrimage to Mecca.

---

[1] Moulay Yezid was the son of Sultan Moulay Mohammed by a renegade English-woman. He was noted for his atrocious cruelty, and in fact only reigned for two years

This feast has had the most melancholy consequences : one of his treasurers, who had been ordered by the Emperor of Morocco to furnish Muley Yesied with two hundred cobbs (or fifty pounds) a day, being later than usual in his delivery of them, and the tyrant wanting them for the feast, ordered him four thousand bastinadoes, and to swallow a quantity of sand. This unfortunate Moor lies at the point of death : indeed those who speak of him hope that he is dead. A servant, whom Muley Yesied thought dilatory during the feast, is likewise dying of the punishment he has received.

A Spanish slave, whom this Morocco prince had taken into his service, escaped from him a few days since, and to recover him Muley Yesied threatens to send fifty men on board the French vessels laying in the harbour, where he thinks the slave is secreted. The Bashaw opposes this measure, as it would be an offence offered to the French flag ; but wherever the unfortunate being is, if Muley Yesied discovers him, he will have a right to demand him of the Bashaw. As the Prince's departure is fixed on for to-morrow with the caravan, it is to be hoped this poor wretch will escape.

August 26, 1787
Muley Yesied, to the great satisfaction of many here, embarked yesterday with his suite for Alexandria. He has prepared luxuriously for the accommodation of the black lady (the mother of his last son), and at the expense of the comforts of the other ladies who are with him, whose accommodations he has considered less than usual, owing to the great expenses he has been at for his favourite. The two unfortunate people whom Muley Yesied had used so ill are dead, and the Spanish slave remained undiscovered in a house in Tripoli. The tyrant is expected to return here again from Mecca next year.

September 20, 1787
We were highly favoured last night with the company of the ladies of Hadgi Abderrahman's family to supper, the only instance of their having so far favoured a Christian house. The ambassador came himself first at nine o'clock in the evening : in about ten minutes after, his lady and his eldest daughter by his first wife, and two Moorish

ladies, relations of the family, with their black and white women attendants, arrived. The gentlemen retired, and none of the male servants were suffered to appear. As soon as the ladies came, the ambassador left us, as, agreeably to the custom of the country, he could not have appeared at the repast with his family. The Moorish ladies, when they entered the house, were so entirely concealed, that it was impossible to discover them, and they could only be known by the crowd of attendants that surrounded them, and by the whiteness and delicate texture of their drapery. When their slaves removed the upper covering, the next transparent web or baracan discovered the most costly dresses, with great quantities of jewels. Abderrahman's Greek was not painted, but the rest of the ladies were. Lilla Amnani gave us a reason for not adding this ornament to the rest of her dress, that being the mother of a family, she was just arrived at that age when the Moorish prayers could not be dispensed with ; and as paint cannot be worn by any one during their orisons, she must, if she painted, be obliged, each time she attended her devotions, to wash it off and paint afresh.

It was very entertaining to us to see the curiosity and surprise every thing through the house excited in our visitors : they beheld in every second article something quite novel. They admired very much the books that were lying about, as they are only accustomed to see, or rather hear of manuscripts, and they seemed hardly to credit that ladies sat down to read through the books they saw. On the apartments being shewn to them which were allotted for officers and gentlemen to sleep in occasionally, some of them manifested no less surprise at male visitors being permitted to sleep in the same part of the house where the ladies of the family were. When they were shewn the beds, they considered the building (as they termed it) of the bedsteads, inclosed with curtains, as distinct apartments : their own beds or couches are laid on the floor of their sedda or bedchamber, filling up an alcove, enclosed with rich curtains, as I have before described. At supper none of the ladies made use of a knife and fork, except Abderrahman's wife and daughter, who seemed to use them with some grace. They touched no wine, but drank sherbet and lemonade ; and were in high spirits, and as much delighted as we were. Supper was not ended when the ambassador returned : a small part of our company attended him in the drawing-room, it being totally against the Moorish custom to have introduced him into the room where his wife and family were. During the conversation, while he was waiting for the departure of the Moorish ladies, he told us that he had caused to be made, when in England, a very costly dress, which was done chiefly by his attendants, for the purpose of presenting it to one of the ladies of the court (Lady Aylesbury), with a very rich sash, and that he had sent another to the court of Sweden after his embassy to that country. Abderrahman's life has been spent chiefly in embassies ; and from having lived so much in the courts of Europe, his thoughts and actions are more refined than the most polished of the Moors here, though he is one of their strictest Mussulmen. He permits his daughter, when she is dressed, to wear many of the presents he has received from Christian sovereigns, which are no small addition to her ornaments ; and she is very proud of them, while they save her the trouble of relating how much Abderrahman is esteemed by almost every crowned head in Europe. Among these ornaments is a gold medal, a present from the King of Sweden : it is four inches in diameter, but the workmanship, which is relative to the history of Sweden, is highly executed, and is much esteemed.

About midnight, Abderrahman, attended by his blacks and two Moorish gentlemen, preceded the ladies home ; who, when they quitted us, having again carefully concealed themselves in their baracans, and putting on yellow leather boots and slippers over them, walked home, encircled by their black slaves, attendants, and guards, with lights.

▨

October 26, 1787

The want of an opportunity for communicating with Christendom has prevented the possibility of sending my last letter ; this, therefore, will accompany it, and bring you an account of the Bashaw having been very ill, a circumstance which is much to be deplored. It has been long suspected that the sword of civil discord hangs imminently over this devoted country, to overwhelm it the moment its present sovereign expires.

The dread, as well as the inveteracy, of the two younger princes against their eldest brother, the Bey, has been particularly conspicuous within the last three days. The Bashaw was taken suddenly ill, and a report was instantly spread of his death. The Moors were shutting up their shops, and the place was thrown for a time into the utmost confusion ; but the true state of the case was as follows. The Bashaw after dinner always retires to his couch or sedda, where he is attended only by those in whom he places implicit confidence. One of these favourites is a black woman, the other a Jewess, who sits by him and tells him tales till he falls asleep. The Jewess is known here by the name of Queen Esther, being considered the head of the Jewish nation, as all favours or petitions granted to the Jews by the Bashaw are only obtained from the sovereign through her influence. This woman goes almost every day from the Jew-Decca (or quarter of the town where the Jews live) [1] to the castle, before the Bashaw's siesta, or hour of sleeping after dinner. She is not young, and so corpulent, that it is thought necessary for five or six men to walk always close to the animal she rides on, expressly for the purpose of assisting her in case of a fall. She was this day at the castle, and after reciting tales to the Bashaw, had, on his falling asleep, retired from his apartment. The Bashaw awaked, and not finding himself well, attempted to rise, and fell from the sedda where he was on the floor of the sala (a height of more than eight feet), in which situation his favourite black woman found him, and ran to call Lilla Halluma. The Bashaw remained insensible for some hours. Sidy Useph hearing of his father's illness, hastened to the apartment, where Lilla Halluma and all her attendants were assembled round the Bashaw. Sidy Useph, despairing of his father's recovery, attempted to stab himself; but Sidy Hamet who was present prevented him. These two princes had declared to the Bey, in a quarrel that happened between them a few weeks since, that whenever their father died they would kill themselves, and not remain to be put to death by the Bey. Sidy Hamet and Sidy Useph now agreed to support each other, and by joining their interest, to act in concert against the Bey : they had never ventured to say so much in public before. Lilla Halluma, when she heard it, protested to all present, her fixed determination to drink the fatal cup the moment her lord expired, in order to avoid witnessing the scenes in the castle, which she knew would follow the Bashaw's death. The day following he continued dangerously ill, and Sidy Hamet and Sidy Useph armed their people. In the morning there was a very full court, as every body went on account of the Bashaw's illness. The Bey appeared perfectly calm, seemed much concerned for his father, but was unarmed, as were all his people. Those who had armed themselves, when the Bey inquired what they meant by putting on so hostile an appearance without his orders, gave for reason, that in the last two hours his brothers had armed all their people. The Bey then asked

1 This quarter was known as the *hara*.

what reason his brothers gave for so suddenly arming ; and, on being told it was the distrust they had of his orders relative to themselves, he immediately desired his people to disarm and convince his brothers of their safety. The throne, he said, was his by right, by his father's and by the people's wishes, and no extraordinary steps were necessary to be taken, and he desired them not to arm again without his orders. It was expected from this conduct in the Bey that his brothers would immediately disarm ; but as they did not, and the Bashaw grew worse, the Bey's people and parties attached to him were extremely uneasy, and from the fear of the Bey being assassinated by his brothers, they would not rest until the Bey permitted them to arm, and had forbidden his brothers to appear in his presence with arms. In the morning the access to the castle was free, but in the afternoon the avenues to it were shut, and every person in it, without distinction, was in a state of defence. A few particular persons only could get in or out, and the castle and town remained in the greatest confusion till the next day. The agitation of Lilla Halluma threw her into a fever, under which she still suffers. The Bashaw is now recovered, and the place tranquillized ; but since his recovery he has shewn himself extremely distrustful of the Bey, for which no reason is assigned.

November 22, 1787

Accounts we have just received from Europe, having explained to us a supernatural appearance that happened here some time since, lead me to tell you of the extraordinary manner in which an eruption of Mount Etna affected this country. Nothing could make a more desolate appearance than this town : the sky was extremely thick and dark, and the heavy rain, as it fell, left the white walls of the houses streaked with black, as if from sooty water tinged with red. This phenomenon appears now, without doubt, to have been caused by the eruption of Mount Etna in July last.

From the great convulsions of the mountain, showers of hot sand were carried towards Malta, and the amazing column of fire that issued took at last its direction across the sea towards Barbary, when the atmosphere on this coast became heated to an alarming degree, and occasioned great consternation ; no one, at the instant, being able to account for such a phenomenon.

December 2, 1787

We yesterday paid a confidential visit to the ambassador's family. As we were not expected, the ladies were bathing. Abderrahman's daughter, Lilla Uducia, was the first that appeared, wrapped up just out of a warm bath ; and her tirewomen were waiting to dress her, in compliment to Hadgi Mahmute her husband, who is going to leave Tripoli for a few weeks. From this circumstance I am enabled to give you an exact account of a Moorish toilet. Nothing was placed on a dressing-table as with us. The whole procedure of Lilla Uducia's toilet agreed, as the customs in this country generally do, with the most ancient descriptions. It was said of the Grecian ladies at Athens, "that they employed whole mornings in dressings and painting themselves." The Moorish lady never completes dressing herself in gala under several hours. The Roman ladies are described to have been very extravagant in their dress : their attendants had each a part of the toilet allotted to them ; one had the dressing of the hair, another managed the perfumes, a third disposed of the jewels, a fourth laid on the paint and cosmetics. In a similar manner the slaves waited around Uducia, with the numerous articles necessary to dress and adorn their mistress, while different tirewomen or dressers, as they term them here, attended, to perform the distinct office of plaiting and perfuming the hair, arranging the eyebrows, laying on the cosmetics and painting the eyelashes, putting on the jewels, placing the head dress, and lastly, adjusting the whole figure.

A profusion of the richest Arabian perfumes and scented waters were used, and cloves reduced to the finest powder, simply by themselves, were prepared in a larger quantity than appeared possible to be used at once ; but they proved only sufficient for the present occasion. The whole of this powder, near a quarter of a pound, was put into two large tresses of hair, descending from each side of the head behind, which were plaited to a size far beyond what the greatest quantity of hair growing on the head could accomplish, by mixing a quantity of black silk in them, prepared with strong perfumes by the slaves present : here they have no idea of false hair. The operation of painting the eyelashes with a black tincture,[1] laid on by a gold bokin, is very tedious, and the method of shaping the eyebrows, by pulling out every single superfluous hair, was evidently most painful.

---

[1] *Kohl*, or antimony, still widely used in the East, both as a beautifier and a preservative for the sight.

Lilla Uducia's patience, and the pain she suffered while having her eyes and eyebrows adorned, proved that the African lady is no less anxious in her endeavours to please, than one brought up at the most splendid of the European courts.

Lilla Uducia, with an interesting countenance and manner, and a fine person, is not strictly handsome ; but when dressed, her face, which had undergone an entire change, wore the appearance of beauty. This lady, in embellishing nature, does not follow the custom of the country. The Circassian and the Moorish ladies adorn and paint themselves with different views : the former endeavour to heighten the beauties or hide the defects of nature ; the latter only to add to the consequence of appearances, and the respect she wishes to shew to those for whom she dresses, leaving nature entirely out of the question. So perfectly are the features altered of some of the Moorish ladies when attired in gala, that their nearest friends meeting them by accident cannot possibly know them.

When Lilla Uducia was dressed, one of her women covered with costly rings her fingers, which had the appearance of shining jet, having been stained that colour with juice of henna, an herb growing here ; another attendant threw over her a string of gold and silver charms ; and a third brought her an embroidered silk handkerchief. In receiving the string of charms, a preference is attached to the taking it from the hands of those they suppose most interested for them ; and this often creates a jealousy among the attendants, each one being eager to deliver them into the hands of their mistress, or to put them on her.

Just as we were about to quit Lilla Uducia's apartment, her husband's approach was announced by an eunuch ; she immediately veiled herself, as did all her attendants, as he entered the sala. After he had remained some time conversing with the Christian ladies, and speaking but little to Lilla Uducia, he left the apartment. We retired sometime afterwards, without having seen Abderrahman's Greek, who had not yet finished dressing.

January 30, 1788

I do not know, my dear friend, how you will approve of the unconnected sketches I give you from this place, but I write them exactly as they occur, and were I to fill up the intermediate time in order to connect them, I must tell you of events that had not really happened ; an imposition which would be too easily detected, where the character of the people is so peculiar to themselves and their country. Many of these events become interesting, and present a true portrait of the person spoken of, chiefly from being related at the moment of witnessing them. On this plan, therefore, the sequel of the following narrative may possibly never reach you.

Ship-loads of unfortunate blacks are frequently brought to Tripoli : they are carried to the bazar, or market house, where they are bought by the rich people of the place, who occasionally sell them immediately to merchants waiting to re-ship them for other parts.[1] We this morning saw a number of them, as we were going through the inner courtyard to the harem of a Moorish house of distinction. Two remarkably fine figures among some newly pur-chased blacks, a beautiful woman and a well looking man, arrested our attention. By their gestures, it was easy to perceive they laboured under some very deep distress : the moment, therefore, our first compliments of meeting the family were over, we inquired the history of these unhappy people, and the reason of their present apparent despair. We were told they had given a great deal of trouble to the merchant's family, so that they were obliged to be watched day and night, and all instruments put out of their way, as they were at first continually endeavouring to destroy themselves, and sometimes each other. Their story will prove that there is friendship and fidelity to be found even among savages. The female, who is certainly beautiful for a black, is about sixteen, her hair long, full, and shining like jet, her teeth beautifully even and small, and their whiteness more wonder-fully striking from the contrast of her face, which is of the deepest black complexion. Her stature is tall, and fuller than that of the blacks in general. She is esteemed to be handsomer than any one that has been brought here for years. This beauty (probably the admiration of her own country) had bestowed her heart and her hand on the man who is now with her. Their nuptials were going to be celebrated, when her friends one morning missing her, traced her steps to the corner of an adjacent wood ; and immediately apprehending she had been pursued, and that she had flown to the thicket for shelter (the common and last resource of escape from those who scoured the country for slaves), they went directly to her lover and told him of

---

1 White slaves underwent a different ordeal : see Introduction.

their distress. He, without losing time to search for her in the thicket, hastened to the sea-side, where his foreboding heart told him he should find her, in some vessel anchored there for the purpose of carrying off slaves. He was just easy enough in his circumstances not to be afraid of being bought or stolen himself, as it is in general only the unprotected that are carried off by these hunters of the human race. His conjectures were just. He saw with distraction his betrothed wife in the hands of those who had stolen her. He knelt to the robbers who had now the disposal of her, to know the price they demanded for her ; but all he was worth did not make him rich enough to purchase his female friend, on whom the high price of two hundred maboobs (near a hundred pounds) was fixed. He therefore did not hesitate a moment to sell his little flock of sheep, and the small bit of ground he was possessed of, and then disposed of himself to those who had taken his companion. Happy that they would do him this last favour, he cheerfully accompanied her, and threw himself into slavery for her sake. This faithful pair was sold with other slaves to the African whose house we were in. The woman was to be sent off from this place with the rest of the merchant's slaves to be sold again, she having, from her figure and beauty, cost too much money to be kept as a servant. The merchant meant to keep the man, on whom a much less price was fixed, as a domestic in his own family.

This distressed pair, on hearing they were to be separated, became frantic. They threw themselves on the ground in the way of some of the ladies of the family, whom they saw passing by ; and finding it was the daughter of their master, they could not be prevented from clinging round her to implore her assistance, and their grief could only be moderated by this lady's humane assurances that she would intercede with her father not to part them. The master, too compassionate in so hard a case to make use of his right in keeping either of these unfortunate slaves by force, expostulated with the man, shewing him how easy his own blacks lived, and telling him that if he remained with him and was deserving, he should have many more indulgences. But the black fell at the merchant's feet, and intreated him not to keep him if he sent his companion away, saying, if he did, he would lose all the money he had paid for them both ; for that, though knives and poison were kept out of their way, no one could force them to eat, and that no human means could make them break the oath they had already taken in the presence of their Deity, never to live asunder. In vain the merchant told this slave, that the beauty of his companion had raised her far above the price of those bought for menial servitude, and that she must soon become the property of some rich Turk, and consequently be separated from him for ever. This barbarity, the black replied, he expected, but that still nothing should make him voluntarily leave her ; adding, that when they were parted by force it would be time enough for him to die, and go, according to their implicit belief, to their own country to meet her, as in spite of those who had her in their power, he knew she would be already gone thither, and waiting for him to join her. The merchant, finding it quite impossible to persuade him by words to stay, would not detain him by force, but has left him at liberty to follow the fortunes of his companion.

Among a number of these new purchased slaves, ordered into the apartment where we were, was the beautiful female black. For some time her attention was taken up with us, but the novelty of the sight did not keep her many minutes from bursting into the most extravagant grief again at the thought of her own situation. She ran from us, and hiding her face with her hands, sat down in a corner of the gallery, while the rest of her companions standing round her, frequently pulled her violently to partake with them of the sight of the Christians, at whom they gazed with fear, amazement, and admiration, while their more polished country-women, who had been longer in the family, laughed at them for their surprise and terror. But in these slaves, just driven away from their native soil, hunted like animals from the woods where they had flown for shelter, and enticed from their dearest connections, the sight of white people must naturally inspire every sentiment of disgust and horror. However, by the time they were a little convinced that their dread, at least of the Christians present, was needless, some of them became quite pacified, and were ordered to make up a dance. About twenty of them stood up. The ablest among them took the lead, the rest, touching the tip of each other's hand and foot, according to their manner of dancing, formed a long line, when each, with the greatest exactness and the utmost grace imaginable, repeated the steps and actions of their leader in perfect time. But neither intreaties nor threats could prevail on the unhappy black to join in this dance. She sat inconsolable by herself, and continued many days in the same sullen condition ; and all we could learn on leaving the house concerning this unfortunate female, lately so happy in her own country, was, that she was destined with her husband, or rather lover, to embark in a few days on board a merchant vessel, the owner of which had bought them both, with several others, to sell them at Constantinople.

◫

February 27, 1788

The dread of rebellion is still very general. Hadgi Abderrahman has just been with us from the Bashaw, to inquire if we had any lights on our terrace last night, as a light was seen in that quarter of the town, which had caused great alarm at the castle : the Bashaw therefore sent to signify by the ambassador, that he wished the Christians to be very particular in not suffering any light to be seen on their terraces after dark. This caution arises from the universal dread occasioned at present by the dissentions at the castle, which makes them suspect rebellion to be brooding in every part of the city.

So many plots are laid by each contending party, that no chief officer can consider himself safe, nor be assured that he is not the one singled out for destruction. If the Bashaw sends unexpectedly for any one of them to the castle, the consternation of his family is beyond description. They take leave of him as if for the last time, and his family tremble with despair till he returns. These fears are rendered natural and unavoidable by the secret and sudden manner in which deaths happen to victims at the castle, who at various times have veen massacred there without a possibility of avoiding their fate.

Hamet Hogia's family still recount one of these dreadful occurrences which happened to the father of Hamet Hogia's wife, whose name was Ben Shabban. He was distantly related to the present Bashaw's family. Some years after the Bashaw came to the throne, this Moor was supposed not to be in his interest. One day a message was brought for Ben Shabban's immediate attendance at the castle. This order came so early in the afternoon, that it was the hour of the Bashaw's siesta (or time of reposing after dinner), when almost every one in this part of the world is wrapped in sleep. When he set out from his house, his son accompanied him as if by accident, the youth knowing if he expressed any fear for his father's safety he would not let him go with him. When they arrived at the castle, they found every thing as they expected extremely quiet ; but they were surprised at not seeing the Great Chiah as usual in his seat in the skiffar, with his officers round him. This minister, even in the still hour of the afternoon siesta, never fails to be at his post, except in case of illness ;

and the present Great Chiah was Ben Shabban's sincere friend. His absence therefore, and this unusual hour of coming to the castle on business, struck them both forcibly, and Ben Shabban observed to his son that he did not like it ; it looked, he said, as if something unusual was to be done. He determined, however, to go in, and his son prepared to follow him, declaring that, if there was any thing to fear, it was certainly a reason why he should accompany him ; but his father forbad his advancing, as their going together would carry the appearance of fear, and confirm to the Bashaw their guilt, whatever it might be that they were suspected of. He therefore obliged his son to leave him, saying he would go into the castle by himself, and hope for the best. While Ben Shabban and his son thus stood debating, they perceived within the skiffar, at the further end of it, two hampers, or guards, looking at them with their hands behind them. These two guards were the only people they saw.

Ben Shabban was highly respected by all the country, and therefore the less suspicious of any plot against himself. He parted from his son and entered the castle. The hampers let him pass quietly by ; but the moment after, they threw the fatal cord over his neck, and strangled him instantly. In the mean time, the rest of the hampers employed on the same dark business went after Ben Shabban's son, and overtook the youth just as he had parted from a friend to whom he had in some degree declared his fears. They told him that his father was with the Bashaw, and desired him to follow them to the castle immediately. The son was struck with surprise : his father sent for to see the Bashaw at such an unusual hour, himself summoned so immediately after, it was too extraordinary to be accounted for. He had loitered much on his father's account after parting with him, and was then but a few steps beyond the castle gate ; he therefore returned with the hampers, who must have appeared to him pale and ghastly, having that moment witnessed his father struggling in the agonies of death. When he arrived at the skiffar, he perceived every thing was still and quiet as before, except that he observed there were a few more hampers. The youth walked forward, looking suspiciously about him, and soon discovered his father's turban, which, in his scuffle with the two hampers, had been thrown from his head, laying in a corner of the skiffar ; as soon as he saw it he started, and knew his hour was come. They attempted to strangle him ; but as he was strong, and more aware of the horrid business than Ben Shabban had been, he defended himself, by which means he was instantly cut to pieces by the knives of ten or twelve surrounding guards : contrary to the intentions of those in the castle, the blood flowing from the murdered youth announced to the town, much sooner than was intended, the tragical fate of the unfortunate father and son. Not one chief officer appeared to have been engaged in this dreadful affair, and it was said to have been perpetrated without the Bashaw's express orders. It is certain that jealousy among the Moors frequently urges them to anticipate the wishes of the Bashaw, and often renders his displeasure fatal, without any orders for so doing ; as in this very case the Bashaw had never granted his teskera, or firman.

Speaking of the political anecdotes of this country : when we arrived here there were two fine youths, named Soliman and Ottoman, one about sixteen and the other fourteen years of age, who were imprisoned, or at least immured, in one of the largest private houses in this place, where they had been kept ever since their infancy, guarded by a confidential eunuch of the Bashaw's and other attendants. Their features were only known to the eunuch, the rest of their people not being allowed to see them. These young captives were provided for at the Bashaw's expense, and every comfort afforded them that their solitary and melancholy dwelling would admit of. We often passed the house where they were ; but the windows of the golphor (the only apartment in a Moorish house, as I have before observed, which has windows to the street) were always kept shut ; and to guard against the possibility of these unfortunate brothers effecting their escape, by having any intercourse with persons passing by, they were never suffered to approach the golphor, or even the lower part of the house. The inner court-yard of their habitation was grated over the top with heavy bars of iron, in the same manner as the Bashaw's harem. Little transpired of these state prisoners, except that they were universally thought to be the sons of the eldest brother of the Bashaw ; and, consequently, they had a prior right to the throne—that throne, which had cost so much of the blood of the Bashaw's family, that he at length shrunk back, and his arm was arrested from hurting these two youths while it was possible to avoid it. For the unhappy lot of these young captives we witnessed the most poignant distress in the countenance of one person only, who we met with unexpectedly at the funeral of the mother of Lilla Halluma. On our quitting the apartment Lilla Halluma was in, we were conducted to a golphor, the windows of which were opposite the house where Soliman and his brother were confined. Among the guests we met there was the youngest and only surviving brother of the Bashaw, whose name was Celeby, and who was then Bey of Derner.[1] He was waiting to accompany the remains of the mother of Lilla Halluma to the turba or mausoleum. On our entering the golphor unperceived by Celeby we found him fixed in contemplation, observing the dwelling of his nephews ; and while the tears fell fast from his cheek, he seemed in silent anguish deploring their case. Celeby a short time after returned to his viceroyship at Derner, where he died of the plague at the time that dreadful disorder began to manifest itself in this devoted place. Soliman and Ottoman caught the fatal infection from the eunuch whose care they were under, and with him perished, leaving the Bashaw free from further anxiety on their account. They died at the commencement of the plague, before the dead (for want of people to bury them) were hurried in confusion to their graves. The remains of these princes joined one of those long and brilliant processions that were yet conducted with order to the burying-ground, and had the great mass said over them at noon.

March 28, 1788

A strange circumstance at Bengazi, which is only a few days' distance from us on the coast, threatens to subject us again to all the horrors of the plague, and shews how little subordination can be maintained here. A vessel with the plague on board arrived at Bengazi from Constantinople. The Bey of Bengazi ordered it to sail from the coast without being permitted to anchor ; but the Bengazeens were so violent, that they insisted on taking the goods out of the ship. The Bey of Bengazi, to escape the contagion, shut himself up in his castle, leaving the Bengazeens to act as they pleased, as he had not troops with him sufficient to oppose them. The vessel has come round to Tripoli under French colours, but the Bashaw has insisted on its sailing from this place immediately. We have only, therefore, to hope that the plague may not reach us again.

The town has been in some commotion to-day, from a general search having been made by the guards for Sidy Hamet's great seal, which was stolen from his person last night. It was of gold, chased with Turkish characters. Each of the princes have one of these seals, or royal signets, as soon as they arrive at a certain age. It is worn near the bosom on the left side of the jileck, next the watch, with a rich

_____
[1] Derna in Cyrenaiaca.

chain hanging from it. The mould is destroyed when the seal is made ; and as they never suffer it to be taken away from their persons day nor night, they do not fear its being counterfeited. When the thief was discovered who had stolen the seal, Sidy Hamet ordered his hand to be cut off. This severe punishment was inflicted on the man on account of the very great danger he apprehended from his seal being out of his own possession, as in these troublesome times any of his confidential officers might have been sacrificed by a forged order sealed with it. The Bashaw's seal is much larger than those of the princes ; it is likewise of gold, and about three inches diameter : he never suffers it to be out of his sight a moment. When it is used, an officer seals the paper before him and returns it immediately.

We went to-day to congratulate Lilla Uducia (Abderrahman's daughter) on the safe return of her husband, Hadgi Mahmute, and his people from Mezulata,[1] where he had been to view his olive estates.

At Mezulata are most extensive plantations of olive trees, which, when ripe, it is requisite for the owners themselves of the plantations (this being one of the greatest concerns in the country), with a number of their people, to protect from the depredations of the Arabs during the time the oil is making and collecting. It is brought in immense quantities to Tripoli, or shipped from the coast of Mezulata for Europe.

One of the Moors belonging to Hadgi Mahmute, who went on this expedition, has married a rich Mezulateen. We found her in the apartment of Lilla Uducia : she was remarkably dark, with very handsome feature ; tall, well-made, and cheerful. She was pleased with the Christians ; but when Lilla Uducia described to her the fine thread lace which the Christians wore, and informed her it was a valuable article, she laughed immoderately at their taking so much trouble and spending so much money to dress themselves with what she termed so many bits of rags. Her own dress was a bright purple and red cotton and silver baracan, of a very thick texture, with a deep fringe at the ends, which were curiously wrought in Egyptian work. This drapery folded most gracefully round her. She wore neither shoes, chemise, nor trowsers. On her ankles and arms she had immense large silver halhals, or bracelets ; her feet were dyed, and her arms, from the wrist to the shoulder, as well as the neck and face, were adorned with a great variety of figures and flowers minutely engraved in the skin with gunpowder. Her cap was set with small gold and silver coins, and a number of silver ornaments mixed with

---

[1] Misellata.

mother-o'-pearl hung from it over her forehead ; her ear-rings were of plain silver, and of these she had seven in each ear ; her necklace was composed of coral, mother-o'-pearl, silver, and glass beads, mixed and strung together in many rows, covering nearly the front of her body, and reaching almost from her neck to her waist ; her hair was plaited in forty or fifty small tresses on each side of her forehead, fastened with a coral or glass bead. She wore a large sash of perfume over the left shoulder, in the same manner as the ladies wear it here, with the difference of the perfume being of a much coarser sort, being composed chiefly of common spices. The divisions of the sash, instead of being formed with gold beads, were made with curious sea-shells ; a ribbon was likewise thrown over the left shoulder, on which a great number of silver charms were suspended. This completed her singular dress.

We have received to-day, from the Greek patriarch at Alexandria, a present of beccafigos (or birds that feed on figs), pickled whole in jars, and fit to eat without further dressing. They are not more than half the size of a lark, and are reckoned very delicious eating when prepared in this manner : the bones are perfectly dissolved. In Egypt these birds are taken in immense quantities, but only at a certain season of the year, when they follow the waters of the Nile, which they never fail to do when that river overflows its banks. There is a most beautiful bird here, natural to the climate, called by the Moors gogalas : its plumage is of the brightest gold-colour on the breast, and its wings and back mazarine blue : it is finely shaped, and about the size of a thrush. These birds are likewise reckoned a great delicacy to eat.

April 12, 1788

The Emperor of Morocco's son, Muley Yesied, arrived here four days since from Mecca on his way to Morocco ; the guns are now firing for a visit he is paying at the castle. He did the Venetian Consul the honour of going on board a vessel of that country yesterday, and during a repast prepared for him there he had the cruelty, for a mere frolic, to compel a very old and respectable Moor in his train to have his beard shaved. This being considered one of the greatest disgraces a Moor can suffer, the poor old man is inconsolable. His great age made the indignity offered him still more distressing. He was reported

to be one hundred and twenty years old ; but Moors and Turks keep
no registers, from the idea that it is unlucky to do so.   They reckon
up their years by guess, from the periods of certain events : it is
therefore no wonder that such uncertain methods should produce the
the strange mistakes we have heard of in their writings.

Muley Yesied was at Algiers when last on his way to Mecca ; and
the liberties he was permitted to take there, such as firing his piece
with ball at the brim of a Christian's hat when he has met one riding
along, and other freedoms equally obnoxious, has rendered him very
troublesome to the Christians here.   When he meets them his diversion
consists of frightening their horses by riding suddenly up to them and
firing at their heels : he frequently desires the Christians to race with
him.   His horses are the finest imaginable, used to stand fire, and
astonishingly swift, and wherever he rides a great number of his blacks
and soldiers instantly follow him.   The horses of the Christians not
being at all used to such violent exercise, makes it extremely disagreeable, and truly dangerous to join him : besides which, as he is constantly intoxicated, and his mirth is not at all civilized, being generally
accompanied with very bad language : every Christian, therefore,
avoids the meeting as much as possible.   He is at present encamped
on the Pianura : he has also one of the Bashaw's gardens allowed
him, where he resides with his eight wives, besides favourites.

Muley Yesied is the eldest son, and, unfortunately for the subjects
of Morocco, will on that account probably be Emperor.   He has no
less than forty brothers.   He is not thirty years of age, and has himself
sixteen children.

The present Emperor of Morocco's sons are brought up in the
following singular manner.   As soon as they are born, the Emperor
sends for a Moor of fortune (not one of the first people of rank),
and delivers his son to him to bring him up as his own.   The child
never sees his father again till he is twelve years old.   The Moor to
whose care he has been delivered is then ordered to bring him to
court, where he is examined by a council respecting the Koran, laws
of the country, etc. ; and upon this examination depends the fate of
the Moor.   If the Emperor approve of the education of his son, the
child's foster-father's fortune is made ; if not, the Moor is immediately
cut to pieces in his presence.

Muley Yesied travels in great pomp, with a number of soldiers,
who are regularly drawn up before his camp on the Pianura every
day.   It is thought he will not make a long stay here this year : he

has been here, however, long enough to shew the depravity of his character.

☒

June 12, 1788

To you, my dear friend, who are always alive to the beauties and effects of nature, I cannot omit describing what an extraordinary impression an eclipse makes on the uninformed part of the inhabitants of Barbary. Of this we had ocular proof during the great eclipse of the sun on the fourth of this month, which was almost total, and occasioned for some minutes a gloomy darkness resembling that of midnight. The beginning of the eclipse was seen at Tripoli at half past seven in the morning : at half past eight, when it was at the height, the face of nature was changed from day to night. The screech-owl, not long retired to its nest, re-appeared, and disturbed the morning with its shrieks. Lizards and serpents were seen prowling about the terraces, and flights of evening birds, here called marabuts, and held sacred by the Moors, flew about in great numbers and increased the darkness. The noisy flitting of their wings roused the Moor, who had been stupified by fear ; and when one of these heavy birds (which often drop to the ground by coming in contact with each other) chanced to fall at his feet, the African would start aghast, look at it with horror, and set up a hideous howl. About eight o'clock, when the lustre of the morning was completely faded, the common Moors were seen assembling in clusters in the streets, gazing wildly at the sun, and conversing very earnestly. When the eclipse was at his height, they ran about distracted in companies, firing volleys of muskets at the sun, to frighten away the monster or dragon, as they called it, which they supposed was devouring it. At that moment the Moorish song of death and *wulliah-woo*, or the howl they make for their dead, not only resounded from the mountains and valleys of Tripoli,[1] but was undoubtedly re-echoed throughout the continent of Africa. The women brought into the streets all the brass pans, kettles, and iron utensils they could collect, and striking on them with all their force, and screaming at the same time, occasioned a horrid noise which was heard for miles. Many of these women, owing to their exertions and fears, fell into fits or fainted. The distress and

---

[1] Literary hyperbole ! There are no mountains or valleys nearer Tripoli than thirty miles.

terror of the Moors did not in the least abate till near nine o'clock, when the sun assured them by his refulgent beams that all his dangers were passed.

During the morning and the day, the atmosphere was uncommonly clear, even for a Barbary sky, which rendered the effects of this great eclipse more striking. We learnt from Hadgi Abderrahman, who paid us a visit when it was over, that the first ladies in the place had trembled at the event, and several were seriously ill. The ladies of his own family, he said, had suffered much less at the appearance of the eclipse, from the circumstance of his being at home with them ; for though he considered it would be useless to enter into a philosophical account of it to them, yet he assured them that the moon went occasionally to see the sun ; and when they met, by their being so close together, the moon always interrupted more or less his light. This account, he said, the truth of which they were convinced of by his great earnestness, considerably abated their fears. To the ambassador it was a serious case, as Lilla Amnani is in a very delicate state of health ; but the account he gave her of the phenomenon entirely pacified her.

August 28, 1788

Muley Yesied is still here. Having described to you his disposition and his exploits, you will not be surprised at the following circumstance which happened a few days since. A French vice-consul, who is acting as Consul till the arrival of his chief, thought the precautions taken by the other Consuls, to avoid meeting with Muley Yesied, were not necessary ; he therefore continued his rides as usual, without avoiding the paths frequented by Muley Yesied. In consequence of this plan, he some evenings ago, met upon the Pianura, the Emperor's son, who rode furiously up to him, and with his usual roughness of manners fired at his horse. The French Vice-Consul, though much alarmed, still supposed the Morokeen savage and his suite would not annoy him further ; but Muley Yesied, completely intoxicated, swiftly passing him a few paces, put himself in a position to leap over the neck of his horse. As this appeared too dangerous an experiment to the Vice-Consul, he suddenly drew back, and the Emperor's son came up with the French dragoman who was following him : this so enraged Muley Yesied, that he drew his sabre, and threatened to cut the

French Consul to pieces. The Tripolitans that were present interfered ; but it was in vain they told him he must not insult a Christian flag in the Bashaw's dominions. Muley Yesied was too much heated with wine to understand reason, and the French Consul perceiving the danger increase, clapt spurs to his horse, and endeavoured to reach the gates of the city, while the Tripolitans and Muley Yeseid were debating the matter. Happily he succeeded and received no greater injury. Muley Yesied finding the next day the Bashaw highly displeased at this behaviour, and being told by his officers that the treatment of the Christians here and at Algiers differs so much, that he must not attempt to take any liberties with them, has conducted himself very differently since, and has even sent to the Christian houses to invite the gentlemen and the ladies to his garden, but has had a general refusal.

You must perceive, by this account, how much better the Christians are treated here than at Algiers. And though you are told in descriptions given of this place, that it is a piratical state, and the inhabitants live by plundering on the seas, and making great numbers of slaves, I am happy to inform you there are but few Christian slaves at present, who have been here for many years ; nor is the number likely to increase.[1] To maintain peace with the different powers of Europe is at present the Bashaw's policy ; and the few slaves who were here before the late peace concluded between Spain and Tripoli, did not at all agree with the numbers reported in Europe. The title of the sovereign here is Bashaw, nor are any tributes paid to the Porte, as is said, by the sovereign of this place : on the contrary, the Bashaw is seldom called upon by the Grand Signior. No piratical vessels are at present sent to sea against the Christians, and the few slaves here belonging to nations who are not at peace with the Bashaw are decently clothed : they walk about the town on their master's business or their own, with only the restriction of returning within the castle walls to the bagnio at sunset, where they are well fed, and are often considerably more in the confidence of their owners than any other dependants.

I cannot better describe to you the Algerine manners, than from an instance which occurred there not long since, and which shews their treatment of the Christians. At the last peace concluded between France and Algiers, it was agreed that no Algerine corsair should be taken on the coast of France. Previous, however, to the peace made

---

[1] The traffic in white slaves was to increase when Ali Karamanli was succeeded by his son Yusef, and piracy revived.

with Spain in 1785, the Neapolitans sunk an Algerine corsair on the coast of France. The moment the news arrived at Algiers, the Dey dispatched his emissaries to the consulary house ; and, without giving any notice, or time for defence or explanation, he had the French Consul dragged away to the common bagnio of slaves. The French sent twenty-one ships to Algiers on this occasion, and the Algerines demanded of the French forty thousand sequins for the injury done them, by the Neapolitans being permitted to take the corsair on their coast. The French dispatched two ships from Algiers to France for instructions to settle this matter ; and ultimately sent, according to the Dey's desire, the rest of their ships to Malta, after having had their Consul liberated, and their trade declared safe from the Algerine corsairs.

September 2, 1788

We had the satisfaction of seeing the Emperor of Morocco's son depart yesterday. While his suite was embarking, the greatest confusion prevailed among his people. Several of them tried to escape from him, owing to his ill usage. He was so much out of humour, that he treated his wives extremely ill before they left him to go to the boat, which was covered over with close awnings. They were entirely concealed from the public view as they were rowed to the vessel, which was elegantly fitted up for their reception.

Muley Yesied's conduct, during his visits to Tripoli, is not in general so boisterous and offensive to strangers as it has been this time ; but, exclusive of this circumstance, we were prevented seeing his ladies, on account of a circular letter sent to Tripoli, soon after their arrival, to announce the coolness that at present subsists between England and Morocco, owing to the Emperor of Morocco having refused provisions to the garrison of Gibraltar. I must here mention an odd trait in his character. By way of proving that he did not wish to quarrel with the English, he ordered his corsairs to look out for the smallest vessel bearing an English flag, and if there were two in company, and they could with ease take them both, they were to bring in but one on pain of his displeasure ; if any one belonging to his empire attempted further to annoy an English vessel without fresh orders from him, they were to be put to death ; but they were not to return without using every exertion to bring with them one English vessel.

₪

October 30, 1788

Since my last, the country round us has become very unquiet ; the Shaiks of the deserts, who are not in the Bashaw's pay, have been making frequent incursions against several of the Arab tribes and Moorish towns belonging to the Bashaw, who has sent the Bey and the two younger princes with troops to different parts of the kingdom to punish these disturbers.[1]

Shaik Alieff, an Arab chief, came with his troops some days ago to assist the Bashaw against his enemies. His demands were so great, and his men so troublesome, that he appeared more in the character of an enemy than in that of an auxiliary. The Bashaw lost time in resisting his demands, while the enemy was gaining ground every hour, and advancing to Tripoli. The absence of the three princes, with the bravest of the Bashaw's agas, or generals, contributed to augment the fears of the inhabitants, the city being unavoidably left in a defenceless state ; and the Arabs of Shaik Alieff, in defiance of the rules always prescribed them by the Bashaw, not to enter the city gates, nor advance within a certain distance of the town walls, when encamped there for his service, entered the town and walked about with an alarming assurance. From the sacrifices the Bashaw made, they at last appeared satisfied and departed, and have already driven back the hostile Arabs.

I shall not tire you with repeated descriptions of frequent skirmishes that now happen near us, which announce a want of power in the Bashaw, and of unanimity in his family, threatening also general commotion in the country. These partial alarms are so common, that I shall mention them only when they present any account of the Moors or Arabs, which I think may be new to you, as you live where the traces of ancient customs no longer exist, while here primitive manners are depicted in the deportment and habit of every Moor and Arab with few deviations. The African chief, Shaik Alieff, before he left the town, paid us a visit. This Getulian, or Numidian, perfectly resembled in his habits and manners the description given of the first

---

[1] The Bey was at Misurata, where at this time Lucas, the traveller, on his abortive attempt to travel to the Fezzan, met him.

inhabitants of those countries. His dress was that of the Jibeleen, or mountain Arab, whose habit is precisely the same as it is described in the time of our Saviour. The fineness of the Arab's dress is proportioned to his fortune, Shaik Alieff's upper covering, or baracan, made of Barbary wool famous for its beauty and whiteness, appeared at first sight to be of the finest muslin, many yards in length, which he had rolled in ample folds around his head and body. He wore a curious wrought belt (of a manufacture peculiar to this country and to the hand of an Arab), ingeniously woven in a variety of figures resembling Arabic characters : it was wound several times tight and even round his body, and one end being doubled back and sewed up served him for his purse. In this belt he wore his arms, and he prided himself much on them, not on account of their richness, but from the proof he had had of their execution. After the manner of the Arabs, he wore sandals, which he took off on entering the apartment, and thus paid a compliment to those who received him ; for among the Arabs no one can approach his superior with his slippers on. His air was noble, his gait haughty, and his figure about the middle size. The Arabs are in general tall. Shaik Alieff's features were perfectly regular and strongly marked ; his complexion nearly black ; his countenance very cheerful, though he was not a young man ; and a settled vivacity seemed to be his characteristic ; yet he retains all the ferocity of the ancient Arabs, and considers himself one of the masters of the desert of Tripoli ; for the Wargummas [1] and the Noilles, the two most powerful tribes known in these parts, hold the sovereignty of the deserts. Both the latter have acted, and are still considered as auxiliary troops to the Bashaw. Shaik Alieff's tribe is of those who were scattered throughout the provinces of Barbary, as descended from those Mahometan Arabians, who, pursued by the Turks, fled to the mountainous parts to save themselves with their cattle and effects, where they still continue to enjoy their liberty. They are divided into a multiplicity of little governments under their respective chiefs, and value themselves highly on having preserved their blood unstained by a mixture with other nations. They pride themselves on being descended from the tribe of Sabeens, who passed from Arabia Felix into Africa, under their king, Melech Afrique, from whom Africa is said to have taken its name.

Shaik Alieff, during his conversation, according to the manner of the Arabs, marked with the forefinger of his right hand on the palm

[1] Ourigemma.

of his left, all the different stops necessary to be made in his narration, and expressed the aspirations by an elevation of his head, while he expected his auditors to attend more to the motion of his hands than to the expression of his countenance. His discourse was interesting, facetious, and lively, except when speaking of war ; it then acquired too great a degree of barbarity. With fierceness in his eyes, and wildness in his manner, he dwelt with delight on the havock he had made ; and he recounted, with the greatest satisfaction, the number of chieftains' heads he had sent to the Bashaw.

The fatigue sustained by his troops and himself, in travelling and in war, according to his description, appeared to us incredible. They traverse the sands for many days with no other refreshment than a small bag of meal and some water ; while at night they are sometimes drenched by heavy rains, deprived of their garments, which it is the custom to throw over their horses, on the preservation of which their own lives depend, and often sleeping under their horses to shelter themselves from the wet. If overtaken by the dreadful hot winds, and if short of water, which they frequently are, when in this dilemma, so much exhausted as to despair of their lives, they have recourse to what they reckon the last expedient, which is, laying themselves flat on the sands, almost buried in them, and with their mouths close to the ground, they endeavour for some hours to inhale a cooler vapour from the earth than that of the burning atmosphere around them ; and rising, after the meridian of the day is passed, endeavour to pursue their journey, when, as the Arab chief said, they were often foiled again ; the sands, like the foaming ocean, put in motion by the winds, following them suddenly in immense waves, and overwhelming them. The chief declared, that, in this manner, he had frequently lost great numbers of his people.

Shaik Alieff's attendants exactly answered the appellation given them by the Moors of the Wild Arabs, and it required no small trouble in the Moorish and Christian servants to watch their actions and keep them in order while waiting for their chief. Their dress was uniformly the same, a brown baracan made chiefly of goat's hair, and manufactured by their women in looms without a shuttle, remarkably thick and of a manufacture not to be mistaken for any but that of the Bedouin women. These baracans, six yards long, and five or six feet wide, serve for their whole dress by day, and their bed and covering by night ; except, as I have said, when they deprive themselves of even this, to cover a favourite or valuable horse. The enormous length of their guns and other weapons, and the fierceness of their countenances, gave them a most alarming appearance. Shaik Alieff, before he left us, accepted of a pair of scissars and a penknife, on which he had bestowed the highest encomiums, as the Arabs much admire English steel work. He came mounted on a most beautiful white horse, but his people were all on foot.

December 20, 1788

Two weddings have been celebrated at the castle this week. Sidy Hamet, the second son of the Bashaw, who has been for a short time a widower, was married to a lady of Turkish extraction ; and a daughter of the Bashaw's, to the Dugganeer's nephew. The present Dugganeer, or officer at the head of the customs, is a Neapolitan renegado : but I have before observed to you, that when Christian slaves become renegados, they often hold the highest offices in Turkey and Barbary.

According to the custom of this country, a Moorish lady's wedding clothes are accumulating all her life, and, consequently, the presents sent from her father's to the bridegroom on the eve of her wedding are most abundant. Among the articles in the princess's wardrobe, were two hundred pair of shoes, and one hundred pair of rich embroidered velvet boots, with baracans, trousers, chemises, jilecks, caps, and curtains for apartments, and many other articles in the same proportion. Each set of things was packed separately in square flat boxes of the same dimensions, altogether very numerous. These would have been taken to the Dugganeer's house, but Lilla Howisha (as the Bashaw's daughter) not quitting the castle, they were conveyed with great pomp and ceremony in a long procession out of one gate of the castle into another, escorted by guards, attendants, and a number of singing women, hired for the purpose of singing the festive song of *Loo, loo, loo,* which commences when the procession leaves the bride's father's house, and finishes when it enters the bridegroom's house.

Two separate feasts for these weddings were celebrated in the castle on the same day : that for Lilla Howisha, the Bashaw's daughter, at her apartments ; and Sidy Hamet's wedding, in that part of the castle where he resides. Sidy Hamet, who could not be seen at his bride's feast, received the compliments of his subjects and the foreigners of rank at court, and was superbly habited on the occasion.

In our way to Lilla Halluma's apartments, the great concourse of people at the castle rendered it as usual impossible to proceed a step without being surrounded by attendants to clear the way.

The apartments of the two brides were entirely lined with the richest silks. A seat elevated near six feet from the ground, in the alcove, the most distinguished part of the room, was prepared for the bride, where she sat concealed from the spectators by an embroidered silk veil thrown over her. Her most confidential friends only went up to speak to her, by ascending seven or eight steps placed on the right-hand side for their approach ; they then introduced themselves to her presence by cautiously lifting the veil that covered her, being very careful not to expose any part of her person to the spectators beneath : the etiquette was to speak but a few words, in order to afford time for other ladies to pay their court to her. Her eyelashes were deeply tinged with black ; and her face was painted red and white, but not ornamented with gold. Lilla Howisha is one of the handsomest women in Tripoli. Her dress was the same as I have already described to you, but the gold and silver jewels with which it was almost covered, left little of its texture to be seen ; her slippers were brilliant, discovering her foot and ankle, which were partially dyed with henna, nearly the colour of ebony ; and she wore on her ankles double gold bracelets. The jewels on her fingers appeared more brilliant from the dark colour underneath them, which also added much to the whiteness of her hand and arm.

Two slaves attended to support the two tresses of her hair behind, which were so much adorned with jewels, and gold and silver ornaments, that if she had risen from her seat she could not have supported the immense weight of them.

Magnificent tables were prepared at each of the brides' houses, furnished with the choicest delicacies of hot viands, fresh and dry preserves, and fruits peculiar to the country. These tables were surrounded with gold and silver embroidered cushions, laid on the floor to serve as seats for the guests, who were served with the refreshments before them, by Lilla Halluma and her daughters, who were constantly moving round the tables, attended by their slaves and confidential women. The black slaves were almost covered with silver, and had nearly treble the quantity of ornaments they usually wear on the head, neck, arms, and feet.

The account of the ceremonies observed at this feast by the ladies of Hadgi Abderrahman's family, will be sufficient to make you acquainted with those performed by other ladies of rank in this place, as all act uniformly at weddings as far as their fortunes will allow.

Lilla Amnani and Lilla Uducia, though they knew their visit at the castle would only take up a very few hours, took with them, notwithstanding, a considerable quantity of clothes to change, reserving the richest and most shewy dresses to put on last. Lilla Uducia's first dress was composed of a chemise made, according to the fashion of the country, of silk, gold, and gauze. She wore two jilecks, the under one of crimson velvet and gold lace, the upper one of green and silver brocade ; and her baracan, which was as usual of several yards in length and width, was made entirely of violet embossed ribbons, nearly eight inches wide, with gold work between each, and a broad stripe of bright gold went through the middle of the baracan from one end to the other, having a singular and rich effect, when wrapped in folds round her body. Both ends of this baracan were embroidered in gold and silver, nearly half a yard in depth. She wore a pair of pale yellow silk trousers, which had also a broad gold stripe up the front from the ankle to the waist, with a rich border of gold round the bottom : she wore all the jewels she could collect, with the addition of some valuable gold orders of her father's.

Lilla Amnani and herself soon after their appearance in the castle changed their dresses, before they " threw," as they termed it, " the first money," to the amount of ten maboobs, to a favourite attendant belonging to the ladies of the castle, who was dressed for the occasion. Soon after they changed their dresses a second time, and presented between thirty and forty maboobs to each of the brides : they then dressed a third time, previous to sitting down to dinner.

The feast for Sidy Hamet's bride was celebrated in the same manner as that of his sister : all the company retired from the castle before sunset.

It is during these large mixed companies, that the female intriguing messengers belonging to the castle find much employment, by delivering messages of gallantry, or introducing, among the immense crowd of visitors, the princes in disguise, who by their assistance are not unfrequently in these meetings closely wrapped up in the baracan of a female, for the purpose of more easily beholding the select beauties of their country, whom they cannot possibly obtain a sight of in any other way.

To render this account more interesting to you, I can with truth assert, it could only have been collected within the circle of those few individuals, whom the Bashaw's family, from a real attachment, admit confidentially to their friendship and acquaintance.[1]

January 18, 1789

Two royal Fezzanners left this place a few days ago : one was a Prince of Fezzan ; and the other, a near relation married to a daughter of the King of Fezzan. They have paid us several visits, and were at three of our evening parties. Both of them were in complexion nearly black, with strong interesting features, and were well made and handsome in their persons : their dress resembled those of the Tripolitans, excepting the turbans. The Prince of Fezzan's turban, instead of being large and of white muslin like those of Tripoli, was composed of a black and gold shawl, wound tight several times round the head, and a long and curiously wrought shawl hung low over the left shoulder. His baracan was white, and perfectly transparent ; and his arms were handsome, with a profusion of gold and silver chains hanging from them. His manner and conversation were not less entertaining than curious. The ideas of the Prince of Fezzan correspond with those of the Abyssinians, who suppose that powerful evil spirits traverse the earth at night, succeeding in their operations against the peace of men, and waylaying their footsteps with plans of destruction ; that they advance slowly over the world at sunset ; and that when dark they make rapid progress over every part of it till daybreak ; it is on this account, the Prince of Fezzan says, that the mischiefs of the night are so swift after dark, that it is impossible for any traveller to escape them, and on that account it is time saved to lay by till morning. He told us his country is the most fertile and beautiful in the world, having himself seen no part of the globe but Africa ; and Fezzan is esteemed amongst the richest of its kingdoms.

In Fezzan there are still vestiges of magnificent buildings, and numbers of curious vaulted caves of an immense size, supposed to have been Roman granaries. But it requires a more enlightened mind than that of the Moor or Arab to discover their origin. These, with many other relics of ancient grandeur in Africa, remain unexplored, to reward the labours of future travellers. Mr. Tully and the celebrated Dr. Ruthman, among the remains of antiquity frequently met with

[1] *I.e.* the Tully family.

about Tripoli, saw near the Friday bazar, out of town, a flat stone with inscriptions, which shewed it was placed there by Cassia, a Roman lady, in honour of her father, but the date could not be made out, being totally effaced.

The Prince of Fezzan says, that in his country it never rains ; but that innumerable soft springs serve to moisten the earth, and keep the country in the state of a beautiful well watered garden. The fruits produced there are remarkably fine, and the Fezzan dates surpass in richness all others in Africa : of them they make the famous date cakes, as I have mentioned to you.

The Prince of Fezzan, in return for some new scissars, razors, and a small looking-glass, with which he is much pleased, proposes to send us some of the best date cakes his subjects can make. This Prince is extremely cheerful in conversation ; his ideas are wonderfully quick ; and he bears an excellent character among his people. One evening, placing himself on a sofa, and musing on the novelty he saw at a Christian assembly to which he was invited, he expressed the highest satisfaction at hearing a select concert of music, performed by a number of ladies and gentlemen. But on seeing afterwards the company dance, he viewed with a great degree of jealousy the liberties, as he was pleased to term them, taken with the ladies in dancing, by the gentlemen being permitted so often to touch their hands. He was so much astonished on this occasion, that it was not easy to persuade him that all the graceful attitudes he saw were only for effect.

This prince confirmed what we have heard before, that human sacrifices are still practised in parts of Africa. To the south of Abyssinia they sacrifice to evil spirits the slaves they cannot sell ; nor were those parts, he said, free from cannibals.

To evince the truth of this too dreadful account, a black eunuch we often see unavoidably, and who is now living at the ambassador Abderrahman's house, is known to have been addicted to this savage propensity, and was with difficulty prevented but a short time since from giving proof of his cannibal disposition.

Notwithstanding the grandfather of the Prince of Fezzan was brought in chains to Tripoli by the grandfather of the present Bashaw, Hamet the Great, and that the King of Fezzan remains yet tributary to the present Bashaw, the two courts are much attached to each other, and the Bashaw has shewn this Prince extraordinary civilities.

The Bey went out lately with a large force against the Arabs ; and no news has yet arrived from him. We were invited to the castle to see him depart : as soon as we got there, the Chiah received us, and sent some of his slaves to clear the place he had allotted for us, which was within one of the round towers of the castle, to which many spectators had crowded. A great number of the Bey's attendants were waiting for him already ranged in the castle-yard in the order they were to march. The part of the procession formed, was preceded by officers on horseback, bearing green silk flags of Mecca, and accompanying a chaoux who was richly mounted, supporting one tail, which is always carried before the Bey : his father goes with three, being a Bashaw of three tails, and the only sovereign in Barbary who enjoys this degree of honour. The Bey's chief officers of state, richly dressed and mounted on beautiful horses, with different groupes of his courtiers, mamelukes, chaouxes, black slaves, and hampers or guards, made up a numerous and brilliant cortege. The quantity of costly ornaments with which the horses were adorned, added greatly to their beauty and to the grandeur of the sight.

During the interval of waiting for the Bey, we were entertained by seeing Sidy Hamet and Sidy Useph with their parties racing on the Pianura, and performing all the manœuvres used by the Moors in war. Their song, or rather cries of war, being so very near us, sounded dreadfully, resembling the description of the war-whoop of the Indians.

After his attendants had waited for him about two hours, the Bey came out of the castle, habited in a loose dress of blue and gold tissue, over a pale yellow caftan, embroidered with gold and silver. His belt was studded with jewels, and his turban was crossed over with gold drapery, leaving long ends pendant from it. He had a very large jewel claw in his turban, which had been newly set, and looked extremely beautiful, with a new gold crescent considerably larger than that he usually wears.

We never saw the Bey better received by the Moors. Their acclamations were loud and incessant for some time ; and the Bey, whose figure is always interesting, looked particularly handsome and majestic. He mounted a spirited black horse. The animal seemed to vie with its master in the richness of its appearance ; and was adorned with no less than four magnificent velvet housings. The broad black chest of the horse displayed to advantage eight solid gold drop necklaces which reached to his legs ; the saddle was chased gold, the front of it set with jewels; and the stirrups were very large, and looked like burnished gold. His whole appearance was uncommonly brilliant.

As soon as the Bey was mounted, the horsemen with the Mecca flags, and the tail carried by an officer on horseback, moved on, followed by the chief of the chaouxes. The front of the chaoux's dress was covered with a plate of silver armour, and his turban was white with a gold claw : he was followed by the corps under his command, who were dressed uniformly in scarlet cloth, with stiff white caps the shape of a cornucopia inverted. Only the chief was on horseback, the rest were on foot. Close after the chaouxes followed the nubar, or royal band, which, as I have said, only plays before the Bashaw and the Bey. The band was followed by many of the chief officers of state ; and after them were three richly caparisoned horses led by blacks. The first in rank of the officers of state then preceded the Bey ; and his body guard of hampers and Mamelukes followed him with the Tripolitan colours flying. The Bey's baggage was carried immediately after the colours, and made a singular appearance. It was in square flat boxes covered with Turkey carpets and placed on the backs of horses, each horse led by a slave. The troops followed, headed by their different Agas.

The greatest number of the Arabs and Moors who accompany the Bey on this expedition, wait to join him where his camp is pitched, eight hours' journey from this place, and where he gives a grand audience to the Arab chiefs, being seated on a superb throne erected for the purpose in his tent. It is said he will depart with near a thousand Arabs this year. They will be composed of a tribe called the Benoleeds,[1] and Shaik Alieff's people.

The Bey is sent by the Bashaw, with his brothers, against Saffanassa,[2] who, taking advantage of the present dissentions at the castle, distresses the Bashaw, by keeping back the tributes which should be paid by the Arabs under him.

The coolness at present subsisting between the Bey and his brothers, is the reason the two youngest princes omitted returning from the Pianura (which it was their duty to do), to join the Bey and his train before he quitted the castle. This want of attention was so striking to every body that the Bey's people murmured much at this

1 The Beniooleeds are the Orfela tribe from Beni Ulid.

2 Seif el Nasser was the famous chief of the Ulad bu Seif tribe. Lucas reported that the Bey went against him with 1500 horse and 6000 foot ; Seif el Nasser had 600 horse and 10,000 foot.

disrespect shewn him by the princes ; but the Bey, with his usual policy, or forbearance, did not appear to notice it. Many of the Bey's friends tremble for his safety ; and the Bashaw is said to be distrustful of all his sons.

〖〗

March 20, 1789

Yesterday morning Hadgi Abderrahman breakfasted with us, and staid several hours. The Shaik, or governor of the town, and Hadgi Useph dined with us ; and this morning we visited Lilla Uducia, the Bashaw's eldest daughter, on account of the birth of her son, and afterwards passed two or three hours with Lilla Halluma and the princesses at the castle ; so that the last two days have been wholly devoted to Moorish company.

Hadgi Abderrahman's account from the Bey's·camp were very bad ; the Bey has been obliged to advance much further into the country than he intended, for want of forage, the Arabs belonging to Saffanassa having burnt every thing near the spot where he had determined to encamp.[1] The three princes do not act in concert ; Sidy Useph's manners are so violent with the Arabs, and he commits such depredations, that he endangers the life of the Bey, whom the Arabs consider responsible for the injuries committed by his brothers.

There is no prospect of peace between the Bey and the Arabs at present. The Bey's army, and that of Saffanassa, have now attained within a few hours, or a short day's journey of each other. The Ambassador had with him a letter from the Caid, or governor of Messurata, which brings the fortunate news of the Bey having formed an alliance with another tribe of Arabs, who are esteemed the most numerous of any in the deserts. This circumstance, it is hoped, may turn the scale in his favour. Shaik Alieff, the Arab chief, whose person I described to you in a former letter, was at that time supposed entirely in the Bashaw's interest, and being one of those chiefs who are considered masters of the deserts, every thing was hoped from his assistance. This Arab, however, a few days ago, very nearly betrayed the Bey into the hands of his enemies, by the following stratagem. He advised the Bey, as the cattle were in want of food, to send the greatest part of the troops belonging to both of them out to forage, before

---

[1] The weakness into which Ali Karamanli's rule had reduced government was emphasized by the governor of Misurata to Lucas. " There was a time when the people of Tripoli knew how to conquer, and the Arab trembled at the sight of an encampment."

the enemy could have time to **advance towards them. The Bey,** some hours after the departure of his people, took his observations as usual with his glasses over the sands, and perceived the enemy rapidly advancing towards him : he asked Shaik Alieff what he would advise him to do in this situation ? Shaik Alieff replied, much unconcerned, that he must remain where he was, for that nothing else could be done, and he would only risk more by moving. By this time, the Bey was informed, that Shaik Alieff had sent secret intelligence to Saffanassa's camp, that the greatest part of the Bey's people and his own were gone to forage, and that this would be a proper moment to attack him. The Bey, to avoid falling by the treachery of Shaik Alieff, instead of taking his advice, ordered his drum to be beat to recall his people instantly from foraging ; and Shaik Alieff, who expected to be cut to pieces on the return of the Bey's people, fled to Saffanassa's camp. A skirmish soon after ensued between the Bey's troops and Saffanassa's, in which the former had the advantage, and eighty heads of the slain are on their way to this place. They are expected to be brought in to-morrow, and to be placed as usual on the gates and walls of the town. Horrid as this custom is here, at Algiers and Tunis it is more dreadful, as in those places they throw them on the ground. Here a Christian may pass the disgusting spectacle without lifting his eyes to behold it, but there he cannot avoid the horror of the sight.

Since the advantage gained by the Bey over the Arabs, he had nearly concluded a peace with Saffanassa ; but owing to an article the Bey insisted on, hostilities have recommenced. The Bey proposed that the Arabs should allow him to build a castle on a part of the sands where one formerly stood, built by Mahomet, the present Bashaw's father ; but to this proposal neither Saffanassa, nor even the Benoleeds, who were with him, would agree.

The Bey's camp is so much in want of provisions, particularly water, that his people and cattle die daily. During a dreadful extremity, when for want of water the heat threatened universal destruction to the Bey's troops, he ordered some of his camels to be killed for the sake of the water contained in their bodies, which, amounting to many gallons in each, was dealt out in scanty portions to the people, who were dying with thirst. This expedient saved numbers from death.

We hope a few days will produce more favourable news from the camp. We hear every day of offerings made at the prophet's shrine at the marabuts, by the Bey's friends, where neither lambs, nor prayers, nor presents, are spared to procure the Bey's success.

His mother and wife suffer extremely from his absence : Lilla Halluma and this princess have almost excluded themselves from the rest of the family, and very few of those who have been at the castle since the Bey's departure with the camp, have been admitted to see them.

After Hadgi Abderrahman had given us the news of the camp, he passed the rest of the morning in giving to us some curious descriptions of the caravans, and a long account of a pilgrimage he had made with his family to Mecca. The caravan with which Abderrahman travelled was in great part made up of his own suite, and numbers of both rich and poor belonging to the caravan of Morocco, joined the ambassador in order to profit by his protection. The pilgrims encamped at that time in the Pianura of Tripoli, accelerated their business to join the caravan of the ambassador's family. Notwithstanding they departed from Tripoli in a favourable part of the year, the difficulties of the deserts proved so great, that Hadgi Abderrahman expected the loss of the greatest part of his family.

The ladies went in carriages inclosed with awnings,[1] and placed on the backs of camels, whence, when the caravan halted, they were in general conveyed into tents, where carpets and every convenience awaited them ; but in many parts of the deserts these conveniences could not be used, as their preparing them required more time than was prudent for the caravan to stop, on account of the wandering hordes.

When this caravan arrived at Grand Cairo, it amounted to upwards of a thousand camels and three or four thousand people. Cairo is a most extensive mart, and is always so crowded, that passengers with great difficulty pass along the streets.

From this vast emporium, merchandise is conveyed through the Mediterranean into Europe and Turkey. Its produce is sent by caravans into the interior of Africa, to Abyssinia, Fezzan, Morocco, and Guinea, and immense riches are transported over the Red Sea into all parts of Asia, Arabia, China, India, Persia, and other places.

From Abyssinia the caravans carry yearly to Cairo nearly two thousand negroes ; these poor creatures having unfortunately been captured in war. Most of the chiefs and sovereigns in the interior of Africa sell or put to death all their prisoners. This caravan also carries

1 The *takhterawan* or *hodej*, the Arab version of the *howdah*.

with it to Cairo, slaves, antelopes, parrots, and monkeys, and some-times wild beasts peculiar to Africa.   Among the valuable articles it takes, is the best gold in dust and bars, ostrich feathers, myrrh, and ebony.   The gold in dust is procured from Abyssinia, tied up in small pieces of cloth, the shape and size of a large nut.   Each parcel is worth a Venetian sequin, or ten shillings and sixpence, and passes current till the cloth is worn out without having once been opened.   The ebony, which is brought from a high mountain near Abyssinia, is said to be the best in the world : it takes a much higher polish than either the black, green, or red ebony, brought from India.

One of the largest caravans which travels through Africa, sets out from Fez and passes along the borders of the Atlantic Ocean, not leaving the coast till it can cross Africa, at the narrowest part, to the kingdom of Sanaar, through which it proceeds to the banks of the Red Sea.   Another considerable caravan sets out from Morocco, in-creasing in its numbers of hadgees and travellers, while coasting the whole of the Mediterranean from Morocco towards Egypt, particu-larly from Algiers, Tunis, and Tripoli.   This caravan encamps for several weeks under the walls round the town of Tripoli, and after-wards sets out from thence over the deserts of Alexandria.   The pilgrims belonging to it range themselves under tents of all sizes and colours in the sandy plain adjoining the gates, which appear at a small distance like a little town of variegated colours.   They receive from the inhabitants of Tripoli what supplies they want, for which they seldom return money, but pay for them with the articles they bring with them, particularly ostrich feathers and Morocco leather.

With one of these caravans the ambassador (Hadgi Abderrahman) and his family went hence to Mecca.   They set out for Grand Cairo, where they joined the caravan of Egypt ; but were detained for three or four weeks, notwithstanding the finest weather imaginable, on account of unlucky days and frightful omens, which were said to have happened from time to time.   These delays are sometimes very serious to those pilgrims who go expressly to visit the holy places, as the Beit-Allah, at Mecca, which is the principal object of their worship, is only open two days in every six weeks, one for the women and another for the men ; consequently such delays often occasion the Mahomedans to be three months longer on their pilgrimage.

The road from Cairo to Suez, though not sixty miles, is among the worst parts of the journey from Tripoli to Mecca, not excepting the deserts to Alexandria.   Many of the pilgrims are then obliged to continue their route by the Red Sea, not being able to carry with them the provisions wanted for the rest of their pilgrimage to Mecca ; for Suez, surrounded with sands and destitute of a drop of water for its own consumption, can furnish nothing to travellers. The inhabitants of Suez are obliged to travel six or seven hours for all the water they use : they go for it to the Arabian shores, and get it from Nuba, on the borders of the Red Sea ; and this, which is the nearest water they can procure, is so bitter, that no European can drink it, without being mixed with spirit. It was, therefore, indispensably necessary for Hadgi Abderrahman to provide himself with pulse, meat, wood, and water, for the rest of his long journey, near seven hundred miles, the greatest part through the deserts of Arabia ; and this circumstance, while it increased the numerous animals of burden in the caravan, obliged the poorer pilgrims, who had no beasts of burden, to proceed by sea.

A pilgrimage by a man of distinction is made at a very heavy expense, as those persons he permits to join his suite almost wholly depend on him for their subsistence.

Nothing can be more curious than the appearance of the caravans when they set out from Grand Cairo, as they are by that time composed of crowds from all nations, as different in their dress as in their complexions. They carry with them besides gold dust, Venetian sequins, silver piastres, corn, wheat, beans, iron, lead and cochineal, to Mecca, Mocha, and other places, and return through Tripoli, with muslins, ostrich feathers, shawls, Arabian coffee, pearls, diamonds from Golconda, silk, cottons, and a sort of paste-preserve, made of roses, apricots, and peaches, which is very excellent but expensive. We have never seen desserts at the castle without this paste ; yet very few people here can purchase it.

Amongst the merchandize brought back by these caravans to Egypt from Arabia, are the beautiful slaves sold at Cairo. These females are brought only from Christian countries, Georgia, Circassia, Armenia, and others ; for no Mahometan, male or female, can be made a slave. Volney observes, it is a very singular circumstance, that Georgia, whence the fairest women are now brought, was anciently peopled with black inhabitants from Egypt, though now that country is so remarkable for the whiteness of its inhabitants.

When the caravans set out from Cairo, they complete their pilgrimage to Mecca and return in one hundred days. Sometimes very good bargains are to be bought here from the hadgees of the caravans, particularly diamonds and pearls.   Of the latter they bring to Tripoli large bunches, and permit purchasers to select out of different bunches the largest and most perfect pearls, at a price much under the value they are sold for in Europe.

The only European traders at Suez now are Venetian merchants, who have been established there a long time : they send to Venice salt, stuffs, silks, etc.   There were formerly English and French merchants there ; but the caravan coming from Suez to Cairo in 1779 being cut off, put a stop to the trade of the English merchants, not one of whom has been seen in either of those places since.   The plundering of this caravan has been much talked of on account of Monsieur de Saint Germain of the Isle of Bourbon.   The caravan was composed chiefly of English officers and passengers, with some French prisoners, who disembarked from on board two vessels at Suez on their way to Europe through Cairo.   The Arabian Bedouins of Tor being informed that these people were possessed of great treasures, determined to rob them, which they effected about five leagues distance from Suez.   The unfortunate Europeans, left entirely naked and dispersed by fear, separated into two companies.   One party returned to Suez ; and the other, to the number of seventeen, thinking they should be able to reach Cairo, struck into the desert, where from fatigue, want of water, and hunger under the scorching rays of the sun, they perished, one after the other ; excepting one solitary object, Monsieur de St. Germain.   During three nights and two days, this unfortunate man wandered about the deserts naked and thirsty, frozen with the north wind at night (it being January) and burnt with the sun during the day.   In despair, he laid himself down on the sands, and would have perished had not the compassion of a Moor saved him.   This man at a distance saw him fall, hastened to him, and having learnt his deplorable situation took him with him to his own cottage.   Under his roof Monsieur de Saint Germain was preserved, and allowed to shelter himself for a length of time till he could obtain an escort to convey him to Cairo.

At Suez, a project was formed to unite the Red Sea with the Mediterranean, by a canal attempted to be made under Sesostris, King of Egypt, and by that means save the voyage round the Cape of Good Hope to India.   The isthmus of Suez being above one hundred miles across, such an undertaking must therefore have been very difficult, and had the canal been of permanent construction and been carefully maintained, it would have totally altered the face of Barbary, by affording a constant communication with those parts of Europe which would gladly have profited by this short cut to the riches of the east. By this means, the hidden treasures of Africa would have been easily explored, nations yet unknown would have been civilized, and the dark Ethiopian and the European would have long ceased to gaze with wonder at each other.

As an opportunity offers to send you this letter, I must reserve the remainder of the anecdotes, gleaned from Hadgi Abderrahman's accounts of his pilgrimage, for my next.

March 30, 1789

As I have no news to relate to you of this place at present, I shall resume the account of the caravans. The Pacha of Tripoli in Syria ought to conduct the sacred caravan himself from thence through the deserts to Mecca, for which conduct, and the furnishing it with corn, rice, and other provisions, he holds his station from the Porte. The former duty he never performs, and the latter very badly.

To supply the dreadful want of water and save the traveller from expiring through thirst, there are in a part of the Deserts of Arabia, about four days' journey to the north of Suez, several ancient aqueducts and many subterranean canals, which have been formed at an immense expense by the Assyrians, Persians, and Medes, who made it a part of their religion to conduct the water into the deserts ; but these canals and aqueducts are nearly rendered useless through neglect.

The Governor of Jerusalem also draws immense sums from the absurdities of the Christians, on account of the pilgrimage to the Holy City. The different communities of Greeks, Catholics, Armenians, Copts, Abyssinians, and Franks, are equally jealous about the possession of the sanctified places. There is a continual strife amongst the different convents and amongst the adherents of each community. The Turks, to whom these disputes are very profitable, never endeavour to lessen the source of them ; but, on the contrary, promote them as much as possible. Each pilgrim going to Mecca pays an entry at Jerusalem of ten piastres, about forty shillings : he then pays for an escort to perform the voyage to Jordan. Every convent pays the Governor of Jerusalem for the right of conducting a procession.

The Catholics send about three hundred chests of chaplets, relics, crosses, sanctuaries, crucifixes, scapularies, etc. from Jerusalem every

year, on which the duties to the governor are immense. The greatest
part of the Christian families and Mahomedans of Jerusalem get their
living by making the above articles : men, women, and children, sit
in crowds round their doors, all employed in sculpture, or in turning
wood, coral, and ivory, embroidering rich stuffs, in silk and pearls,
with gold and silver thread. The convent of the Holy Land sends
every year relics and other articles out of the country, to the amount
of five hundred thousand piastres (about a hundred thousand pounds
sterling) ; and the relics from the convents of the Greeks, Armenians,
and Copts, amount to a still larger sum. These objects exported into
Turkey, Italy, Portugal, France, and Spain, occasion the return of
alms or payments, to a considerable amount, to the religious communities at Jerusalem.

The visits of the pilgrims are not a less important object to these
convents. It is known that from ancient times the curiosity of visiting
holy places brought Christians from all parts of the world to Jerusalem.
For a long time the Popes made it an act necessary to salvation, and
the fervour with which this agitated all Europe, produced the crusades.
Since that epoch, which occasioned so much bloodshed, the number
of pilgrims has considerably diminished. They are reduced now to
some monks from Italy, Spain, and Germany. But it is different
with the Orientals, they continue to regard the voyage to Jerusalem
as one of the most meritorious acts. They even consider themselves
scandalised by those Franks or Christians who come to the East, and
do not follow their example, and stigmatize them with the name of
heretics or infidels, for not fulfilling this part of their religion. To
those who do, the Turks will not give the insulting epithet of Kielb,
or dog, so commonly applied to Christians by them.

The Greeks, more than other nations, believe this pilgrimage to
be productive of the greatest indulgences ; they suppose it absolves
them, not only for the past, but for the future, for not observing feasts
or fasts, and, indeed, for every crime. From these ideas, a prodigious
number of pilgrims of both sexes and of all ages, go from the Morea,
from the Archipelago, from Constantinople, Anatolia, Armenia,
Egypt, and Syria every year. In 1784, the number of pilgrims
amounted to five thousand.

The most simple pilgrimage costs four thousand livres, or near
two hundred pounds, and they often amount to fifty or sixty thousand
livres, or from three to four thousand pounds sterling. Jaffa, which
is about forty-six miles from Jerusalem, is the place where the pilgrims

disembark. They arrive there in November, and go thence directly to Jerusalem, where they remain till after Easter. The pilgrims are lodged all together in the cells of their different communities. They are told their lodging is free ; but it would not be safe if they went away without presenting a much larger sum than it would cost at an inn ; besides which, they must pay for masses, services, exhortations, etc., and buy crucifixes, chaplets, and Agnus Dei's. When the *Jour de Rameau* arrives, they must go to purify themselves in the river Jordan, which costs a very considerable sum. There is an account given in the history of that pilgrimage, of the tumultuous and confused march of this devout crowd in the plains of Jericho, with their astonishment on viewing the rocks of that country. Having compleated this ablution, the pilgrims return to the Holy Land. When Easter is passed, they all return to their own countries, proud of having vied with the Mussulman in the title of pilgrims. Many of them, in order to shew they have made this voyage, have figures engraved on their arms, wrists, or necks, of the cross, crucifix, our Saviour, or the Virgin Mary, etc. This painful, and sometimes dangerous operation, is performed with gunpowder and a hot iron needle made for that purpose.

The convent of Franks, called St. Saviour's, is the chief place of all the missions to the Holy Land that are in Turkey, of which there are at present seventeen, chiefly Italian, French, and Spanish. The administration of this convent is in the hands of three individuals belonging to these nations ; the superior must be born subject to the Pope ; the procureur subject to the King of Spain ; and the vicar subject to the King of France. Each is assisted by a second or one under him, and the convent is directed by these six men and a Portuguese.

The principal revenue of the Bedouins at Tor arises from the pilgrimage of the Greeks to the convent on Mount Sinai. The pilgrims have such veneration for the relics of St. Catherine, said to be there, that they are not sure of their salvation if they neglect to visit them, at least, once in their lives, and they come even from the Morea and Constantinople for this purpose. The meeting place is at Grand Cairo, where the monks of Mount Sinai treat with their correspondents to send Arabs with the pilgrims, to conduct them on to their convent. When they arrive there, the Greeks perform their devotions : they visit the church, kiss the relics and images, go above a hundred paces on their knees up the mountain, and finish by making an offering to the convent of no fixed value, but which is seldom less than fifty pataques (about twelve pounds sterling). The situation and building of this convent is singular. It is placed at the foot of Mount Sinai, and appears like a square prison. The walls of it are immoderately high ; and to the whole building there is but one small window near the top, which in common serves also for a door, and is used in the following singular manner. The person intended to be admitted sits in a basket, previously let down by the monks from this window, and is then drawn up in it with cords. This precaution is on account of the Arabs, who would probably force their way into the convent, and, therefore, it is only on the visit of a bishop that they open a door, which at all other times is nailed up and strongly fastened with ironwork. This convent ought to be visited by a bishop every two or three years, but as those visits occasion a great contribution to the Arabs, the monks endeavour to avoid them as much as possible. Great trouble arises to the monks on being obliged to distribute daily portions to the Arabs, a custom which occasions continual disputes, and often induces the Arabs to throw stones and even to fire upon them. The monks never go abroad into the country ; but by great labour they have made a garden of earth on the rock, on which they cultivate excellent fruit, such as figs, grapes, and pears. The latter are much esteemed at Cairo. The monks lead a domestic life, after the manner of the Greeks and Maronites of Libanus, and are entirely occupied in works of utility and practices of devotion.

Though the Moors never say much concerning the religious ceremonies they perform at Mecca, yet for those they mention they express the highest veneration. They seldom speak to Christians on these topics, except to those in whom they have the greatest confidence, and then it is with circumspection. They dwell with religious zeal on the certainty of the Koran's having been delivered by angels to Mahomet verse by verse. They relate the miracle of Mahomet's tomb, at Medina, being suspended from the earth by an invisible power, and persuade themselves they have seen it in this extraordinary situation. They say, that the lamps have burned constantly round it ever since his death, without ever having been replenished at any time ; that celestial spirits have been seen by the devout Mussulmans who visit with real holiness the Prophet's tomb, the brilliance of which, without the aid of human art, never has, nor ever will be, in the least tarnished or faded in its appearance, and which, they profess, surpasses all that can be imagined. The Black Stone in the Temple of

Mecca, placed there by Abraham the Patriarch, is called by the Prophet the Ruby of Paradise, and passes by that name in all descriptions given of it by the Mahomedans.

The Mahomedans assemble at a mountain not far from Mecca, where they oblige all the Christians, Jews, or Pagans in their suite, to quit them, that they may not contaminate the Holy City of Mecca, to which the Mussulmans set out together in a religious procession from the foot of the mountain. Their pilgrimages are not so expensive as those of the Franks and Christians.

Returning from Mecca through the deserts of Arabia, Hadgi Abderrahman again thought his family would have fallen victims to the dangers of the journey. These deserts are infested with Arab tribes of Christians, a people called by the Moors infidels, and declared enemies of the Prophet. It is only a numerous caravan that can attempt to pass this way on that account. During this part of the journey, Hadgi Abderrahman's family was nearly exhausted with fatigue. The caravan, unable to proceed without resting, halted with great apprehensions within sight of these savage robbers : they dared not pitch their tents, and remained a few hours only. These dangerous tribes are very powerful, wandering over the deserts in all directions, and attacking the largest caravans, too often with success. A space of thirty miles often intervenes without a habitation or green leaf to be seen. From year to year many wretched travellers perish in these deserted tracks, where no shelter is to be met with, nor drop of water to be found, during the whole of the summer months. In the Deserts of Barca, on their return to Tripoli, Hadgi Abderrahman and his family were overtaken by the south winds, which they expected would have buried the whole caravan. These dangerous winds began to blow violently, and after one day's intermission, blew incessantly parching gales for three days, at which period the air became nearly fatal to all those who were exposed to it. Numbers of the caravan died before it reached Tripoli, and the mortality would have been much greater, had they not fortunately been provided with a sufficiency of water.

These dreadful winds are still called by the Arabians the Campsing winds, a name they acquired from the circumstance of Cambyses' [1] army having perished by them in their Ethiopian expedition.

Notwithstanding the danger and hardships of this pilgrimage, the

---

[1] An attractive derivation, but not true ! The wind is so called because it blows for about fifty (*khamseen*) days in March and April.

ambassador has been twice to Mecca since, but without any of the female part of his family.

Not the least news from the Bey's camp has transpired since my last; and notwithstanding the report of the three princes having entirely separated, the Bey is expected in company with his brothers daily at Tripoli.

⚊

April 3, 1789

For our misfortune, we are again honoured with the presence of Muley Yesied, the Emperor of Morocco's son, though it is not seven months since he was here. He seems in his present visit to this country to surpass his former exploits of ferocity and cruelty. Two days before he arrived at Tripoli, on the coast of Zuarra, he performed one of his usual tragedies, for which there was, what is rarely the case, some reason. When he was here last year he had with him a Spanish renegado, in which he confided much : this slave, from being one of his attendants, was raised to the rank of cassnador, or treasurer, and letting him still act in the capacity of a mameluke, he set him to watch over his women, and placed every confidence in him. Muley Yesied had been at Tunis some time, during which period he perceived this renegado had estranged the affections of one of his favourite ladies. He took no notice at Tunis of the discovery he had made of the infidelity of the fair slave, or the treachery of the renegado, but brought the deluded culprits on with him, not altering his behaviour, while his heart was coolly meditating in what manner to sacrifice them, that their punishment might satiate his revenge. By the time he arrived at Zuarra, he had decided the fate of these unfortunate wretches. This cannibal eats not men, but he feasts upon their sufferings : he put the two offenders to death, the woman first, and the man afterwards, with his own hands, in a manner the most heightened description of cruelty could not exaggerate. But a detailed relation of such crimes as his would be criminal in itself ; the pictures of cruelty, which frequently stain the pages of good authors, appear to serve no other purpose than to excite the curiosity, add to the ingenuity, and increase the ferocity of the wretch prone to cruelty, who may chance to read or hear of them. A display of the machinations, by which an unhappy being might be entrapped and slaughtered, may prove of eminent use, to warn the unwary from falling a prey to those of this race, who resemble or belong to the fiends ; but to count the sufferings of a martyr by the seconds of a watch, and minutely dwell on every groan, seems merely explaining, as I have said, the inventions of cruelty. Feasts have been reported to be given in the interior of Africa, at the bare relation of which the savage African has shuddered, while the quickness of his ideas has obliged him to smile at the invention of the author who related them ; but it is no more than truth to say, That Muley Yesied's conduct at present is such, that nature recoils at the idea of treading (even by accident) in the footsteps of such a barbarous savage.

About two years ago, Muley Yesied carried off by violence the daughter of an Arab chief of one of the most considerable tribes of the Deserts of Barca ; he brought her back in great pomp last year as his wife, and to pacify Shaik Saffanassa, her father, has sworn to him that she shall be empress when he comes to the throne.

This prince is so very eccentric in his manners, that it is difficult to discriminate when he is sober or inebriated. He this morning rowed round the harbour of Tripoli in great state, and went on board several of the vessels anchored there, where, though he cannot commit any enormities, as each vessel is protected by the national flag, yet he makes most troublesome visits. At a vessel just come into port he fired a pistol, and the captain, when informed it was the Emperor of Morocco's son, saluted him with guns.

Contrary to Muley Yesied's custom of landing at the Pianura, he landed to-day at the Mole, and rode through the town. It was therefore apprehended he would pay a visit at the consular houses ; but probably, owing to not finding himself pressed to enter them, and thinking the Christians looked coolly on him, he contented himself with stopping to converse for some time without dismounting. He partook of the refreshments of coffee and sherbet presented to him, which was done merely out of respect to his father, by those nations with whom the Emperor is at present at peace.

An unfortunate slave carrying the prince to-day from the shore to his boat, slipped with him, and threw him into the sea. The prince was soon brought to land ; the poor unfortunate slave who fell with him attempted to drown himself, but the prince's attendants seized on him and dragged him away. Orders immediately followed from Muley Yesied to bastinade him so severely that the man is dying.

Muley Yesied has a grand tent pitched in the Pianura, and about five hundred troops with him, besides officers.

The Bashaw causes this prince to be treated with every attention out of the town, but never invites him into the city. He is not a bad figure ; his gait is fierce and haughty, his eyes are black, and his teeth extremely white ; but his complexion nearly copper-colour, with a dark and savage countenance fitted to his actions. He is just turned of thirty ; and the following accounts, with the different anecdotes you will have found in my letters concerning him, will serve to shew you the progress of his life for the last eleven years.

Muley Yesied, in the year 1778, was in open rebellion against his father, and owing to his machinations, was proclaimed king by the negro army at Mequinez : his mother, a Hessian [1] slave of the Emperor's, and who became one of the Emperor's favourite wives, then interceded for her son and saved him from his father's anger. The Emperor ordered Muley Yesied to atone for his crime by making a pilgrimage to Mecca, telling him that he would allow him to be attended by a proper retinue, and that he would appoint officers to accompany him, to whom he would entrust large sums of money, with orders how to distribute them to the shreefs of Mecca and Medina, as an atonement for his unnatural and savage behaviour. Some days after the Emperor had ordered this pilgrimage, he determined that several of the family should accompany Muley Yesied to Mecca, and, in 1779, the prince set out with Muley Aselmn, his brother, Lilla Largitta, his mother, Lilla il Sebiba, his sister, and the princess Lilla Loubaba. As the latter princess had been betrothed for some time to the holy shreef of Mecca, the greatest part of the grandeur displayed in this pilgrimage was considered to be chiefly upon her account. On the arrival of Muley Yesied at Mecca, Lilla Loubaba was married to the shreef. These princes and princesses, besides being accompanied by the grand caravan, were escorted by five hundred and fifty horsemen.

The Emperor entrusted the officers, who accompanied Muley Yesied, with two hundred thousand Levant piastres, or fifty thousand pounds sterling. They had not completed half their journey before Muley Yesied, by promises and threats, extorted sixty thousand piastres from the officers who had the care of it ; and those who opposed this sacrilegious breach of trust to the Emperor, Muley Yesied used with savage brutality. In vain his mother, Lilla Largitta, with tears and prayers, implored him to restore the money, reminding him it was intended for sacred purposes. He was equally insensible to her

[1] His mother is believed to have been an Englishwoman.

remonstrances, the anger of his father, or the vengeance of his prophet. Before he returned from Mecca, the Emperor was informed of his sacrilegious deed, and sent messengers to forbid the Prince's returning to his dominions, and to tell him, that, enraged at his conduct, he had sworn in the most solemn manner by the Prophet, never to see him again, till he had performed three successive pilgrimages to Mecca.

Muley Yesied accordingly remained accompanying the caravans, and passing his time, sometimes at Tripoli, and sometimes at Tunis, for near three years, committing all sort of depredations wherever he went. He determined at last to return to Mequinez, and arrived there in September 1781. It was in vain that at his intercession his mother tried again her influence with the Emperor to see him. He in an agony forbid him his presence, till he had completed the three pilgrimages he had ordered him to make.

Muley Yesied, finding all endeavours fruitless to approach his father's court, determined to join the caravan then going off. The Emperor again sent, as before, two hundred thousand Levant piastres, to expiate the offences his son had now committed against the Holy Prophet and Mecca, ordering those he entrusted with the money not to accompany Muley Yesied, nor to join him till they arrived at the Holy Land. But Muley Yesied waylaid them in the deserts, between Alexandria and Cairo, massacred several of them, and robbed them of seventy thousand piastres. On his return from Mecca he passed as usual through Tripoli, and staid here several months that summer. Knowing how much cause he had given for the Emperor's displeasure, and fearing his resentment, he took letters with him from the Bashaw of Tripoli and Bey of Tunis to plead for him ; but these, with every deception he could employ, did not succeed in persuading the Emperor to receive him. His father ordered him to quit his dominions and finish his pilgrimages, of which he had only yet performed two.

Once more he set out with seven of his wives, besides favourites and black slaves, and went with a numerous caravan in great pomp to finish his third pilgrimage. The Emperor sent again large sums to appease the Prophet, and gain his ferocious son a favourable reception at Mecca ; but took the precaution of sending those he entrusted the treasures to by sea, that they might not be again assaulted by Muley Yesied, who was gone by land. Enraged and disappointed at not being able to profit on the way of the treasures carried for him to Mecca, he determined on robbing the caravan under his protection, and by extorting from the principal people in it forty thousand piastres, or ten thousand pounds, he remained at Mecca and in Egypt nearly three years ; and in 1787, on his return through the kingdom of Tripoli, committed the violence I before mentioned, of carrying off by force the daughter of the Arab chief, Saffanassa, whom he still obliges to accompany him. She, relying on her father's consequence, is less afraid of Muley Yesied than any of the other unfortunate females with him. She detests his manners, and, if she dared, would escape to her father, but that would be risking too much her father's life, who might fall a sacrifice through treachery to Muley Yesied's revenge.

An order has been sent to the court of Tunis from the Emperor of Morocco, to oblige Muley Yesied to quit that kingdom ; and it is now expected he will embark for his father's dominions, whence he has been absent near four years. I should not have written to you so much of this detested prince, had I not been induced to it from the singularity of his character.

June 20, 1789

We went to the castle yesterday. Lilla Halluma was more out of spirits than usual : she was on her couch surrounded by her slaves, but none of the ladies of the family were suffered to approach her, except Lilla Howisha, the Bey's wife ; and Lilla Halluma said, she only permitted this princess to be with her, because she thought her as unhappy as herself. The reason of their being so depressed was on account of the news brought from the camp in the morning ; for though the Bey is returning victorious, the two younger princes are so disaffected to him, that it is said the Bey's life has been twice attempted through the treachery of his brothers. The Bey's daughter, Lilla Zenobia, was with her attendants in the gallery before Halluma's apartment, waiting for her mother. This princess is now thirteen years of age, and more beautiful than can be described. She doats on the Bey, and though so young, feels so strongly the afflictions of her father, that it is feared they have already undermined her constitution ; and the Bey often says with great distress, he fears the delicacy of her frame will not support her through the present turbulent times.

After we had been with the Bashaw's wife some time, one of her daughters, Lilla Fatima, the widow of the Bey of Dernier,[1] came into the apartment, and Lilla Halluma permitted her to go and superintend

---

[1] Derna in Cyrenaica.

the supper that was preparing for the Bashaw. Lilla Fatima invited us to accompany her on this occasion, which we readily did, expecting to find a great deal of amusement. The Bey's daughter and two of the princesses joined her. After passing through several apartments and passages, where we met from time to time only a solitary eunuch, the clinking of whose arms announced him before we could perceive him, from the gloom of the places we went through, we came to a large stone building covered with domes and supported by columns. Here a number of slaves were occupied in preparing different dishes of meat, in grinding corn, kneading bread, making fine pastes, and dressing fruits. Each of the princesses was followed by several of her attendants, but no one interfered in what was doing but Lilla Fatima, who seemed to be very particular in examining everything. The negroes attended Lilla Fatima with fans to prevent insects annoying her. The sight of royalty employed in this manner, called to our mind what has been said of the ancients.

The attentions paid here by the princesses to the food prepared for the Bashaw, though a duty that cannot be dispensed with, is unattended at present with that great degree of dread and suspicion, that prevails where the sovereign's death is every moment anxiously looked for by his subjects and by those allied to him, which is too often the case in Moorish states. At Algiers and Constantinople, the sovereigns live in continual dread of poison being mixed in their victuals. The Grand Signior is said, in troublesome times, to eat only of such dishes brought to his table as are put in a silk handkerchief, and sealed with the seal of his chief cook.

When we returned with the princesses to take leave of the Bashaw's wife, she told us news had arrived of more conquests made by the Bey over the Arabs, and that he was expected alone in town in a day or two, his brothers having separated from him. On account of this latter news, we left Lilla Halluma and the princesses more uneasy than they were before, for fear the circumstances of the Bey's returning without his brothers should procure him an ill reception from the Bashaw.

July 28, 1789

A black prince of Bornou is here at present : he is come from Tunis, and is returning to Bornou. He has with him three of his wives : one of them, in her travels with the prince, has learnt enough of the Italian language to express herself in *lingua Franca* ; but the prince is so jealous of his wives, that the Christian ladies have tried in vain to see them. The prince has one of the best houses in the town allotted him by the Bashaw. We called there one day, unexpectedly, in hopes of gaining admittance to these princesses, but the servants were hurried out with the usual excuse, that the prince was sleeping, and therefore no one could be admitted. He has been at the Christian parties in the evening, but all attempts to see his wives have been in vain, and he leaves this place to-morrow for Bornou. From the accounts given us by the Moorish ladies who have seen the prince's wives, they are extremely pretty for black women, not the least of the negro cast, cheerful and pleasant in their manners, and mild to their attendants. Their dress is modelled after the Tunisian fashion, as they wear caps, jilecks, and baracans, which they have bought in their late visit to that country. They wear the gold cap wound round with a coloured silk Tunisian handkerchief, in the form of a turban. This is an idea of their own, not from the Tunisian or Tripolitan mode of dressing.

The Prince of Bornou, considering he comes from the interior of Africa, is extremely well informed, and much acquainted with the state of Europe. The most striking part of his dress was the pearls he wore, which were all of an uncommon size. He had large gold ear-rings set with the most valuable jewels, but no nose ring, as it is said the great people of Bornou have. His attendants were composed of Turks and blacks, and all perfectly well accoutred.

The Moors are in the habit of recounting such fabulous stories of Bornou and its king, that it is impossible to rely on their accounts. The prince, whose intelligence is probably correct, describes the kingdom of Bornou as a most fertile country with good fruits, particularly grapes, apricots, and pomegranates. He says, though some wild beasts are seen there, they are not so numerous as in the deserts between Tunis and Tripoli ; to cross these deserts being reckoned among the most dangerous journies in Africa, on account of the number of lions and tigers that issue from the woods and mountains near Tunis. The prince says, his subjects are free from the dreadful customs of the nations surrounding them, who eat, sacrifice, and sell the blacks, and that only those who call themselves Christians and the Pagans commit such enormities. It is from the Christian merchants and the Jews on the south-west coast of Africa that the Emperor of Morocco chiefly recruits his negro army : the factories there send to purchase and kidnap these unfortunate creatures from the negro states and other kingdoms. This black prince represented the government of Bornou as extremely mild, and the subjects very pacific. They do not wish to let out their troops for hire, and seldom lend them ; when they do, it is only to Mahometans. They seek after no conquests, are content with their own situation, and for many years have not stood in need of auxiliary soldiers. They could raise, if required, great armies expeditiously, from the number of their subjects and the goodness of their horses, which he reckons superior to those of Arabia or Barbary, as they possess the best qualities of those animals, being as serviceable as those of Arabia, and as beautiful as those of Barbary. The Moors here have such an idea of the forces at Bornou, that among the fabulous stories they recount of that kingdom, they say when the King of Bornou sends out his troops, the body of a large date tree is laid down before the gate of the city, on which the troops step as they go out of the town, and as the foot soldiers go through the gate they wear out the body of this tree. These ignorant stories owe their continuance in circulation among the common people at Tripoli, to the difficulty of their being contradicted, as the kingdom of Bornou is divided from Tripoli by almost impassable deserts, at the distance of near one thousand miles, and the roads from Fezzan to Tripoli are unfrequented by caravans. The little intercourse, therefore, between Bornou and this place, renders every account given of it by the Tripolitans erroneous, and the appearance of a prince or even chief person from thence is at Tripoli very rare indeed.

July 29, 1789

By private letters from Tunis, it is said that an expedition is fitting out, with the consent of the Grand Signior, to convey the Pretender to Tripoli. He is a Tripolitan, who has lived at the court of Tunis for many years, and declares himself to be an uncle of the Bashaw, one who escaped out of seven who fell at his accession to the throne. This prince, if living, fled from Tripoli so very young, that it would be difficult for any one here to ascertain his being the same person. Many who have gone from Tripoli to Tunis on purpose to see him, say he is an impostor.

Some days after these accounts arrived that the Pretender was on the point of setting off for this place, a Moor came into town from a neighbouring village, called the Sucara, who reports that he is the son of the Gebeleen (Mountaineer), at whose cottage the Bashaw's uncle took shelter when pursued by the Arabs ; and that the Bashaw's blacks forced their way in, and returned soon after, saying they had driven the Bashaw's uncle into a well in the garden, where he was drowned. Owing to the very great confusion in Tripoli at that period, the body of this prince was not sought for till many days after the event, when a quantity of rubbish was taken out of the well resembling spoilt habits, but nothing like the remains of a human form appeared. By half the people it was asserted that the Bashaw's uncle had perished in this well, and the other half declared he had escaped ; but the Moor adds, that, previous to the above circumstance, this prince, while secreting himself in the Messeah (the part of the country adjoining the town) where he was waiting to join a caravan and escape to Tunis, was one day loading his piece, when it went off, and took away the first joint of one of his fingers, a mark by which he could not fail to be known, and which circumstance his father, a very old man, is still living to assert.

This report has made so strong an impression on the people, that should the Pretender arrive without any defect in his hands, though with the Grand Signior's firman, he will be repulsed, from his having imposed upon the court of Tunis and the Porte.

August 12, 1789

Tripoli has been, as it generally is when frigates are here, gayer than usual for the last week. *The Pearl*, commanded by Captain Finch, came here some days since, and remained a week. A son of Earl Paget and a son of Lord Bagot were on board, both midshipmen : the latter a proficient in painting and drawing ; and, having an artist with him, lost no time in copying every thing that struck him to be worthy of notice, among which, you may be sure, the curious and antient arch [1] I have mentioned did not escape. It has been correctly drawn and coloured, and he professes himself highly gratified that the English Consul's taste led him to persuade the Bashaw, some time since, to have the shops and rubbish removed out of the arch, which

---

[1] Lyon, the traveller, did a drawing of the arch in 1818. It appears in his book, *Travels in Africa*.

had almost choked up the inside, and concealed the beautiful ceiling. Every body says this is the only drawing that has been taken by the Christians in the memory of any one here, which seems very probable, as from the great jealousy, the Moors displayed on the present occasion, it must have been impossible for Christians to stand and take any observations or models of antiquities, without appropriate precautions for their ease and security. In the present instance, a direct leave was procured from the Bashaw himself, and such of the Moors as were concerned in it were induced to consent, by persuasion of its being natural for literary people to examine ancient customs, without any hostile view on the country, or want of respect to the prophet.

September 18, 1789

The Bey is returned from the camp, and, to the great satisfaction of the people of Tripoli, he is so well received by his father, that they yesterday went round the town in state together to the different mosques, to return thanks at the altar of their prophet, and invoke his further favour, and to strike more forcibly the minds of the populace. The dresses of the officers and those who attended the Bashaw and Bey, had much more an appearance of state than usual ; but as I have before described to you the Bashaw's procession to the marabuts, I shall only say he was on this occasion particularly brilliant. On these days, the Bashaw honours his nobles and chief officers of state, in successively calling at their houses. He yesterday stopped at the residence of Hadgi Abderrahman ; and this honour cost him as usual a negro. When the Bashaw stops at any of the consular houses, sherbets, coffee, and cakes, are presented to him and his suite, which, in general, consists of about two hundred persons.

In the procession were carried the standard of Mahomet, of green satin embroidered with gold, and the Mecca flag of green silk, with sentences of the Koran worked round the edge. The Imam, or Mufti,[1] attended in his robes ; the royal nubar, or band, followed, and no person was mounted on horseback but the Bashaw and Bey. All their suite, guards, and slaves, were on foot, according to the usual respect paid to the Sovereign and the Bey, when passing in state through the town.

When the Bey returned from the camp, the heads of some

[1] The author must mean the Mufti. An *imam* is merely a prayer-leader in a mosque.

particular chiefs of the enemies slain in battle were brought with him, and in order to preserve them they had been salted. This is not an uncommon practice among the Moors and Turks. Muley Yesied, while on his travels, sent two curious looking chests, carefully packed, directed to the care of the English Consul, with letters requesting he would immediately forward them to the Emperor of Morocco. The captain of a man of war, who lay in the harbour of Tripoli, took charge of them. To the surprise of every body, during the few days the boxes were in the consular house, they became so offensive, that had they not been embarked they must have been removed ; and after they were on board, the captain of the frigate feared they would infect the ship. Nobody had the least suspicion of what these chests contained, even at the time they were delivered at Morocco to the Emperor, but these dreadfully offensive packages proved afterwards to be human heads.

Hadgi Abderrahman, from the letters he had received, informed us that before the Bey left the camp he punished six of his people who had behaved cowardly, in the following whimsical manner. He had their baracans put on in the stile the women wear them, their hands and feet painted with henna, and ordered them to be led with their faces covered with silk handkerchiefs, in the manner of brides, all round his camp, and then insisted they should wear that dress till they had recovered their credit by some signal service. This mode of punishment had such an effect upon one of them, that the man who had not sufficient courage to face the enemy, had false courage enough to quit the world rather than bear the scorn of his companions, and shot himself.

The two younger princes are expected in town daily, but it is feared not without intentions of again sowing dissentions between the Bashaw and the Bey.

November 11, 1789

Since the Bey's return from the camp, the country round being clearer than usual from the incursions of the Arabs, it was determined by the Christians to take a ride to the eastward, of a greater distance from the city of Tripoli than has been practicable to ladies for a long time. Our party for this excursion consisted of twenty, and though our guards or dragomen and servants, with those belonging to the other Consuls who went with us, amounted to more than that number, yet it was not thought safe to go without some of the hampers, or Bashaw's guards, from the castle, which was granted for our further security. The place where we dined was an olive grove, with grounds belonging to the Bashaw's first minister, Mustapha Scrivan, where Moors are stationed to take care of his lands. Mustapha Scrivan's eldest son, and a shreef of Mecca, accepted of an invitation to join the party, accompanied us with our attendants and dined with us, sharing the amusements of the day, which were rendered more pleasant, as their presence gave greater security to our excursion by contributing to keep the Moors and Arabs in order.

For some miles after we left the town of Tripoli, the soil the greatest part of the way was a white silver sand, apparently chrystallized, the brilliancy of which, in a long journey, is often fatal to the eyes of travellers. This appearance is peculiar to the sands and deserts nearest Tripoli ; their extreme whiteness makes the contrast between them and the deep red sands brought by the campsin [1] or hot winds from the interior, too striking to pass unnoticed.

In our ride, where the foliage of the Indian fig was in abundance, the roads, fields, and other inclosures, to which it served as fences, made a most extraordinary appearance. This immense leaf grows here to the length of sixteen or seventeen inches, and eight or nine in width ; its consistence renders it nearly the substance of wood : while it is young, it is of a beautiful green, growing without stem, one leaf out of the other. This extraordinary shrub forms a hedge of fourteen or fifteen feet high, and eight or nine feet thick, making a much stronger fence than either brick or stone walls. This being the season for it to blossom, its appearance was truly curious ; every leaf was set close round the edge with the full blossoms of the fruit, which were orange colour tipped with crimson ; and the shape of the leaves forming large scollops, the extreme brightness of the sun gave the hedges and fields an appearance of being every where richly decorated in festoons of gold and red.

The cultivated grounds we passed were not laid out with method or design, but were inclosures of trees of all sizes and qualities, and placed in all directions, among which the towering date tree was every where conspicuous, displaying close to its summit luxuriant branches of the ripe date, resembling amber : cabbages, turnips,

---

[1] The *Khamseen* only blows at one time of the year. The normal desert wind is known as the *ghibli*.

wheat, and barley, grew in variegated and confused patches beneath them. The gardens of people of distinction, by being chiefly confined to the orange, lemon, and citron trees, made a most beautiful appearance, heightened by the effect of the sun.

At the distance of a few miles from Tripoli, the greatest part of the Moors we met had on no other garment but the red cap and the dark brown baracan of web or woollen, which served to cover them from the shoulders to the middle of the leg, placed in ample folds, according to their own taste, around their bodies, but leaving the right arm and shoulder exposed. Coral, bits of tin, and beads ornamented the women's heads, and a lighter baracan, generally black, wrapped tightly round them, composed the whole of their dress. These women stared at us as much as we did at them, and did not seem over diligent to conceal their features from our party, but were careful in covering themselves when the shreef of Mecca, or Mustapha Scrivan's son, or any of the guards who were with us, approached them.

Just before we reached Sahal, we stopped to look at a small mosque in a village that was open at the time we passed. It was remarkable for its great neatness, and the gay china tiles with which it was lined throughout. The floor was covered with bright Tunisian carpets ; and the pulpit, with the steps ascending to it, was of the brightest marble ; yet the congregation that came to this little neat mosque was wholly composed of the unclad peasantry of a mud village. To nothing, however, are the Mahomedans more attentive than to the beauty and cleanliness of their mosques and burying places.

The handsomest mosque in Africa is the one at Fez, which a Moor of distinction, who lately came from thence, described to us. This extraordinary edifice is covered with seventeen principal arches, or roofs, besides a vast number of inferior ones. All these are sustained by no less than fifteen hundred large columns of white marble ; upwards of a thousand lamps, some of a very considerable size, are kept continually burning within it ; and the cisterns, which are prepared for Mahomedans to wash in before they go to prayers, are to the number of five hundred.

When we first arrived at Sahal, we stopped only to examine the olive plantations, where we were to dine, and found, as had been described to us, that the olive trees formed a shade impenetrable to the sun's rays, and promised us a delightful shelter from the atmosphere which was getting now intensely hot ; but we still continued our ride to view a salt lake in the midst of the sands, called the lake of Tajura,

not far from the village of that name. At this time it was nearly dry ;
but when full, it covers a mile and a half of ground, and is in most
places half a mile across. When this lake is dry there remains a bed
of salt round the edge as hard as stone ; it is broken with great difficulty, and brought in bars to Tripoli. This lake produces a great deal
of salt, and is the chief place whence this article is taken which is
exported from the kingdom : it is much finer, both in flavour and
colour, than the salt from the two famous lakes of Delta, on this side
Alexandria. The beds of these two extraordinary lakes are a sort of
ditch, from ten to twelve miles in length, and near a mile in width :
they are dry nine months in the year, but in the winter there comes
from the ground a deep violet-coloured water, filling the lakes to
five or six feet. The return of the heat dries this water up, and there
remains a bed of salt above two feet in thickness, and so hard that it
is broken by bars of iron. They procure from these lakes thirty-six
thousand quintals of salt every year, a quintal being about a hundred
and twenty pounds weight.

The lake of Tajura is nearly surrounded by sands, but on approaching the village of Tajura there appeared innumerable small clusters of
trees at considerable distances from each other. In the middle of each
clump the sands carried thither by the winds lay in a conical form,
nearly as high as the tops of the trees, presenting an appearance of
having been brought there by human exertion for some particular
purpose.

The Mahomedan peasantry, though slaves to their lords in every
thing but name, appeared contented and happy. Whole families
were laying round the doors of their cottages, laughing, smoking,
singing, and telling romantic tales. They brought us out fresh dates,
bowls of new milk, and jars of sweet lakaby.

In these mixed circles of peasants, it was worth while for persons
more refined than the Moors to observe, through the rudeness of their
manners, the attentions paid from the young to the aged, and from
the son to the father. But Moors, Turks, and Arabs are remarkably
kind to their children ; and, in return, children are eminently obedient
and affectionate to their parents, and submissive to their superiors.
It was easy to discern in a moment, by his manner, when a young
man was speaking to his father, his superior, or an older man than
himself : to each he used a different sort of marked respect, both in
his gesture and words.

The Moors are very tenacious and jealous of their consequence, but they are not in general addicted to boasting, and cannot bear it in others. The dragomen who were with us took great exceptions at one of their corps, who gave the following extraordinary account of himself. This man, who is not thirty years of age, is a renegado, and took the name of Hammed when he apostatized : he declares he is the Marquis Saint Julian, whose marriage with the daughter of the first minister of Naples was celebrated a few years since in great magnificence. The marquis held a high command in a corps of Neapolitan guards, of which the privates are all persons of distinction. Hammed describes with enthusiasm the personal and mental charms of the lady he married ; but says the passion he had for her blinded him too much to listen to the numerous reports spread through Naples of an illicit correspondence which took place, during his absence from that kingdom, between his wife and the Prince of Calabria. He says he gave no credit to this report, till observing narrowly the Marchioness one day at court, he was convinced she was culpable. Being obliged to remain on duty near the king, he set spies to watch the conduct of his wife, who soon informed him of the Prince's being with the Marchioness at her own house. He immediately went home, when the first person he met in a corridor leading to his wife's apartments, was one of her women with an infant in her arms belonging to her mistress ; an infant, whose birth and existence the Marquis was an entire stranger to. He, in a paroxysm of rage, stabbed the attendant, and the infant falling on the marble floor, instantly expired at his feet. He immediately proceeded to his wife's room, where the Prince of Calabria was attempting to support the Marchioness, who, on hearing the Marquis's voice, had fallen senseless on the sofa. The Prince perceiving the Marquis so near him armed with his sword, stained with the blood of the victim he had just slain, made a spring to the window, and saved himself by jumping from the balcony. The Marquis turned to the sofa, and plunging his sword through his wife's body, left his house and fled. He sailed from Naples ; was taken by a Turkish corsair, and brought a slave to Barbary, where he directly embraced the Mahomedan faith. He is young and handsome, but proud and ferocious, and speaks with a sanguinary exultation of the dreadful revenge he procured himself.

Our admiration of the village marabut, or mosque, near Sahal, gave an offence to the Moors, which had nearly proved more serious than we at the time imagined. Several Moors came up to us on our leaving the marabut ; but when spoken to by the guards, and seeing two persons of such distinction with us, a shreef of Mecca and the son of the first minister, they retired, though evidently much discontented. Several other parties advanced to us, one after the other, and retired in the same manner : we thought little more of this circumstance, and continued our ride. Several hours afterwards, while we were dining under the olive trees at Sahal, some Moors appeared at a distance, apparently from the curiosity they in general have to see Christians. They hailed us with a compliment paid here from inferiors, " *Salum alicum* " (may there be peace between us), and received from our party the appropriate answer to it of " *Alicum salum* " (there is peace between us). Our servants carried to them, as usual, dishes of meat, and the Moors greeted us often in return with the expression of " *Alli bark* " (God prosper you). This cordiality seemed to speak all well. As the number of the Moors increased, we perceived their good-will towards us declined, and from the time we had finished our repast, and prepared to mount our horses, till we nearly reached the town, they followed us murmuring and expostulating with our dragomen ; and it was certainly owing to the rank of our two Moorish friends who were with us, that they did not molest us. As a proof of their hostile intentions, the Governor of Sahal reported this circumstance to the Bashaw yesterday, saying, the Moors would have attacked the Christians if he had not prevented them in time. As we did not know exactly the extent of our danger, we arrived in town satisfied with having spent a very agreeable day.

February 24, 1790

All is again quiet in Tripoli ; but there is very little hope of the place remaining long undisturbed. The Bashaw is very ill ; the Bey is very reserved ; and the two younger princes, who were united in the strictest bonds of friendship together against the Bey, are now at variance with each other. We this morning visited the castle, and, I am sorry to say, the cheerfulness of Lilla Halluma and the princesses seemed more the effort to check melancholy ideas, than the natural result of the heart. These ladies described to us the castle as a scene of anarchy and confusion. Lilla Halluma says, she has not time allowed her to recover between the succession of frightful visions which the present dissentions at the castle raise, regarding the future fate of her three sons. While she was speaking to us, a message being brought that the Bey was coming to his mother's apartment, his brother's (Sidy Hamet's) wife and other ladies retired, and there remained only Lilla Halluma, two of her daughters, and the Bey's wife, besides our party. When the Bey entered the apartment, Lilla Halluma remained nearly unveiled : indeed, from their afflictions, the princesses also attend less than usual to the etiquette of concealing their features from their brother. The anxious inquiring look Lilla Halluma bestowed on the Bey, and the affectionate manner in which he accosted them all, could not fail to be painfully interesting to us, on account of the news we had just heard. The Bey attempted to be cheerful, inquired the reports from Europe, and talked on indifferent subjects ; but he was austere to his attendants, and the deep melancholy impressed on his features bespoke him not at ease. When he departed, his eunuchs, who waited for him in the galleries, seemed to watch his movements with eagerness, and the motion of his lips with terror. Lilla Halluma hid her face in her baracan for some time after the Bey's departure ; but recovering herself, she intreated us to come often and see her, and not stay away on account of troubles at the castle ; saying, she would send the most confidential of her women to acquaint us if there was any thing to prevent our usual visits.

We could not help being much struck with the many suspicious and fearful countenances we passed in leaving the palace, which foreboded no favourable change to calm the fears Lilla Halluma had expressed.

March 10, 1790

An Algerine chaoux, sent from the Dey to the Bashaw, has been here some days. Like most of the Turks and Algerines, he is extremely insolent and troublesome. He had the effrontery to demand of the Bashaw, for his master, a very fine black eunuch, who had been lately presented to him, and who from being extremely handsome, was intended as a present from this court to the Grand Signior. On the Bashaw's refusal, the chaoux made no ceremony of saying among the people, that as the Bashaw would not give him the eunuch for the Dey, he should take him, and he accordingly enticed the black out of the castle, and forced him on board the vessel, which waited to take him back to Algiers. The Bashaw sent directly a message to the Consul to whose nation the ship belonged, requesting it might be detained till he recovered the eunuch. The Consul, of course, sent word to the castle, that the ship should not sail till the Bashaw was satisfied. The chaoux finding an embargo laid upon the vessel, sent his people to the Marine, and had the black brought on shore again.

॥॥

March 20, 1790

We are seldom many days, I am sorry to say, without unpleasant accounts from the castle. A relation of what passed in the palace yesterday afternoon will convey a much clearer idea than I could otherwise give you of genuine Moorish sentiments and manners, and the existing dispositions of the royal family to each other, who were too hastily collected together on this occasion to disguise their real sentiments.

Sidy Hamet had not long parted with the Bashaw and retired to his apartments, at the hour of the afternoon siesta, when one of his officers came in hastily to him saying, " *ye Sidy Uras el Bashaw* " [1] (by the Bashaw's head), " Sidy Useph has ordered a servant of yours to be bastinadoed, for having quarrelled with one of his attendants." Sidy Hamet wishing, if possible, not to notice or resent the liberty his brother had taken, desired they would not disturb him, saying, " he has done well, in saving me the trouble of doing it myself." In a few minutes another message was brought, that Sidy Useph had ordered his blacks to kill the servant wherever they found him, and that they were then searching the castle to find him. There was with Sidy Hamet a Moor, to whom he is particularly attached, called Hadgi Hamet : this Moor is a Gibeleen, or mountaineer, remarkable for his courage and his attachment to the Bashaw's family. Sidy Hamet rose from his couch, called for his arms, and turning to Hadgi Hamet said, " what can this mean ? My brother orders his servants to kill my servant, and will not trust to me for justice. Did you not see, according to my orders, a servant of mine under the baston for having offended one of my brother's blacks two days ago, and did you not take him to my brother to beg his pardon ? " Hadgi Hamet replied, every thing was done as he had ordered. Sidy Hamet then directed Hadgi Hamet to go to Sidy Useph, and tell him he expected him immediately to recall the order he had given to kill one of his servants. The Bashaw, he said, did not take this liberty with any of the princes, but left them to chastise their own domestics ; and that if his servant's life was with justice required, it should not be denied.

---

[1] Literally " Ya Sidi bi ras el Bashaw," an exclamation affirming the truth of what was said.

Hadgi Hamet went, but returned immediately, having been refused admittance to Sidy Useph. Sidy Hamet then desired Hadgi Hamet to arm himself completely, and wait his orders. Nobody in the castle is permitted to wear arms but the people about the Bashaw, even the dragomen when they go with the Christians to the castle, take off their arms on entering it ; therefore Hadgi Hamet concealed his arms under his caftan. Sidy Hamet returned in a few minutes with his knives and two pistols, bidding Hadgi Hamet follow him. They went to Sidy Useph, whom they found armed at the door of his apartments. Sidy Hamet inquired of him why he had given orders to kill his servant, and to what lengths he meant to go ? " Do you begin," said he, " by cutting my servants to pieces, and then mean to end with me ? " Sidy Useph making a short answer, said, " Sidick [1] (the Bashaw) is alive ; he will protect me " ; and immediately turned round, calling to his people, who had already armed themselves, and only waited for his orders to act : for in an instant fifty men rushed out of Sidy Udeph's apartments and set up the scream of war, which according to the Turkish custom always precedes their fights. Sidy Hamet's people, fortunately for him, aware of his danger, had armed themselves without his orders, and in a few moments were collected round him, when he ordered them to be silent, and not to return the scream of war ; but remarked to his brother, that the disagreeable task of assembling his people to arm in his own apartments, he was happy to say, was not a necessary measure for himself to take, and that, asleep or awake, Sidy Useph must not expect to find him unprepared, as every man he had would be with him in time of danger, without being summoned. He then went up close to his brother and said, " Sidy Useph, what shall we get by cutting our servants to pieces here, who are all friends, *wield el bled* (sons of the town) ? We may fill the castle with blood, and frighten the women, but here we shall escape each others' arms ; if we fall, it may be by some of our own people, and our private quarrel will remain unrevenged. Call for your horse, mine is ready, and let us instantly go out in the Pianura, and there settle this dispute between us." Sidy Useph seemed to agree to this proposal, but the Bashaw appeared amongst them at the moment they were preparing to leave the castle. He was summoned to this scene by the voice of Lilla Uducia, the wife of Sidy Hamet, who when that prince left his apartments followed him, tearing her hair and throwing off her ornaments as she accompanied him to the utmost

[1] Literally *Sidik*, " Your lord."

extent of the harem ; and when she saw him quit it, ran to Lilla Halluma's apartments, screaming in despair, that Sidy Hamet was gone out armed to meet his brother. All the attendants and slaves repeated her cries ; and the Bashaw, who was retired to sleep, was awaked by the sounds of *wulliah-woo* (the song of distress), which ran through the castle. He started up, and slinging one of their long knives across him, he took a pistol in each hand, and supported on one side by a black woman, and on the other by a black slave, left his couch and entered the castle-yard in his sleeping apparel, without caftan or turban. The Bashaw is old and infirm, and thinking (as all must do at present on any alarm at the castle) that his sons were destroying each other, he appeared too much affected to be able to stand. Out of respect to his father, Sidy Hamet seeing him approach, dismissed all his people, and ordered them not to appear till he called for them ; whilst Sidy Useph remained opposite his father with his servants, who were still increasing in numbers. One officer alone remained with Sidy Hamet. The Bashaw in his agitation seemed not to notice the hostile appearance of Sidy Useph, and when sufficiently recovered to speak, directed himself only to Sidy Hamet, desiring him to lay down his arms, saying he had one foot out of the grave and the other in, and his beard falling one hair after the other, " yet," said he, " Sidy Hamet, you will not let me enjoy in peace the few last days of my life ! " It was in vain Sidy Hamet observed to the Bashaw, that he had, out of respect to him, dismissed his people, and that he remained with only one officer, while his brother had all his people armed by his side, even in his father's presence, against the rules of the castle. Sidy Hamet said he was there to protect the lives of his people against the orders of Sidy Useph, and requested the Bashaw to order his brother to dismiss his people and lay down his arms first, as he was the aggressor and the youngest ; but the Bashaw again desired Sidy Hamet to disarm the officer that was with him, saying, he being the eldest must set the example. " Twice," said the Bashaw, " I have told you, Sidy Hamet, to disarm ; this is the last time ; do not make this a day of blood for you and for me : I am armed as well as you, and am still Bashaw in this castle. This drawing of knives while I am alive, this calling me from my sedda (or couch) with pistols in your hand, is aiming at my life, and against all the laws of our Prophet." Sidy Hamet replied to his father, " Ye, Sidy, it is that you do not or will not behold my brother surrounded by arms, while you order me to disarm—but you gave me life ; if you chuse that my brother should take it away in your sight, it is enough ; there are my arms, and here are those of my servant."

The Bashaw then called to Sidy Useph, and ordered the brothers to embrace each other. Sidy Hamet and Sidy Useph approached the Bashaw : they each kissed his hand and laid it on their heads, then kissed his head and the hem of his garment, and wished him in the Moorish manner a long life. They were retiring and did not offer to salute each other : the Bashaw seized both their hands in his, and said, " By the Prophet, by my head, by your hands, and by this hand that holds them, there is peace between you." The Bashaw then desired Sidy Useph to go to his apartments, and taking Sidy Hamet by the hand led him to his chamber, where Sidy Hamet's sister, Lilla Howisha, the Rais of the Marine's wife, was anxiously waiting, and whom, of all his sisters, Sidy Hamet is the fondest of. The Bashaw ordered her to go and sit by her brother, and not to leave him till he was calm.

They say at the castle that Sidy Useph is the Bashaw's favourite, and that he takes an advantage of that to usurp more power than belongs to him. This was hinted to the Bashaw by the family during this disturbance, when the Bashaw very angrily expressed himself as follows : " How many wives have I married ? [1] Where is the Greek slave of whom I have made a queen ? Have I given to one jewels, and dressed up her son, and forgot the rest ; or are they not all Lilla Halluma's children ? Is there any other Lilla Kebbiera, or Bashaw's wife, in the castle but herself ? " This disturbance was so serious, that every inhabitant of the castle was called to the scene of confusion, except the Bey, who is hurt at the power the Bashaw permits Sidy Useph to assume, and is with reason suspicious of his brother's intentions towards himself. The Bashaw retired to Lilla Halluma's apartments, accompanied by herself and two of her daughters ; and the silent hours of the siesta not being yet over, the castle resumed its usual stillness, and all appeared tranquil during the remainder of the afternoon.

April 26, 1790

For the last ten or twelve days, we have been living at one of the Bashaw's palaces in the country, which I need not describe, as it is

---

[1] The Bashaw, contrary to the Mahomedan custom, has had but one wife though many favourite blacks, and some Circassian slaves. (T.)

the same where the Consul entertained the officers who brought the ambassador, Hadgi Abderrahman, from England ; and on this account, some of the lower class of Moors in the neighbourhood still mention the circumstance. I informed you in that letter, of a midshipman having been wanting in respect to the Bey, and now and then a Gebeleen, or Mountain Moor, passes us with a severe look, and is heard to wonder at the Bashaw's lenity to the Christians, which indeed is uncommon, and renders the living in this country in that respect very pleasant. It is seldom we meet a Moor, from the highest to the lowest, who is not perfectly anxious to oblige and serve us.

As soon as the Bashaw heard of our dislike to go to any of the Moorish ambassador's country residences, on account of their families having occupied them during the plague, he obligingly offered us one of his palaces, which had remained shut up at the time of the sickness, as none of the royal family left the castle while the plague lasted.

During the violent heats, and before the hot winds set in this season, a party was made and we came here, with three Consuls' families besides our own. Our number, therefore, together with the guards and servants belonging to each family, renders us formidable enough to feel ourselves very secure from common occurrences ; and to outward appearance, the princes have remained tolerably reconciled since the last disturbance at the castle. Nor are we afraid of being molested by Muley Yesied, who is at Fez, and in open rebellion against the Emperor of Morocco. Circular letters were received a few weeks since from the Emperor, to all the Consuls in Barbary, desiring that none of his subjects might be shipped for any place but his dominions, on pain of breaking the peace with him.

The palace we are in is very large ; and every family is perfectly well accommodated with a detached suite of rooms to themselves, all spacious and lofty. We breakfast apart, but ride and walk in the morning, and dine all together, and do not separate till the evening.

The Bashaw's chiosk, or Belvidere, which I have not before mentioned to you, is carried up a considerable height above the top of the palace. It is built in a square form, with windows round it ; and the walls and every part is lined with the finest and most beautiful tiles peculiar to the Persian manufactory, of which no seam or joints are visible, and which represents pleasing landscapes. Under a burning atmosphere, the comforts of this chiosk are not to be described : it forms a cool, clean, and pleasant retreat, which renders it a delightful shelter from heat, insects, and sand. From its height, it commands a view of the country round. On one side, the summits of the dark blue mountains at Gerrain are distinctly seen from the windows ; on the other side, the deserts beginning from the Bashaw's garden wall bound the horizon. In this vast space, no other objects are seen but two great marabuts, or mosques, whither most of the criminals of Tripoli fly as a sanctuary ; and a few shrubs at great distances appear like small black specks in the sand. Hence with glasses we have seen the caravan at so great a distance, that it appeared at first sight, on these sun bleached deserts, like a crooked line from the stroke of a pencil.

⛭

May 12, 1790

We are still at the Bashaw's palace in the country : the three princes are often out to take the diversion of riding on the sands ; but the Bey visits us more frequently than either of his brothers. He came to see us to-day and had nearly two hundred mounted guards with him. Most of the horses belonging to the chief persons had as usual their harness studded with gold and silver, and were covered with housings of costly embroidery ; the customary number of relay horses for the Bey, richly caparisoned, were led by the blacks. The Consuls went to receive the Bey as soon as he dismounted. When he entered the apartment, he was conducted to a sopha, and the Christians were seated in chairs round him : his sword-bearer, treasurer, and other officers of state, and his two favourite mamelukes remained standing. The Bey partook of the refreshments offered him, and appeared in much better spirits than usual.

In the course of conversation, he expressed a wish that his youngest brother, Sidy Useph, was older, as he did not doubt but that a few years would correct his fiery temper (he being now about seventeen). He said, " though my brother is so mad now, he will be, if he lives a few years longer, a great man." The looks of some of his officers expressed their great regret at the Bey's thinking so mildly of Sidy Useph, whom they suspect of harbouring the worst intentions towards his brother.

Sidy Useph's courteous manner to his brothers, and the high favour he at present enjoys with the Bashaw, is the talk of every one. No one else gives credit to Sidy Useph's professions ; but the Bashaw places implicit confidence in all he says. The Bashaw a few days ago observed to his courtiers that Sidy Useph never speaks to him against his brothers, while he is continually hearing of Sidy Useph's offences from the Bey and Sidy Hamet; but, from Sidy Useph's conduct, most people think that it is only to gain favour with the Bashaw, and by that means to augment his own power.

The Bey's dress to-day was lighter than usual, on account of the extreme heat. The Bey's mamelukes were more shewy than any other persons in his train : besides the lustre of their arms, their habits were covered with gold and silver, and fitted close to their bodies. They wore no turbans, but had in general black and gold shawls wound tight round a scarlet cap, and one end of the shawl, entirely of gold, hung low over the left shoulder

When they left the palace, as a compliment to the Christians, the Bey and his suite raced with their usual swiftness for some time before they departed.

Sidy Hamet went out to the sands yesterday with his people, without either of his brothers (it being now the fast of Ramadan, the princes ride daily) : he called on us as he returned from the sands, and rested for a long time. Only one of his officers accompanied him into the room, and the rest remained in the garden. Sidy Hamet acknowledges that Sidy Useph's power increases, as well as that of every body under him; but his expression was, "the Bashaw lives, and while he lives we are to consider ourselves safe." The Bey (he says) cannot attempt to increase his own forces without an appearance of rebellion; and Sidy Useph's manners are extremely changed, not merely to the Bey, but his conduct in the castle does not leave any reason for complaint. He concluded by saying, "with the Prophet all things are possible, he may have changed Sidy Useph's heart." The ideas of the chief officers of state are, that the family are all of them afraid of each other; and they express the most dismal forebodings on the occasion. They say, the long and quiet reign of the Bashaw, for upwards of thirty years, has rendered the people so peaceable and so attached to the whole of the royal family, that no treasonable plots against any parts of it can be dreaded from them; and that if the princes are determined to act unfairly against each other, or against their father, they must call in the assistance of the Arabs, for they say, the "Wield el Bled" (sons of the town) will not assist them.

Sidy Useph has lately married a young lady of Turkish extraction. Her mother is extremely sensible, and remarked by the whole country for her honourable principles; but she is proud, ambitious, and fond of meddling in politics. It is feared, therefore, by many, from the great influence she has already gained over Sidy Useph, that she may rather increase than diminish the violence of his measures. Neither Sidy Useph's bride, nor her mother, are in the confidence of Lilla Halluma or the princesses, who are afraid of both of them, and speak to them with the greatest caution and reserve.

Sidy Hamet speaks in the highest terms of the fidelity of his own people. He says, though they are few, they are all attached to him, and as he has nothing to ask of them that is forbidden by the Koran, he has a right to expect their support. On the other hand, it is not uncommon, when the Moors speak of Sidy Hamet, and declare their apprehensions of his danger, to see a tear accompany their professions of loyalty.

June 1, 1790

We have had for some days a dreadful heat in the atmosphere, which no description can give an idea of to those who have not been in this climate. During the excess of it, after we had been for some hours watching the slow progress of a caravan over the sands, we were shocked at the horrible state it arrived in. For want of water many had died, and others were in so languishing a state, as to expire before any could be administered to save them from the parching thirst occasioned by the heat. The state of the animals was truly shocking ; gasping and faint, they could hardly be made to crawl to their several destinations, many dying on their way. This destructive heat lasted seven days, since which the weather has become as pleasant as it was then horrible.

We have just returned from a long ride, during which we passed a place called the Acas, from a tribe of Arabs of that name who inhabit it, and who have all the Bashaw's sheep and cattle confided to their care and management. At this place, a chaoux always meets the Bey when he arrives from the camp, and presents him with a new caftan, as a compliment from the Bashaw, at an ancient castle, where the Bey goes through the ceremony of receiving it and putting it on, and then makes a considerable present to the chaoux in return.

The castle is still very strong, and was once formidable to the Moors themselves when in possession of their enemies, at the time the Emperor Charles the Fifth gave Tripoli to the Knights of Rhodes, after their expulsion from the Island of Rhodes by the Turks, in 1522.[1] From 1311, when this order, under the name of the Knights of St. John of Jerusalem, became a military order, fifty-one years after they had opened a house in Jerusalem for the reception of pilgrims, their name did not lose its terror in this part of the world. A period of more than four hundred years had not obliterated the horrors of the crusades ; and the Moors beheld, with terror and dismay, the Maltese gallies commanded by the successors of the Knights of Jerusalem, continually committing ravages round their coast. During these depredations, while the Knights of Rhodes were settled in the town of Tripoli, a celebrated Moorish corsair, not being able to land on the coast and relieve his countrymen, on account of the Maltese being in possession of the above-mentioned castle, he determined to take or destroy it. For this purpose he brought his gallies to that part of the coast opposite the castle, which stands a great way inland. In the night he caused the gallies to be dragged on shore, and brought by their crews as far over land as they could, where he made them serve as a fortification from which to fire on the Maltese, and from thence he mined the rock to the castle. This dislodged the Maltese without blowing it up, when the corsair entered, and gained still greater advantage from possessing it in a perfect state. This man's extraordinary ideas of bringing his gallies over land, and his great success, gained such credit in those days, that the Maltese gave him the name of *Chasse Diable*, and the Moors that of *Rais Draieco*, or dragon captain. The ground at a great distance from this castle sounds frightfully hollow under the horses' feet. The Moors say in some parts it is mined almost to the surface. Rais Draieco was at this time made Cyde of Tajoura.

June 2, 1790

To our very great surprise, the Bey, Sidy Hamet, and Sidy Useph rode on the sands together to-day. The Bey's people were nearly double the number he has in general with him, while Sidy Hamet and Sidy Useph's attendants were not near so numerous as usual.

The Bey's friends are much alarmed for his safety, and are very sorry to see him so reconciled to Sidy Useph. When they wish to caution him, the Bey's language is : that Sidy Useph has no power

---

[1] According to Feraud, the historian, the date was 1530.

to injure him, as he can bring in no Arabs without his father's leave ; and as the Bashaw's life is expected to terminate daily, he will not have it on his conscience to shorten its duration. The people, he says, know and acknowledge the throne to be his ; therefore, while his brothers do not openly molest him, it is time enough when the Bashaw's life is ended to set limits to their power and possessions ; "and then," continued he, "unless they aim at the throne, they will have every reason to be satisfied with what I shall do for them."

The Bey depends on the vigilance of his people to guard his person from treachery ; and it is impossible for them to give greater proofs of attachment to him, or to be more on the alert than they are. Those who are not at the palace with the Bey, keep watch at night in their own houses, in case of the least alarm at the castle, and this they do without any orders from their prince.

The Bashaw is going to send out a force to settle some accounts with the Arabs ; and yesterday one of the famous marabuts went to the castle to pray for the Bashaw, as they do sometimes on public occasions, when every body present prays with him. This man, in his prayers, conveyed political advice to the Bashaw (a liberty these holy men sometimes take) ; saying, if a force was sent out to the Arabs, at present, it would ruin the country, as all the Bashaw's troops were wanted at home ; that the Bashaw must not think of sending Sidy Useph on any account ; if he did, he would repent it when it was too late. The Bashaw advised the marabut not to open his mouth again upon that subject, and scolded the saint very much. Mustapha Scrivan, the Bashaw's first minister, whispered to the sovereign, endeavouring to soften the matter, by saying it was not proper to speak to this marabut so severely in public, he being one of their greatest saints ; but the Bashaw told the Scrivan, that if he heard the marabut say another word on that head, both the marabut and himself should repent it. This silenced them ; and the marabut, in solemn prayers, finished his oration, without touching on political subjects.

We are preparing to return to town, owing to an unpleasant and alarming affair. The princes have been out with their people on the sands almost every day since we have been here ; sometimes all three together ; sometimes two ; and often only one of them. Some days ago, the Bey and Sidy Useph rode out in company. The Bey, as usual, had the whole of his people with him, and Sidy Useph very few of his. When they returned, Sidy Useph stopped at his own garden, close to where we reside : when the Bey had left the sands, we heard the report of a pistol from Sidy Useph's garden, and in the same instant an exclamation that the Bey was shot. Our being at the Bashaw's palace increased our alarm, from the circumstance of not being able to shut the gates against Sidy Useph, with the Moors and Arabs, who would have joined him and rushed in with him. The person who had fired at the Bey from Sidy Useph's garden could not be found amongst the crowd. The Bey's suite were enraged against Sidy Useph : they said, as there were but two parties out, the wretch who had aimed at the Bey's life could only be a creature of Sidy Useph's. The Bey, incensed and persuaded by his people, proceeded to his brother's garden, but seeing Sidy Useph waiting to receive him with the greatest appearance of cordiality, he turned to his own officers, and said to one of them who was near him : " his blood shall not be upon my head ; this ball may have been fired by some one unknown to him, out of a blind zeal to serve his cause ; if he refuse to go with me to the altars of our Prophet and take the oaths for our mutual protection, he will be then our acknowledged enemy, and if he must fall, let him fall by open vengeance, not by treachery." When Sidy Useph saw the Bey enter his garden, he came forward to meet him, and ordered his servants to search for the offender, whether amongst his people or the Bey's. He readily agreed to go to the marabut and swear at the altar, and gave no reason to suspect that he was privy to this diabolical act. Many days have passed since this event, but the Bey and Sidy Useph have not yet been to the marabut to confirm their oaths.

⚇

June 12, 1790

Sidy Useph is gone out to his cyderies, or government, and is expected back in a few weeks. Every thing has been perfectly quiet since his departure ; but we shall set off for town in a few days, as it is thought too dangerous to remain here on Sidy Useph's return.

⚇

August 2, 1790

It is some time since we returned to town from the Bashaw's palace in the country, whence my last letter to you was dated. At our return all was calm and quiet. The Bashaw, the Bey, and Sidy Hamet went to the marabut's together ; and, during our late visits to the castle, we have found Lilla Halluma and the princesses happy, in comparison to what they were when we left town. There was only a little anxiety apparent to know how Sidy Useph was engaged whilst out of Tripoli ; but that no person in or out of Tripoli could divine. It was thought by the family that Sidy Useph went out only to gather his tributes from his cyderies ; but it was suspected by many that he was going about to the chiefs of the Arabs to engage them in his interest against his father and the Bey. After his return, he remained at the Bashaw's garden in the Messeah, and at the palace at which we were, whence he went at different times, apparently in the most amicable manner, to visit the rest of the Royal Family at the castle ; and no one suspected the scene he meant so soon to bring forward. Sidy Useph's success in a plot so diabolically laid against the Bey, is amongst those wonders which cannot be accounted for. Tired of waiting longer for the annihilation of the Bey, he came to town, more determined and better prepared to complete the dreadful act than he had been before. He brought with him his chosen blacks whom he had well instructed. The moment he entered the castle, he proceeded to his mother Lilla Halluma's apartments, to whom he declared his fixed intention of " making peace " with his eldest brother, and entreated her to forward his wishes by sending for the Bey to complete their reconciliation in her presence. Lilla Halluma transported with the idea of seeing her sons again united, as she flattered herself, in the bonds of friendship, sent instantly to the Bey, who was in Lilla Aisher's (his wife) apartment, a confidential message informing him that his brother Sidy Useph was with her without arms and waiting to make peace with him ; that she would herself join their hands together ; and that, by the Bashaw's head, the Bey, if he loved her, would come to her directly unarmed. The Bey, actuated by the first impulse, armed himself with his pistols and sabre, to obey the summons.

Lilla Aisher knowing the impartial tenderness of Lilla Halluma for all her children, was sure no open danger could threaten his life : her only apprehensions were from secret plots, but this the Bey would never listen to. At the present moment, Lilla Aisher trembled for fear a report of the Bey's passing through the harem, to Lilla Halluma, with so hostile an appearance, so contrary to the rules of it, might give a pretext for the Bey's being treacherously assaulted by Sidy Useph's people ; she, therefore, observed to him, that as he was going to his mother's apartments, where it was at all times sacrilege (according to the laws of Mahomet) to carry arms, his going there armed, after the message Lilla Halluma had sent him, would seem as if he meant to assassinate his brother, and thereby draw the vengeance of the castle upon him. The Bey, after hesitating a moment, unarmed himself, embraced Lilla Aisher, and was departing, when she threw herself at his feet, and, presenting him his sabre, entreated him not, however, to depart wholly defenceless ; and she would not let him go till he had yielded to her supplications. When the Bey came to his mother's room, she, perceiving his sabre, begged of him (assuring him his brother had no arms) to lay it aside before they entered into conversation. The Bey, to whom there could not appear the smallest reason for suspicion, willingly delivered his sabre to his mother, who placed it upon a window near which they stood ; and she, feeling convinced of the integrity of the Bey's intentions, and being completely deceived in those of Sidy Useph, led the two princes to the sofa, and seating herself between them, held a hand of each in her's ; and, as she afterwards declared to us, " looking at them alternately, she prided herself on having thus at last brought them together to make peace at her side."

The Bey, as soon as they were seated, endeavoured to convince his brother that, though he came to go through the ceremony of making peace, yet there was not the least occasion for it on his part ; for that, as he had no longer sons of his own, he considered Sidy Useph and his brother as such, and would always treat them as a father whenever he succeeded to the throne. Sidy Useph declared himself satisfied, but observed, that, to make Lilla Halluma completely happy, there could be no objection, after such professions of friendship from the Bey, to seal their peace with sacred oaths upon the Koran. The Bey replied, " with all his heart " ; that " he was ready " —upon which Sidy Useph rose quickly from his seat, and called loudly for the Koran—the word he had given to his eunuchs for his pistols, two of which were brought and put into his hands ; when he instantly discharged one of them at his brother, seated by his mother's side. The pistol burst, and Lilla Halluma extending her hand to save the Bey, had her fingers shattered by the splinters of it. The ball entered the Bey in the side : he arose, however, and seizing his sabre from the window made a stroke at his brother, but only wounded him slightly in the face ; upon which Sidy Useph discharged the second pistol, and shot the Bey through the body.[1]

[1] This account of Miss Tully's is used in all subsequent records of the period.

What added to the affliction of Lilla Halluma at this tragical event, was, that the Bey, erroneously supposing that she had betrayed him, exclaimed after being wounded, "Ah ! Madam, is this the last present you have reserved for your eldest son ? " From her favourite son, what must these words have produced in the breast of the mother ! Sidy Useph, upon seeing his brother fall, instantly called to his blacks, saying, " There lies the Bey—finish him ! " In a moment they dragged him from the spot where he was yet breathing, and discharged their pieces into him.[1] Lilla Aisher hearing the sudden dreadful sound, broke from her women who endeavoured to keep her from the sight, and springing into the room, clasped her bleeding husband in her arms ; while Lilla Halluma, in endeavouring to prevent Sidy Useph from disfiguring the body, fainted over it from agony of mind. Five of Sidy Useph's blacks were at the same moment stabbing it as it lay on the floor ; after which miserable triumph of their master, they fled with him.

This wanton barbarity, in thus mangling the Bey's remains, produced the most distressing spectacle. Lilla Aisher, at this sight of horror, stripped off all her jewels and rich apparel, and throwing them into the Bey's blood, took from the blacks the worst baracan amongst them, making that serve for her whole covering. Thus habiting herself as a common slave, and ordering those around her to cover her with ashes, she went in that state directly to the Bashaw, and said to him, " that, if he did not wish to see her poison herself and her children, he must give immediate orders that she might quit the castle, for that she would not live to look on the walls of it, nor to walk over the stones that could no longer be seen for the Bey's blood with which they were covered."

As Sidy Useph left the castle he met Bey Abdallah, the great chiah,[2] a venerable officer, the first in power, and beloved by the people. This officer, seeing the dreadful state in which Sidy Useph was, expressed his fear that something fatal had happened. Bey Abdallah was known to be particularly attached to the Bashaw's family ; and, from his religious principles, could not be supposed to approve of this day's deeds. The moment, therefore, Sidy Useph saw him, he stabbed him to the heart, and the chiah instantly expired. Sidy Useph's blacks, who were following him, threw the body into the

---

[1] The Bey had eleven balls in him when he died ; one in his head, three in his left arm, and seven in his side. (T.)

[2] No doubt seated at his usual post in the *saqifa*, or entrance hall of the castle.

street, before the castle gate, and the hampers (the Bashaw's guards), who were standing by, conveyed it to his unhappy family. It was buried at the same hour with the Bey. Sidy Useph had been three times into town to perpetrate this dreadful deed. The last time, he came at an hour he expected to find the Bey unarmed and alone ; but meeting him, on the contrary, armed and surrounded with his people, he kissed his hand ; and, after paying him the usual compliments, returned disappointed to his residence at the Bashaw's garden. On the 20th of last month he, however, accomplished the act, and nothing could then equal the confusion of this place. The people hurried in distressed groups through the streets, with their families and cattle, endeavouring to reach the city gates and quit the town, not knowing where the scene of havoc at the castle would end ; and numbers crowded into our house besides those who had a right to shelter there from being under the protection of the flag. One of our dragomen met Sidy Useph with his trowsers and bernuse stained with blood. He was followed close by his blacks, and riding full speed from the castle through the city gate, dreading at the moment the vengeance of the people. Various were the reports of the Bey's existence for several hours. When the people were certain of his death, they began to arm, and passed through the streets in great numbers ; the Arabs and Gibeleens with their long guns and knives, and the Moors with their pistols and sabres, making to the inhabitants a most terrific appearance ; each dreading to meet an enemy in his neighbour, and not knowing what party he was of.

The general alarm in town made it necessary to shut the consular houses. Ours had been closed but a few minutes, when two of the Bey's officers hurried in despair to the door, and intreated us to let them in ; expecting, as they said, to be massacred every moment by those attached to Sidy Useph, for being the favourites of their late master. One of them was Sidy Hasseen, the nephew of the ambassador, Hadgi Abderrahman, whom you have seen in England. His feelings for the fate of the Bey were so acute, that he would have sunk on the floor had not our people supported him. In a moment after he entered our house, the Bey's funeral passed, and Hasseen instantly rose to join the procession, determined (as he said) to pay the last attention in his power to the Bey's remains, by supporting his coffin ; though he thought it so hazardous, that he had not the least expectation of reaching the grave alive. He called to the other officer to accompany him ; but he declined it, saying it was only sacrificing their lives to no purpose ; and Hasseen went by himself.

The Bey was buried at three o'clock in the afternoon—the short space of little more than four hours had witnessed the Bey in the bloom of health—in the midst of his family—murdered—and buried !

The colours at the consular houses were hoisted half-mast high, as soon as the Bey's death was announced ; and all the ships that were in the harbour fired minute guns till he was interred, when the colours were hoisted up and the ships fired a salute of twenty-one guns.

The Bey's widow freed every slave that followed his remains ; but the people were so panic-struck, that the Moors of the highest rank seemed afraid to follow the body ; and few accompanied it besides those who were ordered by the Bashaw to do so.

So little judgment could be formed of the Bashaw's state of mind at this critical moment, that the shaik could not act in any way without sending first to the castle for orders, and waiting to hear from the Bashaw until he thought the town unsafe. Such was the agitation and dread the whole mass of people were in.

As soon as the Bey was interred, chaouxes went through the town, proclaiming an order from the Bashaw for every one to be silent, not to assemble in the streets on pain of his displeasure, and to fear nothing. The chaouxes' words were, " To the Bey who is gone, God give a happy resurrection " ; and " none of his late servants shall be molested or hurt." But to the surprise of every one, with this order no Bey was proclaimed, which was unprecedented ; as, at the moment a Bashaw or Bey expires, his successor is expected to be announced.

Sidy Hamet was from Tripoli when this shocking catastrophe happened ; but was in town before night, and brought with him from Mesuratta [1] a chief of the Arabs (Shaik Alieff), and several hundreds of his people. They were encamped round the town during the night. Before Sidy Hamet reached town, however, the Bashaw had sent one of his confidential officers to Sidy Useph, desiring him to come to the castle. On word being brought that he was afraid, the Bashaw sent him his beads,[2] to serve as a pledge for his safety. But even with this safeguard, Sidy Useph would not trust himself within the town.

[1] At Mesuratta, Sidy Useph has been rejected as Cyde very lately, on account of his extortions and persecutions the last time he was sent there by the Bashaw. (T.)

[2] The beads by which the Bashaw says his prayers are considered so strong a talisman in the hands of the greatest criminal, that they render his life sacred while they are in his possession. (T.)

When Sidy Hamet arrived with his Arabs, he went immediately to the Bashaw, who was so much alarmed at seeing him come into his presence armed, that he expressed his displeasure at it; but Sidy Hamet observed that he had that moment seen the officers whom the Bashaw had sent with his beads, to render the person of Sidy Useph sacred, after he had *cut the Bey in pieces!* " This then," said he, " is a moment when no person or action can be understood : every way is dark and uncertain, and therefore requires a strong guard, for fear of stumbling."

Sidy Hamet retired to his apartment, where, fatigued with travelling and overcome with agitation, he fainted upon the sofa. This accident happening so soon after his arrival at the castle, gave rise to a report that he had been poisoned, and threw the town again into confusion for some hours during the evening.

Were I not writing from a country where the ideas and manners are so totally different from those you are accustomed to, I should almost fear that you could not credit the following account of Sidy Useph's conduct. The grave was scarcely closed over the brother he had mutilated, when he sent to town for Jews and a turbuka,[1] to make a feast at the Bashaw's garden, where he was. The sounds of music, firing, and women hired to sing and dance, were louder than at the feast of a wedding. This was soon known at the castle, when, during the atrocious circumstance, the Bashaw retired, giving orders for no one to approach him, till he called for them. From one of our rooms, which commands a view of a covered gallery leading to the Bashaw's apartments, we saw him seated, in deepest thought, alone !

Sidy Useph, during the above feast, sent word to Lilla Howia, widow of the murdered Chiah (whose garden is not far from that of the Bashaw), that if he heard her women scream for Bey Abdallah's death, he would have her instantly strangled. She therefore came to town, and performed the obsequies for her departed husband's remains, in company with the Bey's widow, at the castle.

At the time the Bashaw sent out his beads to Sidy Useph, he ordered his garden to be guarded by the four Shieks of the Messeah, to protect Sidy Useph from the rage of the people, who he thought might be inclined to resent the Bey's death.

The Consuls kept additional guard on their houses, and the streets were more strictly watched than usual during the night.

[1] A sort of drum. (T.)

The day following the Bey's murder, Sidy Hamet (now Bey) went with two hundred horsemen to the Bashaw's garden, to have an interview with Sidy Useph, who had by this time extended his guards to the end of every street that led to the Bashaw's palace, at the gates of which he sat. His people stood in double line round him, under arms, and the wretched blacks, who helped him to assassinate the Bey, stood close at his side, not only armed, but with their blunderbusses pointed. A long time was spent in messages sent backwards and forwards, before the brothers met. It was at last agreed that Sidy Useph should send all his people out of the garden, and that Sidy Hamet should enter it without his horsemen. They then had a long conversation, during which, each of the princes stood in the midst of a few of their chief officers, who formed a circle round them the whole of the time they were together.

After the Bey's death, Sidy Hamet, and every body in the place, in vain expected, from hour to hour, to hear him proclaimed Bey. Sidy Hamet was however silent : he could not have borne to hear the festive song, and the nubar sounding, whilst the Bey's widow, and every one in the castle, were performing the obsequies and the *death song* for the loss of the Bey ; but when the time was expired that was allotted for an act that could not be dispensed with, Sidy Hamet applied to the Bashaw, to order the ceremony of proclaiming him Bey. The Bashaw gave his consent ; but on condition that *Sidy Useph would likewise give his !* Sidy Hamet, at this unexpected answer from the Bashaw, retired to his golphor for some hours, and his people could not persuade him to give up the strange resolution he had formed, of going, accompanied by a few attendants, to know Sidy Useph's sentiments. He entered the Bashaw's garden, where Sidy Useph was (with three hundred men under arms) with only four of his officers, and told his brother that the Bashaw had consented to his being proclaimed Bey, but that if Sidy Useph, though the youngest and having no right to it, wished for the title, that he (Sidy Hamet) would cede it to him, without further bloodshed, and would swear by all the oaths directed by their Prophet never to molest him. Sidy Useph protested by the Bashaw's head, that he had killed the Bey only because he had quarrelled with him, and not because he wished to succeed him ; that he was ready to acknowledge Sidy Hamet as Bey ; and that he disclaimed, on his part, all pretensions to the throne.

After this extraordinary interview, Sidy Hamet returned to town, and received from the Bashaw, a new caftan,[1] and the late Bey's horses, slaves, arms, etc., etc., and was proclaimed Bey on the 29th July. The castle guns were fired, the nubar played, and the Moorish colours and those of all the nations here were hoisted, and all the Consuls went to the castle to compliment him on the occasion.

Before a week had elapsed after the Bey was murdered, his disconsolate widow was delivered of an infant, which, from its being a boy, was a renewal of affliction to its mother ; for having no son living at the time of his death, she could not help reflecting on the joy the Bey would have expressed at her presenting him with an heir, and the cannon that would have announced through the kingdom the birth of her infant, formed in her distressed mind, too cruel a contrast to the mournful silence of the present moment. It hurt us extremely, when the messengers from the castle brought us the news, and added that they wanted no *buona mano* [2] but were sent by their Lilla, only because she thought we should be anxious for her safety.

The state of the town and of the castle is at present so precarious, that it has precluded the possibility of our seeing the family since the Bey's death. The series of tragical and extraordinary events during the last eight days, have made my letter longer than I intended ; but as there is no prospect of our quitting this place for the present, and as these events are much connected with what I may have to write to you hereafter, I have determined to send you a full account of them as they pass.

August 30, 1790

Sidy Hamet has been out again to visit, at the Bashaw's garden, Sidy Useph, who still keeps a great number of men under arms. Sidy Hamet went to advise him to send the blacks who assisted in the murder of his brother to the great marabut,[3] merely to content the people,

---

[1] A caftan, among the Turks and Moors, is a mark of royal favour bestowed by the sovereign on many different occasions. The Grand Signior sends one to the different courts of Tripoli, Tunis, and Algiers, on the birth of his son, which great presents are returned. (T.)

[2] It is customary at the birth of the Bey's sons, particularly of the heir to the throne, as in the above case, to give a present of money to those who bring the news, which is called a *buona mano*, and some handsome article of dress is presented to the mother of the prince from each of the Consuls. (T.)

[3] Where criminals go for protection, or to screen themselves from justice. (T.)

who were not only enraged with them on account of the unfortunate Bey, but on account of their forcing their way into the Harem, which is considered as a violence that every Moor ought to resent, as they cannot reckon their women safe while such an outrage is suffered to go unnoticed.

Sidy Useph, however, seems to act entirely independent of the Bashaw and the Bey. He has ordered his people to massacre the late Bey's servants wherever they meet with them, and has sent to the Bashaw to desire that an officer, named Bourga, might be ordered to surrender up some beautiful arms the late Bey had given him, which was done. Sidy Useph then went to the garden of Sidy Bourga's ukiel,[1] or steward, and took away some fine horses which were likewise a present from the Bey. The Bashaw, in consequence of these liberties taken by Sidy Useph, has ordered him not to come to the castle armed ; but notwithstanding this order, when Sidy Useph came into town, a few days since, to congratulate Sidy Hamet on being proclaimed Bey, he brought with him two hundred men under arms : they remained, however, outside of the castle, where they were very near murdering a Mameluke belonging to the Bashaw, who had fired his piece unintentionally. He would not have escaped but for the friendly hand of a common Moor who stood by him, and threw a black baracan over him, by which means he saved himself.

The place the unfortunate Bey Abdallah held of Great Chiah is now filled by Hadgi Murat, the husband of the eldest princess, who refused taking it, unless the cyderia, or government of Sahal, which he had, was given to his son : this was done, but no sooner had the nuba played [2] and the guns fired for his promotion, than the cyderia was taken from his son, and a favourite of Sidy Useph's, Ali Napolitan, a renegado, made cyde of Sahal. As the chiahship of Tripoli is honorary and produces no emolument, Hadgi Murat had reckoned on supporting the dignity of his family with the cyderia of Sahal. He consequently attempted to shoot himself in the presence of the Bashaw, who had been induced from the danger of the times thus to deceive him and distress the family of his own child. The Bashaw considered Hadgi Murat the only safe person to trust with the important post of

[1] Literally *wakil*.
[2] The nuba, or royal band, is allowed to be played at the creation of a Bey, a Chiah, and a Rais of the marine, governor of the port, otherwise it plays only for the Bashaw. None of the sons have a nuba but the Bey, and that only when he goes out to the camp. (T.)

Great Chiah ; but he could not refuse Sidy Useph the cyderia of Sahal for his favourite renegado.

Sidy Useph is still so much on his guard and so alarmed, that besides his people watching close by him under arms while he sleeps during any part of the day, the garden of the palace where he is kept shut, and no one can get in or out without application to himself.

When Sidy Useph went last to the castle, the Bashaw desired Sidy Hamet, though Bey, to go to the skiffer and meet him : a compliment not paid from the Bey even to the princes of Morocco, when they come here. Another message was sent to Lilla Halluma to meet Sidy Useph in her apartment, and to receive him without signs of grief or mourning. The same orders were sent to all the princesses and their children, the Bey's widow only excepted.

Sidy Useph has in his suite a person of a very bad character, a famous or rather infamous marabut, of the name of Fatasie, who to command more homage calls himself a Fatamite.[1] It is now said this wretch instigated Sidy Useph to the murder of the Bey.[2]

🕮

September, 1790

Sidy Useph still keeps away from the town, notwithstanding the Bashaw sends him repeated messages to come and reside in the castle. The Bashaw is very uneasy at his remaining out of it, and at his making so many excursions to the Arabs.

Sidy Useph, at present pays frequent visits to the castle, but always leaves his soldiers without the city gates : his wife and family continue to live out of town.

Since the Bey's death, Sidy Useph's disposition develops more and more, and he is as whimsical as he is arbitrary : of this he gave a proof in the following instance a few days ago. The Bashaw had a full grown lion and two very large tigers brought from Algiers, for presents to the Grand Signior. They were confined in separate large cages, strongly made of wood and iron. Sidy Useph sent to desire that the Maltese slaves (almost all invalided old men) might be made to carry each cage out to him at the Bashaw's garden on their shoulders.

---

[1] A dynasty of *Khalifahs* who ruled in Egypt and North Africa from A.D. 908 to A.D. 1171. They took their name from their founder, Abu Mohammed Obeidallah, who alleged he was descended from Fatimah, the Prophet's daughter.

[2] Feraud believes that the Bashaw himself was privy to the murder of his eldest son. (*Annales Tripolitaines.*)

This was done at the serious risk of those who carried the animals, to save Sidy Useph a short ride into town.

October 18, 1790

Since my last, Sidy Useph has continued his visits frequently to the castle. Previous to the Bey and Sidy Useph being at variance, and long before the late Bey's death, they took the sacred oaths of allegiance to each other at the shrines of their saints ; and they went together a short time since to renew and confirm their oaths in a still stronger manner, by performing the last ceremony resorted to in this country of, what they term, the mixing of blood. To accomplish this barbarous idea, they approached together the altar of Mahomet, and after swearing by the Koran each to hold the other's life sacred, they wounded themselves with their knives, and mixing their blood in a vessel, shocking to relate, they both sipped of it.

The procession for this purpose was extremely grand : the princes were attended by every chief officer and person of consequence in Tripoli.

The whole corps of chaouxes preceded the Bey, and loudly proclaimed him as they went through the town, as is usual in all public processions of either the Bashaw or Bey.

The princes after going to the marabuts continued together, and went out of town to spend the day in company at Sidy Useph's garden. Sidy Useph was attended by four hundred horsemen, and besides his own chief officers, most of those belonging to the Bashaw followed him.

When the princes arrived at the garden, Sidy Useph brought his son, an infant, to Sidy Hamet, saying, " you see I trust you with my boy ; his infancy makes it impossible for him to resent any thing that is done to him ; take him for an hostage ; and I ask in return not for your son, but only for your daughter, to divert and keep my wife company." Sidy Hamet's daughter is a sweet little girl about five years old : he would not consent to her remaining many days at Sidy Useph's garden, but he agreed to her sleeping there that night. Besides the officers appointed to attend her, two of the people Sidy Hamet has the greatest confidence in, the selectar's[1] brother and another Moor, had private charge of the princess, till she was brought back to the castle the next day.

[1] Selectar : the sword bearer ; a Turkish title.

The Bashaw's family remained in friendly intercourse with Sidy Useph's for several weeks, till he declared his intentions of going to his cyderies at Mezurata, after the Mezurateens had sent repeated messages to Sidy Hamet, as Bey, to say that they would not receive his brother on any terms, on account of the outrages committed by his people the last time he was there, but would accept cheerfully of any other governor he might chuse to send.

After several debates in the castle, the Bey refused his consent to his brother's going to Mezurata. Sidy Useph then proposed to send his people to treat with them. This was acceded to ; but it was discovered that they had orders to fall on the Mezurateens and cut them to pieces if possible. The Bey seeing the danger of this step, as the Mezurateens might persuade the neighbouring Arabs to revenge such an act of injustice on the Bashaw, used his exertions again, and prevented the slaughter of the Mezurateens, and probably the loss of his throne.

Not long after this, Sidy Useph gained the Bashaw's consent for the Bey and himself to be sent out with a strong force, aided by the Arabs in the Bashaw's pay, against the Mezurateens. Sidy Hamet refused to go ; and Shaik Saffanassa, one of the most powerful of the Arab tribes, sent a message to the Bashaw that he would not see the Mezurateens ill treated, and if he sent a force against them, he would attack the princes and would bring the pretender, Mustapha, from Tunis (whose history I have before given you), or one of the Beys from Egypt, to take the throne.

Sidy Useph still persisting in his determination of going in person to his cyderia at Mezurata, and the Bashaw being equally desirous he should go, the Mezurateens sent one of their chief people to the Bey to say they would not see the man again who had taken away their property, had suffered his people to abuse their wives, sisters, and daughters, and had murdered his brother ; but that they would open their gates, by day or night, to himself, and if he chose to bring Sidy Useph to them, they should know what to do with him. The Mezurateens concluded by saying, that if the Bey would accede to their proposals, they would call in sufficient Arabs, and bring him safely back and set him on the throne of Tripoli. Treachery is certainly not a part of Sidy Hamet's character ; he has not yet shewn it in any one instance ; he did not, therefore, accept of the easy means presented to him by the Mezurateens of mounting the throne by shedding the blood of his relatives.

The Bashaw became enraged at the prince's not going out as he ordered ; and having sent several severe messages to the Bey, the Bey at length sent for the Caitibe (the first minister), and desired him to go to the Bashaw and tell him, he was resolved not to accompany his brother against the Mezurateens ; that his people would support him ; and that he would not lead them to be sacrificed in an unjust cause. If his life, he said, was to be forfeited on the present occasion, he would fall alone, without having the lives of his people to answer for.

The Caitibe, fearful of carrying such a message to the Bashaw, reminded Sidy Hamet that the late Bey lost his life for saying much less.

Sidy Hamet, hurt at the Caitibe's refusal, told him, if by bringing the Bey's death to his recollection he intended to frighten him into an approval of the measures, he was mistaken. " My brother," said he, " was off his guard—I am not. Hear me, Caitibe ; if you know of any secret hand pointed against my life, let him be careful. My people, as I told you, are all mine ; there is not a man amongst them who would spare one drop of his blood that he thinks can be of use to me. *Uras el Boui* [1] (by my father's head), I order you to go—deliver my message instantly to him and bring me his answer."

The Caitibe, much against his inclination, carried Sidy Hamet's message to the Bashaw, and returned in a short time with an answer : " That the Bashaw would think about it ; but must see the Bey and Sidy Useph at his levee that afternoon." Hadgi Hamet, the Bey's confidential attendant, was with his master during this interview with the Caitibe. When it was ended, Hadgi Hamet left the prince to execute some orders he had received, and returned to the castle in the greatest anxiety at the situation of Sidy Hamet, on which his own fate and that of his wife and children might depend, as is frequently the case with the favourites of Moorish princes.

Hadgi Hamet, instead of finding the Bey returned from the levee, and alone as he expected, found him with the Bashaw and Sidy Useph, and all of them much irritated. The Bashaw's people and those of the two princes were armed in the castle without orders, and no notice was taken of this circumstance (though against the rules of the palace) by the Bashaw or either of the princes : each of them seemed to approve of their own people being in readiness. Hadgi Hamet, who was obliged soon to depart, placed himself opposite to the Bey, in

---

[1] Literally " *ala ras abuyi.*"

hopes of getting a look or sign from him for further directions in case he meant to go with the forces ; but this he despaired of till Sidy Hamet called to him to fasten his sash, which, while Hadgi Hamet was doing, the Bey told him all was unsettled, except his own determination, not to head the troops to Mezurata ; but that at present his life depended " on the balance of a barley-corn." [1]   He desired Hadgi Hamet to remain at the castle and watch till morning, saying he should not stop in the harem, but would return to his golphor and stay there all night.

From these events the town was again in a state of alarm the whole evening ; Mustapha Scrivan (the Caitibe), the Shaik and the Chiah were much agitated : and we were very sorry for Lilla Howisha, the second daughter of the Bashaw, a most amiable princess ; for it was plain from the expression of the Caitibe, that her husband, the governor of the port, was safe from the confusion only at the castle, but that his life was aimed at by the Caitibe or the Bashaw.

The next morning the Bashaw postponed sending out the troops. A few days before this event, and four days preceding the feast of Ramadan, the famous marabut who attends Sidy Useph prophecied at the castle, in presence of the court, that one of the late Bey's friends would make the first day of the Ramadan a day of revenge for his death.   This prophecy occasioned no small consternation till the first day of the feast was passed.

If the town remains at all quiet, we shall attempt to go to the castle and see Lilla Halluma, which has not been practicable for Christians since the Bey's death !

October 25, 1790

In the following account you will find a description of the visit of a Moorish princess and her family to the tomb of her husband. The Bey is buried in the royal turba (mausoleum), within the great mosque, both of which I have described to you in my former letters. According to the prevailing custom here, of periodically visiting the tombs of the dead, the late Bey's widow went from the castle yesterday, about sun-set, for that purpose.   The way from the castle to the mosque was lined by the Bashaw's guards, and several of Sidy Hamet's officers attended.   Many of the late Bey's officers were in sight, but

[1] Barley-corns are used by the Moors to weigh diamonds.   (T.)

durst not approach too near for fear of being observed by Sidy Useph's people, and thereby incurring his anger by publicly shewing their compassion for the Bey's widow.

The grave of the Bey had been previously strewed with fresh flowers for the second time that day ; immense bouquets of the choicest the season could afford were placed within the turba or mausoleum, and Arabian jasmine threaded on shreds of the date-leaf were hung in festoons and large tassels over the timb ; additional lights were placed round it, and a profusion of scented waters was sprinkled over the floor of the mausoleum before Lilla Aisher entered the mosque. Her eldest daughter, the beautiful Zenobia, was not spared this dreadful ceremony ; she accompanied her disconsolate mother, though this princess was so ill from the shock she received at her father's death that she is not expected to live.

What a thought to carry such an object as this to her father's grave ! But the customs of the Moors drive them to despair ; and instead of endeavouring to soften the hand of affliction, they are in-genious in finding out new horrors every hour to heighten their mis-fortune. Lilla Aisher's youngest daughter, not six years old, was likewise present at this scene of distress ; and when this infant saw her mother weeping over the Bey's tomb, she held her by her baracan and screamed to her to let him out, refusing to let go her hold of her mother or the tomb (which she was clinging to at the same moment) till she saw the Bey again ! The wretched Lilla Aisher, who went there in a state of the deepest dejection, was naturally so much afflicted at this scene of useless horror, heightened by the shrill screams of all her attendants (who were expected to pay the compliment to herself and their late master), that she fainted away, and was carried back senseless to the castle in the arms of her women.

Notwithstanding the Bey's refusal to take the command of the troops against the Mezurateens, as no proper measures have since been taken to reconcile those people, it is now feared his going will be unavoidable. Shaik Saffanassa, the most powerful chief of the Arab tribes, favours the cause of the Mezurateens, while Shaik Alieff is in the Bashaw's pay. The latter has promised to join the princes ; but the people suspect that when they are out he will betray them and join Saffanassa and the Mezurateens.

Preparations have been carried on with the greatest expedition, during the last two or three days, for the camp, which the Bey at last agrees to head, and Sidy Useph goes as second in command.

We went yesterday to the castle, and parted, as usual, with the gentlemen who accompanied us, at the Bagnio where the Christian slaves are kept. I have observed to you there are but few slaves here, and those chiefly Maltese, some very old and infirm ; but as we are always obliged to pass them, it is a great alleviation to our feelings on their account, to see them easy and well dressed : and so far from wearing chains, as captives do in most other places, that they are here perfectly at liberty.

Near the Bagnio we found the eunuchs waiting, who accompanied us with lights through the passages to the Harem. Lilla Halluma was standing at the door of her own apartment ; she was leaning on the arm of Fatima, the third princess, and widow of the Bey of Derner ; one of the blacks stood close by the other side of her, with a new silk handkerchief put over her shoulder, on which Lilla Halluma rested her head. I must remark to you that Lilla Halluma has never been seated (unless from illness) when we have first approached her ; for, as her dignity will not permit her rising to receive those who visit her, her delicacy and affability make her avoid, as often as she can, this distinction ; and except the compliment of saluting her in the manner of her country, which cannot be dispensed with, she lays aside all further ceremony. After the married ladies had kissed her head, and the rest her hand, as usual, she desired her ladies to conduct us to Lilla Aisher, the Bey's widow ; saying she would herself join us directly.

We found Lilla Aisher, as we expected, very melancholy. According to the customs of the East, her dress bespoke the state of her mind ; deprived of all its lustre, by methods taken to deface every article before she put it on. She wore neither ear-rings, bracelets, nor halhals round the ankles, nor ornaments of any kind except the string of charms round her neck. The moment she saw us she burst into tears, and one of her blacks was going to scream ; but Lilla Aisher had the presence of mind to prevent her, as such a circumstance would have thrown the whole harem into confusion, and frightened Lilla Halluma, besides renewing her distress. Lilla Aisher's two daughters were with her : the eldest, Lilla Zenobia, is so strong a likeness of the late unfortunate Bey, that it was distressing to look at her. She had lost all her vivacity, and was the fixed image of grief, rendered more interesting by her extreme beauty.

In a short time after we had entered the apartment, the blacks came to say Lilla Halluma was in the adjoining galleries, coming to see Lilla Aisher. The Bey's widow rose and hurried out to meet her, having first desired her blacks to darken the room on account (as she had been telling us) of Lilla Halluma not bearing the light since the Bey's death. To render you better acquainted with Lilla Halluma's state of mind, before I say more of her, and the singular manners of this place, I must inform you of some circumstances Lilla Aisher had just been relating to us.

During the Bey's life, Lilla Aisher (from her proximity to the throne) was very jealous of her own dignity in the castle, and sometimes thought the princesses did not shew her a proper deference, which occasioned a slight degree of coolness between her and the family ; but Lilla Halluma's tenderness to her since the Bey's death, and their mutual afflictions, have rendered these royal mourners inseparable friends. Lilla Halluma's sufferings were so aggravated by the cruel impression the Bey's last words (suspecting her of betraying him) had made upon her feelings, that her life was despaired of. From the superstition that prevails in this country, Lilla Aisher thought of an expedient which proved her knowledge of the human heart, her affection for Lilla Halluma, and the ingenuity of her own invention, by which she has relieved Lilla Halluma from a state of distress that threatened the loss of her senses, or her life. Lilla Aisher, to effect her plan, sent a message one morning (previous to the second Friday after the Bey's death) to request of Lilla Halluma a private audience, saying she must speak to her directly, and quite alone. When they met, Lilla Aisher told her, that as the widow of the murdered Bey, she came to implore her not to heap additional sorrows on her head by thus persecuting the spirit of her departed lord. Such an address increased Lilla Halluma's sufferings ; she asked her in the greatest agony to explain what she had said. Lilla Aisher replied, she had last night seen the Bey, who had no hopes of joining the celestial assembly of departed spirits on the approaching Friday,[1] unless his mind was tranquillized, which was impossible while his mother's lamentations reached him beyond the grave, and justly reproached him for having in his last moments, for an instant, thought such a mother could have betrayed him—that being out of this world he had been shewn the truth, and was now wandering among the tombs of his ancestors, in the same disconsolate state in which Lilla Halluma was exploring the

---

[1] Alluding to the feast which is imagined to be held by the spirits of the departed in the burial places on Friday evenings (the Sabbath of the Moors) ; and it is for this cause the Moors are so anxious to dress their dead as richly as they can afford. (T.)

castle, and renewed his grief in proportion as she did hers every moment—that he was permitted to send his beloved parent only this one message from the grave, and that he should enjoy all the blessings of a happy departed spirit the moment she recovered her tranquillity, and believed his affections for her the same as they had ever been during his life.

This ingenious and affectionate expedient of Lilla Aisher's had the desired effect. Though she could not entirely suppress her sorrows, Lilla Halluma became more reasonable and partook of food, from which she had before almost entirely refrained.

But to return to the subject whence I began this digression. Lilla Aisher and Lilla Fatima entered the room with Lilla Halluma and led her to the sofa. As soon as she was seated, Lilla Aisher's children knelt to kiss her hand; for which purpose she presented them the hand that was wounded when the Bey was killed, and which was still bound up and in a sling. Her hand is terribly mangled, but her finger was saved, as the splinters of the pistol struck against her ring.

The custom here, to dwell upon and nourish the recollection of misfortunes, induced Lilla Halluma to mention several instances of branches of the royal family being put to death unfairly. Among others, the most atrocious was an uncle of the late Mohamed Bashaw, father to the present Bashaw. Mohamed Bashaw, who had long waited for an opportunity of privately putting his uncle to death, sent his physician to the prince, who had been wounded, with a poisoned plaster, with orders for the physician to put it on and remain with his uncle an hour and a half, by which time it had taken effect, and the unfortunate victim died in great agony in a few days.

Lilla Halluma desired the princesses, Lilla Fatima and Lilla Howisha, who had entered the room after Lilla Halluma, to take us to the apartment where the Bey was killed. Dreadful as this favour appeared to us, we could not refuse to go for fear of offending her. We found the sight as strange as it was terrible; against the walls on the outside of the apartment had been thrown jars of soot and water mixed with ashes. The apartment was locked up, and is to remain in that state except when opened for the Bey's friends to view it.[1] All in it remained in exactly the same state as when Lilla Halluma received the Bey to make peace with his brother; and what was dreadful, it bore yet all the marks of the Bey's unhappy end. Not an article of any description had been suffered to be removed since the Bey's dissolution.

[1] This apartment, now a museum in the castle, is still shown to visitors.

All that the apartment contained was doomed, by Lilla Halluma, as she said, to perish with the Bey, and like him to moulder away in darkness.

Among the number of the late Bey's horses, which were never mounted by any person but himself, he had one remarkably handsome and perfectly white. During the obsequies performing for the Bey's death, where all was wretchedness and nothing to be seen but mourning, this beautiful horse formed a painful contrast. It was the last object that appeared in the midst of this scene of horror to which it was brought richly caparisoned, and with the same state as when it belonged to his late master ; but soon the lustre of its appearance was tarnished. Those who were mourning for the Bey's death, sprinkled it with their blood and strewed it over with ashes, and it was led from the place covered with dismal tokens of his master's fate, with which it was honoured in preference to the rest of its species, on account of its having been its master's favourite. The Bey was accustomed when he returned from riding to place his little boys (who died in the plague) on this horse, while the slaves led it round the yard.

We returned with the princesses to Lilla Aisher's apartments. Lilla Halluma deplored the present state of the castle, so different from what it was a few years since, when the passages to it were clear and open and every face free from suspicion ; but that now the passages from the harem to Sidy Useph's apartments were locked on his side, and Sidy Hamet, from this caution of his brother, has insisted on Lilla Halluma's ordering them to be fastened on his side : every place, she says, is so watched and guarded in the castle, that she considers it only as a state prison.

We saw none of the princes during this visit. Refreshments were as usual profusely and grandly served, but none were touched, and we left the castle as late as we could before sunset.

⠿

October 30, 1790

We rode out yesterday to see the camp, which is at last pitched for the Bey and Sidy Useph. It was formed nearly in the shape of an angle, the centre of which was marked by two handsome spacious tents communicating with each other, and which were erected for the Bey. We dismounted and entered them where he received us with his usual affability. He informed us that Shaik Alieff's people, to the amount of four hundred, were expected to join the camp every moment, with Shaik Alieff's son at the head of them ; and that a considerable number of the Krowailes, another tribe of Arabs, were to come in from the deserts the next morning to accompany him in this expedition. He told us he was obliged to find them each a cap, a baracan, a shirt, and a pair of shoes, as soon as they arrived, and to supply the chief Arabs amongst them with a sum of money in small piastres, which at the time it was fixed many years ago, amounted to a maboob (seven shillings and sixpence) ; but this sum being still obliged to be paid in small piastres, is increased to ten times as much from the fluctuation in the value of the coin.

Sidy Hamet expressed his disapprobation of the groops going out against the Mezurateens, and he regretted their not having been brought to terms before they had been so exasperated ; but concluded by saying the force would be strong enough to silence them with very little trouble.

The inside of the first of Sidy Hamet's tents was lined with light blue silk, and the top with crimson satin, embroidered with gold and silver flowers. The inner tent, which was intended to sleep in, was more simple than the first, the inside being chiefly composed of blue and white silk. On each side of the entrance of the first tent were placed the colours and the silver stick bearing one tail.[1] In front of the tent, at some distance from it, were the cannon. The nuba plays every day at the same hour as at the castle ; and was leaving the tent when we entered it. Sidy Useph's tent could not be distinguished from those of the common men ; except from its being newer and there being an awning before it.

We went this morning to the castle to see the princes set off. As the procession of officers, etc. was in every respect the same as the last I mentioned, I shall not trouble you with a description of it. I shall only acquaint you with the circumstances that attended it. When the troops were at a considerable distance, we saw Sidy Useph return full speed to the Arabs, who with their chief had not moved from the walls of the town. Sidy Useph seemed to be much agitated, and after speaking to them for some time, he sent off a chaoux, or aid-de-camp, to the Bey. By this time it was known that the Arabs, not having received of the Bashaw all they had demanded in advance, would not stir ; and Sidy Useph had sent for the Bey's consent to

---

[1] One horse tail, or *tugh*, being the insignia of a Bey, as compared with three for the Bashaw.

fire upon them, but the messenger returned with contrary orders. The Bey said he had agreed with them that they should follow in the evening.

When the troops were entirely gone, Shaik Alieff, before he would suffer his Arabs to move, exacted such hard conditions from the Bashaw, and was so exorbitant in his demands for ready cash, that the Bashaw, who was obliged to make him join the camp at any rate, was under the necessity of submitting to the most unreasonable sacrifices with a good grace, fearing if he did not satisfy Shaik Alieff, he would go over to Shaik Saffanassa, who is already on the side of the Mezurateens, and turn the scale entirely against Tripoli.

Owing to there being various parties for and against the government here at present, the most trifling circumstances gives rise to serious alarms. While the consuls were taking leave of the Bey this morning before he left the castle, an Arab made his way to the prince, and hastily kneeling snatched at his hand as if to kiss it. At his sudden and rough manner, and from the neglect of his people in permitting a common Arab to approach him without notice, Sidy Hamet gave so significant a look of anger and surprise, that his selectar, or sword-bearer, and other officers, caught hold of the man instantly, and pushed him with such violence from one to another to get him out of the way, that it was every moment expected he would be thrown over the galleries, in which case he must have been dashed to pieces. The Arab was so out of breath from the fright and rough treatment, that he dropped down senseless, and was thought dead for some time.

᎚

November 10, 1790

Letters have arrived from the princes to the Bashaw. The Bey's letters were brought into town in the morning, but Sidy Useph's letters did not arrive that evening. It was in vain that the Caitibe, the Chiah, and the Shaik, waited to hear the contents of the Bey's letters ; the Bashaw was alarmed, and said he would do no business nor open any letters till those from Sidy Useph arrived, which they did the next morning. The news they brought was quite favourable, and relieved the minds of the people, who had been in a state of despondency for many days.

The Mezurateens attacked the princes in great numbers on this side of Mezurata. Shaik Alieff did not desert the Bashaw's cause as was expected. He fought against Saffanassa's Arabs and killed his son, whose head is brought here to be placed on the walls of the town. The princes and the Arabs whom they had with them, drove the Mezurateens back with great loss to the town of Mezurata. The chaoux who came with the accounts went about to ask, as is the custom here, for a *buona mano* (money) from the Moors of distinction, and from the Consuls, as a reward for bringing such good news. The Bashaw gave fifty sequins (nearly thirty pounds).

With the Bey's letters there came an order to the governors of the port to stop a Jewess, named Mezeltobe, who was ready to embark for Malta. She is daughter to the famous Jewess I have mentioned to you, known by the appellation of Queen Esther, and who is so great a favourite with the Bashaw.[1]

Mezeltobe had endeavoured to betray Lilla Howviva, wife of the present Bey (while he was Sidy Hamet), to the late Bey. She had brought several messages from the Bey to Lilla Howviva, for which she was forbid her presence, and on this account Lilla Howviva determined not to visit in the castle for some time, unless accompanied by one of the Bashaw's daughters. Mezeltobe with unremitted toil watched a long time the princess's motions, and one night she informed the Bey that Lilla Howyiva would in a few minutes pass through a passage in the castle to her own apartments quite alone. The Bey, profiting of Mezeltobe's intelligence, concealed himself in a baracan and went immediately to intercept Lilla Howviva in her way. Deceived by Mezeltobe's information, the Bey had formed an erroneous idea of Lilla Howviva's conduct, and flattered himself he should meet with a favourable reception from her. He followed a female figure through the dark passages of the harem for some time, not daring to accost her for fear of a mistake ; till by the light of the moon which reflected on Lilla Howviva as she passed by a window, he was convinced it was her. He addressed her, and terrified her exceedingly, from his extreme anger at finding himself disappointed in her unexpected behaviour, which he supposed was merely assumed.

This female messenger, like the rest of those nuisances in the castle, acted only from mercenary views, and though she had seriously incurred Lilla Howviva's anger, yet the expectation of a valuable reward from the Bey made her determine on procuring a meeting between them, as she hoped the Bey's persuasions would do more in his favour with Lilla Howviva than the messages she had carried from him.

---

[1] Feraud alleges she was also the mistress of Sidi Yusef.

From the sternness of the Bey, and his disbelief of her real sentiments, the timid Lilla Howviva was near fainting, when the approach of servants at a distance obliged the Bey to retire for fear of being discovered by them. Lilla Howviva, freed by this fortunate circumstance, returned unperceived to her own apartments ; but as soon as she entered them, she sunk senseless on a sopha. When she recovered, to quiet the solicitude of those around her, who were both surprised at her situation and alarmed for her health, she attributed her illness to the extreme heat of the evening, and cautiously concealed this unpleasant event, aware that its discovery must terminate the life of Sidy Hamet, or the Bey, or perhaps both. This lady is extremely handsome, without being regularly beautiful. Her complexion is fine, her eyes are black and wonderfully animated, not with haughtiness, but with sweetness ; she is not very tall, but finely made ; her character is unimpeached, and her disposition softness itself. How dreadful, that owing in a great measure to the customs of this country, such a woman should often be dangerously exposed to the machinations of infamy. There is no doubt that the Bey was perfectly deceived from the account he had heard of her, and yet it is certain that this meeting was fortunate, both for his peace and that of Lilla Howviva, as it displayed their real sentiments to each other. Mezeltobe was instantly forbid the castle by the Bey, but her infamous conduct remained unknown to the present Bey till a very short time since. When the Bey was setting off with the troops for Mezurata, some person disaffected to Mezeltobe, knowing she was going to quit the kingdom with a good deal of money, related the story to him, which they had heard from Mezeltobe herself. The Bey was so exasperated at her conduct towards Lilla Howviva, that notwithstanding her having failed in the object she wished to accomplish, he determined on her death, and for this reason sent the order above mentioned to the governor of the port, forbidding him to permit her to leave the kingdom ; but from the great influence of Mezeltobe's mother (the Queen Esther) with the Bashaw, an order was procured from the castle for her sailing, and she is gone to Malta.

山

November 29, 1790

The troops are returned successful from Mezurata. The Bey and Sidy Useph came in together. They had disagreed in their measures a few days previous to their return, and it was feared that Sidy Useph would have made this a pretext to have gone off to the Arabs, and have brought them with him to Tripoli against his father and brother ; but at length the princes returned amicably. The guns of the castle and the batteries fired, and the consular flags were hoisted when they entered the town. Among other spoils, they have brought with them one hundred dogs, which have been used to hunt the gazels or antelopes, and are, therefore, reckoned of great value here.

We paid a visit to Lilla Halluma yesterday, and had a very narrow escape from being obliged to see and speak with Sidy Useph at his own house. Your feelings will give me credit, when I assure you, that to us a more shocking circumstance could not have happened. To those who have known so intimately the late Bey, as we have, while the dreadful circumstances of his death are still so fresh, nature recoils at the sight of Sidy Useph.

You are informed as to these visits being in the style of the ancients, and, therefore, will not be surprised, or shocked, when I tell you, that we found Lilla Halluma superintending her blacks while they were making fine bread. Lilla Halluma offered to send her women with us to her apartments, there to wait her coming ; but we objected to this. After some time, when she was coming away, her blacks stopped her to say that some workmen, who were repairing a building, had had notice, and would be out of the way in a few minutes. This precaution was necessary, as Lilla Halluma could not pass through the harem while men were in sight.

When we came to her apartments, we found ready prepared, on a Turkish table of mother-o'-pearl and silver, curds and whey and Fezzan dates. This light repast was placed on a gold embossed waiter, nearly the size of the table, about three feet in diameter. I do not mention this to draw your attention to the grandeur of the castle, but to shew you the difference between the customs here and at Constantinople, where the plain manner meals are served in has, by writers, been attributed to the tenets of Mahomed, which they say have denounced vengeance against those who eat off gold or silver ; whereas, here they seldom present the most trifling article but on one of these metals. Coffee, though served in the finest china, is placed in a gold chased cup. At Lilla Halluma's, the tea and coffee placed in those cups are put on gold trays, so large that they are carried round to the company by two black eunuchs. Soon after we entered the apartment of Lilla Aisher, the late Bey's widow, Lilla Howisha came in. Lilla Aisher was spinning wool, to divert, as she said, a melancholy moment.

Lilla Howviva, Sidy Hamet's wife, we knew waited for our paying
her a separate visit in her own apartment, as it was the first visit of
ceremony after her husband being proclaimed Bey.   Lilla Halluma,
knowing our intentions, begged us not to omit going to the wife of
Sidy Useph first, saying, she knew Lilla Howviva would excuse it.
We were very sorry to do this ; but there was no alternative, as it
was Lilla Halluma's wish and order.   She sent some of her most confidential women with us to conduct us there and back to her again.
This was a very great favour, as none of her people have been suffered
to go near Sidy Useph's residence since the murder of the Bey.

In going to Sidy Useph's house, we passed through some subterraneous passages almost entirely without light ; and the superstition
of the Moorish women with us (who were convinced that we should
meet the ghost of the Bey at every dark corner we passed) did not
serve to enliven our minds, which were depressed with the fear of
meeting more animated beings than spirits.   When we arrived at the
entrance of the last of these gloomy passages, a door nearly all of iron,
securely fastened, prevented our advancing further till our names were
reported.   After some time, we heard the eunuchs advance, push back
the iron bolts, and, with great difficulty, remove two immense heavy
bars, with which this pass had lately been guarded, to screen the guilty
heart from the vengeance of all but its Maker.   As soon as this gate
was opened, a lantern, carried by one of the eunuchs, gave just light
enough to discover a part of their formidable figures and the glare
of their arms ; but when they held it up to take a better survey of
those to whom they had given entrance, it shone fully on their faces,
which, black as jet, were rendered more striking by the fierceness of
their eyes and the whiteness of their teeth, and thrilled us with horror,
while we reflected, as we followed them closely through the gloom,
how lately their hands had been stained with the blood of the Bey.
We rejoiced when we saw day-light again, and found ourselves at a
greater distance from these murderers.   The tirewomen and blacks,
who were sent to meet us, took us to an apartment, where we waited
for the princess, Sidy Useph's wife.   The floor of the apartment was
covered first with Egyptian matting, over which were Turkey carpets ;
and, before the sofa, were laid over the carpets quilted sattin mattresses
with gold flowers.   The sofa was crimson velvet embroidered with
gold, and the cushions were of gold tissue.   Contrary to the taste of
the country, this room was not hung with tapestry, but nearly covered
with looking-glasses, and gold and silver fire-arms, trinkets, and

charms. About the room were a number of large costly cabinets of mother-o'-pearl, tortoiseshell, and ebony, some mounted with gold and others with silver. Before the sedda, where the couch or bed is for sleeping, four silk curtains richly embroidered were hung, one over the other. Upon the whole, the apartment was grander than any in the castle, except that of Lilla Halluma.

In a few minutes after we were here, the wife of Sidy Useph entered the apartment superbly dressed. An etiquette was observed when she entered which we have not seen practised in this place before: her people ranged themselves regularly on each side, her white attendants nearest to her, and her blacks the farthest off, forming a double line, through which we passed to meet her. It was the first time we had seen her. She is of Turkish extraction, young and handsome, but nothing soft in her manner, and her face has too much of the fierceness of a Turkish countenance to be pleasing. She was very reserved at first, but grew more familiar afterwards, and was so importunate with us to wait for Sidy Useph, who she said was expected every minute, that we quite despaired of quitting her before his arrival. When we parted, and before we got to the end of the galleries belonging to her apartments, we heard him with his blacks entering the court-yard below. The eunuchs who were with us wished us to return; but we desired them to go on, and soon reached the outside of Sidy Useph's harem, when the eunuchs quickly closed the tremendous door after us at the end of the subterraneous passages, with as much grating and difficulty as it had been opened.

On our return from Sidy Useph's we went with Lilla Halluma's women directly to Lilla Howviva the Bey's wife. The contrast was striking between the Bey's apartments and those which we had just quitted. Here every countenance was open, and the servants looked easy and free from suspicion. Lilla Howviva received us in the most courteous manner. Though this was merely a visit of form, a consciousness of her own dignity had satisfied her, without manifesting any outward sign of etiquette or ceremony that could be dispensed with. Her dress was more costly than usual, and she wore some additional jewels. She was engagingly affable but not cheerful; for who, as she said, can trust Sidy Useph? and she trembles for her husband's safety. We had not been long with her before the Bey came in. We saw him cross the yard as we entered the galleries. He was then going to his father's levee; but Lilla Howviva sent to tell him we were with her, and he returned to her apartment.

Sidy Hamet has never been out of Tripoli, nor is he in the habit of conversing much with Christians ; yet his behaviour was mild, polite, and courteous. His dress alone bespoke him a Moor. His manners to his family were not less affectionate and delicate than those of the most polished European. Lilla Howisha, his favourite sister, wife of the Rais of the Marine, came into the apartment : as soon as she entered she went up to the Bey and kissed the top of his turban, which instead of his not deigning to notice, as is the custom of the country, he directly saluted her cheek and offered her his chair ; this she did not accept, but made a sign to her blacks who instantly brought her another. Chairs, which do not enter into the list of furniture for a Moorish sala, had been previously brought in for us, and it was the first time we had seen in Moorish company all the guests sitting on them. As soon as Sidy Hamet was seated, they brought him coffee and a pipe ornamented with gold, coral, amber, and silver.

Moors of distinction hardly ever sit in company without their pipe and coffee. If they visit you, they are immediately presented with both.

As this was a visit of etiquette, all the ceremony of coffee, sherbets, and perfumes were served, although we had already partaken of them at Lilla Halluma's. The Bey did not leave the apartments till a very few minutes before we went away, which was at sunset ; he must therefore have been absent from the Bashaw's levee, for which he must have accounted to him, as the omission of this ceremony by the princes, without some particular reason, is considered a great mark of disrespect.

Sidy Hamet conversed with his wife and sister in a manner which shewed he considered them as rational beings : he told them the news of the day, and heard their opinions on different subjects with a complacency uncommon to the Moors. He desired Lilla Uducia to send her women for some new gold bracelets for the feet that were making for her in the castle, which the Jews came there to manufacture. They were brought for us to see ; the pair weighed nearly five pounds of solid gold curiously wrought, and from their weight they have literally the effect of fetters ; but a Moorish lady walks very little, and with great caution when she wears them.

When we left the apartments of the Bey, Lilla Howisha, the Rais of the Marine's wife, accompanied us through the harem as far as the house allotted for the black female slaves. This place, though within the precincts of the harem, is farther than the ladies are accustomed to go. In consequence of this, a circumstance occurred that might have proved very serious, had it happened to any other than the parties concerned. From the long time we had spent with Lilla Howisha, we were considerably beyond the hour appointed for us to quit the harem. The Consul came to meet us as far as this place, a liberty, I believe I may safely say, that would not have been permitted to any Christian but himself; but the Moors look up to him as answering the title they give him of "*Boui*" (protector), while they call his daughters "*Bint el bled*" (children of the country). Lilla Howisha's terror and surprise at finding herself so fully exposed to the eyes of a Christian, is easier conceived than described, in a country where the laws make it death for a Moorish lady to be seen by a male stranger. She instantly veiled herself and retired; but declared all the fault was hers, as it was indiscretion to wander so far through the harem, without sending to the house where the blacks are, to warn them of her approach. She intreated us to come again soon, and smilingly said she should take care no such accident should happen in future. I hope the anecdotes of this visit may make amends for the length of my letter.

ⓌⓌ

December 20, 1790

Since Sidy Useph's return from his expedition with the Bey against the Mezurateens, the following circumstance has happened, which shows how much he is feared and looked up to at the castle.

A woman named Fatima, a favourite attendant of Lilla Halluma's, soon after the late Bey's death, went from his widow to the present Bey to intercede with him to save his late brother's children from the ignominy of pulling off all their ornaments, according to Sidy Useph's order, who had said they were condemned blood, and that if they lived, they should appear dressed like the children of the slaves. Besides this offence, Fatima is likewise accused of having spoke too freely of the late Bey's death in the castle: Sidy Useph, therefore, ordered two of his infamous blacks to strangle her and her infant. The heart-broken Lilla Halluma, hearing of the order for the death of her favourite confidential servant, ventured to conceal Fatima in her apartment; but during the evening, being convinced she could not save her, she ordered her to seek for other shelter, or the result would be that of seeing her and her infant killed before her eyes, as it was by this time known they were in Lilla Halluma's apartment. The poor unfortunate woman then sought refuge in the Bey's widow's house, who at the risk of her life ventured to detain her the whole night ; but not daring to befriend her longer, she also sent her off in the morning, advising her to attempt to go secretly round the castle to Lilla Howisha, the wife of the governor of the port. Sidy Useph being informed by those sent to search for Fatima where she was concealed, sent word to his sister, Lilla Howisha, that her husband's life should be the price of her attempting to screen Fatima and her infant from his vengeance. The poor creature was again turned out instantly with her child, but she was now advised to quit the castle, and take refuge at some consular house. Watching her opportunity she escaped from the castle, and knowing she was pursued, as she ran by the house of Lilla Uducia, the eldest princess (who as I informed you, quitted the castle two years ago and lives in the town), she left her infant there, not being able to carry it farther : she laid it in the skiffar, or hall, hoping some one would protect it, and reached the Venetian Consul's home, that being the nearest. She just touched the door (which was sufficient to protect her) at the instant Sidy Useph's servants were about to seize her. The event was truly distressing to the Consul. His feelings would not permit him to give Fatima up to Sidy Useph's rage, and the protecting her might eventually embroil his nation with Tripoli. All the Moors of rank advised the Consul to go at once to Sidy Useph, as the Bashaw does nothing at present but what is sanctioned by him. This marked attention to Sidy Useph had the desired effect. He gave his word to the Consul that he would not only revoke his orders for Fatima's death, but would himself return her to his mother. Fatima was instantly conveyed to the castle, for fear any change might take place in her destiny, and Sidy Useph kept his word in delivering her himself to Lilla Halluma. But certainly all these circumstances prove that Sidy Useph is gaining more power in the castle than he is entitled to as youngest son of the Bashaw.

January 18, 1791

To-day, Sidy Amorrah, the eldest son of the first minister, and Hadgi Useph, an officer of the Bey's, dined with us. Sidy Amorrah is just arrived from Spain, where he went as ambassador from this country. I have before remarked to you that the Spaniards have paid enormously for this their first peace with Barbary. Sidy Amorrah has made so much advantage of his embassy, that he has left a considerable sum in the banks of Spain, in reserve for himself, besides great property which he has brought here. I regret to say that he is a great usurer, putting his money out at so high an interest as to make eighty per cent. of it, to the complete ruin of those who apply to him for assistance ; but he has not returned in time to save himself from some great losses incurred from the enraged and artful Arabs, in return for the infamous interest he wished to make them pay for sums of money he had advanced them. Sidy Amorrah, though so lately arrived from a brilliant European court, was a complete foil in point of politeness to his countryman, Hadgi Useph, who has never been out of Tripoli. The former spoke but little at dinner : he had not since he went away accustomed himself to the use of a knife and fork, or made any alteration in his manners, which are not the most polished for a Moor. The latter has adopted many of the European customs ; in company he is easy without rudeness, and courteous without annoyance ; and is always a welcome guest with the Christians for his cheerfulness and good humour. As a specimen of Moorish witticism, Hadgi Useph, on seeing one of the company where he dined carve a fowl, not quite with the adroitness which is usual among Europeans, observed that the fowl was still suffering for the sins it had committed in this world, and the leg which was now taking off with such difficulty, was certainly the same with which he had scratched up the barley-corn in the farmer's yard where he went to steal it.

A disagreement has lately taken place between Sidy Useph and the Bey. The former proposed to assist in placing Sidy Hamet on the throne, deposing the Bashaw, and remaining himself Bey, till Sidy Hamet's son (now an infant) grows up. This proposal not being approved of by Sidy Hamet, Sidy Useph immediately left the town, and placed all his family at one of his country residences in the Messeah.

A few nights after Sidy Useph was seen disguised in a black baracan, going to all the shaiks of the Messeah. He told them that in case of wanting their assistance, those amongst them who obeyed his summons he would pay highly and protect, and those who refused to join him, his people should massacre and plunder. By promises and threats he easily induced them to agree to join him ; in the mean time he is gone to the mountains, and his family, who were expected to return to the castle during his absence, remain still out of town.

We heard this news from the Bashaw's eldest daughter, with whom we went to spend a few hours this afternoon, it being the fast of Ramadan, a season rendered very tedious to her. Her slaves and servants were most of them prostrate on the ground, some asleep, while others looked as if fetching their last gasp, from not being able longer to resist the violent heat of a land wind, which (added to their abstinence from food) they have had to contend with for the last three days.

This princess employed herself in directing her women, who were giving out the provisions necessary for the meals of the night—the only time they can eat during the fast. Among other articles, they divided five baskets of bread, containing one hundred and fifty small loaves each. The slaves then portioned out large pitchers of sherbet of raisins boiled to a strong juice ; and this liquor was put into above a hundred diegers or antique vessels. In making this sherbet, from forty to fifty pounds of raisins are consumed every night in one family, during the month of Ramadan.

⊞

January 19, 1791

To-day the ceremonies begin for the bridal feast of Hadgi Abder-rahman's niece, a lady named Bint el Trabaltzi (the child of Trabaltzi), who has married the ambassador's son, the same who was with him in England. As I have before described to you the marriage cere-monies of people of rank here, I shall have little to say on this occasion. We found assembled at the ambassador's house between three and four hundred women ; and among the people of consequence, Lilla Zenobia, the wife of Sidy el Buny, did not fail to make a magnificent appearance. This is the lady I have before mentioned as a favourite of the late Bey. She has not ceased since his death to excite jealousy at the castle ; and owing to her influence in this place, is by Moorish ladies of rank admitted into their houses. To-day her bracelets, not confined to the size usually worn by the nobility, exceeded those worn by the princesses. Zenobia first made her appearance in a gold flowered baracan, exactly the same as one Lilla Halluma had sent as a present for the bride ; and this circumstance, though it would not appear to you to be of consequence, is considered here as an affront to Lilla Halluma : this baracan Zenobia soon changed for one equally rich and handsome. A great quantity of money was given by the company to the singing girls at this assembly ; for which one of Lilla Amnani's confidential women carried a silk handkerchief round to the company : the larger sums were afterwards given by the guests, and put into a silver plate, as offerings to the bride.

The bride takes her meals alone for the first seven days after she is married, as she is not allowed to eat, during that time, with any of her relations.

While the bride occupies the seat erected for her during the cere-mony, it is a crime for her to smile ; but the Lilla Bint el Trabaltzi was so much inclined to laugh, that Lilla Uducia, the ambassador's daughter, to screen her from observation, threw the veil over her again, which had covered her face while she walked to the seat. Before she ascended it, one of her blacks was sent to clear it by charms from the effect of any bad eyes, that might, by gazing on it, have rendered it unlucky to the bride. She was enveloped in the baracan sent her by Lilla Halluma, and had a silk veil thrown over her face : she was supported by the ambassador's wife and daughter ; six wax lights were carried before her by her slaves ; and she was conducted to her bridal seat, through an immense crowd of ladies who were assembled to see her. At this moment the music and singing increased, and the festive song was so loudly vociferated, as entirely to drown every other sound for the time it lasted.

During the feast, the bridegroom was employed in his choaish, or golphor, receiving the compliments of his friends. The Consuls visited him on this occasion, and they afterwards came at sunset to join us on our return from the ambassador's house.

The feast for the bride lasts seven days, during which period she does not see the bridegroom ; such is the etiquette here.

May 29, 1791

Last night a Jewish Bible was presented to the synagogue by a Jew, at whose house we were present to see the feast made on the occasion. The ceremony there will be more novel to you than a description of the presentation of it in the church, which has been so often and so correctly described by others.

This donation is always accompanied with a great deal of cere-mony and expense. Grand suppers were provided for immense numbers of Jews at the house of the donor for seven nights previous to the carrying of the Bible to the synagogue ; and the night before it is removed from the house, a general supper is also given there, to as many Jews as think proper to attend.

The Jew who gave this Bible not being married, the wife and daughters of the governor of the Jews did him the favour to come to his residence and superintend the dressing of the viands, and to perform the honours of the house on this occasion.

All the Jewish priests assembled at the house, to examine the book, and dress it with flowers ; and the Jewesses of the highest rank who may be present, lighted a number of wax candles, which were previously placed before it, and burnt incense. Silver vases with flowers were placed on the top of the ark which contains the sacred manuscript, and it was covered with most expensive drapery.

The donor was obliged to go to bathe previous to touching it, and when he returned they put over him a purple mantle, surrounded with a deep white border and a fringe. These mantles are chiefly made at Cairo. As soon as he was dressed, the Bible being his present, he was entitled to hold it up to the people (in imitation of Moses lifting up the tablets on the mount) : even the rabbies could not deprive him of this honour. He took the Bible out of the ark, and carried it with great veneration to the door of the apartment, where it had been deposited ; here the rabbies first, and the chief of the Jews next, kissed it. He then made a sign for those to approach whose distinguished rank in their different tribes had previously entitled them to be called up to the Bible by the chief priests at the synagogue, and presented it to them to salute also. Again receiving the sacred volume, he held it extended before him, never lower than his breast, and carried it from the door of the apartment into a gallery opening into the square area of the house, to show it to immense numbers of people who were assembled below. Those who had a right to salute the Bible received it from the Jew, and in the same manner as he had done, they took it by turns to lift the sacred manuscript to the people. When the Bible was brought back to the door of the apartment, it went through the same ceremony as before, of being saluted by the Jews. It was then replaced in the ark.

On the third day, the general supper was given at the house of the Jew, and the Bible, attended by the rabbies and the chiefs, was carried with great ceremony to the synagogue at the adan (or break of day).

The Bible might have remained seven days longer with the donor, but in that case, he must have given up the chief part of his house for that use only ; refreshments must have been provided for all the Jews of distinction, none of whom could have dispensed with coming every day to pray by it ; and the Bibles from the synagogue must have been brought with great expense and ceremony to have kept it company. All these considerations induced the donor to convey it to the synagogue as soon as it could be sent with propriety, which was on the third day after the feast had commenced.

June 4, 1791

A single gun was fired last night to announce the finishing of the fast of Ramadan, and the commencement of the feast of Beiram, and the dragomen to-day received double presents, one for their feast of Beiram, and the other for our King's birth-day.[1]

In the afternoon, the Consuls went to the castle to compliment the Bey on the birth of a son, who was born this morning. They found a marabut with the Bey, whom the Bey's people were perfuming with aloes. The Bey held in his hand a gold censer of incense for the purpose, and was shewing the greatest veneration for him, who with an air of haughtiness received all his attentions as only his due. The marabut came to the castle on account of the new-born prince, to perform writings for him, and offer up prayers and sacrifices to the prophet for his future welfare, for which a lamb was sacrificed. At the feast of Ramazan, at houses of distinction, a quantity of lambs are sacrificed, according to the number of the family ; and these lambs must be sacrificed at the door of the habitation. At the last feast of Ramazan eight lambs were killed, drest, and given away at the house of Hadgi Abderraham. Among the middling class of people, one lamb for a family is deemed a sufficient offering.

It is some days since Sidy Useph returned from the mountains, and fortified himself at the Bashaw's garden, in the same manner he did after the late Bey's death. The gates of the garden, or grounds, are shut before sunset, and not opened the next day until Sidy Useph rises, which is seldom before noon. He has with him at present near three hundred Arabs.

Among the subterraneous passages through which we passed, belonging to the Bashaw's and to each of the prince's harems, and

[1] George III.

communicating with other parts of the castle, the Bey has caused those leading from his harem to be closed up. This singular order was occasioned by the following event. During the fast of Ramadan, about a fortnight since, the Bey went to pay a visit to his sister, Lilla Fatima, the widow of the Bey of Derner, who had sent for him. On entering the apartment, the Bey perceived an Arab woman sitting in the room, wrapped in a dark baracan : this did not strike him particularly, but the terrors of Lilla Howviva his bride, who was there, and had purposely unveiled herself, surprised him ; and she, at the same instant, made a signal to him with her eyes to leave the room, which he directly did. Lilla Howviva followed the Bey as soon as she possibly could, and informed him, the figure in the dark baracan was Sidy Useph, disguised as an Arab woman. She said it was the third time he had been conveyed in disguise into Lilla Fatima's apartments, for the purpose of meeting the Bey there, and hearing his sentiments ; and that she had seen the same figure each time, but never discovered it to be Sidy Useph till the present moment, when an aukward plait in his baracan shewed her a part of his countenance, after the Bey had entered the apartments. On this account, the Bey had all the subterranean passages that led to his harem securely closed. The Bey's precautions can never be too great, while events continually prove Sidy Useph's intentions to ascend the throne at any price ; the following illustration of which this day has furnished.

This being the first day of the feast of Beiram, Sidy Useph came to town to pay his compliments to the Bashaw and Bey, an etiquette which could not be dispensed with while Sidy Useph keeps up the least appearance of cordiality with his father and brother, as one of the strongest of their religious tenets is that of reconciling all differences at the feast of Beiram, and the least neglect or coolness at that period is considered as a declaration of open hostility. When the princes were at the Bashaw's levee, it was noticed that Sidy Useph was uncommonly agitated, and was eagerly pressing to get near the Bey, as if to speak to him in private, which could not easily be accomplished, as the brothers were too much at variance to accost each other without ceremony. Sidy Useph at length came up to one of the Bey's most faithful attendants, who with the keen eye of affection as well as of duty, watches over the safety of his master in all critical moments, and desired him to tell the Bey, that when their father's court was over he would go to the Bey's golphor, where he much wished to be permitted to say a few words to him. The attendant excused himself from going at that moment, by observing to Sidy Useph that the Bey was speaking with his father, and he durst not interrupt them. Sidy Useph finding this man unwilling to deliver his message, sent another Moor, and in a few minutes after the brothers were proceeding to the Bey's golphor, whither they were instantly followed by the infamous marabut Fataisi, and several of Sidy Useph's people ; which this attendant perceiving, instead of accompanying them, he went directly to the Bey's chief chaoux, and told him to go instantly up with his blacks and take possession of the golphor to clear it from intruders, as the Bey was gone there with Sidy Useph. The chaoux lost no time, but on his arrival he found that Sidy Useph's blacks, after the princes had entered, had already crowded round the door of the golphor, with their chief (Sidy Useph's chaoux) at the head of them. In consequence of the information he had just received, he ordered Sidy Useph's chaoux to draw off his blacks and leave him room to pass, but finding it impossible to prevail on Sidy Useph's blacks to permit them to gain a foot of ground without open hostilities, which at such a moment would have proved fatal to his master's life, he had recourse to stratagem to effect his purpose. He took the hand of Sidy Useph's chaoux, as if in a friendly manner, and contrived by one squeeze to dislocate the man's little finger, the excruciating pain of which deprived Sidy Useph's chaoux of all strength, and, knowing he was usurping a post, for which if he said a word he might be cut to pieces, he led off his blacks directly, and left the door free to the Bey's chaoux.

Sidy Useph, who was already in the golphor with the Bey, on seeing the apartment on a sudden so completely guarded, not by his own chaouxes and blacks, as he had expected, but by those of the Bey, rose quickly from his seat, and with his marabut (Fataisi) took instant leave of his brother, who has for the present escaped any mischief intended him, through the vigilance of his watchful attendant.

June 10, 1791

I am sorry to observe disturbances are again beginning at the castle. The marabuts occasion a great deal of mischief. The one who went to the castle previous to the late Bey's death, entered it unexpectedly some days ago ; ran screaming through the apartments of Lilla Halluma, and, spreading out his hands, pointed to where the blood of her children was, in a short time, to run " in rivers through the rooms " (that was his expression). Lilla Halluma, prone to super-stition, as they all are here, fainted in the arms of her daughters, and has remained very ill ever since.

One of the Consuls, who has great claims at the castle, and is uneasy about them, went there to-day, and found the family in very great confusion. The Bey and Sidy Useph had met, and could not agree in any of their points. The Consul endeavoured to persuade Sidy Useph to let his own son and the Bey's son be placed as hostages, while Sidy Useph and his brother had another conference. This Sidy Useph would have consented to, but was prevented by his marabut Fataisi.

It was thought Sidy Useph would have slept at the castle last night, but, on the contrary, when the Bashaw's levee was finished, he re-turned very late to his garden, where his people have increased during the night, from three to six hundred.

The Bey talks of shutting up the town to-morrow. He has sent his hampers to advise the Consuls to make their houses as secure as they can, in case of being attacked by the Arabs. From this account you will perceive our situation does not mend ; but I hope my next may bring you better news.

❦

June 23, 1791

The town has been in a state of great alarm. The twentieth of this month was fixed for Sidy Useph to meet the Bashaw and Bey in the castle, and make peace again with the Bey in the Bashaw's presence ; but Sidy Useph sent a letter to his brother the preceding evening, to say he should not come to the castle without his arms, and desired the Bey to remember the words of the prophet, which declared that nothing could shorten or lengthen the life of man, and that if the Bey believed in their strongest tenet (mughtube, fate), he could not want courage. The Bashaw sent immediately an answer to Sidy Useph, to tell him that he would not suffer him to come into his presence armed ; but, notwithstanding this order, Sidy Useph approached the town next morning with three hundred men under arms. In conse-quence of Sidy Useph's approach with such numbers, a proclamation was issued from the castle to the Moors of the town, that if they were molested, every one had the Bashaw's leave to defend themselves, not only against Sidy Useph's people, but against Sidy Useph himself.

Such a defence, without this edict, would have been considered high treason.

Before Sidy Useph appeared in sight, his famous marabut Fataisi came into town with some of his holy followers. They were admitted to the sovereign, and Fataisi told the Bashaw that Sidy Useph was on his way to town with twenty people only, and without arms, and implored him by the prophet to send the Bey out to meet him, and make terms with him for the peace of his family and of his people. The Bashaw instantly agreed to it, and had the prince gone he would certainly have been murdered. But the Bey having received certain information, that Sidy Useph was near the town with several hundred people, he seized the marabut, though in the Bashaw's presence, and, holding his sabre over him, he told him, that had he not been a marabut he would have laid him dead at the Bashaws' feet for his treachery, and then informed the Bashaw that his brother had with him upwards of four hundred men under arms. The Bey turned the marabut out of his presence, and the officers presented their arms at him, but the Bey ordered them not to fire. He desired they would see the marabut out of the gates of the town, and give orders that, on pain of death, no one should suffer him on any account to enter it again.

In the evening, the castle was crowded with people, and strongly guarded at the sandannar, or guard-house; and, at the zook, a sort of guard-house in the bazar, the guards were trebled.

From our house, we saw the Bashaw sitting in his golphor, at five in the morning of that day, and he remained almost wholly there till evening. The Bashaw dispatched messengers to the different cydes of the Messeah, to send the Moors of the adjacent villages into town that night; but Sidy Useph sent immediately to tell them, that if they did not come to him, or if one of them attempted to go into town, he would massacre their families and burn their gardens.

A body of Mezurateens and Arabs came in that night to assist the Bey, whose situation is truly distressing. He can get no resources from the Bashaw, and was so short of cash when the Arabs arrived, that he was obliged to borrow money to provide provender for their horses, and to get the necessary provisions for his family.

In the evening the Shaiks of the streets were ordered to arm the inhabitants of the town. In the Messeah, the Moors joined Sidy Useph's people, and committed dreadful ravages all the night, plundering the palaces and gardens belonging to the Bashaw, and to those people who remained attached to him.

Before sufficient assistance could arrive from the Arabs for the Bashaw, it was feared Sidy Useph had Moors enough on his side to enable him to enter the town, and the whole of the night of the twenty-second he was every hour expected to have forced his way in. The agitation of the Tripolitans, as well as the Europeans, during the whole of that night, is not easy to be conceived.

The town being on the sea coast, the inhabitants could have fled no where, from the rapacity of a banditti of Arabs, had they made their way into the city.

At half past ten the next morning, Sidy Useph appeared for the first time in open hostilities against his family. All the atrocities he had as yet committed, received a ten-fold addition of guilt, by their having been achieved under the mask of friendship.

On the appearance of Sidy Useph the second day, all the consular houses were closed, as were the shops and the houses of the inhabitants, who turned out with their arms, and ranged themselves in the streets.

The Bashaw sent forces out early in the morning, to preserve the villages of the Messeah from the further ravages of Sidy Useph's people. In the afternoon they brought in the governor or cyde of the Messeah, who was carried to the castle to be strangled, but he is yet living. This man, instead of assisting the people and protecting them, had given every assistance he could to Sidy Useph. When the cyde arrived at the town gate, the Bashaw ordered his chaouxes to proclaim Sidy Useph a rebel, and that it should be lawful to seize him wherever he could be taken, excepting in the marabuts or mosques, which may not be violated.

A noble Moor came into town in the evening of the twenty-second, and pretended not to have joined Sidy Useph, or to have approved of his measures ; but he returned again to him early in the morning, and, a short time after his departure, a quantity of provisions and ammunition was stopped at the town gate, which he had endeavoured to send out to him.

About an hour before noon, Sidy Useph's people attacked the town. We saw Sidy Useph for some time seated as cyde of the Messeah in the Pianura, in the place the cyde should have occupied had he been present. Just at this moment, the cyde of the Messeah was brought into the castle-yard to be strangled ; but he was remanded back. This is the second time in one day that he has undergone the terrors of being put to death.

The Bashaw has sent round the coast to collect the Arabs. We saw a number of horsemen at a very great distance, approaching from the west : this circumstance gives courage to the people here, who were much cast down. The cannon from the town were fired at Sidy Useph's people during the whole of the day, which had the desired effect of keeping them back. But though the firing was incessant, it did little execution on either side. Sidy Useph lost only five men, and a few horses belonging to the town were killed, notwithstanding there were upwards of three thousand shot fired. The cannon were not even mounted upon carriages ; and they were fired by a Russian so badly, that he frequently pointed them into the sea on his left, instead of into the Pianura exactly before him. This account, I assure you, extraordinary as it appears, is true, for we saw every one fired.

From the situation and strength of the English consular house, it was at this critical juncture considered as the only safe asylum among the consular houses. It is very large and chiefly of stone, being built for the Bey's residence many years ago. The side of the house which commands the harbour, Hamet the Great employed to contain a part of his garrison, having shut up all communication thence to the house, in which at that time resided two of his queens. This part was afterwards restored to the building. It is now considered strong enough to make a tolerable resistance, and is favourably situated, being isolated on three sides. On the fourth, it is joined only by Moorish houses, not sufficiently high to annoy it, therefore the flat terracing at the top of the building is very safe, being inaccessible except from the inner part of the house ; so that, in the midst of the present troubles, we can in general walk on it with security. It is built exactly on the plan of all Moorish houses, with a square area in the middle, and a piazza, which supports an open gallery into which the apartments lead.

As soon as Sidy Useph arrived within sight of the town, the Greeks, Maltese, Moors, and Jews, brought all their property to the English house. The French and Venetian Consuls also brought their families ; every room was filled with beds, and the galleries were used for dining-rooms. The lower part of the building contained the Jewesses and the Moorish women, with all their jewels and treasures. There was likewise a great quantity of jewels in the house belonging to the Bashaw, which were in the possession of some of the Consuls, to be returned him at a future time. All these circumstances rendered it highly necessary to guard the house as much as possible, for which purpose a number of Sclavonians, and other sailors, with small cannon from the Venetian ships, were ready with their arms to be stationed on the terraces.

Sidy Useph discontinued his assault upon the town about six in the evening. His people retired out of sight, and the cannon from the town ceased firing ; but it was expected he would return in the dead of night. The cry of the town-guard was without interruption till daylight, and at our house the Consuls watched by turns the night through.

As Sidy Useph and his Arabs are still at a distance, our house is already empty of the greatest number of its guests ; but it is not easy to divine how the town may be situated before I write to you again.

📖

July 14, 1791

Since my last, the Bashaw has shewn such an extraordinary distrust of the Bey, as seems to threaten the life of the latter. The Bashaw gave orders to the Chiah, to let only two or three attendants come in with the Bey, and if he had already three attendants with him in the castle, no more were to join him at the Bashaw's levee, where, when the Bey arrived, the Bashaw's officers increased in numbers, and on the Bey's appearance they made a circle round the Bashaw, and the hafsadar [1] (or treasurer) kept in his hand, what is very unusual here, a blunderbuss. This marked distrust of the Bey rendered his situation very dangerous, as the Tripolitans were at a loss whose part to take while this lasted. The Bashaw's suspicions, however, gradually disappeared in a few days, and the Bey seems restored to his confidence.

Accounts are received that Sidy Useph has overrun vast tracts of the country and was endeavouring to gather forces ; but that as yet he was every where repulsed. He was ill received by the tribes of the Benoleeds and the Tahownies. At Mesalata he reckoned much on the governor of the place, who is the husband of the famous Zenobia, the late Bey's favourite, but this man still retains his resentment for the Bey's death, and finding it impossible to oppose Sidy Useph, he fled. Sidy Useph laid all his property waste and returned again to the mountains, leaving Lilla Howia, his wife, with his infant and her mother at the marabut of the Seide. At this trying moment, Sidy Useph discovered a greater degree of feeling than he was

<hr>

[1] *Khasnadar.*

supposed to possess, as he returned three different times to the marabut, before he could resolve to part with his wife and child. After his departure, their distresses were so great for want of provisions and clothes, that the Bashaw was induced, from a relation of their sufferings, to offer the princess an asylum for herself, her mother, and her son at the castle ; but of this alleviation to her distress Lilla Howia would not accept : she says, she is ordered by Sidy Useph to remain at the marabut till he comes to take her from it, or till she hears he is dead. If the latter misfortune should take place, Sidy Useph has ordered her to take his infant to the Bashaw and go herself to the castle ; if she be still permitted to profit of such an asylum. These being the last directions given her by the prince, she says, nothing but death will prevent her strictly following them. No person can force her from the marabut ; but they might starve her to death there, as it is lawful to prevent the conveyance of either food or clothes to those who fly to these sanctuaries, by which privation criminals must either die, or deliver themselves up, when nature can resist no longer. After this princess had refused to quit the marabut, the Bashaw, touched with her sufferings and those of his little grandson, permitted clothes and provisions to be carried them from the castle.

The Bey has been obliged for the last few days to send his horsemen to the bazar, or market place, which is held every Friday morning within a few miles of the town, and is termed the Great Bazar,[1] as he feared its being molested by Sidy Useph's people during the hours it lasted.

August 3, 1791

We have seen nothing of Sidy Useph or his troops since the attack they made upon the town in the last month ; but since that time he has sent three letters to the Bashaw to solicit peace on any terms. One of these letters was brought by the son of an officer, named Busseneener, who is entirely in the interest of the Bashaw ; a second came by the grandson of the Bashaw, who is as much in the interest of Sidy Useph ; and the third was brought by the Dugganeer's son, whose head it was expected by his family and all here, would have been taken off by Sidy Useph, as his father had been particularly assiduous in the Bashaw's service, in assisting to drive him from the

[1] Suk el Jum'aa.

walls of the town ; but, according to the custom of this country, of not infringing on the laws of hospitality, Sidy Useph gave the following message to the Dugganeer's son to deliver to his father. " Tell your father that I have not to learn that it was he who pointed the guns at me the other day from the castle, and that I might now take your life as a forfeit for his ill intentions towards me ; but, as that would be violating the laws of hospitality, tell him that I will not let pass the first opportunity that offers to revenge myself upon him."

Not long since, Sidy Useph, compelled by his mother-in-law, gave a still stronger instance of not breaking through the laws of hospitality. Before he quitted his gardens to attack Tripoli, the Bashaw wishing to make terms with him, sent out his chief officers, at Sidy Useph's own request, to treat with him ; among these were the Cataibe, the Chiah, the Rais of the Marine, and the Selectar, four persons whom it was said, some time before, Sidy Useph was determined to put to death, whenever an opportunity offered. On his mother-in-law being informed that it was intended they should be poisoned on the present occasion, she called to Sidy Useph from a gallery that surrounds a marble court-yard, and stretching out her arms with his son in them, declared she would drop the infant into the yard, unless Sidy Useph swore at that instant not to violate the laws of hospitality at her house, he being then at her gardens ; " let these officers fall," said she, " in any other manner, but not now ; they are come as friends, and under your avowed protection, to see you under my roof." Her determined manner prevailed, and for that time these devoted people escaped with their lives.

〽

August 16, 1791

Some letters, with three changes of clothes, sent to Sidy Useph by Lilla Fatima, have been intercepted. On this occasion a marabut, not Fataisi, came to the Bashaw to say that Sidy Useph had not a change to wear, and scarce any thing to cover him ; but the Bashaw withstood all entreaties, and ordered the clothes to be deposited in Sidy Useph's apartments in the castle.

Since the above, accounts are arrived that the Tahownees [1] have joined Sidy Useph : these are a tribe of Arabs of near three thousand men, each possessed of a gun, and who have about five hundred horses. Besides this addition to his strength, the Messulateens have declared,

---

[1] *I.e.* the Arabs from Tarhuna, a town inland about sixty miles from Tripoli.

that though they will not fight against the Bashaw, yet if Sidy Useph comes among them, they will defend him from his enemies. On account of the above news, Soliman Aga, one of the Bashaw's commanders-in-chief of the Arabs, has been sent to defend Tajura.[1] A quantity of ammunition has been sent hence to that place, where there is a strong castle with a good drawbridge.

To shew you how unsafely or with how little judgment they act here, I may mention that the Bashaw yesterday banished three persons, friends of Sidy Useph, to Tajura ; but as they were embarked without chains, or in any way secured, and have servants of their own with them, it is certain they may get the better of the crew of the vessel they are in, and be landed on the coast just where they please.

Lilla Halluma has forbidden Lilla Fatima her presence, on account of that princess meddling so much in the dissentions between her brothers : her great partiality for Sidy Useph makes her act unjustly to the Bey, which renders this circumstance still more distressing to Lilla Halluma. These accounts cannot affect you as they do us ; we feel for every part of this unhappy family, yet see but little of them at present on account of the times, though much solicited to go to them : the continual intercourse there is now with the Arabs, would make it unpleasant, and, perhaps, indiscreet, to enter the castle at this period.

⚏

September 21, 1791

After I closed my letter to you, the Consuls had determined on embarking their families on board the ships in the harbour, with orders to sail from the coast if necessary on the appearance of Sidy Useph, as he has at present with him the most rapacious of the Arab hordes, and as they were expected to commit every excess had they entered the town.

The day on which Sidy Useph was expected to attack this place, a party of Knowiales [2] came into the town under the command of Shaik Alieff to assist the Bashaw. These people suddenly departed, on pretence of being dissatisfied, but they went away only to plunder the Moors in the Messeah. Shaik Alieff sent his son after them to bring them back ; but, instead of returning, they carried off their booty.

Sidy Useph, by appearing frequently within sight, keeps the town

---

[1] A coastal oasis a few miles east of Tripoli.
[2] Nouail : a semi-nomad tribe located in the Zuara area, west of Tripoli.

in constant alarm, but does not attack it. Profiting by his forbearance, we have been to visit the Bashaw's eldest daughter, Lilla Uducia, who, as I have before mentioned, lives out of the castle in the town. We found with her, her sister, Lilla Howisha, the Rais of the Marine's wife, and a number of other ladies from the castle. They came to visit Lilla Uducia on the recent birth of two sons in the family ; one her own, and the other her daughter's ; an event which happens oftener here than with you, from the circumstance of the ladies in this part of the world marrying so young.

In Lilla Uducia's apartment, we saw the wife of the Cyde of the Messeah, one of the three black sisters, who were favourites of the Bashaw. This woman, who is a singular instance of good fortune in having been married by the Bashaw to a Moor of rank, has by her husband's disgrace experienced a sad change. The Cyde of the Messeah, who was several times brought out of the castle, as I have mentioned, to be strangled, has been at last banished the country, and all his property forfeited to the Bashaw. Lilla Uducia has had the generosity to receive his wife into her house, and this black beauty (as she is called) is as comfortable as she can be in her fallen state.

There were in the apartment two fine blacks just purchased from the bazar, as nurses to the infants of Lilla Uducia and her daughter : these two slaves were as usual richly dressed, but were not so wild as the new purchased blacks are in general.

Among other decorations in the apartments, we were struck with the appearance of several gold-headed canes, hung without order on the walls ; but they were described to us as badges of honour, shewing their owners to be among those of the first rank in the government ; for it is only the Chiah, the Captain of the Port, and the Selectar, that receive one of these gold-headed canes from the Bashaw or the Bey, to be carried when either of them go out to head the troops.

The accounts from the castle given at Lilla Uducia's were very melancholy ; every one spoke of Sidy Useph with dismay, and they fear the present Bey will fall a sacrifice to his brother as the late Bey did.

Lilla Halluma was too ill to visit Lilla Uducia on this occasion. The princesses lamented exceedingly that their sister, Lilla Fatima, was so very much in the interest of Sidy Useph. They say, she took so great a part in every thing that concerned him, that the Bey, who is lenient and circumspect, found himself obliged, some days ago, to send a message to his sister by a confidential person, to tell her that if she meddled any more in what concerned the government or Sidy Useph, he, though her brother, would put her to death. But private messages are still conveyed from Lilla Fatima to Sidy Useph.

Neither the widow of the late, nor the wife of the present Bey, were at this feast. The former is still in a state of deep mourning, and the latter too unhappy, from the precarious situation her husband is in at present, to see any company.

〓

October 3, 1791

We are just returned from visiting the wife of a Moor of distinction : he was one of the late Bey's favourites. His lady, Lilla Zelluma, from being received among the most welcome visitors at the castle, is now excluded from it, by the jealousy of those around the Bashaw, who prevent as much as possible any of the late Bey's officers approaching him, least the Bashaw's compassion might lead him to provide for them in preference to themselves.

In the late Bey's life-time, Hadgi Useph, the husband of Lilla Zelluma, lived in splendour. To use her own expression, the females of her family were covered with gold, and their slaves basked in the sycamore shade ; but fallen under the neglect and oppression which has awaited all the late Bey's favourites, Hadgi Useph is become a monument among many vicissitudes of fortune. He has left, by compulsion, an extensive house and gardens in the country, and brought his family to town to a place almost in ruins, where he has been waiting for a long time for a post promised him by the Bashaw's ministers ; but as this offer was made only as a screen to the appearance of open persecution, it has added considerably to his distress. Hadgi Useph entered the apartment before we left it.

This lady is his second wife, having lost his first, and all the children he had by her, in the last plague. His description of his situation at that time was as remarkable as it was distressing. His family were then living out of town. After his wife had fallen a victim to the illness, his servants died so fast that there remained nobody to attend his children. He was at this time himself attacked with the disorder and incapable of passing the night in walking from one apartment to the other where the children lay. He was however averse to putting them together in one apartment, hoping that some one might escape by being divided from the rest. Unable to remain with them all, when he took leave of them in the evening he placed only a jar of water by each of their beds. In the morning, hardly able to support himself, he anxiously went from room to room to visit them, and daily found one dead, or dying, till the whole had expired. His next great trouble was their interment, which from his own illness, and the scarcity of people near him to assist, was so long delayed as to render it almost impossible to remove them. He continued himself for many days without the sight of a living object, and was deprived of food for such a length of time, as to be aware that the want of it impaired his senses : he would then, from necessity, rise and supply himself with such grain or meal as he could find in the house, and in this manner existed till he succeeded in getting strength enough to have the remains of his children interred, and to change his dreadful abode !

Hadgi Useph, when he entered the apartment of Lilla Zelluma, was just returned from the castle, where he had been disappointed as usual, and put off with promises. He talks of taking his family to Tunis. He observed, while lamenting the Bey's death, that no event had ever proved so strongly the force of their prophet's assertions delivered in the Koran, that all is mughtube (destiny) ; for, he said, the Bey was continually warned by his friends of the fatal stroke that awaited him, while, with courage, talents, and power to oppose it, he never for a moment could be brought to apprehend it, or think himself the least in danger.

In this visit, very little more than their habits reminded us that those we were with were Moors. Zelluma leaned on her husband's arm unveiled, and talked with easy confidence. Their conversation was rational, and their ideas almost wholly coincided with ours. An invitation was given to Lilla Zelluma to bring her daughter and sup at the English house. On her being told no male servants should be in the way, and that even the Consul would absent himself from the house, for the hours she would be there, she expressed herself highly sensible of this civility shewn her ; as such attention from the Consul is expected only during the visits of the princesses, or of an ambassador's wife.

I fear we shall not long enjoy the liberty of visiting our Moorish friends, as it is reported that Sidy Useph is again approaching Tripoli, and all the respectable Moors in the Messeah are bringing their families into town.

November 20, 1791

Sidy Useph is so near the town, that his people are heard from the adjacent hills,[1] beating the tambura, and singing the song of war every night, to collect together all those willing to join them. The Bashaw has sent out again for troops ; and sailors from European vessels have been brought on shore to assist at the castle in pointing the guns. This will not give you a high idea of the Tripolitans as warriors ; but the long period of peace which preceded these times, has rendered the people of Tripoli unused to warlike preparations.

For many months we have not been able to ride, except to a very short distance from town ; but at present there seems a prospect of our being even deprived of the possibility of passing through the gates of the city, as Sidy Useph and his people are continually in sight.

Sidy Useph has removed his family from the marabut of the Seide to his own gardens. He often mixes among his people in a common baracan, so wrapped up as not to be distinguished from them, and for many hours they have not the least idea where to find him. It is thought he does this to learn exactly how the Arabs he has with him stand affected to his cause.

The town is badly off for articles from the country : none are brought in, as the Moors cannot venture out for fear of being plundered by Sidy Useph's people. A fowl, fresh meat, or even an egg, cannot be had without great difficulty and danger, and at an enormous expense : vegetables and other provisions have already been procured, at the risk of the lives of those who have been sent for them.

Tripoli may now be said to be overrun with strangers, and those of the most dangerous cast. Arabs from the mountains, who never saw Tripoli before, now walk about it daily, not without impressing terror on all the inhabitants. Many of these people are of what is termed the unvanquished hordes ; a people who live in places where none can penetrate but themselves. Many are the sovereigns that have attempted to subdue them, but have retired with their armies unsuccessful. The Arabs, when pursued, fly before the enemy to their secure abodes, in thick impenetrable woods, in frightful hollows between high mountains, or they descend into the sloping caverns I have mentioned, which they have formed within the bowels of the earth, where their enemies cannot follow them, except singly, in which case they would be massacred by those waiting for them within these dreadful retreats.

---

[1] Probably the low sandhills about five miles south-east of the city.

These Arabs descend from their mountains to rob the adjacent villages, and plunder caravans coming from those countries which do not pay them for their friendship.

They have something in their appearance peculiar to themselves, and are easily distinguished from the Arabs who are called here Gibeleens (mountaineers). The latter carry more arms, and are better clad ; but these unvanquished hordes have a martial, fierce, and artful look, distinguishing them from others. They are not black, but of a deep copper colour, and are in general tall and well made, with good features : a dark baracan which at times but ill conceals them, and an immense long gun, is all they are usually burthened with. Many of them have received their arms, with a horse, as an invaluable legacy from a dying parent, to whom, while on his death-bed, they have sworn to revenge him on his enemies.

These Arabs never fall upon their prey but in large bodies. It is only by passing them quickly and unexpectedly, or in such large parties as to overawe them by their numbers and force, that travellers are safe.

December 8, 1791

The Bashaw sent for the Cyde of Messalata, either because he suspected him, or to consult him ; but the Cyde refused to come, alleging as an excuse that he must remain at Messalata to guard the people. His reason for not obeying the Bashaw's summons has, however, appeared since, by all the Messalateens having gone over to join Sidy Useph. But accounts were brought in to-day much more distressing than these, not only to the Bashaw but to all here, which were that Sidy Useph has gained the Acas [1] over to his side. These are a people who have the care and management of the Bashaw's flocks ; they, therefore, carried with them all the animals they had belonging to the Bashaw, among which were several thousand sheep : this is a loss that will be severely felt by all the people of Tripoli, and can be remedied only by sending to Malta, and other parts, for provisions.

In the last four or five days, upwards of a thousand musquets have been manufactured here, which is reckoned a wonderful effort. They say the town is in a better state of defence than it has been for many years, and it is expected to make a sufficient resistance against Sidy Useph's attacks.

---

[1] Probably a misprint for the *Akkara,* a tribe from southern Tunisia.

To add to the Bashaw's troubles, and the confusion of the country, it is said the Grand Signior is displeased with the present state of government in Tripoli ; and continual accounts are brought of his intentions to re-establish a Turkish garrison, similar to what was here formerly, under a Turkish Bashaw, who is said to be appointed and on his way to this place.

It has been our fate to reside in Tripoli during a period the most unfavourable to Christians in the memory of any one here. Famine succeeded by pestilence, and that by war, have ravaged this unfortunate kingdom, from almost our first arrival on its shores, where its inhabitants had been healthy and trade flourishing, and where peace and fertility had enlivened the country for the best part of a century. I am sorry to say we have no prospect of witnessing better times.

January 18, 1792

This year, like the last, finds Tripoli involved in accumulated difficulties. A day does not pass without hearing of families despoiled, and wandering into town, reduced from affluence to beggary. Such a general consternation reigns, that it is impossible to discover who are friends or enemies, and war surrounds us with increasing horrors, aggravated by the dreadful consideration of its being between father and son.

Sidy Useph still exerts his utmost efforts to excite the Arabs to arm for him, and they are joining him very fast : they are so much in his interest, that when the Bashaw sends to any of the Arab chiefs to assist him, their terms are so cruelly unreasonable, that it is often impossible to employ them. Sidy Useph is at present at Zuarra on the coast, a short distance hence ; but he is so continually expected here, that every outlet leading from the suburbs of Tripoli to the sands is kept blockaded with stones, to impede the approach of his people.

With all the present disadvantages of this place, we have still frequently reason to acknowledge that it is not so bad for Christians as other barbarous states. We have just heard that at Morocco, Muley Yesied, who, to the terror of his subjects, has ascended his father's throne, lately put to death the man who was his father's first minister ; and, because he suspected this minister to be too much in favour with the Spaniards, he caused his head to be placed on the Spanish consular house, and his hand nailed on the door, to the dreadful annoyance of the family.

What is most to be dreaded here by the Christians, is a sudden burst of the Arabs into town, as these people will receive no check to their depredations by the sight of national colours, to which they would pay no attention unless restrained by the Moors, whom they would certainly overpower.

◫

February 1, 1792

Some Tunisians, who are just arrived, and who have been sent from Tunis to the Bashaw, have brought the following extraordinary account of the Bey of Tunis. Owing to disturbances in the country, the Bey had for several days secluded himself from the people. One morning, a few weeks ago, near the adan, or break of day, his officers hearing a dreadful scream from the room where the Bey slept, summoned the guards immediately to the place. The Bey's apartment being fastened, they fired into the lock, which burst open the door : here they found the Bey, who is a very stout man, struggling with his Mamelukes, three boys, the eldest of whom was not seventeen years of age. They secured only one of these assassins, who died half an hour after he was taken : the other two, finding they could not succeed, and having previously fixed on a signal between them, at the same instant snatched a pistol from their sides, shot each other, and dropped down dead together, to the amazement of those present, who could scarcely believe the scene they witnessed to have been acted by mere children ; and from this dreadful circumstance it was concluded, that the third youth had swallowed poison unperceived, which had occasioned his death so suddenly.

To-day letters arrived from the Venetian envoy at Russia to his brother here, with the news of Prince Potemkin's death, the particulars of which you may not have heard. This Prince has been one of the most victorious of all the Russian generals in the present war against the Turks ; and notwithstanding his life was spent in continual war, he attained nearly the age of eighty years. Being unwell, he undertook some weeks ago a journey from the Crimea to another part of the country, for change of air, accompanied by the Countess Potemkin, a near relation. After some days travelling, they one morning got out of the carriage for the pleasure of walking ; the Prince not finding himself well, leaned on the Countess's arm, and proposed their resting under the shade of some trees, where, seated by her side, he expired in a few minutes.

He has left immense treasures to the Empress of Russia, to whom the news of his death was immediately brought. The account reached her while at her levee, when the empress dismissed her court, retired to her apartments, and remained very ill for several days.

Though Prince Potemkin has left treasures worthy the acceptance of his sovereign, he lived at all times in great splendour. He was remarkable for being whimsically expensive in his entertainments : not long before his death he gave a dinner, at which in the middle of the dessert was placed a large orange tree, full of blossom, and also fruit of the richest flavour : of this tree, reared in the middle of winter in the frozen region of Siberia, each orange was reckoned to have cost more than its weight in gold.

♱

March 10, 1792

It has been reported that Sidy Useph has gone to Tunis, to solicit the Bey's assistance ; but it is now known that he is in the Messeah, though he does not discover himself to any but his confidential people.

Provisions are scarcely to be had here at present at any price, and the Jews are so cautious, that they secrete their money, or offer it at so high an interest, that those who want it cannot avail themselves of it.

♱

March 18, 1792

On fresh alarms yesterday from Sidy Useph's people, who were seen at a distance in great numbers, the Venetian Consul went to the castle, and offered the Bashaw the assistance of the forces on board the Venetian galliots which have put into the harbour for provisions, and are employed in the Venetian war with Tunis. A well disciplined body of men, most of them Sclavonians, with plenty of ammunition, might have made a great difference in the present state of these disturbances ; but, to the surprise of every one, the Bashaw rejected this offer : and, strange to say, the cause of his refusal appears to arise from his wishing Sidy Useph to succeed in coming into town. He does not, however, openly avow these sentiments, fearing the resentment of the Bey and his friends.

Sidy Useph's wife and child are again at the marabut, where she is dressed as a common Bedouin Arab, having nothing but a brown baracan to cover her. How different from the last time we were with her, when she appeared decorated with a greater quantity of jewels and gold than any of the other princesses, and received us with infinitely more pomp than even the sovereign herself.

𝕎

April 16, 1792

In my last letter but one, I mentioned the atrocities of Muley Yesied, then Emperor of Morocco. Happily for the peace of his subjects, this inhuman character is no more. We have received the following accounts of him, by some Moorish friends just come from Morocco. Immediately after Muley Yesied's quitting this place, finding his father was still determined to punish him for his infamous proceedings, he resolved, when on his return he reached the coast of Morocco, to take refuge with his family in one of the most revered sanctuaries in his father's dominions, from which he might be sure of not being taken on any pretence whatever.

He fixed on the marabut of *Muley Absalem ben Jensies*, or Muley Absalem the son of Jensies, which was near Tetuan, and continued his voyage from Barbary to that part of the coast.

His father, the Emperor Muley Mahomet, had previously set out for Sallee, to inspect his black armies, and to head them against his rebellious son, whom he had not been able to soften, by all the indulgence and immense treasures he had wasted on him. During the last part of the Emperor's journey he grew ill so rapidly that he was obliged to be carried in a litter, and within a short distance of Sallee, worn out with fatigue and vexation, fell a sacrifice to the afflictions he suffered from the unnatural conduct of his son. He expired on the eleventh of April, 1790, near the river Cherattas, in the midst of his officers, who, fearing his remains might be insulted by the brutish disposition of Muley Yesied and his soldiers, kept his death a profound secret. They placed the dead body in the same litter from whence the Emperor had descended but a few hours before, and continued to manifest the same attentions in accompanying it as they had done whilst he was alive.

The next morning the Emperor's death was proclaimed at Sallee, and he was buried in the palace of Robat, according to the last orders he gave to the officers who were with him when he died. The people of Morocco, paralized with terror and dismay, then heard the Effendi in pomp and magnificence proclaim Muley Yesied Emperor, on the fourteenth, three days after the death of his father.

Not even a barbarous nation could accustom itself to the cruelties of Muley Yesied, and as soon as he ascended the throne his subjects placed his brother Muley Ishem at the head of an army against him.

The enraged Emperor Muley Yesied, after having in the most savage manner forced immense sums of money from all classes of his subjects, headed an army of thirty thousand men, and set out on the fourteenth day of February 1792 to meet Muley Ishem. The dreadful career of Muley Yesied's cruelties was now drawing to a conclusion ; for on the same day on which this monster set out with his troops against his brother, he was mortally wounded with a barbed arrow from a private hand. As soon as he was wounded he was brought back to his palace of Dar-Beida at Morocco, where he arrived the same evening. Here he lay in agonies till his death, as the arrow could not be extracted ; and during his sufferings he caused more people to be sacrificed, and committed more crimes and outrages, than he had ever accomplished in his life, in so short a space of time, as he survived only till the next evening.

· On the day following, the sixteenth of the same month, it was with universal joy that Muley Ishem was proclaimed Emperor, and on that day the body of the barbarous Muley Yesied was carried to Messia in Morocco, to the mosque called the Coba Ysheesfu, where, to the great relief of his people, this tyrant was interred. He was said to be forty-three years of age ; for, as already observed, the Moors never register their ages, it being against their religion. Muley Yesied had been Emperor twenty-two months when he died. His wives and all his female slaves were immediately after his death conveyed to the palace of the Emperor Muley Ishem. Among the widows is the Arabian he took hence by violence from her father's house, the daughter of Shaik Saffanassa, who, it is supposed, will return to him again.

May 20, 1792

Sidy Useph is again with the Arabs. He had taken possession of
a great part of the suburbs of Tripoli, in retaining which he would
have been entirely master of the Messeah, and have kept this place
in a state of famine. The Bashaw sent off forces to drive him away,
which was with great difficulty effected.

So great at present is the difficulty of procuring barley here, that
after a hard day's fighting yesterday on the Pianura, the Bashaw's
horses, and the greatest part of those belonging to the town, were
constrained to pass the night without their food ; a cruel circumstance
when one reflected on the exertions they had next day to go through.
At sunset the Bashaw sent out several hundred men with cannon to
attack a body of the enemy who were stationed within his own
gardens, whence they were not driven till late to-day.

We remained till near day-break this morning on our terrace,
observing the efforts made in both sides to maintain their ground.
The Consuls went to the coffee bazar ; for it being at present the fast
of Ramadan, the principal persons assemble there every night after
midnight to drink coffee. It is, therefore, the most favourable time
for the Consuls to learn from the officers authentic accounts of the
state of the country, which at such serious times as these is of the
greatest importance to the Christians.

While we remained on the terrace, we had a most perfect view
of all that was passing in the Pianura. It was one of those clear still
nights known only in the Mediterranean : the bright beams of the
moon from a brilliant sky, distinctly discovered to us the greatest part
of the Messeah with every object in it. The silence in the town was
striking ; nothing denoted a night of cheerful relaxation after a long
day's fast in Ramadan, at which time the Moors are seen in their
yards and on their terraces, profiting by the few hours' relief they can
enjoy from sunset to sunrise, to prepare them for another day's abstinence. The greatest part of the inhabitants were without the ramparts
guarding the town, and the rest of the Moors, instead of being seen
sitting on their terraces, were, by their fears and the Bashaw's orders,
retired within their houses. In the streets no objects were visible but
the town guard with their hungry pack of dogs, prowling about in
vain for some strolling victim to repay them for their vigilance. Near
us, not a sound broke upon the ear but that of the slow-swelling wave
that washed the walls of the town ; while, at a great distance on a
calm sea, the white sails of the passing vessels were distinctly visible

by the clearness of the night. Opposed to this calm, were the confused screams and the incessant firing in the Pianura and in the country round, accompanied by the loud song of war and the continual beating of the tambura, or drum, to call the Moors and Arabs to arms. Frequent parties of Moorish horsemen and foot soldiers, we distinctly saw by the light of the moon, passing with swiftness over the sands in pursuit of the Arabs. The death song breaking from different parts of the country, often announced to us the loss of some distinguished person on either side, who at that moment was numbered with the slain.

The enemy found a great quantity of ammunition and provisions in the remains of the old palace of Hamet the Great, where they had stationed themselves with the hope of subduing the country round the town of Tripoli. The resources they discovered in this palace had been left for them purposely by the Cyde of the Messeah (Scanderanni) when he deserted his charge and fled. A Moor, named Bussnina, a general of Sidy Useph's, during the night continually declared from the walls of the palace that they had within plenty of supplies, and that it was in vain to attack them. The Moors, when they find themselves in imminent danger, frequently adopt desperate expedients without even a prospect of succeeding. Bussnina at day-break proposed to his soldiers an extraordinary measure, which they agreed to ; and with less than two hundred men, in defiance of seven hundred of the Bashaw's people, they made a sortie from the palace, firing all their pieces at the same instant, which for the moment drove back their enemies, and gave them an opportunity of escaping in detached parties. One of Sidy Useph's captains, a Russian renegado, and four heads of the slain, is all the spoil the Bashaw's people have brought into town. This skirmish has freed the Messeah in part, and left it again open to the people of the town.

The escape of this handful of people belonging to Sidy Useph, from nearly four times their number, is among the examples of courage on the one side and deficiency on the other, which happens here alternately to either party.

When the cannon was sent from the town on this occasion against the enemy, instead of being conveyed hence by carriages, horses, or even camels, as they usually are, each cannon was drawn from the castle out of town by thirty slaves, mostly decrepid old men ; and when they met with any impediment, it took the slaves at least two hours to get the gun into a position for moving forward again. This is an instance of bad management ; but the following circumstance is a still greater instance of bad policy. Late to-night four hundred Arabs arrived from Zavia,[1] having been sent for to assist in recovering the Messeah from Sidy Useph. The Bashaw was so much displeased with them for coming too late to be of use, that he ordered them all back without any recompence or refreshment. The Bey, however, ordered them supper ; but the Arabs were so angry at the reception they met with, that they all went off, and, as might have been imagined, have joined Sidy Useph, by which he gains to his cause four hundred Arabs who came from the mountains to fight against him.

The Bashaw, on the following day, was so extremely ill, that his physician did not expect him to live. The Bashaw told the Consuls that he had been poisoned, and he appeared to suspect the Bey so much, that nobody could speak to the prince at the levee for fear of offending his father.

Yesterday Sidy Useph and his people surrounded the great Friday Bazar, where meat, oil, vegetables, and all provisions are sold in the gross. The people had previously been driven from it, and were glad, after losing what they had purchased, to escape with their lives. You may conceive what a serious misfortune this proves to all here, as none of the above articles are to be had in town at the present moment for money, and we have every prospect of being terribly distressed before these disturbances are over.

June 2, 1792

Sidy Useph, since the last skirmishes, has left us tolerably quiet : and it is some weeks since any of his people have been seen from hence. The gates of the town are open again daily, and the excursions of riding and walking a short distance into the country are again permitted us ; but we do not expect this indulgence to continue long. Profiting of this short interval of liberty, and the town being more tranquil than usual, we have been to see a Grecian lady at the house of a Moorish merchant, who brought her here for himself a few months since. The merchant having sold some pearls and diamonds to the Christians, was induced to comply with the wishes expressed by the ladies present to see his fair Greek, their curiosity being greatly excited from the account he had given of her.

1 These would be the Nouail.

His mother and aunt received us : the latter regretted that she could not accompany us to her nephew's apartment, because he was at home, as, according to the custom of the country, she could not be seen in his presence in company with strangers ; and his mother, she continued, could not go with us, as that would be considered too great attention paid by her to a Greek slave : we were, therefore, under the necessity of being conducted to the apartments by an attendant. The lower part of the house was not so nice as Moorish houses are in general, but we found the merchant's apartments, which were under the direction of the Greek, neatly arranged and richly furnished. In the one we entered, we found the merchant and the Greek seated on a costly sopha ; the Greek, who did not expect us, evidently appeared to have been weeping ; on perceiving us she immediately rose. She was most elegantly dressed in the Moorish costume, and appeared very handsome. She stood the whole time we were there, not daring, in the presence of others, to sit down before her master, while he remained supinely stretched upon his satin sofa. On discovering that she was near her accouchement, Mrs. Tully was shocked at her standing so long, and intreated the merchant to order her to sit down, adding, that we must otherwise shorten our visit ; he at length told her she might be seated, but not in a manner (as we perceived) to permit her to accept his offer, and she continued standing until Moorish sweetmeats and perfumes had been presented to us. Immediately after the collation was ended, the Greek retired, probably too much fatigued to stand any longer. It being the fast of Ramadan when we paid this visit, though the Moors themselves cannot eat, they could not dispense with the etiquette of offering refreshments and perfumes to us.[1]

This merchant was born here, but he had resided the greater part of his life at Constantinople, where he made a great fortune by dealing in black and white slaves ; and he put on all the airs of one of those inhuman traders, when it was observed to him, that as the Greek was so very handsome, and as he appeared so content with her, it would probably not be long before he would give her her liberty by marrying her. " Oh ! no," said he, " if she has a boy now it may be lucky for her ; but even then I may wish to sell her, which I could not do were

---

[1] Here, as in the east, they cannot omit offering refreshments to those persons they wish to shew respect to who come to their houses, as it is considered the means by which they mark the degree of honour necessary to be paid their guests, and the refreshments and perfumes offered are always prepared according to the rank of those they entertain. (T.)

I to marry her." He told us she was not above sixteen years old, and that she was brought up at a magnificent house at Constantinople, under a Grecian woman who lives by educating slaves and selling them. She bought this beauty, who was taken by the Turkish soldiers, at the age of six years, and brought her up among others expressly for the Seraglio. She had been treated by her with all the delicacy and luxury imaginable, and had been instructed in the fine arts and accomplishments, which the ladies of the Grand Signior are expected to possess. The merchant said, that the quickness of her comprehension and the brilliancy of her wit, had rendered her an object of particular admiration to those with whom she was educated, and that it was owing only to the circumstance of the woman who had possession of her being distressed for money, that had induced her to let him have her at the price he gave for her, which he owned was not more than an eighth part of her value, had an opportunity offered for disposing of her to the Seraglio.

We took leave of the merchant soon after the Greek retired, not expecting to see her again ; but on going to take leave of his mother, we found the Greek with her : she still looked very melancholy. A lady of our party spoke to her in Greek : on hearing herself addressed in her own language, she seemed to recover her spirits, and spoke confidentially of herself. She complained of her great disappointment in being sold to this slave trader, as she termed him ; and she confirmed what the merchant said, that had her mistress been more wealthy she would have kept her for a better offer, when she might have been purchased for the Seraglio, or for some high officer about the Porte.

She observed, the obligation she formerly had to study the taste and elegance of her dress was no longer necessary, as it was her fate to live among those who neither admired dress nor even found cleanliness necessary. " My music, my voice, my painting," said she, " and all the little accomplishments which I have learned, are lost upon this trader : he is pleased with none of them, as he is perfectly ignorant of them all." She complained that he would not let her go to the baths, as he said it was too expensive to send her there regularly, in the style she ought to go in as belonging to him, and therefore she was obliged to get up at the adan (break of day) to bathe, to avoid having a parcel of awkward dirty people about her ; while at Constantinople, even at her mistress's house, there were fine baths, which she went to with a number of blacks to attend her, who carried with them rich perfumes and muslins for her use. She told us she wore the Turkish habit, till mughtube (fate) had made her the merchant's property ; he then obliged her to change her dress for the Moorish costume, and alter her name from Celatia, which she was called at that time, for Mahbooba. A mahboob [1] is a Turkish coin made of fine gold without alloy, the merchant therefore gave her this name, as emblematical of herself. She brought us some of the caps she wore with her Turkish dresses ; they resembled a bright crimson beaver, made upon a block exactly like those worn by the Moorish men here, with the addition of a large tassel at the top of different coloured silks, and an embroidery of gold spangles round the foot of the tassel : those who can afford it use jewels instead of spangles. Round these caps are worn a large turban of painted or gold and silver muslin, with long rich ends to it ; of these turbans she shewed us some very beautifully painted and embroidered by herself. She described to us the situation of herself and companions as very happy under the tuition of the woman they were with, whom none of them left, even to go to the Seraglio, without regret. After talking with her some time, we left her in better spirits than we found her ; but she wept when we departed, and entreated us to come and see her again.

July 20, 1792

As the suburbs of Tripoli still remain clear from Sidy Useph's people, we rode out yesterday afternoon to the westward. Though we have often taken the same ride, I have not mentioned to you the antiquity of this part before. Here is one of the famous Roman highways, leading from this place to Tunis : it is called by the Moors the great western road. For some miles from Tripoli it has undergone no change whatever, but remains in the same state as the Romans left it. It is extremely broad and smooth, and there are still existing remains of houses the work of former ages, many of them built of stone by the Romans ; this country being inhabited at different periods by the Carthaginians, the Phoenicians, and Vandals, and forming one of the provinces of the vast empire of Rome. The ruins of edifices built by each of these nations are found at no very great distance all around us : and what once formed the region of Tripolis is yet easy to be traced. Of the three famed cities, Leptis Magna, Sabrata, and Æo,

[1] The name in Arabic also means " beloved one " ; a more likely explanation.

which gave the name of Tripolis to this district, the site only of the latter is at present an inhabited town : but the ruins I have already mentioned at Leptis, the relics of the Vandal towns and fortifications seen thence, including the vestiges of Sabrata, still remain ; and at Tripoli, the magnificent arch I have described, and other remains of antiquity, remind us of its former possessors.[1]

A part of the great western road from Tunis to Tripoli cannot be passed without great danger on account of wild beasts, which not unfrequently attack passengers, in spite of the precautions taken to prevent their approach.   The Bashaw's physician, a Sicilian, performed this tremendous journey by land with his wife and two children not long since.   He joined an immense caravan ; that being the only method by which he could traverse the deserts, and proceeded in safety to this place.   One of these caravans, consisting of from four to five hundred persons, which are increased soon after they set out to as many thousands, sets out every year from Tunis to purchase slaves in Guinea.   The whole of them sometimes perish from the dangers and fatigues of the journey ; or, buried altogether under mountains of sand, are heard of no more.   The Sicilian has often described to us the gloomy and impenetrable forests they passed, where the repeated howlings of wild beasts, excited by the scent of the cattle accompanying the caravan, were increased and heightened as it drew nearer their horrible dens.   Sometimes the caravan was constrained to remain for several days near these woods, to avoid the approaching hurricane in the desert they were about to pass through ; for by the aspect of the heavens, those who frequent the deserts can often foresee these dreadful winds many hours before they happen.   No sooner were the tents pitched and the caravan become stationary, than a peculiar noise in the forest announced the wild beasts verging to the borders of it, there to wait a favourable opportunity to rush out and seize their prey.   The dreadful roar of the lion was not heard during

1 The ground between this and Tunis is enriched with great treasures of money, buried by Arabs, Moors, and Turks, to secure it from their despotic masters, to save it from the rapacity of their enemies, or to conceal it in the hour of pestilence, when rendered by sickness unable to defend their property from such as might be inclined to take advantage of their distressed state : and as only the head of the family, or the chief of a tribe, knows where this wealth is deposited, it frequently happens that he dies without divulging the spot where it is laid.   This extraordinary custom is prevalent in most parts of Africa, which by this means contains many curious articles, and large sums of money, deposited in the bowels of the earth for many centuries back, which may never be found.   (T.)

To this day the Tripoli Arabs believe there is buried treasure in the western suburbs of the city, and sporadic attempts to dig for it occur.

the day ; but when the darkness came on, continued murmurs announced him, and his voice, getting louder, broke like peals of thunder on the stillness of the night. The panther and the tiger were seen early in the evening to make circuits nearer and nearer round the caravan. In the centre of it were placed the tents with the women, children, and flocks ; the cattle were ranged next ; and the camels, horses, and dogs last. One chain of uninterrupted fires encircling the whole, were kept continually blazing every night. On the least failure of these fires, the lion was instantly heard to come closer to the caravan. At his roar, the sheep and lambs shook as if in an ague ; the horses, without attempting to move, were instantaneously covered with a strong perspiration from their terror ; the cries of the cattle were distressing ; the dogs started from every part of the caravan, and assembling together in one spot, seemed endeavouring by their united howlings to frighten away the savage devourer, from whose tremendous power nothing was able to save them but a fresh blaze of fire. Twice during this journey the lion was seen to carry off his prey, each time a sheep, to the universal terror of the affrighted spectators, who in vain with fire-arms endeavoured to prevent him. Fortunately for the caravan, sheep are the lion's favourite food, therefore, though he passed their horses, camels, and cattle, and was in the midst of their tents, he was satisfied with selecting a victim from their flocks.

The Sicilian observed that to the caravan the sight of a tiger would have been infinitely more dreadful, since his favourite food is man.

To return to our ride in that part of the Messeah where the great western road begins, we saw patches of ground making the most singular appearance. The land seemed every where thickly set with the finest cut chrystal, acquiring beautiful colours and lustre from the sun, in the manner of jewels. The plant that occasioned this extraordinary effect was called by the Moors, as it is by us, the barilla, which they burn to ashes and use in making soap. The Moors gather and burn it on the coast, and the Christians pay the Bashaw for leave to carry it away. It forms a very considerable trade from this place to Europe. Though they are in possession here of the barilla plant, no soap is made in Tripoli ; all that is used is brought in jars from Tunis, where it is made ; and that kingdom draws hence an immense sum annually for the soap consumed here.

We saw in the fields, among the barilla plant, many of the famed devouring locusts, which in clouds actually darken at times the rays of the sun in Egypt. They resemble in shape a grasshopper, but are thicker and larger, and are of a light brown colour. Fortunately for this country, they seldom commit depredations here as in Egypt ; yet they sometimes occasion serious apprehensions to the Moors, who dread their numbers increasing so as to make their approach fatal to the harvest.

We have had some weeks respite from Sidy Useph's attacks ; but we again expect his return hourly, as the Moors come in continually from the Messeah with accounts of having seen parties of his horsemen on the sands.

Ⱳ

August 17, 1792

Sidy Useph's famous marabut Fataisi arrived to-day, with letters for the Bashaw. But as he was not permitted (on account of his last intended treachery to the Bey) to enter the town and deliver the letters himself, he would not part with them, and carried them back, saying that Sidy Useph, finding his letters returned unopened, would consider it as a signal for renewing hostilities, and that he expected reinforcements from Tunis, which were already on the way : and this evening we saw, to the westward, Sidy Useph's people with their horses in great numbers.

The Venetians have a second time offered their assistance to the Bashaw, which he has again declined. The Venetian galliots sailed hence some weeks since, carrying ostriches, antelopes, and parrots, as presents from the Consul for the Doge of Venice.

It is asserted that the ostrich will eat iron. That they may, but that they do not always digest what they eat, we have had a recent and singular proof. While the above-mentioned ostriches were at the Venetian house, some days previous to their being embarked, a silver snuff-box was missing. One of the ostriches died soon after it was on board ; and the captain of frigate, regretting the loss of the ostrich consigned to his care for the Doge, had the bird opened on board, to ascertain the cause of its death. Within the stomach was found some pieces of a broken lantern, nails, keys, and the identical snuff-box, which from its size and shape, proved too much for the ostrich to digest, and consequently caused its death.

The Arabs, when they go to hunt these birds, carry with them no other provision than wheat wetted with water. They take no other nourishment than this sorry food [1] till they find an ostrich, which they

---

[1] *Bazeen.*

roast and feed on, while enjoying the thought of the treasures its feathers will yield them. The Arabs will follow an ostrich for six or seven days successively, by which time it is so fatigued for the want of food and rest, that it easily suffers itself to be taken, and the feathers are considered as a full reward for the laborious trouble of taking it. The prime feathers, in the first state they are taken from the bird, will fetch from one to three sequins here. While the ostrich is pursued, to annoy its enemies, it makes use of an ingenious expedient, which often proves efficacious ; it is that of kicking up large stones with its foot, and casting them with great strength and dexterity behind it, by which the dogs are often stunned or wounded. The ostrich is as quick in its pace, when pursued, as a horse. They are too heavy to fly, but their wings serve them as sails, and they partly glide over the sands while endeavouring to escape their pursuers. One of these birds was lately dressed here, merely out of curiosity. The most delicate part of its body resembles the coarsest beef : one of its eggs made three large dishes of omelet, too strong in flavour and smell to be tasted without disgust : and another egg was made into cakes and fried, and appeared like toasted crumpets. The whole repast was too disagreeable to be partaken of by Europeans, but some Moors who were present ate of it with pleasure.

August 19, 1792

The Bashaw and Bey, being in continual fear of Sidy Useph's attacks, are obliged to keep constantly a party of Arabs here to oppose him. This is done at an enormous expense, and with much annoyance to the place, as the manners of the Arabs are better suited to their wild hordes among the mountains, than to the more civilized inhabitants of towns. The liberties taken by the Arabs here often occasion dreadful disturbances between them and the Tripolitans.

Notwithstanding the great charge the Bey is put to at present, he has little or no support from his father, nor is he ferocious enough to exact so much from his subjects as to leave them without food for themselves in order to supply him. His resources have hitherto been drawn from the people in so mild a manner as hardly to resemble the laws of a Moorish prince. He is so extremely embarrassed at present, that after being greatly distressed for many weeks past, he to-day thought of calling the Consuls together, to raise a contribution or loan for him on any terms they pleased. But some of his friends persuaded him against this measure, and advised him to oblige the Jews to open their coffers, they having refused to lend him more money. Nothing being yet determined on, his people are going round the town, and actually planning the means to procure victuals for the Bey's family, barley for his horses, and provision for the Arabs, who are without the gates round the walls of the town, and expected every moment to revolt and go off, on account of their provisions being so long delayed. A few hours will bring to a crisis this unpleasant situation.

In the mean time, that you may form an idea of the alarms in which the Christians live here, I shall give you an anecdote of this evening. In the first place, I must inform you that it is at present customary to have a general party, or (as the Italians term it) a conversazione, alternately at each of the Consuls' houses, where all the rest of the families meet. As the consular houses are so extremely well guarded and secured, and a number of servants in them, they are always considered perfectly safe.

To-night, the party not being at our house, there remained but one lady and myself at home. An attendant, who was waiting on us at tea, suddenly left the room ; we immediately heard an unusual noise below, and as the voice of a Greek servant was predominant, we concluded it was a quarrel between him and the Moors, and were much terrified for fear of mischief, as the Greeks are dreadfully vindictive. On our enquiring the cause of the noise, we learnt that twenty-five Moors had entered the skiffar (or hall), and that more than double the number were endeavouring to force their way into the house. The guard, who is stationed in the skiffar, had ordered the door to be shut on those who were in, to prevent more from entering. The first object that struck us was a Moor in a most violent passion, with a knife absolutely bent double in his hand, which he was straitening against the wall, where he stood. There was so much confusion at first, that it was not understood whether the people in the skiffar were this man's enemies or friends : we therefore expected every minute to see him stabbed at our feet. Before our surprise and terror had subsided, an alarm having been given, we were consoled by the appearance of the Consul : the house and the front before the doors was immediately cleared of the Moors : only the dreadful wretch who was still straitening his knife remained, a pale and ghastly object. While he was endeavouring to give an account of himself, and while the violence of his feelings rendered every explanation vain, his master, who proved to be the Bashaw's grandson, Sidy Mahmoud, arrived. He directly asked the Consul if he would save his favourite servant (pointing to the Moor, who had still the bent knife in his hand). He entreated him to let him remain in the house, which being a sanctuary, he would be safe even from the Bashaw's guards, till something further could be done in his favour. Sidy Mahmoud assured the Consul that his servant was not the aggressor, and that he was perfectly excusable in the affray that had happened. While the Bashaw's grandson was yet speaking, intelligence was brought that the man was dying whom his servant had stabbed : his master now applied more strenuously to the Consul to protect him, but he was told his servant would be given up the moment it was known that the man he stabbed was dead ; yet that he might take the Moor with him, if he did it instantly, while there was a chance of the other man's recovery. The Bashaw's grandson was then going to take the Moor with him, but the son of the Dugganeer, who had accompanied him to our house, told him it was hazarding his own person too much, and that it would incur the Bashaw's displeasure were it known. He then desired him to wait a few minutes, and he would himself return with a sufficient force to fight the man's way out of town, without his appearing in the matter. He returned immediately with several men armed, and himself disguised in a black baracan ; and having brought the servant of the Bashaw's grandson another knife and two pistols, he placed him in the midst of his people, and walked off with him. Sidy Mahmoud, after making many apologies for the disturbance his servant had occasioned, returned to his house.

⚏

August 20, 1792

The walls of the town were too well guarded last night, on account of Sidy Useph, for the servant of Sidy Mahmoud to get past the gates, but this morning, at the adan, or break of day, he was conveyed out of town to the great marabut on the sands, where he will remain while they intercede with the Bashaw to pardon him.

To conclude the account I gave you of the Bey's distress last night, the Jews, to avoid being compelled, advanced of themselves further sums of money to the Bey's treasurer ; but the food for the Arabs, the barley for the horses, and the provisions for the Bey's own family, owing to these difficulties, were not ready till many hours after the usual time, which occasioned such confusion among the Arabs, that it was hardly possible to prevail on them this morning to remain.

ᙡ

September 25, 1792
Though in a remote part of the world, distant from Europe, we lately witnessed some of the effects of the revolution in France.

On the fourteenth of last July, the crews of several French vessels came on shore, to celebrate the anniversary of the destruction of the Bastile, and of the general oath of allegiance taken in the Champ de Mars. They sung the horrid song of *ça ira*, and danced the festive dance on the sea-side ; but on discovering their intentions of planting the tree of liberty on shore, the Consuls applied in time to the Bashaw, and easily persuaded him to prevent this from taking place. Exasperated at finding all endeavours fruitless to accomplish their design, the French sailors became insolent to the Tripolitans ; they came on shore constantly with concealed arms ; and some evenings ago they rose upon the Moors, and occasioned such a riot in the Piazza, that it was with great difficulty we were safely conducted through the square, while returning to our house. Some Moors having suffered in this affray, the Bashaw sent for the French Consul, to desire that no Frenchmen should land, unless the Consul would be responsible for their not bringing arms with them. The Consul is a loyalist, and as the commanders and crews of the French vessels are all *sans-culottes*, it renders the situation of the former very serious ; and this affair may probably end in the Consul being denounced to the National Assembly in France, by some democrat of these crews.

A number of the French sailors went some days ago to measure with cords one of the castles of defence here. The Bashaw was very angry at this, and again ordered them to be kept on board ; but, averse to discipline, the crews regard no command. Since this event, a son of one of the French captains carried a gun with him into the Messeah, and shooting about at random, wounded a Moorish youth, for which he very narrowly escaped falling a sacrifice to the vengeance of the Moor. They pelted him with stones, and drove him to the castle-yard ; where he was detained by the guards till the sum of four pataques had been paid for him to the Moorish boy's friends, four to the servants of the Chiah, and two to the hampers, or guards, who had charge of him, in all about four pounds sterling, and he was at length dismissed with positive orders not to appear on shore again. This circumstance rendered the French crews a little more circumspect, and they sailed a few days since.

♦

October 5, 1792

The seasons have been particularly dry at Tripoli for the last two years ; but the fatal effects of the want of rain has never struck us so forcibly as to-day. Owing to a strong land-wind, which has blown incessantly with increasing heat for the last five days, several Moors coming off the sands into the town have perished, who might have been saved could they have obtained in time a draught of water. Four people died to-day literally of thirst : they were with a caravan just arrived from the deserts, and expired a few minutes before they reached town. Not a drop of rain has descended from the atmosphere for several months, and such a dearth of water occasions the intense heat of the air to become in many instances fatal. The air here is heated to that degree at present, that the insects cannot resist it. Scorched to death, they drop in numbers from the burning atmosphere. It is not usual for these extraordinary winds to blow here successively for more than three or four days : if they do, the heat, which is then dreadful, increasing rapidly to the ninth, sometimes to the tenth day, renders respiration so difficult as to occasion death. Since we have been here, we have not witnessed the violence of these winds so strong as at the present period. On account of their dreadful effect, the generality of the Moors wear a silk handkerchief tied over the face when they walk the streets, to prevent blindness, occasioned by the burning sand, which comes in such quantities as to darken the sky, the azure blue of which, and the brightness of the sun at intervals, shew more strikingly to what a degree the finest sands brought from the deserts obscure their lustre.

At such a distressing period as the present, the ruins of a fine aqueduct near the gates of this city, which was in high order in Hamet the Great's time, and conveyed plenty of water to town, reproach the Moors with their shameful neglect of it. This useful edifice has been suffered to moulder away arch by arch, ever since we have been here,[1]

---

[1] No trace of this aqueduct now exists, but there is a coloured drawing of it in the first edition of Tully.

though it at first appeared easy to be repaired ; but the Moors never think of repairing, and will often build upon accumulated rubbish rather than take the trouble of removing it.   This apathy to industry is not confined to the Moors of Tripoli : in Egypt some of their finest harbours are lost, while others are daily destroyed for want of removing the rubbish, which from time to time unavoidably accumulates in them.   From the want of this aqueduct, Tripoli has for many years been supplied only with rain-water collected in cisterns, which in taste, brightness, and coolness, is the finest imaginable.

                                                          November 22, 1792

A few days since the melancholy news arrived from Morocco of the death of the ambassador, Hadgi Abderrahman, sincerely lamented by all those who knew him, Christians as well as Moors.   According to the etiquette of this country, every body visited immediately his disconsolate family.

Were I not to give you a minute description of what passed during the visit we paid them, you could not imagine a scene so extraordinary and melancholy as that we witnessed on this occasion, or suppose customs so barbarous could still exist among people in any degree civilized.

When we entered the house, we found it filled with an immense crowd of mourners : the ambassador's sisters and other relations were there.   His widow and daughters, besides the natural sorrow they felt for their loss, were wound up to such a height of agony and despair, that their countenances and figures were entirely changed.   Abderrahman's widow was weeping over the bier raised in the middle of the court-yard, fitted up with awnings for the purpose ; and round it the blacks were deploring her loss.   As soon as she perceived we were there, she came towards us, but immediately sunk down, and was carried senseless into the apartments.   Lilla Amnani and Abderrahman's eldest daughter had ashes strewed upon their hair, but the youngest daughter was almost covered with them.   The sufferings of this family, so aggravated by the dreadful outcries of their friends and the strangers round them, were shocking to behold.

To such scenes we may suppose for our consolation the greatest number of people here are become accustomed, and do not suffer so acutely ; but there are many, who, from their great affection for the departed, and their delicacy of feelings, are by no means capable of bearing these strong emotions : they either fall a sacrifice to them at the moment, or languish out the remainder of their days in a debilitated state.

The lamentations of the servants, slaves, and people hired on this occasion were horrid. With their nails they wounded the veins of their temples, and causing the blood to flow in streams sprinkled it over the bier, while they repeated the song of death, in which they recounted all the most melancholy circumstances they had collected on the loss of Abderrahman, and ended every painful account with piercing outcries of " *Wulliah woo !* " in which they were joined by the whole of the immense numbers of Moorish mourners who were present.

The real sufferings of the nearest relations of the deceased had not a moment's respite : even that stupor which nature yields to, when nearly exhausted, was roused into anguish by every new condoler ; many of whom came up to Abderrahman's widow and his eldest daughter, and locking them in their arms, screamed over them till the poor exhausted mourners sunk from their embraces to the earth, overwhelmed with these cruelly repeated horrors.

Unable to bear this scene longer than a short hour, we left them, promising to see them the next day, which was unavoidable, as a refusal would have been considered most unfriendly. When we departed, Lilla Amnani was conducted by her attendants to the skiffar to meet Sidy Hamet, Abderrahman's son, who was waiting there to embrace his mother. He hung upon her and wept, and endeavoured to console her in the most tender and affectionate manner ; his condolences forming a striking contrast with those she had just been receiving. His not being able to proceed farther into the house than the skiffar was the reason Lilla Amnani went to meet him ; for though the lower order of females might have veiled themselves while he passed, he could not enter within the house, on account of the women of distinction who were assembled there to mourn for his father.

We went the next morning as we had promised, hoping to find them a little calmer, but, on the contrary, they were still more agitated. The first deplorable object we beheld was Lilla Uducia, Abderrahman's eldest daughter. Her countenance was so altered that we ssarcely knew her : her temples were not injured like those of the hired people, but her face was disfigured by excessive grief ; her hair hung uncombed and unplaited ; she was pale and emaciated ; and not being able to support herself, was leaning on her blacks. She accompanied us to an apartment where we found the Greek (Lilla Amnani) and her daughter, who had sat up all night, and looked very ill. We had been there but a few minutes when Lilla Amnani and Lilla Uducia returned to mourn over the bier. We endeavoured to keep them away from it, but could not attempt to dissuade them much from what they considered a duty and a compliment to the departed. They endeavoured themselves to prevent the youngest daughter from going to the bier, particularly as this young lady, not having been married, was under the necessity of keeping a silk handkerchief tied close over her face, to avoid being seen by any strangers, and the great heat would now render her situation insupportable. She insisted on being led to the bier, promising to return very soon ; but when they attempted to lead her back she threw herself on it. As it would have been sacrilege to force her from the bier, they were obliged to let her remain till they perceived she had fainted ; they then brought her to her mother's apartment, where Lilla Amnani and Lilla Uducia lamented over her a long time before she recovered. It is incredible to relate, that no sooner did she resume the appearance of life, than a Moorish friend of consequence, who was sitting by her, began describing to her the situation of her father in the grave, which this lady, in figurative language, painted in the strongest colours ; saying, that his eyelids were closed never to be again opened, that his fine beard lay neglected and uncombed, that the sand had filled the hollow of his ear, that the worm was feasting on his cheek, that he died from his family in a distant kingdom ; and various similar ideas, sufficient, one would have thought, to drive to madness the unfortunate listener, who, at the end of her friend's speech, sunk again senseless by her side.

To shew further the manners of this country, on these occasions ; when the news of the ambassador's death was received at the castle, the Bashaw, to testify his friendship to Abderrahman, and as a compliment to this family, sent his black women and servants with orders, the moment they reached the yard of Abderrahman's house, to set up an outcry altogether ; which they did. Lilla Uducia and the Greek hearing the noise, came in alarmed from their apartments to learn the cause. The Greek was immediately surrounded by the black women, who pulling off her baracan, threw it with rage upon the ground ; they then unfastened her ear-rings and threw them down ; and, taking off the rest of her jewels, ended with the words, " Scream for your husband ! scream for your father ? " to Lilla Uducia, who stood motionless by, " scream for the ambassador, he is dead ! " The blacks then vociferated the usual lamentations of " *Wulliah woo !* " altogether. In this unaccountable manner were Lilla Amnani and Lilla Uducia first made acquainted with their loss.

When we left them to-day, the family were mourning over biers erected in three different parts of the house. The youngest daughter, who could no longer bear her face covered, had one placed in her apartment, where she remained to mourn over it with her slaves and servants. The Greek and Lilla Uducia, with ladies from the castle, were mourning in Lilla Amnani's apartments ; and the rest of the people were round the bier we first saw in the court-yard.

These dreadful lamentations not long since were extended to seven days, they are now reduced to three : how happy for the unfortunate sufferers were they altogether abolished. When this ceremony ends, a dinner will be dressed and given away to all who come for it. To-day they send bread and oil in great profusion to the marabuts, as an offering for the peace of the departed ; and to-night they dress the supper of the grave, which is portioned out to the crowds of poor who assemble at the gates of the house.

$$\text{［◯◯］}$$

December 20, 1792

We have been to-day to see the royal family, after having been absent from the castle some months, owing to the very unsettled state of the place, which has made it impossible for Christians to go thither.

We found Lilla Halluma and the princesses in tolerable spirits ; and though we went to pay them but a short visit, they detained us till after sunset, alleging that there was nothing to fear, as Sidy Useph was not in the castle. The Bashaw and the Bey came in each by himself. The Bashaw remained till the hour of his retiring to dinner, when he dispenses with the attendance of Lilla Halluma, who, according to the custom of the country, should stand by him while he eats ; but the Bashaw is only accompanied by his black women and his favourite Jewess Queen Esther.

Soon after the Bey and the Bashaw had departed, a collation was served in the covered gallery before Lilla Halluma's apartment. As the party to-day consisted only of Lilla Halluma, three of the princesses, and our family, we had the pleasure of seeing them all sit down with us, instead of Lilla Halluma walking round the table, attended by the princesses, and conversing alternately with the guests ; which she does if there are any Moorish nobility at dinner, as it is considered too great a condescension in her to sit down and eat with her subjects. Lilla Halluma's urbanity, and the dignity of her manners, were as usual equally engaging and fascinating, nor could those of the most polished sovereign in Europe have been more striking ; with this infinite advantage, that court duplicity forms no part of her character. You would have smiled to have seen us seated on costly cushions on the ground, round an ivory table inlaid with gold, not twelve inches high, with plenty of variegated spoons of coral, ebony, ivory, mother-of-pearl, and tortoise-shell, chiefly inlaid with pearls and precious stones, but according to custom, all of us without knives, forks, or plates.

The number of attendants exceeded by far that of the company : not less than two or three blacks attended on each of the guests, and supplied them amply with gold embroidered towels and scented waters.

The table is always covered with forty or fifty dishes, each of which is taken off by a black and handed round to the company, to help themselves ; but to-day, Lilla Halluma, to let her company have the dinner hot, ordered it to be served in the true Turkish style. Only one dish was brought in at once, and they extended to a number not easy to be remembered accurately. This mode of serving caused a very considerable time to be spent at the repast.

Another table was ready prepared, where among dried and fresh fruits, and various sherbets (instead of wine), were some curious specimens from Constantinople, Egypt, and this country, displaying different ways of preparing confectionary, and light beverage. Among the confectionary, were orange and lemon flowers, the cocoa-nut highly preserved, and the juice of numerous fruits converted into hard cakes of sweetmeat.

Anecdotes, similar to several in the Arabian tales, in all but fiction, enlivened the glass, not of wine, but of sherbet. To many of the pieces of china, or other ornaments of the dessert, was annexed some interesting account. Lilla Halluma bid us observe some china vases, which contained preserves of orange flowers. These vases, of the most beautiful Neapolitan china, were a present from her favourite grandson, Sidy Mahmoud ; but she told us at the same time, they were the gift of the Prophet, to remind her how near she was losing him, at the time he was collecting them for her at Naples, where he lost his heart to Lady Hamilton, and brought back her miniature set with brilliants. Lilla Halluma, who was extremely religious, shuddered to think how far his Mahomedan faith might have suffered by that fascinating fair one, and bid the princess next to her relate to us the following events, which she did nearly in these words.

When Sidy Mahmoud left this country as ambassador for Naples, he was betrothed to a young lady named Selima, of Turkish descent, and his remorse for having neglected her, nearly cost him his life after his return to Tripoli. You will ask whence this acute feeling in Sidy Mahmoud for his disappointed bride, whom, by the laws of his country, he could not have seen till after the celebration of his marriage with her. But notwithstanding the severest restrictions of the Prophet Mahomet on this point, and the seclusion of a female's life, yet by the help of emissaries (which for money are to be found in this country on all occasions), those betrothed sometimes obtain, with difficulty and danger, a distant view of each other, and even learn each other's sentiments. From intelligence procured in this manner, the parties after being engaged, will often, one or both, so strongly oppose their intended nuptials, as to sacrifice life and fortune, rather than submit to the union, which their parents, on both sides, have frequently planned from the moment of their children's birth. Sidy Mahmoud, accustomed to the extravagant ideas of this country, considered his being betrothed to a stranger as a matter of indifference. He heard the lady had youth and beauty, he knew she was rich, and he felt himself satisfied in inquiring no farther. It was not so with his destined bride : she left nothing undone to discover his character, and gain a sight of his person. She soon satisfied herself in both these wishes, and was enraptured to find the result surpassed her warmest imaginations. But on repeated inquiries, finding Sidy Mahmoud betrayed not the least curiosity relative to herself, Selima grew melancholy, and was offended at the coldness of his conduct, so ill suited to her own ideas.

When the Bey with his suite took the diversion of racing on the sands, Sidy Mahmoud generally accompanied him. The road the Bey took obliged them always to pass the residence of Selima. From the moment this lady learned she was intended for the bride of Sidy Mahmoud, she never failed, by different contrivances, to gain a sight of him from her father's golphor, which required the greatest circumspection ; ladies not being permitted to enter it, though it is known they often infringe this rule. Selima used to see from hence the Bey and Sidy Mahmoud pass leisurely on their horses close under the walls of her father's garden, where the golphor was situated, and had the latter experienced the slightest wish to see his intended bride, he might have here expected a chance of satisfying his desires. One day, in particular, the Bey stropped to talk a long time with the father of Selima, who had been riding out with him. The agitated Selima watched Sidy Mahmoud ; but he turned no inquiring eye to the building, nor bestowed a look on the jealousies of the golphor, whence the anxious Selima had been so often disappointed, by Sidy Mahmoud's want of curiosity, that she was at last confined by illness, and not able to continue longer her visits thither.

For Selima's declining health, in vain were all the Dervizes [1] in Tripoli consulted. Lambs were sacrificed ; oil and provisions were carried daily to the mosques ; sentences from the Koran were written by the sacred hand of the Imam, burnt to ashes, mixed in wine, and drank by the fair sufferer ; but nothing availed. The bloom of Selima's cheek disappeared, and her friends trembled for her life : she became too ill to leave her apartments, and saw none but her nearest relatives. At length an ingenious plan was contrived to satisfy her scruples with regard to Sidy Mahmoud : but whether the means by which Selima gained the satisfaction of being seen by her intended lord were contrived by her own relations, or that one of her attendants, who is very much attached to her, had ventured to accomplish such an event without her mistress's orders, remains a profound secret.

At this time the brother of Selima, who was very fond of her, and the most intimate friend of Sidy Mahmoud, gave an entertainment to the latter in his father's golphor (the same whence the anxious Selima had so often watched him). On these occasions, when feasts are given by the gentlemen of the house, the greatest precautions are taken that none of the ladies of the family may risk being exposed to view.

Selima considered the entertainment her brother meant to give Sidy Mahmoud as an addition to her sufferings, as it was given solely in consequence of her intended nuptials ; at the thought of which she now shuddered, being fully persuaded that Sidy Mahmoud's extreme indifference about herself was the effect of an attachment he had to some happier object.

While all in the house were anxiously busy, preparing for her brother's guest, Selima's most confidential attendant, named Ismaini, came to her and sat down by her side as she lay on her couch. Selima,

___

[1] *I.e.* Derwishes : holy men.

out of humour, did not wish to be disturbed, and ordered her attendant to retire ; but Ismaini informed her that her favourite Gibeleen (mountain woman), the wife of one of her father's gardeners who lived in the garden, was dying, and in the greatest affliction, because she wished to see Lilla Selima on some particular occasion, and knew she durst not ask a thing so impracticable. When the voice of affliction called, Selima was all attention ; she concluded it was some last favour this poor woman had to ask, and she determined to wrap herself cautiously up in her baracan, and venture with Ismaini into the garden, to a little cottage she had given to this Gibeleen.

Selima found the poor woman in the state she was led to expect, apparently very ill, and laying down ; but it was not till after she had been with her a considerable time, that she noticed the figure of a country woman who sat on the bed-side and supported the invalid. Struck with this figure remaining closely veiled all this time (which conduct amounted to a mark of disrespect in her presence), she hastily inquired who this woman was, and why she remained with her face concealed before her, and was told it was a friend from the mountains to see the Gibeleen, who was ashamed to uncover herself in Selima's presence ; and she was entreated to forgive her ignorance and not to be angry with her. While this was passing, the figure suddenly disappeared. Selima felt herself uneasy and alarmed, and immediately left the cottage. As she retired, she questioned Ismaini and threatened to forbid her her presence, but could gain no further intelligence concerning the stranger till the next morning ; when Ismaini brought her a message from Sidy Mahmoud, entreating her to pardon the Gibeleen, whom he was told had displeased her ; saying, he should consider her taking the Gibeleen under her protection again, as a favour done to himself.

Whether Selima received any other message in addition to the above, to inform her that Sidy Mahmoud was the figure in disguise who supported the sick mountaineer, is not known ; but not only the Gibeleen was forgiven, but Ismaini became a still greater favourite.

After this event the fairies, or Sidy Mahmoud himself, kept Selima constantly informed of his proceedings ; and on the days he went with the Bey to ride on the sands, she was always prepared beforehand with some new ornament of dress, and her toilet was infinitely longer than usual ; while Sidy Mahmoud, accustomed to ride with ease the finest chargers, could not now get one to pass Selima's residence without difficulty : they were obstinate, took offence at the bridle, and occasioned such delays as led him frequently to alight, while his horse was examined and put to rights.

At this time the Bashaw fixed on Sidy Mahmoud to go as ambassador to Naples, which he endeavoured to avoid, disliking to leave the country which now held all that he esteemed worth living for, and he also dreaded the effect it would have on his fair Selima ; but as the time for celebrating their wedding was yet distant, the Bashaw would not admit Sidy Mahmoud's refusal, and he was obliged to depart for Naples.

While he was stationed in this vortex of dissipation, the charms, the very licentious manners of the Neapolitans, the brilliancy of the court, and its courtezans, had such an effect on the heart of the young ambassador, that he became for a time alive only to the delusive scenes in which he was engaged. During this period, malice brought an exaggerated account of his conduct to his faithful Selima. She had nearly fallen a victim to her feelings when Sidy Mahmoud returned to Tripoli, who, satiated before he had quitted the shores of Naples, and remembering no more the syrens he had left behind, thought again solely on his Selima, but dreaded the probability of her having heard of his amours.

When he arrived at Selima's residence, he was told her life was despaired of ; and instead of preparations for his nuptials, found them busy preparing for her hourly expected dissolution. Artificial flowers lay about in abundance, and when his foreboding heart led him to ask for what purpose they were intended, he was informed they were to ornament the bier of Selima. This unhappy account had such an effect on Sidy Mahmoud, that he was for several hours senseless and at the point of death. As soon as he recovered his reason, he had once more recourse to disguise. Concealed again as a female in a common baracan, he went to the faithful Ismaini, to whose assistance he owed the first sight he had obtained of Selima at the Gibeleen's cottage. Ismaini conducted him to the apartments of her mistress, and told her that this was a Tunisian woman with news concerning Sidy Mahmoud, and that she would not confide what she had to say to any one but herself ; adding, that she would keep the avenues to the apartments clear till the Tunisian had delivered her message. It was with the greatest difficulty Ismaini prevailed on her mistress to let the stranger approach her, which when she did, Selima, with an emaciated look and feeble voice, desired she would not be too long in delivering what she had to say, as she was not able to attend to her, and hardly wished to waste any of the few moments she believed she had to live in talking or thinking again of Sidy Mahmoud, who had long forgotten her, and was too far off to reach her, even if he wished it, in time to see her before she fell a sacrifice to his infidelity : besides, said she, I am so altered, that he who was once surprized to see how beautiful I was, would now find no resemblance of me. Sidy Mahmoud, who under his disguise had attended to all she said, could hardly recover strength of voice enough to acquaint her with the events he wished to relate before he discovered himself. He succeeded, however, and while she wept at the account of his repentance and sufferings, he seized the favourable moment to shew himself to her. An event so unexpected called for the immediate assistance of Ismaini, who was nearer to her mistress at this crisis than she imagined. She caught the fainting Selima in her arms, and Sidy Mahmoud, wrapping himself closely up in his baracan, hastened to leave the house without being discovered by the attendants. Selima, to the surprize and joy of her friends, recovered her health rapidly from this hour, and they had soon the satisfaction of seeing her united to Sidy Mahmoud.

This strange circumstance, added the princess who was relating to us the story, has converted these artificial flowers, which were meant for bouquets to ornament the bier of Selima, into garlands to adorn these Neapolitan vases, and they were given so adorned to my mother by Sidy Mahmoud, saying they would be a memento, that it had been in his power to change the destination of these flowers, and he hoped that circumstance would procure his pardon for having so nearly sacrificed the fair Selima, to whom he had long ago delivered Lady Hamilton's picture.

The sun had set before Lilla Halluma would suffer us to leave her. She had been in excellent spirits, but, unhappily, previous to our departure, very alarming intelligence was brought again of Sidy Useph. When the accounts arrived, contrary to the custom of not disturbing the Bashaw after sunset, the news was carried to him before we deaparted, that Sidy Useph with a strong force had halted within five miles of the town. Chaouxes were sent off to call in the Arabs from the west ; the avenues to the harem, which had been left more open than usual latterly, were ordered now to be closed ; and when we took our leave of Lilla Halluma all was suspicion and anxiety.

January 19, 1793

Though it is near two months since the funeral ceremonies were performed at Lilla Amnani's for the ambassador's death, yet she would not herself put on mourning till letters with the fatal news came directly to the family, according to the etiquette of the country. These letters are received, and the afflicted Lilla Amnani commenced her mourning yesterday.

The ceremonies performed by a Moorish lady when putting on and quitting her weeds will to you appear singular. Lilla Amnani, accompanied by her blacks and attendants, and perfectly concealed by the multiplicity of the coverings she wore, went to the seaside, where her hair was combed with a gold comb, and the tresses plaited with white silk mixed with them, instead of black ; and she put on a white binder over her forehead, instead of a gold one ornamented with jewels, which she usually wears.

The period fixed for a widow's mourning is four months and ten days. At the expiration of that time, Lilla Amnani goes again to the sea-side. The same gold comb she had used before is carried with her, and four fresh eggs ; the eggs she gives to the first person she meets, who is obliged to receive them, were it even the Bashaw himself. With the eggs, it is imagined, she gives away all her misfortunes, consequently no person likes to receive them ; but this custom is so established, that not any one thinks of refusing them. She then proceeds to the seaside, where her hair is combed a second time, and the comb thrown into the sea by herself ; and she is then, and not before, at liberty to marry again.

We were with her yesterday : all superfluous articles of dress were put away, as well as those of furniture. To denote the house being in a state of mourning, neither curtains, looking-glasses, tapestry, nor carpets were to be seen, except what could not be dispensed with. The blacks had their caps turned the wrong side outwards, and wore neither silver nor beads. Lilla Amnani had neither her feet nor hands painted with henna ; she wore no bracelets on her hands or ankles, nor had she any jewels. No perfumes or scented waters were allowed to be used, being considered articles of dress.

Hadgi Mahmute, the husband of Lilla Uducia, is expected daily from Morocco, where the ambassador died. Lilla Amnani feels now the very great advantage she has over Moorish widows, from having possessed so entirely Hadgi Abderrahman's confidence till his death. From this circumstance, she remains without being in the least subject to any of his relations, but entirely mistress of his children and all that he has left.

January 23, 1793

For some days continual messages have passed from Sidy Useph, at the Messeah, to the Bashaw, who is very strenuous with the Bey to have another conference with his brother ; but to this the Bey entirely objects, and has been so alarmed for his own safety, that he has increased considerably the town-guard at night.

In consequence of the advice of a famous dervise, who came very lately from the mountains, and who was closeted with the Bashaw several hours yesterday, the Bashaw to-day, accompanied by the Bey, has been to the mosques to worship and make offerings to the prophet. In his way, he stopped at the residence of the shaik, who, according to the etiquette of the country, presented two of his blacks to the Bashaw, as an acknowledgment of the honour done him by his sovereign. On his return from the mosques, the Bashaw and the Bey passed our house and drank coffee and sherbet with us. A friend in their suite sent to advise us of their coming, and the time was quite short enough to prepare refreshments for two or three hundred persons. The Bashaw appeared in good spirits, and said, in the Bey's hearing, that he did not doubt of Sidy Useph's returning to his duty, and that he yet hoped to see him live peaceably in the castle, and leave his brother in quiet possession of the throne. This speech, which every body was convinced was the effect of the conversation the Bashaw had had yesterday with the dervise, seemed to make a sad impression on the Bey, and indeed upon all present. Some of the Bashaw's officers of state told us they were sure the dervise had not come from the mountains without his instructions from Sidy Useph ; and others expressed their serious fears that the Bashaw meant to give up the Bey, and that he would share the fate of his brothers Hassan (the late Bey), and fall by the hands of assassins. Though they stopped some time, neither the Bashaw nor Bey alighted. In the way from our house, three marabuts (or saints) joined them, who were immediately led to the side of the Bashaw, and walking close by his horse, accompanied him to the castle.

Nothing can be more melancholy than to behold the country torn by such intestine broils as inevitably must destroy it.

☒

February 28, 1793

In consequence of the arrival of Hadgi Mahmute with the wreck of the presents for the Bashaw of Tripoli, which had been consigned by the late Emperor of Morocco to the ambassador Hadgi Abderrahman, we went to see his daughter this morning. Hadgi Mahmute gives the following account of the few last days of Hadgi Abderrahman's life, and the events which occasioned his death.

The late Emperor of Morocco was, as I have told you, exceedingly attached to the Bashaw, and in consequence of the present afflicted state of Tripoli, and the striking similarity of the Bashaw's sufferings and his own, both being occasioned by the unnatural conduct of their sons, the Emperor ordered immense presents to be given to the ambassador for the Bashaw, among which was an invaluable clock nearly covered with jewels, seven of the finest horses, rich saddles, arms, a number of beautiful slaves, men and women, and several large cargoes of wheat.

A vessel demanded by the Emperor from the Christians (which is always done on these occasions), was laying sumptuously fitted up in the harbour to convey the ambassador to Tripoli, with the greatest part of the presents on board. Hadgi Abderrahman had had his last audience of the Emperor, and gave an entertainment to his friends at Morocco the evening before he intended to depart. During this entertainment unexpected news was dispatched to the ambassador by some of his friends from the palace, to inform him that the Emperor had suddenly set off to head his troops at Sallee against his rebellious son Muley Yesied, and that since his departure some of Muley Yesied's chief officers had arrived in town, and, by threats and persuasions, were endeavouring to prevail on the Emperor's ministers to lay an embargo on the vessels in the harbour, with a view to plunder them, if any accident befel the Emperor on his way, or in meeting with his son Muley Yesied.

The ambassador's health had been declining from repeated fatigues, and the many long and arduous embassies he had completed for his country. His frame, at his advanced age, was too weak to bear the shock this news gave him, at the moment his loyal heart was distended with joy at the great success of this embassy, which he had considered as the last he should be able to undertake for his beloved master. He sunk back in his seat at the table, when he was instantly bled and put to bed. In the morning, as no embargo had yet been laid on the vessels, the ambassador, not being able to support himself, ordered a litter to be prepared to convey him immediately on board, without waiting for the part of the presents that were not yet embarked. His suite were assembled, and all things ready for his departure ; when, in consequence of news having arrived at Morocco of the Emperor's death, on his way to Sallee, a royal mandate was presented in form, by the satellites of the new Emperor Muley Yesied, to prevent all persons from leaving Morocco on pain of death, and from removing an iota of their property from the capital, until further orders ; and an embargo was laid at the same instant on all shipping in the port. Sinking under this last stroke of ill-fortune, the ambassador was carried back to his couch. He sent off couriers to the new Emperor, two of which were pursued and brought back in chains when thirty miles on their way to Sallee ; and before the third was dispatched, the worthy Abderrahman, who had been four days speechless, had fallen a martyr to the loyalty of his feelings.

Owing to the great confusion throughout the whole kingdom of Morocco, Sidy Mahmute, the son-in-law, and Hassead, the nephew of Hadgi Abderrahman, were threatened with being despoiled of all belonging to them, if they did not immediately leave Morocco without any of the presents.

A third courier was dispatched by Sidy Mahmute, at the hazard of his life, secretly at midnight, with hopes that the darkness of the night might be favourable to the beginning of his journey, and enable him to reach, undiscovered, the camp of the Emperor Muley Yesied, with petitions and remonstrances from Sidy Mahmute to recover the presents assigned for the Bashaw by his father. But though this courier succeeded in delivering his message to the Emperor, a watch, and a white horse caparisoned, were all that was obtained, out of the immense treasures destined for the Bashaw ; and owing to the auk-wardness of the Rais's fregategees, or sailors, in disembarking the horse from the vessel, it was obliged to be killed the moment it reached the shore.

Before Sidy Mahmute left Morocco, a great number of Muley Yesied's slaves, and some belonging to his sister, were brought for sale to the public market. The sister of Muley Yesied, out of respect to her father's memory, had freed five of her slaves ; but they had, notwithstanding, been seized, and their papers of freedom taken from them ; they were then stripped of their habits and all their ornaments, and, covered merely with a coarse woollen shift, were sent to the slave market and sold. Nothing could equal the distress of these unfortunate people, after having, for a few short hours, enjoyed the sweets of freedom, to find that, in. defiance of the established custom of the Mahometans, who, when they free their slaves, free them for ever, they were thrown again immediately into slavery. Yet they consoled themselves with having quitted the country where Muley Yesied reigned, and that they were not taken back to his palace. They envied the fate of a very fine young woman who, with themselves, was freed at the Emperor's death. She had had the courage to set off instantly from Fez to Tunis, where, after having walked many hundred miles with the caravans across the African deserts, she was, through the compassion of Şidy Mahmute, brought with his blacks to Tripoli. They spoke with despair of the difference between their situation and hers. She being free, is going in a few hours to join the caravan from Tripoli to Fezzan, her own country, at the moment her old companions in slavery will be embarked for different parts of the globe. Among the latter is a most extraordinary person : she was born in Asia at the foot of Mount Caucasus, a white negress, extremely mild in her manners and uncouth in her figure. Her hands, when she stood up, reached beyond her knees ; her legs were likewise very long ; her waist very short, and her shoulders as broad and as athletic as those of a strong man. Her hands and feet were astonishingly small for her size ; her head was covered with white wool instead of hair ; her complexion white, without a tinge of red in the cheek ; her eyes light, with white eyelashes, and without the mark of an eyebrow. She spoke in a mixture of the Moorish and the black's tongue ; the dialect of her native country, which is a nation of the Kesty, and has no resemblance to that of any known language, while their. origin and manners are also totally unknown. She was stolen from her parents in her infancy by a party of the Offi, another of the Caucasian nations who live by the plunder of youth, whom they carry out of the country and sell. This woman gave us a singular description of her situation in the family of Muley Yesied's sister.

When Muley Yesied used to visit his sister, which he generally did without being expected, all the blacks in her palace on his arrival immediately ran to hide themselves in chests, behind sacks of wheat,

C.T.—11*

behind doors, or in any place, to escape being of the number the tyrant would wantonly and cruelly sacrifice on this occasion ; and Muley Yesied, aware the blacks were afraid of him, would himself penetrate into all the parts of the palace he could, to search for them. One day this Caucasian seeing Muley Yesied approach the place where she was, and not being able to fly further out of his way, got behind a large wood-fire, on which was a great pot boiling, suspended by an iron hook. She concealed herself behind this pot and the smoke, and though she was dragged from thence the moment the tyrant disappeared, she was so dreadfully scorched, that she has remained marked with deep scars, notwithstanding it is a twelvemonth since this dreadful event happened. This poor slave was not alarmed that day without reason ; Muley Yesied amusing himself with the blacks in a game of ball he had desired them to play at (and none dared refuse him), they were, unhappily for them, struck with such panic, that many of them appeared in an ague fit, while diffidence in Muley Yesied's eyes always merited death. He accordingly destroyed six of the blacks, and a handsome Greek youth (one of his sister's mamelukes) who could not help shuddering at his atrocities. To make up for this loss he sent twelve of his finest blacks to his sister that evening.

This princess, from the beauty of her person and the amiableness of her disposition, was named by her husband Cobah (or the morning star) ; her sister, for the same reason, was honoured by the high epithet with which the Mahometans adorn in letters of gold their cakes of opium, that is " Mashallah," or the Gift of God.[1] These two princesses, reputed without a fault in their hearts or tempers, were, with the tyrant Muley Yesied, born of the same mother, who is as remarkable for the urbanity of her manners as her daughters, while Muley Yesied's talents, which might be reckoned bright, prove him any thing but a human being.

The dresses of the ladies at the court of Morocco are much lighter than those worn by the ladies of Tripoli. The favourite habit of the Lilla Cobah is pale pink satin, covered with drapery of transparent muslin, fastened under each arm with braces of light blue velvet, almost covered with precious stones, and gold embroidery between each row of jewels : even her sandals are set with precious stones. She does not wear a cap like the Moorish ladies, or any thing on her head but a band of jewels ; and her hair, plaited in numberless small

---

[1] *Masha'llah* means literally " by God's wish " and is usually an exclamation of appraisal or surprise.

tresses, is confined by strings of large pearls. She dyes her fingers as the ladies do here, perfectly black under the rings she wears, and likewise dyes her feet to show off the jewels of her sandals.

The daughter of Shaik Saffanassa, at present Empress of Morocco, whom Muley Yesied stole from this country, has, since his death, petitioned the new Emperor, Muley Ishem, to send her back to her father. Nothing can abate the desire this young Arabian princess has to find herself again in her native deserts. Disgusted with the atrocities and injustice she has seen, she eagerly seeks the residence of the African chief her father, which, among steep and craggy mountains, offers her more charms than she can find in her palaces at Fez or Morocco.

To return to Hadgi Abderrahman's family. The immense sums the ambassador has spent on this embassy has rendered them severe sufferers. The Bashaw and Lilla Halluma shew every mark of attachment and protection to Lilla Amnani, and both these sovereigns mourn sincerely for the loss of her husband.

March 10, 1793

We have been earlier and oftener harassed with land winds than is usual. It has blown a perfect storm from the deserts for the last four days. The ground and air contained a degree of heat insupportable : travellers have perished lately who were even supplied with water : the great heat killed them. We fear this wind will last seven days, as it generally does when it exceeds three. Its serious and fatal effect, when lengthened to seven and nine days, I have described to you, but it oftener subsides in a few hours. Many jars of water have been thrown by the blacks over the floors of our apartments, which are of stone, and each room is left for a time empty, with the doors and windows close shut. In a short time, by this method, they acquire a most salutary coolness, which relieves the respiration. But in this case, as the sand finds its way through the smallest crevice in the apartments, and no particle of it enters without its proportion of heat, every opening, though ever so trifling, must be attended to, that none may enter, as it would frustrate all attempts to cool the apartment ; the door being opened only once or twice even this temporary comfort is over. The apartments, though it is now midnight, are as intensely hot as ever ; nor can these winds be described so as to communicate any just idea of them, which can only be done by feeling their force and effect. The deserts near Tripoli resemble the finest and whitest silver sand, but that brought by a land wind is quite different : it is equally fine but of the deepest red, and only to be met with in Tripoli at these times, when it lies in such quantities on the floor of the galleries and ridges of the windows, as to be swept up and carried away in baskets several times in the day. There is no eating nor sleeping in this weather : a fan of palm leaves, and a glass of lemonade, are all the sufferers seem alive to. The Moors add to these reliefs the enjoyment of a cold bath, but that often proves a dangerous expedient.

By relating to you how we passed a day last week, in an excursion into the country, you will be able to form a general idea of the many days we have spent in this manner since we have been here. It has been usual for a general party of Christians to dine out of town, in different parts of the country, about once a week, for many years past, till some time after the present troubles began, which rendered it impossible for them to go unaccompanied by Moors of consequence, and with more guards than were always convenient. This recreation was therefore quite given up for the present. It is the custom here, whenever Sidy Useph retires with his people from before the town, if it be but few days, to throw open the gates, and every apprehension appears to be removed : in consequence of these ideas, the Bashaw's first minister, Mustapha Scrivan, invited a large party of the Christians to dine at his gardens, about three miles out of town. As it was known he had taken trouble to prepare every thing in the best manner he possibly could for our reception, and that no excuse could be made through fear or doubt of safety under his protection, his offer could not be refused ; besides which, after having been shut up for many weeks in the town, the temptation was irresistible to enjoy the aromatic perfumes and luxuriant shades of the orange groves at this season, when the air, if free from land winds, is most salubrious.

We were accompanied in our excursion by some Dutch and Venetian officers who happened to be here. Horses were sent from the castle for these gentlemen, an indulgence the Bashaw often shews the Christians on such occasions ; but some of the gentlemen paid severely by fright, from their distrust of the Moorish bridles, the mouth of the Arabian horse being much too delicate to bear the European ones substituted for them.[1]

---

[1] Nothing could be more severe than the Arab bit. Unless these horses had been only halter ridden, it must have been poor horsemanship, and not the European bit, which was responsible.

When we arrived at Mustapha Scrivan's garden, we were all escorted to his golphor, which is built in the middle of his garden at a distance from the dwelling house. A pleasing light penetrated into this apartment through the thick foliage of the orange trees, as well as the jasmines, honeysuckles, and roses, that covered entirely the lattice windows which surround this golphor on all sides.

The hours before dinner were passed by the gentlemen in playing at chess with the Moors of rank, the Bashaw's first minister, the Cataib, and the Dugganeer. The ladies went into the dwelling-house to pay a visit to the minister's young bride : her age, with that of the Spanish Consul's bride, who was in our party, did not amount to twenty-four years ; the former being eleven, and the latter not thirteen. It was singular to hear these two children (as one must term them) talking of their babies, both of which were very fine infants, about six months old.

Dancing women, and refreshments of all sorts, were immediately produced on our arrival at the bride's apartments, who, with her mother and sisters, were superbly dressed : her jewels, gold, and silver, displayed the opulence of the minister.

While we were entertained in Mustapha Scrivan's harem, he ordered men and women dancers into the garden, to gratify the curiosity of the officers and those gentlemen who had not seen the extraordinary feats performed in these dances, and other violent exertions peculiar to this country.

We remained with the Moorish ladies till a mameluke from the minister came to the dwelling-house, and informed us that the gentlemen had waited dinner for us some time. We left them with regret, the bride's mother being extremely agreeable, and the scene altogether novel. The brides had exchanged presents : a quantity of Genoa velvet, with gold and silver lace and coral buttons, for a jelick, were presented by the Spaniard's bride to the minister's, and she received a valuable ring from her young Moorish friend in return.

Sherbets and coffee, together with walking in the gardens, filled up the time from dinner to sunset, when we mounted our horses and returned to town, and were obliged to pass through a very large caravan, encamped in the Pianura, which had arrived since the morning. Numbers in the caravan, unused to the sight of Christians, expressed their surprise at our appearance, which engaged so much of their attention as to render it difficult for the Moors to clear the way for us to pass by them and their merchandize. Our curiosity was no less excited. In some places, groups of Moors were seated on the ground playing at chess, having marked a chessboard[1] in the sand, and substituted pebbles for the pieces of the game ; others sat around a straw fire by the side of a tent, which the Moors were hastily erecting. Circles of women were cooking. These latter groups, by the confusion we occasioned, were quickly dispersed, putting down, or throwing away, whatever they had in their hands. Some of them, on seeing us, ran away through fright, and others advanced with exultation to meet us. They invited us into their tents, and would have given us the best they had, if we would have partaken of their fare.

As the Moors and Arabs of the lower class are, in their manner of living, but a few degrees above animals, and are content without any of the conveniences of life, they would be by far the dirtiest creatures which are found in their tents, had not Mahomet wisely ordered them to wash as often as three times a day, and to have made this indispensably necessary to their salvation. Of these ablutions the one called abdest,[2] which is preparatory to their prayer, is considered the most sacred ; therefore, they are expected to attend rigidly to the rules laid down for it in the Koran, which directs them at this ablution to begin by washing their head and arms, next their neck, face, and feet. Hundreds we saw who, not being near enough to where there was water, to be in time to perform this ablution before the sun was set, prostrated themselves on the earth, and made a semblance of washing, which they afterwards performed in reality the moment they could get it. On their crowding round us, we were glad to find ourselves so near the gates of the city, on entering which, we were free from their importunities.

It is more than ten days since the people of the town have had free access to the Messeah, during which period they have gone out daily for provisions ; but they have by no means laid in the stock they were expected to do, to provide against the time that must shortly arrive, when all supplies will be again cut off, by the approach of Sidy Useph's people.

April 28, 1793

We have had the place in great confusion for some days past, by circumstances distinct from the usual cause of alarm, and were near

---

[1] More probably the ancient Bedouin game called *mangoul*.
[2] A Persian word. The Arabic is *wudhu*.

having a tragical Parisian scene acted here by the *sans-culottes*. Some months since, a very serious affray happened between some Spanish and French crews here. Several men on both sides were nearly cut to pieces, and the French, the greatest part of whom were *sans-culottes*, went away dissatisfied with their Consul, who is a loyalist.

This week, to the great surprise of every one and to the French Consul, a French frigate appeared with a new Consul on board, sent by the French Republic. It is not easy to conceive the consternation and terror of the French family ; the Consul, Vice-Consul, and Chancellor were considered to be in the most imminent danger. The officers of the French frigate, the captain of which had been a hairdresser some years back, hurried on shore, and the new Consul with them. After the Consul had been received at the castle, the French assembled in the court-yard of the Consular house. Here they made an enquiry into the former Consul's conduct. The sailors were outrageous ; they planted the tree of liberty in the yard, and held a sham trial of the French family, whom it was expected would be sacrificed by these abandoned people. The new republican Consul, fortunately, behaved well on this occasion. A long speech was composed partly by the French, and partly by the rest of the Consuls here, and was delivered with such success to the mob at the French house, as to arrest and turn their intentions ; and after a short time, a loud cry of " *vive la Nation ! vive la Republique ! et vivent les Citoyens !* " meaning the former Consul, Vice-Consul, and Chancellor, announced them all to be out of danger. But a continued scene of rioting ensued till these people left the shore, to the great satisfaction of every one. They were detained by the Bashaw twenty-four hours after a Spanish cruiser had sailed, to give the latter time to clear the coast, according to the treaties of the powers at peace with the Bashaw, that none of their ships shall be molested from this port, within a certain time after their quitting the harbour.

May 10, 1793

This morning, at four o'clock, the unwelcome news was brought us that Sidy Useph had arrived within four miles of the town, with a much more considerable force than he has yet appeared with, consisting chiefly of Arabs, with the addition of the Moors of Sahal and the Seide, two considerable districts belonging to the Bashaw. The guards stationed at the town gates closed them as soon as it was known. Remonstrances were made to the Bey to open the gates again, as many people belonging to the town were shut out, and the Bashaw ordered them to be opened immediately. The Bey was heard to say, that as his father was in Sidy Useph's interest, the gates might be left open constantly, that his brother might walk in quietly, without the trouble of cutting his way to the castle through a handful of troops kept for the mere ceremony of opposing him. A Moor, named Bunny, went up to the Bey for directions, saying, he was ordered out by the Bashaw with a party of horse to scour round the walls of the town, till the Arabs arrived in sufficient numbers to oppose Sidy Useph, and he should then go out with them. No sooner had Bunny quitted the castle, than the Bey suspecting his intentions, sent a hamper, one of his guards, after him, desiring him to return for further orders. The hamper found this officer at the gates of the town, surrounded by a few of his attendants ; and, while he was yet speaking, Bunny shot him, and rode off full speed to Sidy Useph, with the few people he had with him.

During the first hours of this alarm, the Bashaw would not allow of any additional guards being called to the castle, nor did the Chiah give orders to barricade the streets, which has been always done on these occasions. At length the Bey seemed to have the full command of the town allowed him by his father. Before daybreak the next morning the Bey sent his brother-in-law, the Rais of the Marine, to the coast, with vessels and orders to fire upon the Pianura. By some mistake the guns fired from the Rais's vessels were directed against a party of the Bashaw's soldiers instead of Sidy Useph's, which threw them all into dreadful confusion ; but such a circumstance is less to be wondered at here than in Europe. Arabian troops are so similar in appearance, that sometimes it is only a particular flag, or a small difference in their arms and manner of wearing them, that distinguish the enemy, and they are recognized among the Moors by a striking difference in the complexions and persons of one tribe of Arabs from another. We saw the whole of this engagement from our terrace, where curiosity leads us to pass a few hours every day during these extraordinary times. The Moors retain in their combats much of the manners of the ancients.

Cyde Mahomet, the Bey's wife's brother, was nearly taken under the walls of the town about noon to-day, while Lilla Howviva, his sister, was looking at him from one of the towers of the castle : his people lost seven of their horses, and his own horse was shot dead under him. From his sudden fall at this instant, Lilla Howviva imagined he was killed, and the attendants ran to her assistance and saved her, while fainting, from falling off the ramparts of the castle. They were severely reprimanded by the Bey for having accompanied her to so dangerous and exposed a spot. One of Cyde Mahomet's guards came to us this morning from his master : this man's horse was wounded, yet they are so much in want of horses at the castle, that the hamper was ordered out in the afternoon with the same unfortunate beast.

The English Consul, who was with the Bey in the morning, saw a prisoner richly dressed, dragged into town from the Pianura by the hair. The Moors assigned as an excuse for this act of cruelty, that the man had deserted from the Bashaw's troops with a large party under him but a few days before. Orders were given, if he survived the present punishment, that he should be hanged to-morrow as a traitor in front of the Pianura.

The Arabs who were coming to the Bashaw's assistance are not yet arrived, and Sidy Useph's people increase so much, that all the force they could collect in the town appeared inadequate to succeed in repelling him. The Bey ordered the town gates to be shut closely at four o'clock in the afternoon, and all the force that could be collected employed to defend them till more Arabs arrived. The tribes of the Knowiales are expected to-night. These people come from the westward, between this place and Tunis.

Sidy Useph's people finding the Bey did not give them battle, turned about to plunder all the huts and gardens near the Pianura. On this occasion, the extraordinary groups that flocked to the town were equally distressing and singular. Some were composed of large families, men, women, and children, entirely despoiled of all they had. They came wringing their hands and tearing their hair, but were forbid to scream when they entered the town, on pain of being shut out of it, that the enemy might not exult in the advantages he had gained. Behind a Gibeleen family from the mountains were two females, carefully concealed in baracans, with a few women round them. These excited much curiosity, as there being so totally concealed denoted them to be much above the groups they were accompanying : they proved to be women belonging to a rich Tripolitan merchant, who not expecting Sidy Useph, had remained out at his garden, and these ladies at the risk of their lives had escaped in the night with the

Moors they were now accompanying. To give you a further picture of this distressed party, a family, which had escaped being plundered, passed under our windows : of this group a man came on driving two camels heavily laden with corn, barley, oil, eggs, and vegetables of all sorts, and many other articles of clothes and lumber. His wife, a pretty Beduoin, followed him, driving three cows : behind her were four small children ; the eldest of them a little girl not seven years old, was leading four lambs by one string : and two others had bundles on their heads, as large as their little limbs could support. Three Bedouin men, armed with guns and knives, leading two large dogs with chains, brought up the rear.

Such parties, some smaller and some larger, continued to pass through the town, the whole of the afternoon. Their increasing numbers were seen with great distress by the people here, as there are no provisions whatever in this place, and the little these people have saved from the ravages of Sidy Useph, is insufficient to form any proportion to their numbers.

Every one is so extremely apprehensive of Sidy Useph's entering the town to-night, that the Rais of the Marine, who is afraid of being sacrificed by him if he succeed, keeps himself in readiness to depart at a moment, and has a vessel laying close to his golphor at the marine, to take him to Tunis or Malta, with every article on board prepared for his instant departure.

The list of persons said to be devoted to death on Sidy Useph's entering the town, are his brother, the Bey : the Chiah, his sister's husband ; the Selectar ; Cyde Mahomet (another brother-in-law) ; the Cataib and the Rais of the Marine (his third brother-in-law).

This place is so dreadfully in want of corn that some of the Consuls have agreed to freight a vessel for Tunis to return with some. Another vessel sails for Leghorn to-day, by which I shall send you this.

June 30, 1793

From the time I closed my last letter, the state of this place is grown worse and worse. Sidy Useph was expected to make his way into town every hour ; during which period the Consuls were continually preparing to send their families to Malta, without being able themselves to accompany them, as they could not quit their posts. You may conceive the horrors of such a situation : nothing worthy of the name of a ship was in the harbour ; we could only look forward to what was little better than a boat wretchedly equipped, and worse manned, for our voyage.

Notwithstanding all the Bashaw's messages, teskerers, and firmans, sent with threatenings and rewards, no Arabs came to his assistance for several days. Boats were sent by the Bashaw to bring the Moors from Bengazi, but Sidy Useph had the address to send his people in time to Tajura to drive the boats off with their guns. On the 27th, Sidy Useph, finding the Bashaw still unable to send a force from the the town against him, attempted to pass his people over the Jews' burying-ground (which is adjoining the town) to a weak part of the walls ; and it cost all the exertions possible to prevent their succeeding, as the walls, beside being in a bad state, were without cannon : but this part was immediately guarded and rendered secure. On that day all the force that could be collected in the town made a sortie against Sidy Useph. They at first drove him back, but were afterwards nearly cut to pieces before they could make good their retreat into town, which was impeded by the town gates being by mistake closed against them at the moment they were returning.

The Bey was so constantly importuned by his people for resources, that it was quite painful to the feelings of the Consuls, who were with him at the castle, whence, in much distress, he was viewing the battle. Being pressed for powder and ball by the Moors, he told them in a rage to gather up the stones and fight with them if they could find nothing else. Sidy Useph approached so close to the town at this moment, that the Christians left the castle, and the Bey retired from the ramparts. One of the Bey's own people had fired at him : the man was taken and brought into town. They said he was intoxicated ; and immediately the chaouxes proclaimed an order through the town, that five hundred bastinados should be given to every Jew who attempted to sell a drop of brandy.[1]

Owing to the insupportable heat of a strong land wind, the Bey, fearful of losing his men and horses, ordered them in during the middle of the day. On this occasion, Sidy Useph's people hooted and sung the song of victory round the town walls, and made their bravadoing feasts, which consisted in roasting dogs and eating them.

The enemy were ancious to drag away the body of a man who had been killed by a gun from the castle. Their eagerness determined

[1] The sale of spirits is limited to Jews and Christians, it being contrary to the tenets of Mahomet for the Moors to vend them. (T.)

the Bey to send out a party of fifty men to recover the body, which they supposed to be one of Sidy Useph's generals ; but Sidy Useph's people succeeded in carrying it off. During this interval of the battle, some curious circumstances happened, which mark the Moorish manner of thinking and acting in war. A party of Arabs carried a fine mare with its murdered master to Sidy Useph, who asked them why they had killed a man not fighting against them, as he had ordered that none but those armed against him should be molested ? On their replying they had killed him for the sake of his mare, as the soldiers were so much in want of horses, Sidy Useph ordered the animal to be brought forward, had it shot in their presence, and desired them for the future to observe his orders better. Another extraordinary event was, that a Tripolitan, one of the Bashaw's people, having, on going out of the town, met with an old friend who was fighting on Sidy Useph's side, the latter began to reason with him and endeavoured to persuade him to join Sidy Useph ; but the Tripolitan told him to profit of that moment in which they were speaking amicably to save himself, for he considered it now his duty to take his life if possible whenever he should meet him afterwards ; on which the Arab instantly departed. The third circumstance, not less singular than the two former, was, that the Bey, after he had given orders for his soldiers to go out against his brother, perceiving Sidy Useph's people busy in carrying away their dead, prevented their going, saying he would not have the enemy disturbed till their present work was over.

The Arabs being short of ammunition, we saw them sifting the sands on the Pianura for balls, which had been previously used, and they are offering great prices at present for flints for their guns.

Parties of Arabs, who came to assist the Bashaw, have behaved so unruly and have taken such liberties, that the Bashaw has ordered the streets to be paraded by armed Moors to keep them in order.

On the 28th, after hazarding a great deal by not being able to make any resistance to Sidy Useph's attacks, the Bashaw and the Bey had the mortification to see Shaik Alieff come into town with one hundred men, instead of a thousand, which he had promised to bring, and to hear him say, that none of his people should fire on Sidy Useph, for that he knew his intention was only to retire to Bengazi, of which place the Bashaw ought to make him Bey and leave him in peace. Soon after Shaik Alieff arrived, the chief of the Knowiales came in with all the Arabs he could muster, and Shaik Alieff, won over by his persuasions and the Bashaw's promises, at last sent for his Arabs who had halted not far from Tripoli, and agreed to join the chief of the Knowiales against Sidy Useph. No sooner was this done than disputes arose between the chief Arabs of the Knowiales, and those of Shaik Alieff. These tribes had been sworn enemies for many years, and therefore declared they would not go out to fight together, but that they would go out alternately. They were at last persuaded to go to the mosques and swear by the prophet that they would not turn upon each other in the battle. This done, they all went off together ; but a whole day was lost in adjusting these matters.

At this time a reward was publicly offered to the Arabs, by the Bashaw's orders, before they quitted the town, of two thousand sequins to any one of them who brought in Sidy Useph's head. We saw to-day Sidy Useph's men gathering up the sand on the plain and throwing it by handfuls towards the town. The meaning of this action was to show their contempt of the Bey's people, and to excite them to come out. When the guns fired from the castle to-day the Arabs ran off ; but as soon as the balls fell, some of them returned and fired their pieces at the balls as they lay on the ground, hallowing and hooting at the town for having missed their aim ; and last night, when the Bashaw's horses were taken out to water at the wells, an Arab, in the Bashaw's pay, mounted one of the very best of them and rode off at full speed to Sidy Useph. The Bey was at the same time so distressed for horses that he sent to one of the Consuls for one to replace that taken off by the Arab.

To-day the town gates have not been opened, the chief of the Knowiales not being sufficiently recovered from a severe wound he received yesterday, and the Bashaw would not trust Shaik Alieff to head the Arabs alone, for fear of his deserting with them to Sidy Useph ; while, on the other hand, Sidy Useph's people are exulting round the walls and braving the people to fight.

A courier sets off for Tunis immediately, sent by the Bashaw on account of the great distress of this place. He takes a few letters with him from the Christians, among which this will go, but I have little hopes of sending you better news by the next.

July 10, 1793

This week the Bashaw has been expecting Soliman Aga, the son of Ramadan Aga, a name renowned in Tripoli for his attachment, and the services he has rendered, to the reigning family. He has shewn his friendship very strongly to all the princes separately, when they have been out with their troops to collect the revenues ; therefore when the Bashaw sent for him now to assist him against Sidy Useph, Soliman they say wept. He gave no answer to the Bashaw's repeated messages for several days ; at last the Bashaw's chief officers, with himself and the Bey, wrote him a long supplicating letter, " to take the cause to heart, and come with all the forces he could muster." After reading this letter, Soliman ordered his people to prepare for his departure to Tripoli, and when his favourite horse was brought for him to mount, he clasped it round the neck, and after a silence of some minutes, he himself fastened under the gold necklaces round the neck of the horse, a token of mourning, which consisted of black cloth covered with wet ashes, to shew his sorrow at engaging in this cause. He then made a solemn agreement with Shaik Saffanassa to protect the countries to the eastward during his absence, and set off for Tripoli. He was expected here yesterday from one hour to another, having slept on this side Tajura the night before ; but to-day a boat arrived from the east, which was dispatched in the middle of the night by Soliman Aga from the coast, to say, that the numerous tribes of the Tahownees had intercepted him at a river near Tahowna,[1] and now, as he cannot advance till Saffanassa joins him, he is not expected for some days. This news has thrown the town into the utmost confusion, as the assistance of Soliman Aga seemed a last hope. In this extremity, additional forces from the westward have been sent for by the Bashaw, and they are advancing quickly, to the great terror, not only of the Christians, but the Tripolitans, as the western Arabs are all banditti. The Arabs from the eastward are much quieter, though worse soldiers.

A fortunate circumstance happened for the Bashaw last night. His brother-in-law, the Bey of Bengazi, arrived here, and has brought with him not only considerable sums of money, but a great supply of wheat and barley, and at present feeds all the people under arms, Arabs and Moors, who are maintained at the castle. They have only a hundred measures of barley a day for the horses. Wheat in this place is so scarce, that it sells at two thousand four hundred piastres the measure instead of eight hundred which is its usual price. We are reduced to eat black bread at more than ten times its value, and obliged to buy up all the hard biscuit that can be got at any price from the

[1] More correctly Tarhuna.

ships in the harbour. We lost a man yesterday, and another was wounded to-day, who ventured out of the town to purchase greens, eggs, and poultry, for us, luxuries which we have not been indulged with for some time. To-day six men were seized at the gate by the enemy : they were loaded with fire-wood for the town, for which we are terribly distressed. Sidy Useph's people bound them, set fire to the wood, and were going to burn the men alive, when one of Sidy Useph's generals, named Sidy el Mair, rode up full speed to save them, telling the Arabs to remember that Sidy Useph held the life of every person sacred, and that he would put to death any man who killed another, except in battle.

The Bashaw has been solicited, by sixty wounded Arabs, for leave to join their families, not being able (from the state they are) to keep the field any longer. They were put into a boat to-day with provisions, and sent off to the eastward.

Six Marabuts came into town yesterday with great ceremony, to claim the protection of the Seid, a Marabut district which the Bashaw has always protected ; but the Chiah told them, the Bashaw would no longer protect them, as they had all been traitors to him, and the Chiah ordered them to quit the town immediately.

July 14, 1793

To-day, though it is the Moor's sabbath, prayers have been dispensed with at the church for the first time, on account of the people being employed in guarding the town. The western Arabs are arrived, and are to go out commanded by the Bashaw's officers to-morrow, against Sidy Useph. These Arabs have been here but a few days, and are already intolerable. They have so little regard to subordination that they can scarcely be kept from incommoding the Bashaw's person, when they are permitted to approach him at his levee ; and yesterday an Arab threw down one of the Bey's guards who opposed his approach to the prince. The Bey gave orders, notwithstanding the Arab's impetuosity, for him to be brought forward, and after hearing his complaint, afforded him redress. Every body seems afraid of offending these Arabs at present. A number of them crowded round the Rais of the marine to-day, and one of them offered to take a pistol out of his sash, which he was quick enough to prevent, and asked the Arab if he meant to steal his pistols, when another Arab replied, "No, he only wanted to look at them." But had the man ran off with the pistol the Rais must have let him go, as the government is too much in awe of these thieves, to offer to punish one of them. This must prove to you what a state we are in ; and if more of these Arabs come from the westward what we shall have to dread.

They say here that Sidy Useph is quite short of ammunition, as several men who were shot yesterday near the gate were proved to be killed with bits of iron and not ball. Sidy Useph presented his general, Sidy el Mair, this morning, with a rich saddle, the back of which was gold embossed, the stirrups burnished gold, gold trappings, etc., a pair of pistols set with jewels, and a gold handled yatagon set with diamonds and emeralds.

The beautiful Zenobia, the wife of Sidy el Bunny and favourite of the late Bey, of whose gay conduct I have written to you, is at her husband's garden out of town. Sidy el Bunny is one of Sidy Useph's generals, consequently he is fighting against the Bashaw. Zenobia has been continually sending secret intelligence to the castle concerning him ; and she gave notice to Cyde Mahomet this morning, to send thirty men to a garden where her husband is, to assassinate him. What a part for a wife to act ! but with such extreme immorality as her character presents, such crimes are compatible. Sidy Useph has told Bunny that he shall be made captain of the port if he enter the town.

The Jews, some days since, offered some Moors a considerable sum of money, to escort them to their burying-ground to inter a body ; but, notwithstanding the sum they offered, the Moors would not venture to accompany them. The Jews then attempted to carry the body themselves to the grave round by the seaside, hoping to avoid Sidy Useph's people by this precaution ; but the poor Jews were met by a party of Arabs, and were so frightened that they left the corpse and ran away, and it remains there yet unburied.

The Bey lost a favourite attendant this morning in the following manner. We saw from our terrace this officer follow a party of fourteen Arabs, whom he thought had deserted from the Bashaw, and under that impression went to encourage them to return to their duty, when, on a sudden, we perceived the Arabs surround him, and carry him off by violence. They proved afterwards to be Sidy Useph's Arabs.

June 20, 1793

Late this evening a party of Sidy Useph's people called loudly under the walls to three of the Shaiks of the Messeah, by their names, who had lately fled from the Messeah, telling them from Sidy Useph, that if they returned to their several gardens, and brought back with them the people of the Messeah, whom they had enticed to follow them, they should all be safe, and well received ; but if they did not return, that Sidy Useph had fresh forces from Terhona and Gerrianna, that he should be in the town with the Arabs directly, and would certainly put them all to death.   To these menaces the Bey conde-scended to answer them from the castle ramparts, telling them they should be brought into town the next day, and made to suffer for their insolence.

The smoke of several fires round the walls of the town, loud songs, and the beating of the turbuka (a sort of drum), announced the enemy to be celebrating their barbarous feast of roasted dogs, which is con-sidered among the Arabs as one of the greatest proofs of bravado an enemy can give.   The riotous noise of these feasts began several hours since, and still continues.   The Moors this evening led the castle horses, and those of the Arabs, to water at a well without the gates of the town :   not one of the animals would touch the water.   The Moors examined the well, when they found that Sidy Useph's people had contrived to throw into it a dead horse, to spoil the water.   The Jews (whom the Moors force to perform all hard or unpleasant offices) were immediately seized upon and set to work to drag the horse out of the well.

🔲

July 24, 1793

Sidy Useph still keeps his ground without retiring a step ;   parties of his people constantly come close to the walls of the town, but the main body of his troops remains on the other side of the Pianura. To-day, when one of Sidy Useph's chief officers was killed by the Bashaw's soldiers, Sidy Useph's Arabs fought over the body on horse-back, against twenty of the Bashaw's people on foot, till the former obtained the body, and carried it off in triumph ;   saying, that not a head of any one of their people should be brought into the town to-day.   One of the bravest Arabs they have had here belonging to the Bashaw, named Alli Benamoor (a Tunisian), was brought into town to-day by his friends laid on a baracan, mortally wounded, his wife and family accompanied him. They were making loud lamentations over him, but the Bashaw's officers came up to them and prevented their outcries, as orders have been daily issued from the castle, that no one must scream for those killed in battle, in order not to augment the exultations of the enemy for the slain. The Moors belonging to Sidy Useph, for want of other methods, pile the horses that are killed one upon another, and fire from behind them. They likewise bring out all the chests they can get from the Moorish cottages, fill them with sand, and make them serve for a defence.

Yesterday we were disturbed by the cries of a Moorish family who were accompanying the body of a fine youth about sixteen years of age, apparently dead. They had just brought him from the sea-side where he had been bathing, when, by some accident, he could not extricate himself from the waves. His friends considered him a corpse, and his mother followed him tearing her clothes. The English Consul, reflecting on the customs of the country, which would cause this youth to be rapidly interred, took with him two Dragomen, and went to the house of the young man's disconsolate family, who were already taking measures to bury him, and in a very few hours he would have been laid in the earth, notwithstanding there was every reason to suppose he would recover by the proper methods being taken to save him. The superstition and ignorance of the Moors did not fail to induce them to raise frequent obstacles while endeavours were used to restore the youth, and they pronounced these measures useless, notwithstanding the terror and surprise they evinced at the momentary signs of life produced by them from time to time ; but the family imbibing hopes that the Consul's exertions might recal life, used every method in their power to repel the Moors who crowded into the house, many of whom were indignant at the unnecessary experiments (as they termed them) practiced by a Christian on their countryman. Although the Consul had taken every precaution ; and had ordered the servants to carry with them plenty of camphor and vinegar, to prevent the fatal effects of a too crowded apartment in a country hardly free from pestilence, yet he was obliged several times to quit it, with strong apprehensions that the fear and jealousy of the Moors would, in his absence, render what he had done of no effect, as they would not wait the issue of the medical proceedings.

The Consul almost losing his patience, and to recover himself from the effect of the confined air of the house (which had become quite oppressive from the concourse of Moors who had assembled there), returned home for a short time. The Moors, frightened at the thought of his having, perhaps, given up the project of trying to restore the youth, eagerly sent to implore his return, and solemnly promised to fulfil his orders, which were to clear the house of every person except the family. The next time the boy was left, the English broker and two guards were set to watch by him. Before the morning he was perfectly restored to life ; and the effusions of gratitude, and the extreme astonishment of the Moors, at what appeared to them so very extraordinary, was not less curious than pleasing, and rendered them thankful to the Consul, almost to adoration.

To-day, at the hour Sidy Useph was expected to attack the town, we were surprised to see his horsemen, in great numbers, galloping in the cultivated gardens of the Messeah. The reason for this extra-ordinary manœuvre was to find out where the ground was soft, and discover hidden barley, which the inhabitants, some days before, had buried in their grounds when they fled from their houses. Sidy Useph had discovered immense quantities of grain by the above method. The reason so much barley is sown in all the gardens near the town is owing to the impossibility of extending arable land to any distance from the capital, unless it were possible to protect the produce of the earth from the ravaging hand of the Arab. From this circumstance, Christians are entirely precluded from farming.

I have before mentioned to you how successfully barley grows in this country, producing five times as much as it does in Europe ; but owing to the depredations of the powerful tribes of Arabs, an European settlement here would require a standing army to gather in the grain they raised.

It is thought Sidy Useph has received supplies of cash from the court of Tunis. He is certainly at present better furnished with re-sources than either the Bashaw or the Bey. A very short time must finish these cruel dissentions as the town cannot hold out much longer for want of provisions.

July 28, 1793

We receive messages every day from Lilla Halluma and the princesses. They send their confidential women to say how sincerely they wish to see us ; but the insolence of the Arabs continues so very great, and the castle is so crowded with them at all times, that it is impossible to venture there.

These western Arabs are so very assuming, that the Bashaw seems as much afraid of their going out in a body and returning with Sidy Useph, as he was of Sidy Useph entering the town before the Arabs arrived.

Sidy Useph has succeeded in bringing his cannon near enough to bear upon the Bashaw's castle and the harbour, and if he had any body about him as clever as himself, he must have been in the town long ago ; but his engineers are so unskilful, that they hit every object but the one they aim at. Already their balls have struck the Swedish and Venetian houses, and entered the Swedish Consul's bed-chamber. Such circumstances render our situation very alarming, although our house is, as I have told you, in many parts bomb-proof.

July 29, Monday 10 at night, 1793

This has been, my dear friend, a very extraordinary day with us, and we are for the present moment most dangerously situated. Though we are so near quitting this place, we are destined to see an entire new government, and the whole of the Bashaw's family driven from Tripoli, before our departure, by a Turkish invader : even Sidy Useph, with all his efforts against his father, must leave the throne to this usurper, who came into the bay at five this afternoon. We were taking our usual afternoon walk upon the terrace, when we perceived a fleet of Turkish vessels anchor in the harbour. As the Turks are never welcome visitors here, the dragoman was sent directly to inquire what Captain Pacha commanded the fleet that was just anchored. We were immediately informed that a Turk, named Ali Ben Zool,[1] was on board, with a firman from the Grand Signior to depose our Bashaw, and mount the throne himself. The confusion this account has thrown every body into is not easy to describe, besides being perfectly distressing to those concerned with the government, as it puts an end to all business at the castle.

As hazardous as we considered our situation a few hours since, it is now infinitely more so, and increasing in danger from one moment to another. The commodore, with whom we are to return to Europe, with that delicacy of feeling and attention which he displayed from

[1] Ali Bourghol. See Introduction.

the first moment we saw him, and from which he has never in the least deviated, sent to us, the moment the arrival of the Turks was known, the most pressing messages by his officers, to come on board his ship. They informed us, that the frigate's boats would lay in waiting for us at the Marine, as late as possible ; and that afterwards, they would be kept in readiness during the night, when on any signal being made from our terrace, they should be at the mole again before we could get there ourselves. It was then agreed that a light should be hoisted at our flag-staff, as a sign for the boats to come off for us if necessary. The officers, who came to spend the evening with us, did not remain half an hour, as our dragoman came to say that orders had been given to shut the Marine gates two hours earlier than usual.

The Marine was already crowded by the Turks, who were walking about without any opposition from the Moors.

Ali Ben Zool was still on board, and messengers were passing continually from the castle to and from him. At seven in the evening, it was thought quite necessary for us to take advantage of the commodore's offer, and go on board the frigate. The Venetian Consul's lady came to join us, and the dragomen were sent once more to reconnoitre the way before we set out. They returned, and to our great disappointment were in the utmost despair. They declared that the Turks were not from Constantinople, but that they were a banditti, and came only to sack the place ; that the Marine gates were strongly guarded by the Turkish soldiers, and not a Moor was to be seen near the spot. It was with great difficulty they themselves escaped being detained by them, as the Turks would not let them go till they were convinced they were guards belonging to a consular-house, but no person was suffered to go in or out of the gates ; the Turks stood with their sabres drawn. They had nearly killed a Jew, who was under the French protection, for endeavouring to pass the gate in his way to the Marine. He lay on the ground almost lifeless ! This news was rendered infinitely more dreadful to us, as a confidential officer from the castle had just informed us, that the Bashaw had determined to open the gates of the town to the Arabs and Sidy Useph, that they might join with him in driving off the Turks, which the Bashaw considered the only remaining step to save himself ; and every body agreed that if the Arabs were let in, not a house in town that could furnish them with the smallest booty for their labour would escape their ravages. Indeed, they have all been long promised by Sidy Useph leave to plunder the town for three days whenever they enter it ; from which violence not Sidy Useph himself now could restrain them.

The dragomen have been sent every half hour, for some hours past, to the town gates, to the Marine gates, to the Shaik's golphor, or apartments, and to the castle, but nothing is more impossible than to know what is going on. They report that the Bashaw and the Bey have sent for Sidy Useph to lead his forces into town. We can only ascertain that the Turks are in the castle, as we have seen them on the ramparts.

𝕨

July 30, *Tuesday morning*, 2 *o'clock*, 1793

Worn out with anxiety and fears, the greater number of the ladies of our party are retired to rest for a few hours. The Consuls have determined to keep watch themselves through the night, relieving each other every two hours. Not a servant in the house, whether Christian, Moor, or black, but is completely loaded with knives, guns, and pistols ; and little else is heard at this moment but the din of arms. The dead silence of the night at intervals is surprizing, while so much is going forward. Nothing is seen or heard in the town, except from time to time a sudden burst of noise, from the clinking of the arms of large parties of Turks, who parade the streets.

Three hours ago the Grand Signior's firman was read at the Marine, to announce the arrival of Ali Ben Zool and the abdication of our Bashaw ; and the Rais of the Marine, and several of the Bashaw's chief officers, were obliged at that time of night, near twelve o'clock, to go on board the vessel in which the Turk still remains. Guns were fired about an hour since from the Turkish fleet, as signals that some of the Bashaw's officers were strangled. As we know them all personally, and are intimate with their families, these reports are very afflicting to us.

During the darkness of the night we ventured on our terraces : early in the evening, it was not thought right for the ladies to go there, for fear of being seen by the Turks. The town and the harbour still wear a directly opposite appearance to what they did before the Turks' arrival. All continues perfectly quiet, as a calm before a storm, except at the Marine, where we hear continual talking.

The strength and the situation of our house rendering it the safest asylum in the town, not only those who have a right to the protection of the flag have been admitted into it, but it was thought policy not to refuse the relations of the Gibeleens who were settled in the town, who came to solicit a shelter for their women and property. In return for which, nearly two hundred of them have surrounded our house, well armed, and declare they will be cut to pieces before they quit its walls. All the Consuls who have ladies in their families are with us.

Ꮂ

12 at noon

At the adan, or daybreak, this morning, a party of the Turks were sent from the castle to our house, to guard, as they say, the English flag, which risks no insult but from themselves. These men are now laying stretched in different parts of the court-yard, calling about them to the servants to light their pipes, and bring them coffee and sherbet. They are loaded with costly arms, and their habits are rich, but their arrogance is intolerable.

At midnight the Bashaw, the Bey, the Bey of Bengazi (the Bashaw's brother-in-law), the Cataib, the Chiah, with the ladies of the Bey and the Chiah's family, left the castle. Lilla Halluma remained in a house in the town, not being able to proceed further. This unfortunate sovereign was so ill, as to be carried out of the castle by her attendants ; but the late Bey's eldest daughter, Zenobia, is still there, with two of the princesses ; Lilla Fatima, widow of the Bey of Derner, and Lilla Howisha, the Rais of the Marine's wife. As the persons of female royal prisoners are held sacred in this country, it is to be hoped their lives may be spared.

There cannot be a stronger proof given of the degree of consequence attached to the Grand Signior's firman, than the manner in which the Tripolitans have bowed their heads to it on the present occasion ; for as the Bashaw and the Bey at last ventured out of the gates defenceless to Sidy Useph, the Bashaw might have let Sidy Useph in, as he at one time intended to do, with his forces, to have driven the Turks off ; but under the idea that the Grand Signior's firman cannot be resisted, all has been submitted to.

By half-past six this morning, the officers of the frigate we are to go with were with us : they congratulated us on the ease with which the Turkish troops had been permitted by the Moors to enter the town, without harassing it with a battle ; but every thing is to be dreaded from the ferocity of the Turk, who, known to be a great enemy to the Christians, will always endeavour to insult them, except when restrained by interest. We breakfasted in a party of thirty, most of whom had passed the night in hourly expectation of the Arabs entering the town from the land-side, or the Turks from the sea-side. Before we had finished our breakfast, we were summoned to the terrace, to see the Turk come up from the Marine in the character of Bashaw ; for, by this time, every person in Tripoli doubts the authenticity of the firman.

On the Turk's landing, all the Moorish flags were immediately changed for the Turkish colours ; every where the crimson flag, with the gold crescent in the middle, displayed itself. As the Turks advanced, we saw them drive, with violence, the Jews from every part of the town, not suffering them to remain in sight while the Turkish Bashaw passed by, who was attended by a great number of Turks. The castle music, and the same corps of chaouxes which had for so many years announced to us the approach of the Bashaw and Bey, preceded him ; all the Turkish vessels saluted him, and the batteries at the Marine fired, till he reached the castle. In his suite we had the satisfaction to see the Rais of the Marine, who, they last night said, was strangled.

The despair and confusion of the Jews cannot be conceived : they expect to be stript of their property, and happy for them if they save their lives by discovering all their treasures.

Every thing is quiet in the Messeah ; and so few of Sidy Useph's people are seen, that it is thought by some of the Moors, he has determined to go to Tunis with the Bashaw and Bey. Others say he is collecting more Arabs to make head against the Turk, whom he speaks of and considers only as a ruffian.

At present we are as much limited to our terraces for taking the air, as we were lately during the plague. We cannot get into the Messeah nor walk at the Marine, and the town (at no time agreeable to walk in) is now quite overrun with Turks ; but we have not to lament this circumstance long, as we expect every day to embark for Europe.

August 11, 1793

We yesterday witnessed a more painful and alarming moment than we have yet felt here, from a circumstance that seriously threatened the life of the Consul. We perceived an English ship sail out of the harbour in the morning after a French tartan (a small vessel) which happened to be bringing in Turkish troops for Ali Ben Zool : the Turks were running the vessel on shore to save it from being taken. The castle batteries fired as a warning, it being irregular to take the vessel under the guns of the fortresses. In the mean while, a very menacing message was brought from the Turk to the Consul to come directly to the castle. Had the Turk's order been complied with, he would afterwards have demanded an exorbitant ransom for the Consul's release ; and we are too well acquainted with the manners of the Turks and the accommodations they would afford to a Christian they were displeased with, not to know that the Consul's life might ·have fallen a sacrifice in this instance. I leave you to paint our situation to yourself with that humanity you always feel for others. It was necessary for the Consul to go immediately on board till the matter of taking the vessel could be adjusted ; and, as owing to this accident, he did not think his family safe at the English house, he went with us to the Venetian-house. Our own dragomen accompanied us, and as many of the Turkish guards as were sufficiently in their senses to be able to stand ; for by this time most of them lay intoxicated about the skiffar (hall) and court-yard. The streets we passed through had quite a novel appearance to us : they were almost lined with Turks. The guard at the Sandanner, instead of the old Aga who used to treat us with the greatest marks of respect as we passed, was a set of fierce armed ruffians who seemed scarcely able to refrain from insulting us. We met the dugganeer going to the castle, but he could not say the least word in confidence to us, being surrounded by armed Turks instead of his own attendants. Immediately after we had parted with him, we met one of Sidy Useph's generals, Sidy el Bunny, the husband of Lilla Zenobia, the late Bey's favourite. This officer told us he had come into town during the confusion of the morning, and trusted he should get out again before night, as he is not known to the Turks, but he could not stop to say a word more for fear of being discovered : he was disguised, and wrapt up close in a dark baracan. The Consul left us at the Venetian house, and had but just time to escape on board our ships and acquaint the commodore with the issue of what had happened. Every thing was adjusted in a few hours, and our dreadful apprehensions for the Consul's safety relieved. After remaining at the Venetian house some hours, the Turks being satisfied, we returned home to dinner.

The rest of the Turkish guards were still rioting in our house. The Consul insisted on their leaving it, as he told them he had no further occasion for them, but their chief informed him he must be paid a pataque (five shillings) an hour for their services. This imposition being acceded to, we had the happiness to see them depart.

These wretches, while we were gone to the Venetian house, got hold of a Jew, and would have killed him for not executing some orders they had given him ; but the man was saved by the interference of our servants, who remonstrated with them, and told them that no such work was permitted near the doors of the English house.

The Turkish Bashaw begins by treating the Christians with great haughtiness : he has already declared he will not see the infidels (meaning the Consuls) till to-morrow. On his being applied to, to see and receive the English officers to-day, an etiquette necessary on the present change of government, the Turk, endeavouring to copy the Dey of Algiers, had the effrontery to propose that the English officers should leave their swords behind them ; but on being informed by the Consul that no such proposal would be agreed to, he gave up the project.[1]

During the two last days hostilities have ceased in the Pianura and in town : not a Jew or a female is to be seen in the streets, and very few Moors. The shops are all shut, the trading Moors have retired, and nothing can appear more empty and desolate than the town ever since the Turk landed and paraded through it to the castle.

Sidy Useph's forces have entirely withdrawn themselves from the Messeah, and what his next movements will be nobody here can imagine, but the Arabs continue coming over the deserts in great numbers, from the east and west.

A circumstance which occurred this morning after our return from the Venetian house, induces me to give you an anecdote of a black, as a specimen of their great attachment to their employers. A black slave, named Zur, came to intreat that he might be received into the Consul's service, and would not take a refusal, though he was repeatedly told the family were on the point of leaving the country. His eagerness to be employed (if it was but for a few days), and his dress, though shabby, displaying the remains of too rich a habit for a slave, led to an inquiry into his history. He proved to have been the property of a Moor of distinction, named Sidy Hassana, a confident of the late

---

[1] He also, according to a French consular report, demanded that the European Consuls should remove their shoes before entering his presence.

Bey's, who, like the rest of his favourites, was ruined by his attachment to his master. At Sidy Hassana's death, which happened very soon after the Bey was murdered, his property, not excepting the jewels of his family, and all his slaves, were seized. His widow, a beautiful Circassian, was left with three small children destitute of bread ! She was named by her husband Sebbeeba,[1] and had been brought by her lord himself from Asia, who, owing to his fears of her being seen or talked of on account of her beauty and accomplishments, had secluded her from all intercourse but with himself and her domestics. The unfortunate Sebbeeba, therefore, found herself in an instant, not only deprived of her protector, but without a friend or connexion in this country.

At the time the hampers (guards) were plundering his master's house, the black ran to Lilla Sebbeeba and implored her to give him his liberty instantly, before the hampers had seized on him with the rest of her slaves. She opposed a request so totally against the black's own interest, as he would have been taken immediately to the castle to be fed and clothed, and considered (being so fine a black) as a domestic of royalty. She reminded him that she had nothing to give him, and that for want of better protection than she could afford him at present without a master, he would starve. But the faithful black replied, that it was for herself and his master's children he begged for his liberty, saying, if Lilla Sebbeeba gave him his freedom he could not be taken from her ; and he would, by business or employment, procure provisions for her family, and endeavour, besides, by his labour, to prevent as much as possible her missing the servants she had lost.

The unhappy Circassian, totally friendless, gladly complied with his generous proposal, and when the hampers appeared to order him to the castle, she declared him free, and proved to them he had been given to her by her lord after her marriage, by which she was enabled herself to give him his freedom. The Circassian, obliged to leave Sidy Hassana's possessions in the Messeah, was, by the black, conducted with her three infants into town, where the latter has helped to maintain them all to the utmost of his power ever since the Bey's death,

---

[1] Sebbeeba, in the Moorish language, means raisins. The Moors give to the Circassians, and other Asiatic beauties, when they marry them, Moorish names of their own invention meant to be endearing and complimentary ; as, " Mabooba," a coin of pure gold ; " Cobah," the morning star ; " Halluma," sweetness, etc. On this account Hassana gave his fair slave, at the time he married her, the name of " Sebbeeba," *a raisin.* (T.)

without the smallest deviation from the obedience he was formerly accustomed to shew his unfortunate mistress ; and he considers the mentioning of her name even a want of respect, giving her, when he speaks of her, only the distinguished epithet of his Lilla. The faithful black's request was complied with, and he is to remain with us till we go from hence ; when the Dutch Consul will take him into his service, and find him a lucrative employment in the purchase of Arabian horses for the Emperor of Austria, which the black is to take to Vienna in a few months.

We have heard nothing of Lilla Halluma, though it is four days since this unfortunate sovereign has left her castle, and we dare not yet endeavour to find out her residence for fear of discovering it to the Turks.

August 17, 1793

A few days after I closed my last to you, the people of Sahal (a considerable district a few miles from town) were sent by Sidy Useph to salute, as they said, the new Bashaw ; and Sidy Useph sent many compliments, saying, he was coming to see him immediately : but these two chiefs knew each other too well. On the message being delivered from the Caid of Sahal, the Turkish Bashaw desired they would all retire for a few days, till he had considered in what manner to receive them and Sidy Useph.

A Shaik, with a large body of Turkish soldiers, parades the streets of Tripoli at night : we met them late this evening as we were returning home. They talked a great deal to our dragomen, who were unwilling to answer them, knowing it was unusual for them to take the liberty of stopping and talking in the streets while in attendance on the Consul's family. The Turks were very troublesome in persisting to escort us home, though repeatedly told that our own guard was sufficient, and that their services would not be accepted. On a sudden, their attention was called off by the arrival of a person whom we were sorry to see had just been seized by the Turkish guards. This was a confidential officer of the Bey, who had ventured into town in the afternoon, intending to leave it again at sunset. The Shaik and the Bashaw's satellites carried him immediately to the castle, whence I fear he will be heard of no more.

Sidy Useph is at his father's garden with the Bashaw and the Bey.

The Turk sent him to-day a message with a rich caftan, desiring, or rather ordering him to come to town, saying, he expected him to join the divan which was to be held this day at the castle ; but Sidy Useph would not venture himself so much in the Turk's power, and entirely declined coming.

· This morning another of Sidy Useph's generals came into town in disguise. Among the very few people he has ventured to discover himself to, he did so to us. He told us, that the night the Turkish fleet anchored in the Bay of Tripoli, Sidy Useph had not the least suspicion that a new Bashaw was on board till after midnight, when the town was guarded by the Turks and completely in the hands of the usurper. When Sidy Useph saw his father and brother take refuge in the Messeah, and learnt the cause of their flight from the town, he was almost distracted at having neglected taking the town by storm, which he could easily have done had he not waited to make terms with his father.

This officer expressed himself highly pleased with the hope, that the Moors would yet enter the town and drive the Turks away. He informed us, that Sidy Useph, with a stronger force than usual, and his Arabs animated by seeing the Bashaw and his sons now united in the same cause, meant to attack the town, with all the exertions he could possibly make, that very night ; and that an agreement was made between Sidy Useph and the chief of the Arabs, that if the latter succeeded in getting into the town, they should be at liberty to plunder every house in it three days, for their pay, " And is this the friendship," said Mr. Tully, " we are to expect from you ? " " What greater proof of friendship," replied the Moor, " can I give you, than telling you a secret, that if you chuse to put my name to, my head will be placed on the gates to-morrow, if even I get through them alive to-day ; and though I tell you this, that you may prepare for the alarm, Sidy Useph, for his own sake, will, I suppose, respect the consular houses." His kindness was readily acknowledged by Mr. Tully, and every attention and assistance afforded him to forward his departure from the town ; but the information this officer had given us was so alarming, that all the Christians began a second time to think of retiring to the harbour. This last resource was, on reflection, relinquished by the Consuls ; for as there remained no European ships of force in the harbour, which is now filled with Turkish gallies manned with riotous and savage crews, it appeared to them a more dangerous expedient than trusting to the protection of the consular flags, which are thought safer, if Sidy Useph enter the town, than they are at present, as these Turkish invaders are considered nearly as banditti. The great danger apprehended by the Christians was from what might happen in the first moments of confusion, on the Arabs entering the town before their chiefs could have time to restrain them ; and, owing to this, the rest of the day was spent in the greatest agitation and terror. We saw Sidy Useph's people advancing every hour, and by the evening they were close to the town. The Turks drove them back at different periods during the day, by firing bombs, of which many burst over the town, to the distress of the inhabitants. The Moors being much harassed by the use of this implement of war, retired for that night. The next day Sidy Useph annoyed the town so much with his cannon, that the Turks sent three strong armed boats to land at the Messeah and endeavour to spike them. After much difficulty this was effected, but it was only owing to Sidy Useph's being absent for a short time, having left his brother to take his post. When he heard what was going forward, he returned immediately to take the command. His conduct during the time the Turks have been here, obliges every body to own that, though his heart is bad, his talents are superior to the rest of his family.

Notwithstanding the repulses Sidy Useph received from the Turks, he continued to keep his ground close to the town gate all that day.

The Christians have no means of guarding their houses at present, as they did on former occasions, when Sidy Useph approached with his Arabs. There were but few Moors in town, and these all subject to the Turks ; and we had only to hope the Arabs might be restrained in time by Sidy Useph or his generals from assaulting the Consuls' houses. At night every body assembled on their terraces in the greatest agitation, to observe what was passing, and be apprized of the moment when victory would prove decisive either to the Moors or the Turks. Just after midnight, Sidy Useph's people succeeded in getting so close to the town gates, that every one thought they had entered them, and all were dreadfully alarmed who knew of the permission Sidy Useph had given his Arabs to make the best of their time to enrich themselves at the expense of the inhabitants.

At half-past twelve, under a heavy fire of the Turks, Sidy Useph crowded with his Arabs close to the gates. He had formed a plan of entering through some old magazines, under which he had mined a way into town, unobserved by the Turks ; but at the moment his people were preparing to enter this subterraneous passage, the Turks unexpectedly set fire to some large branches of trees dipt into boiling pitch, the immense glare from which instantly discovered every part of the Messeah, and particularly what the Moors were doing, which consequently prevented their success. The firing from the Moors formed a continued line round the town, and the Turkish ships kept up an incessant fire on the Messeah. I suppose this is the last alarm we shall experience from that quarter during our stay in Tripoli, as we expect to quit it in a few days.

An officer much attached to the Bashaw, and who was in the castle the whole of the night he was destined to quit his throne, gave us a minute account of all that passed there from six in the evening till the moment he left the castle.

Both the Bashaw and the Bey may be said to have fallen sacrifices to the fatal effect of believing in destiny. When the unexpected news arrived at the castle of a new Bashaw being already in the bay, accompanied by a strong Turkish fleet, these princes were so paralised with the thought of what they considered impending fate, that they seemed to wait without attempting to make any resistance till the storm reached them. When it was known that the Turk, who had arrived in the character of sovereign, was possessed of the Grand Signior's firman, the Bashaw and his ministers appeared motionless, and ready to bow their heads to the irrevocable decrees of the Porte. After some time, however, doubts were entertained of the validity of the firman, and of its having been obtained from the Grand Signior ; orders were therefore issued from the castle for the Shaik and Rais of the Marine to collect all the force they could, and oppose the Turk's landing : but neither the Bashaw nor the Bey came out to animate the people, who feared without a chief to resist the man who in a few hours might hold their lives in his hand. An hour and a half passed after these orders were issued from the castle, without any appearance of their being put into execution. Messages were again sent to the Shaik and Rais of the Marine to arm, while neither the Bashaw nor Bey approached near a window or gallery of the castle to see what was going on, or to shew themselves to the people. From eight in the evening, the time was passed in fruitless messages from the Bashaw to his ministers, till midnight ; when the firman was sent from the Turk on board the fleet, with great ceremony, to the castle, and the Bashaw ordered to quit it, or receive his death there.

The Bashaw, the Bey, and the Bey of Bengazi went off, accompanied by a tribe of the Knowiales, headed by their chief Shaik Alieff.

This officer confirmed the accounts given us, of the Bashaw having fainted three times in his way from the castle to the gates of the town. He felt severely for not having sent the females of his family, at any risk, to the Messeah, which it was now too late to do ; but they comforted the Bashaw by reminding him that all royal female captives must be safe according to the tenets of their Prophet, who forbids their being in the least violated in cases of war. The subsequent conduct of the Turk and his men, however, proved the Bashaw's fears just, and themselves to be banditti, and not authorized from the Porte ; for, contrary to all Mahomedan laws, they took not only from all the ladies of the castle, but even from the Bashaw's daughters, their jewels and every valuable article they had about their persons, and of those ladies who were not detained in the castle few had more than a baracan to cover them. One of the princesses, Lilla Fatima, had the courage to resist the ruffians, and declare, that as she was a Bashaw's daughter, she would submit to death rather than leave the castle in such a state. They yielded to her remonstrances, and afforded her some more of her clothes. Lilla Halluma, who was very ill, was carried out in the arms of her blacks, to whom she had formerly given their freedom, for all the slaves in attendance were detained at the castle, male and female, for the Turk's service, or to be sold. These blacks, some living within the castle and some in the town, now gratefully flocked round their afflicted mistress to offer their services to her at this unfortunate moment. They bore her from the castle, accompanied by the widow of the late murdered Bey, and these two royal fugitives are now secreted in town, but as yet we know not where. The late Bey's beautiful daughter the Turk has detained in the castle, having declared his determination to marry her, and place her on the throne ; but his intentions, instead of affording consolation to the family, can only distract them, as every body seems convinced that this usurper, who calls himself Ali Ben Zool, and has risen under sanction of some of the pachas to a command in the Grand Signior's navy, was noted for his piracies, and has formerly been considered as the chief of a banditti of Arnauts, a people who are the refuse of the Turkish dominions.

This Turk put into the harbour of Tripoli with his ships several times lately, in his expeditions from the Porte to Egypt, which afforded him an easy opportunity of becoming acquainted with the dissentions in the Bashaw's family, and consequent disorder of the kingdom. Ali Ben Zool, perceiving the general confusion, determined to profit by the defenceless state of the country, hoping to silence the Grand Signior's ministers by the rich presents he will send hence, amassed by murder and rapine ! I fear I shall have no better accounts to give you during the remainder of our stay here.

In the last eight days, atrocities have occurred, which, thank God, while residing in this country, we had as yet been strangers to.

We are waiting for the return of the commodore, with whom we shall embark for Europe ; he is gone to look in at Tunis. I close this with the intention of writing to you once more before we leave Tripoli.

August 17, 1793

In order to give you a final account of the state we leave Tripoli in, and of the last days we spend here, I determine to keep this, and forward it by the first opportunity that may present itself, on our way from this place.

A few days ago we discovered the residence of the persecuted Lilla Halluma. Mrs. Tully lost no time in sending her fresh roasted coffee, fine loaf sugar, and such trifles as she seemed most to wish for ; confidential messengers went with them, but they found all access to this unhappy sovereign impossible. They were driven precipitately from her residence, and were happy to have escaped without further mischief. They heard loud screams from her house before they reached the door, where they found the Turks dragging out a beautiful youth, a son of Hadgi Mahmute, and grandson of the Bashaw, whom they had imagined to be a son of the late Bey, and were hurrying him to the castle to secure him, supposing him to be the next heir to the throne. The day following, when the bustle of this affair was over, the messengers were sent again, and found an easy admission to the terrified Halluma, who was sinking from the affliction of this last outrage, in seeing her favorite grandson dragged from her bedside by the Turks. The voice of the youth was drowned by the clatter of the tremendous sabres of his assassins, by which Lilla Halluma supposed he was massacred before they left the house ; but they carried him alive to the castle, where he still remains. It is determined for us to make an effort to see once more this worthy relic of royalty, but the difficulty of approaching her, owing to the jealousy of the Turks, makes it necessary to put off this dangerous visit to the last :

C.T — 12*

we however hear from her by her women, and send to her almost daily. Lilla Halluma has none of her daughters with her, but is consoled by the presence of the late Bey's widow, who never leaves her. Lilla Howisha, the Bashaw's third daughter, has ventured to remain at the castle with her husband, the Rais of the Marine, who, from his consequence and weight in the place, the Turk finds it the best policy to retain in his post.

Ⓜ

August 17, 1793

Within the last few days the scenes here have been too shocking to relate, I therefore pass them over in silence ; but I cannot omit telling you of the present precarious state of two persons, for whom we are much concerned, and in whose situation we are every hour anxiously hoping to see a change. One of them is a chief officer of the late Bey, who for many years was in the habit of visiting the Christians and being of their parties. This unfortunate man was seized by the Turk's satellites the night before last and carried to the castle, where, on the Turk's imagining he did not candidly confess what treasures he was possessed of, gave immediate orders to put him down into a deep dry well in the castle-yard, where, shocking to relate, no food had yet been administered to him ; but hopes are entertained, that if the inhuman Turk can be convinced of his error, he will, in consequence of the rank of this officer, have the unhappy man taken out of the well again, in time to save his life.

In the course of the same day, we had scarcely sat down to dinner, not at all recovered from the distress this account had thrown us into, before a Jewish youth, or rather spectre, who had sent to intreat he might be permitted to speak immediately with the Consul, was conducted into the room. Scarcely could he articulate owing to his agitation. His request was that he might be allowed to go with the dragomen, and search the prisons belonging to the English house, for a chain he had seen there to confine prisoners. On being asked for what purpose he could want it, he burst into tears, and said, his mother (the same called Queen Esther, the Bashaw's favourite) was expiring in the castle, chained with so tight a chain, that it was cutting through her wrists and ankles, and that she must inevitably die from anguish, if not immediately relieved ; and that the inhuman Turks had agreed, if he found an easier chain, they would permit him to change it, but otherwise she must remain as she was.

It seemed a dream to hear this distressed youth request as a favour, an iron chain for Esther, who but a short time since was the person most at ease, and perhaps the happiest in Tripoli.   The chain was immediately sent, and as much attention shewn to Esther as possible, that this effort to serve her might attract the notice of those about the castle, who were able to speak in her favour.   Great Esther, as they call her, had been sent for by the Turk, and ordered to produce him one hundred thousand pataques (five thousand pounds) immediately : she has been put in irons till this demand of the tyrant is complied with, in specie or in jewels, as he will receive no paper for the sum he has required.   Her family have offered nearly double that sum to the Turk, if he will spare Esther's life till the money can be sent from Leghorn, as they cannot answer the whole of his demand at present in specie ; but we hope the Jews will make up the number of sequins wanted, and save this unhappy woman from her present impending death.

The Bashaw, the Bey, and Sidy Useph, are going by land to Tunis, from whence they are expected to return immediately, supported by that court.   As, therefore, the reign of this tyrant is not imagined to be long, he is making the best of his time in plundering the wretched inhabitants before his departure, forcing them by every method to declare their property, which he immediately seizes.

August 18, 1793

Sidy Useph has not yet set off for Tunis.   He has kept the town completely besieged ever since the Turk has been here, notwithstanding bombs are continually fired from the town.   With his cannon he keeps the place so effectually blockaded, that these people, though starving, cannot get the least article of provision through the gates ; and are mortified by the sight of the grapes, dates, and oranges, hanging in luxuriance in the gardens, while with the parching heat they are literally dying for want of those salubrious articles.   At the same time, their feelings are distressed in beholding the quantities of cattle and vegetables consumed by the enemy under the walls, while there is literally nothing in the town to eat ; and it is only at the risk of their lives, and at five times the value of the article, that the Tripolitans are sometimes tempted to endeavour to get them for the Christians. From this account I leave you to judge of our situation.

This morning the Moors from the Messeah have been offering a great price for flints for their guns, at the gates of the town. Among the persons who sold these flints one man was detected, and will be hanged as a traitor.

The want of flints was most seriously felt by Sidy Useph, for the common flint that is found in such abundance in most other countries, is not to be met with here.

W

August 18, 1793

Ali Ben Zool is expected to call in the Western Arabs to his assistance, and if he has but treasure enough by him to satisfy these auxiliaries, who surpass as much in avarice, as they do in arms, the rest of the tribes around Tripoli, he will succeed in gaining them to his cause, notwithstanding the allegiance they owe the Bashaw, whose subjects they are. The Western Arab is a composition of the worst traits in the Arabian character, devoid of honour, honesty, or hospitality, which the Arab from the east of Tripoli possesses in a high degree. The former are infinitely less handsome in their persons than the latter.

It is, however, to be wished, for the sake not only of the Tripolitans, but also of the Christians, that Ali Ben Zool will not find money to employ these tribes, who hate the name of a Christian. They have not lost sight of the cause which produced that hatred in their predecessors, who were provoked by the injustice and cruelty of the crusades, when the blood of their countrymen was indiscriminately shed for following the standard of Mahomet, and since which the name of a Christian is held in abhorrence in the different countries of the Levant. The uncivilized part of their communities throughout Africa and Asia have confirmed with their latest breath this hatred to their children. Seven hundred years have not obliterated from the unlettered mind of the Arab, that agriculture, commerce, and the fine arts, were buried by the Christians under the wreck of the Saracenic empires.

The Western Arabs, who, as I have already mentioned, came into town to assist the Bashaw, retired with him when he left Tripoli. Whether they have returned to their deserts, or joined Sidy Useph, is not known here ; but as the last general we saw belonging to Sidy Useph informed us, he certainly had ten thousand men with him ready to oppose the Turk, the western tribes must have made up a part of that number, and will almost insure his getting into Tripoli.

On account of the many enormities we hear of, committed by the Turk, and the still impending fates of the wretched Sidy el Bunny and the Jewess Esther, we are careful not to enquire the names of the prisoners at present detained in the castle, to avoid hearing of the sufferings of those with whom we have been intimate. Lilla Fatima, the favourite sister of Sidy Useph, still continues to send him secret dispatches in spite of the Turk's vigilance, and on account of his spies the family tremble for her safety.

The life of Zenobia, the unfortunate daughter of the late Bey, is despaired of : she is still detained by the Turk at the castle, and scarcely either eats or sleeps, but confines herself to a part of the palace that overlooks the sea, not permitting any of her attendants to be with her but when she is in need of them. Her own apartments, and a part of the ramparts of the castle which commands the Messeah, where night and day she watches, are the boundaries of her walks. Not even the intreaties of any one can induce her to extend them till, as she says, the way is free to her from the castle to join her afflicted mother, who is with Lilla Halluma. The vicinity of her father's tomb in the royal turba (mausoleum), close to the castle, according to the Moors' ideas, would have been to the affectionate Zenobia the highest consolation in her present sufferings, had it been in her power to visit it. There, she says, she would have spent the greatest part of the day, to choose and arrange the choicest nosegays to deck it in the fullest manner, and have bestowed what flowers she had to spare among the graves of her ancestors. But she is prevented leaving the castle by the Turk's orders, against which no one dares act. Already the Turk has sent off all the black and white slaves he could collect in the castle as merchandize, to be sold in Asia, by which he will amass an immense sum, as there were a number of invaluable blacks, men and women, belonging to the royal family.

The Turk has made no public procession through the town yet. He has not been to worship at any of the marabuts, or mosques, on his ascending the throne ; but we see him walking in the galleries and through the castle daily. He has always a number of Turks around him.

By this time the rich Jews would all have embarked for Europe, but the Turk was too much on his guard not to provide in time against any one of them leaving the place ; at least, before he has ascertained what they are worth, and appropriated to himself as much of their property as he thinks right.

The shops are still almost all shut, and there is not yet any re-appearance of commerce. Scarcely any person is seen walking in the streets; and the gates are kept securely closed and guarded by bodies of Turks, the service of all the Moorish guards being dispensed with for the present. The guard of the town gates, the Sandanner, and the nightguards, are entirely composed of Turks, who are riotous and noisy. They have no compassion on the Jews, and ill use the Moors when they meet with any they dare annoy.

The Turkish gallies have been continually going in and out of the harbour. It is supposed they go along the coast to buy what the Moors at different places will sell them. Upon the whole, the Turk is as little expected to maintain his ground here, through embarrassed circumstances, as from the want of supplies and the concurrence of the town, the inhabitants of which seem only waiting to embrace a favourable opportunity of getting rid of him.

August 22, 1793

We expect to embark to-morrow; we have, therefore, been to-day to see for the last time all those of the Bashaw's family who are out of the castle. We went first to his daughters, Lilla Howisha and Lilla Fatima, both of whom had left the castle. The husband of the former of these two princesses retains his post under the Turk, and is still Rais of the Marine. We found Lilla Howisha, as we expected, in the utmost affliction for the fate of the Bashaw and the Bey. She told us, when the Bashaw left the castle at midnight, supported by those officers who were sufficiently attached to him to follow him in his misfortunes, he fainted three times on his horse before he reached the gates of the town. Twice the Bey, in his distress, wished to take him back to the castle, fearing he would die before they could get him out of the town.

The family had collected a box of treasures before the Bashaw quitted the castle, which was carried with him; but this was broken open and plundered at the gate by the very Arabs who accompanied him. These people took advantage of the confusion in their leaving the town to open the chest, and entirely emptied it. They were Western Arabs, who are noted for their treachery and deceit.

Not any of the ladies we visited can learn the least intelligence of what passes at the castle: they have only the satisfaction of knowing that no royal captive has been put to death there; consequently, those of the family who remained at the castle are yet safe. But they tremble for the fate of the young and beautiful Zenobia (the late Bey's eldest daughter) ; she still remains in the tyrant's powers. All her faithful slaves and women have been taken from her, and a set of attendants sent to her from the Turk, of his own chusing ; she is, therefore, not able to communicate a thought to her family but through these spies, whose lives depend on the Turk's will. The royal sufferers told us these afflictions were accelerating Lilla Halluma's death ! " You will find her," said Lilla Howisha, " equally deprived of health and state."

These ladies had saved the greatest part of their jewels from the Turks. In the first moments of confusion they left the castle with all their jewels on their persons, relying on the customs of the East and the laws of Mahomet, which declare the persons of all royal females sacred in war. But though these princesses succeeded in passing from the castle during the entrance of the Turks, orders were instantly given that no more of the royal family should quit it except Lilla Aisher, the afflicted relic of the late murdered Bey, whom the Turks forced from the palace gates, while they detained her daughter there !

After having spent with these unfortunate princesses all the time we could, we left them with great regret, and went to see Lilla Halluma, the Bey's wife ; Lilla Howviva, and the late Bey's widow, Lilla Aisher, were with her.

Here the scene can scarcely be described. The first person we saw was Lilla Aisher, who was in silent anguish, slowly pacing the apartment we were shown into, amidst the few faithful blacks that remained with her ; they were prostrate on the ground, and, in a low voice, lamenting for her sorrows. Lilla Aisher's fine hair, instead of being braided with gold and jewels, as we have always seen it, hung dishevelled over her shoulders, and the tears streamed down her cheeks pale as death. She hastily came up to us, and with a sort of wild agony, pronounced the name of her daughter. " Lilla Zenobia," said she, " remains at the castle in the tyrant's power ; Sidick el Bey [1] (my Lord the Bey) was cut to pieces who should be here now to protect his child ! " The blacks, seeing their mistress's increasing grief, were preparing to scream, when Lilla Aisher stopped them, with a convulsed voice, forbidding them, " Your cries," said she, " will offend the tyrant, and he will murder my child ! " She was so overcome by her feelings that her women led her to a sofa, where she seemed for

[1] Literally : " Your Lord, the Bey."

some time almost lifeless. On her recovery, she accompanied us to Lilla Halluma, and reproached herself for having kept us so long from her. " I see too well," said she, " that the very winds are now gathering which are destined to blow you from the shores of Tripoli, and this is the last time we are to see you."

We had but a short distance to go to Lilla Halluma's apartment. No long corridors nor subterraneous passages, as in the harem of the castle, were here ; no crowds of attendants, so numerous that we have been often obliged to wait a considerable time before way could be made for us to pass them in going to their sovereign !

Lilla Halluma received us with the greatest expressions of kindness. She appeared, as usual, all softness, but her frame is shrinking fast under the shock it has received. She spoke with that patience and resignation which presented a lesson for the best Christian, though given by a Mahomedan. The sweetness of her countenance was not altered from what we had always beheld it ; but a livid paleness overspread her face that betokened the hand of death had reached her ! No massy gold curtains encircled her bed ; no eunuchs waited at her chamber door. What a change ! But a few days since, the happiness of others depended on her smiles ; and to-day, the meanest subject in Tripoli is more at ease, because they have not known her grandeur. Only ten of the faithful blacks surrounded her, while two white women supported her as she sat up on the bed, or couch, on which she was placed.

She thanked us many times, with a feeble voice, for coming to see her again before we left the country ; and in the most pathetic manner, described to us the departure of the Bashaw from the castle. He endeavoured to comfort her by assurances that he would soon send an escort from Tunis for her, and bid her remember, that by Mahomet's laws, persons of her rank were perfectly safe even in the midst of war.[1]

She saw him for the last time from the galleries of her apartments, crossing the court-yard of the harem, where his strength failed him, and she beheld him carried off by his blacks, followed by the Bey of Bengazi and Sidy Hamet. Lilla Halluma's anxiety for the Bashaw's safety now rendered her situation dreadful, till her women hurried to her from the castle ramparts (where they had been watching) to

---

[1] It was not without great reason that the prophet made it one of his strongest tenets, to hold the persons of royal females sacred, in a country where no ready conveyances are provided to transport them instantly over burning sands and steep mountains, from the fury of the enemy : he, therefore, judiciously decreed, that they should pass unmolested in their persons, even through the enemy's camp if necessary. (T.)

tell her that the Bashaw had cleared the gates of the town, and had gained the Pianura.

Immediately after the Bashaw's departure, Lilla Halluma left the castle, in company with her daughter-in-law, Lilla Aisher, and very few attendants, and came to the residence where they now are ; but Lilla Halluma's voice failed her when she was about to tell us of her being forced to leave Lilla Zenobia, her beautiful grand-daughter, at the castle, in the usurper's power.

When this afflicted sovereign had finished the melancholy account of her last deplorable evening at the castle, conveyed in the language of singular oriental idioms, she added (alluding to the English Consul's departure from Tripoli at this period), " Ah ! the Consul's sun and the Bashaw's sun have set together ; their day closes, and their night begins at the same time : but may the Prophet yet wake them to a brighter adan, which I am hardly likely to behold again."

The reign of Lilla Halluma has been marked with continual clemency, and many are the severe and savage laws she has caused to be laid aside during the last years of it, through her intercession with the Bashaw. She prevented the barbarous custom taking place of throwing Moorish women into the sea inclosed in a canvass bag with stones to facilitate their sinking quickly, as a punishment for their being seduced by Christians. All the fandukes (inns for travellers) that have been erected during the Bashaw's reign, have been suggested and built at her own expense. One of the handsomest of them remains at present in an unfinished state.

We staid with the unfortunate Lilla Halluma as late as it was possible to return home without danger, and till she reminded us that the state of Tripoli was changed, and her power no longer existed to insure our safety as it had formerly done, or protect us now from a set of Turkish ruffians. We left her with the deepest regret, fully persuaded of the truth of her own words, that her sufferings would not be long.

□□

August 23, 1793

We spent a parting evening at the Venetian-house last night, where all our Christian friends were assembled to meet us. Several of the officers of the ships we are going with remained on shore till a late hour. During the evening, the Moors were continually coming to express their regret, in the strongest terms, on the English Consul's leaving their country. Many were the Moors of every rank who met us yesterday in the street, and wiped the tears from their eyes as they passed him, while they named him loudly to each other, as " *Boui el Bled* " and " *Wield el Bled* " (father of the country, and son of the country).

The whole of last night Sidy Useph kept up a constant firing upon the town, and every one is quite convinced, that if he is not betrayed into the Turk's hands, he must be in possession of the castle very shortly.

As there is an opportunity for this letter to be conveyed to Leghorn, I shall not keep it so long as I intended ; but I will write to you again on our way from hence.

🛆

At Sea, September 1, 1793

I begin this letter on board the Iris frigate, where the attentions paid to our comforts and feelings would appear exaggerated were I to describe them. We have had the singular good fortune to find one of those superior characters in the commodore, Captain Lumsdale, who commands it, that are but seldom met with, and cannot be delineated with justice.

Before we quitted Tripoli, the Shaik, who ventured to come and take leave of us, informed us that the Bashaw, the Bey, and Sidy Useph were all at the Bashaw's garden ; that the Arabs and the Moors of the country had made a compact with them, to keep the Turk so totally deprived of resources from the Messeah, as to oblige him to give up the town through fear of famine. We were very glad to learn from the Shaik, that the late Chiah, Hadgi Murat, the husband of Lilla Uducia, the Bashaw's eldest daughter, had escaped from the Turk the same night the Bashaw left the castle ; notwithstanding a plot had been laid by the Turk to take him, and for the failure of which one of the usurper's own officers has been imprisoned some days, and is destined to suffer. This officer was dispatched on shore with a message to Hadgi Murat, the first evening the Turkish fleet anchored in the bay of Tripoli. The Turk not seeing the Chiah come on board among those of the Bashaw's officers whom he had sent for, ordered this officer to go immediately to Hadgi Murat, and offer him the choice of any post he would name, which should be given to him the moment of his landing ; but the officer was ordered by Ali Ben Zool not to return on board without the Chiah. Hadgi Murat, fearing he might alarm the Turkish officer by his refusal, and by that means find himself in the power of the Turk, feigned an approbation of the offer made him, and left the officer with the apparent intention of joining him again instantly ; but wrapping himself up in a baracan, and profiting by the confusion of that evening, he immediately walked out of his house to the Messeah, and by that means saved himself. The Shaik, who was never in the Bashaw's interest, insisted that the firman the Turk brought with him was from the Grand Signior ; but he could not help acknowledging his fears that the town would not resist long for want of supplies, as not the smallest article could be had from the Messeah without the concurrence of Sidy Useph's people, and at their price. As we had at this time Moorish friends within and without the gates of the town, they availed themselves of the short intervals of the cessation of arms, to procure us every thing they could for our departure.

We embarked from Tripoli on the 23d of August. All the Consuls, except the French, accompanied us to the frigate, which lay nearly two miles from the mole, in their boats ; where they could remain but for a short time, as we sailed immediately.[1]

We embarked on the Moor's sabbath (Friday). The Marine gate was shut for prayers, and we were obliged to descend the private stairs of the golphor, or pavilion, where the Rais of the Marine sits. This we did at the risk of breaking our necks, as the stairs are dark and out of repair. A short month since, we should have passed through the Rais's golphor, accompanied to our boats by the Rais himself. But the time is past for Christians to expect civilities in Tripoli ; and not to ask a favour of the Turks, which they might have refused, it was thought best for us to pass this way.

A few days has worked a total change at the Marine, or quay. There is a part of it where the remains of an old fortress affords a cooling shade, when the sun is sinking in the west, and by that means presents the conveniency of taking the air there for some time previous to the Marine gates being shut before sunset, a perfect luxury during the summer months. This place, which used to serve as a sort of mall for the Moors of distinction to walk in at evening, and enjoy the cool breezes of the sea, and where we have spent many a placid hour, was now crowded with Turks, who could hardly stand under the weight of their arms, with countenances full of suspicion.

Fearful of seeing some Moor or Jew ill treated by them, we

---

[1] Lucas, the traveller, himself a former slave, took over the Consulate on Tully's departure.

hastened to the place where the boats waited to convey us to the frigate.

Until the day in which we embarked, new scenes of horror and danger to individuals continually occurred, and if the greatest judgment and constant precautions are not observed by the Consuls, to prevent even the satellites of Ali Ben Zool from taking the least liberty with the lowest of those subjects dependent on the consular houses, this uncivilized tyrant will soon lay his fatal hand on the protected, as well as the unprotected. It required the greatest circumspection and moderation, on the part of the Christians, to exact for themselves respect from the Turks, and to protect the Christian servants from insult and depredation, in the short distance we had to pass through the town. A Turkish guard escorted us to the seaside; but the dread of their wantonly striking with their knives, which they carried in their hands drawn, some poor straggling wretch that might chance to come in our way, rendered our situation perfectly painful, till they were dismissed on our reaching the boats.

The evening before we embarked, Gomarti, a Moor of rank, who had been a traitor to the Bashaw, and very assiduous in assisting the Turk in getting into Tripoli, had the honour of being appointed by him ambassador to Constantinople. Gomarti was highly pleased with the consequence of this embassy, and had prepared to set off in the grandest style he possibly could, while in his demands he was flattered with every indulgence from the Turk. But Ali Ben Zool not daring to trust this emissary to Constantinople, with a full account to the Porte of all he had witnessed at Tripoli, determined, as soon as he was embarked and safe on board, to send off an order for his death; and Gomarti no sooner entered the cabin, than two blacks from the castle seized and strangled him. Thus did he pay for his treachery to his country.

The morning we left Tripoli, it was expected Sidy Useph would hazard another attempt to enter the town. The Bashaw had set off with a caravan for Tunis: and his being able to pass unmolested by the Arabs, is another instance of the honour and hospitality of those people. Even the Arab Shaiks, who had acted in opposition to him, and complained of grievances he had not redressed, have agreed to protect him, and restrain the numerous hordes that might molest him in this way; giving for a reason, that the Bashaw has put himself in their hands, and that his present state is a striking instance of oppression, besieged by his own son, and driven from his kingdom by an usurper.

The sovereignty of the Arabs is most formidable. They may be truly said, not only to extend their sceptre over one of the four principal parts of the world, but to extend with success their dominion from Africa far into Asia ; remaining every where in powerful hordes sufficiently numerous to prevent the intercourse of nations, without their special leave. Inured to the hardships of the deserts, they easily undergo there such as none but themselves can resist : priding themselves on the purity of their blood, untainted, as they say, by a mixture with that of any other race, and boasting of their ancestry as Arabians. The Arab Shaiks support and keep up an alliance with each other, from the extremity of Africa on the farthest shores of the Atlantic Ocean, through nearly the extent of Asia.

In the deep recesses of the mountains the Arabs have their dwellings and retreats, which are defended by fortresses of craggy rocks and frightful precipices, rendered inaccessible by nature. The whole of the extensive mountains of Atlas are occupied by them, and in the same manner they inhabit the different chains of mountains in almost every direction throughout two quarters of the globe. While they are dispersed in such powerful bodies, so hardy and savage in their manner of living and possessed of policy and strong judgment, it is no wonder they remain what they stile themselves, masters of nearly all the deserts in Africa and Asia, to the present day. The Bashaws in Egypt, and those in Asia, hold their sovereignty from the Grand Signior, merely to keep the Arabs in temper, by paying them an immense revenue to buy their protection for the different caravans that could not otherwise pass unmolested to Mecca, and other parts of Asia and Africa.

Mahon, Nov. 20, 1793

I have detained this letter some time longer than I intended, as we expected daily the letters that have just reached us from our friends at Tripoli, and I was much interested to give you the latest accounts in my power of that unfortunate place, as this is probably the last time I shall write to you on the subject, hoping very soon to join you.

By our friends we learn, that from the day we embarked the Turkish usurper's reign increased in devastation and horror ; and in his persecution of the royal family, against whom he was more inveterate after the beautiful Zenobia had (assisted by the Moors) found means of escaping to her mother.

Some weeks after our departure from Tripoli, Ali Ben Zool took from the ladies of the Bashaw's family, who were in his power, their jewels, clothes, and every thing they had ; he then put them on board a small French vessel, with one hundred and fifty other persons, and obliged them to put to sea without provisions for the coast of Tunis ; and had not the Christian captains, in the harbour of Tripoli, supplied them with water and biscuit, they must have perished.

Sidy Useph has been betrayed by the Shaik of Tripoli, for a large sum of money the latter received from the Turk. On this account, he and the Bey retreated from before the gates of Tripoli over the deserts to Tunis, to join with their father in endeavouring to engage the court of Tunis in their interest.

The Grand Signior, in consequence of the outrages the Turk is committing in Tripoli, and his having acted without his sanction, has declared, that the Barbary powers have his leave to make war against him. The brother of Ali Ben Zool (Michael Aga), who was with the Grand Signior's fleet at Algiers, has also been disgraced. Tunis is preparing to send to Tripoli ten thousand men against the Turk, headed by the Tripolitan princes (the Bey and Sidy Useph). The Bey of Tunis has shewn great friendship to the Bashaw in his present misfortunes ; he has not only received him and the princes, but has invited as many more of the Bashaw's family as could get away from Tripoli, to take shelter in his dominions ; he also allows a sufficient establishment for the Bashaw, the Bey, and Sidy Useph, during their residence at his court, with leave to remain there till their kingdom can be recovered.

The forebodings of the excellent Lilla Halluma, which she expressed to us when we parted with her, were but too true. Concealed in the same remote quarter of the town where she remained screened from the ruffian hand of the Turk, this unfortunate sovereign fell a sacrifice to her sorrows a few days after we embarked. She died surrounded only by the blacks she had given freedom to, and two of her own family, Lilla Aisher, and her fair grand-daughter Lilla Zenobia, who, as I mentioned in my last, had so recently escaped from the castle.

Lilla Uducia, the eldest daughter of Lilla Halluma, seems destined to share as heavy a portion of affliction as her mother, with the additional misfortune of beginning to taste them earlier in life. I informed you in my last that her husband, Hadgi Murat (the late Chiah), succeeded in escaping from the Turk's hands the first night the latter arrived in Tripoli. Lilla Uducia has a large family by the Chiah, and though, according to the customs of the country, she was obliged to marry a renegado, yet, contrary to most Moorish princesses, she, by indulging, studying, and polishing the Chiah, has lived many years happily with him. Lilla Uducia had not been long in the Messeah with her husband and all her children, safe from the hands of the Turk, and had just escaped being sent with the rest of her sisters to Tunis in the French vessel without provisions, before Hadgi Murat was summoned to defend his sovereign, the father of his princess. In any other case he would have fled with his family to Tunis, but in this he could not refuse ; and, in the last battle fought in the Bashaw's cause against the usurper, Hadgi Murat fell a sacrifice to the Turkish arms before the gates of Tripoli, where he had not (as the Moors said) quitted his post that day from the adan to sunset. Lilla Uducia had been, during the whole time, watching the engagement from Hadgi Murat's golphor, whence her blacks departed and returned every half hour to bring her accounts of the success of the day. Anxiously waiting for the next arrival of her blacks, an uncommon outcry through the whole Messeah announced to the foreboding heart of Lilla Uducia the fate of her husband. The death song of " *Wulliah woo* " (sung for no one now but the chiefs) proved it was Hadgi Murat that was slain. While it resounded through the country, accumulating voices re-echoed the cries as they drew near the residence of Lilla Uducia, who, in addition to her afflictions for the loss of Hadgi Murat, was in agonies at the thought of not recovering his remains. Both Moors and Arabs fought over the body a long while, and having prevented its being mangled by the Turks, they at last carried it off to the unfortunate Lilla Uducia, who had it buried in her own garden.

The savage Turk, soon after we left Tripoli, burnt the agents belonging to the English and Dutch Consuls, who were both Jews, by a slow fire, and seized the English Kitchen-Moor,[1] whom he hung with twenty-one persons at the same time—accused of being concerned in a conspiracy against him.

A respectable merchant, named Serroar, one of the chief of the Jews whom we had known for many years, had been imprisoned on the same pretence, with an enormous chain about his neck and legs, under the weight of which he was near expiring, and has only escaped with life for the present, by paying fifty thousand sequins (twenty-

[1] *I.e.* the cook of the British Consulate.

five thousand pounds sterling). Another Jew, equally respectable, named Abraham, paid forty thousand sequins to save his two sons; but before this unhappy man had quitted the castle his sons were executed !

In addition to the enormities I have mentioned, among the many this tyrant has committed, was the following. After the English Consul's agent had been burnt, the Turk gave his widow, late a beautiful young bride, and who had not been married to him a month before we left Tripoli, overwhelmed with her sorrow, to one of his Arnauts, who are more savage than even the Turks themselves. These ruffians come from the countries between the Caspian and the Euxine Seas, and resemble in person, as well as in disposition, their neighbours the wild Usbec-Tartars, who are as much surpassed in civilization by the Kalmuc-Tartars, as these Arnauts are by the lowest order of the Turks. Many suppose the Arnauts to be the same race of people as the Argonauts that Jason led to Colchis (Mingrelia) for the Golden Fleece. The Arnauts in religion are Mahometans ; in disposition they are ferocious, sanguinary, and arrogant. From their course of life they are known by the name of Turkish banditti, and are employed by the Turks on board their corsairs, in which they commit shocking piracies. They are low in stature, very large boned, and broad in their make, though thin ; they have very prominent features, with fierce black eyes, which are small and round, and they have a very dark sallow complexion.

Of this cast was the Arnaut, who received from the cruel hand of the Turk the widow of the English Consul's agent. Her distracted father, some weeks after this atrocious action, amassed one thousand dollars (five hundred pounds) to purchase back from the Arnaut his unfortunate child, and by this means redeemed her from slavery, in which she must otherwise have remained for the rest of her days.

The Tripolitans, who daily expect the Bashaw and the princes back, supported by the Tunisians, do not at all accustom themselves to the tyranny of the Turk, but oppose him whenever they dare.

The enormous crimes of the Turk will evidently effectually prevent his return to Constantinople, and it is hoped he will be seized and carried to the Porte, before he can save his head in Egypt : the usual place where proscribed Turks take refuge.

His expulsion and the return of the Bashaw's line, may restore Tripoli to its former state of respectability, it having for a long series of years ranked as the first kingdom of the Barbary states ; for Algiers continues a piratical state to the present day, and Tunis is but little better.

But should Sidy Useph persist in depriving a second brother of his right to the regal dignity, which there is great reason to apprehend from the sanguinary measures he has adopted hitherto, wretched may be the state of Tripoli ; for many traits in Sidy Useph's character seem to have been drawn from the tyrant Muly Yesied, the late Emperor of Morocco, who was too much the companion of his youth.

Tripoli, under Ali Bashaw, has experienced for upwards of thirty years a mild government, perhaps too mild for the interest of its subjects. The country was visited by the heavy calamities of plague, famine, and war, unfortunately for us, during the greatest part of the ten years we lived there ; but no tyranny of the Bashaw made up a share of its misfortunes. Moorish families slept unmolested in the open air on their terraces, and waked to peace in the morning ; while the Christians, to whom the highest respect was paid by the Moors on all occasions, lived happy with the natives, and safer here than in any other part of Barbary, till Sidy Useph, by rebelling against his father and brother, tore the country with intestine broils, and laid it open to a series of troubles, which have long rendered it the theatre of murder and desolation ; and it is not easy at present to conjecture when its tragedies will end.

Gibraltar, April 30, 1795

Since you must have had my letters with the journal of Tripoli, we have received in addition to them later accounts respecting that place, and I send them, as they may serve as an appendix to the rest.

A packet of letters reached us yesterday from Tripoli from an intimate friend, with whom Ali Bashaw has held a correspondence in Moorish, ever since he has been at Tunis.

These letters inform us, that the two princes, the Bey and Sidy Useph, have returned to Tripoli with forces from Tunis, and have driven the Turk away. The latter retreated by sea with all his people and ships, and it is thought he is gone to Alexandria,[1] but not before having despoiled almost all the inhabitants of the town of Tripoli of their property, and putting to death numbers of them in the most cruel manner.

[1] See Introduction.

By the decrees of the Grand Signior, the Bey of Tunis and Ali Bashaw, the Bey of Tripoli, and Sidy Useph were jointly to share the throne of Tripoli ; but soon after the two princes had cleared Tripoli of the Turks, Sidy Useph executed one of his schemes against the Bey, which has completely shut him out at present from regal power ; and this was accomplished in the following singular manner.

The Bey, warned by his friends or by his own apprehensions, had for a long time since his return to Tripoli, avoided quitting the town but in company with Sidy Useph, from the fear of the latter acting inimically to his interest while absent, or preventing his entering the town again on his return. But the two princes being out in the Messeah together, Sidy Useph on a dispute with his brother left him, reached the gates of the town some minutes before him, and without further ceremony closed them against the Bey ; he then ordered him from the walls to retire to Derner, of which, he said, he permitted him to be Bey ; adding, that on his refusal, he should be sacrificed before the walls of Tripoli. The Bey having no other resource, turned about with the few people he had with him and went to Derner, of which place he is the Bey ; leaving his brother, Sidy Useph, quietly seated on the throne, as Bashaw of Tripoli.[1]

A disposition in the present Bey to give up his kingdom quietly, seems to promise him a happier life in this retreat than he has before experienced : while he need not envy Sidy Useph the throne, accompanied as it must be by dreadful reflections. Every object around must daily and hourly remind him of the late Bey's murder, perpetrated in the same room in which he himself first drew breath, and which room still remains shut up in testimony of the dreadful scene performed within it.

Fortunately for the fair Selima, whose story you can refer to,[2] a few weeks previous to the Turks arrival in Tripoli, her husband, Sidy Mahmoud, went to Sweden, from whence he has now returned, escaping by his absence falling a victim among the numbers destroyed by the invader's cruelties. But Sidy Mahmoud, when he returned from Sweden, had nearly as much affliction to encounter on the beauteous Selima's account, as he had after his embassy from Naples, when he thought he had lost her by his own neglect.

---

[1] Yusef, in fact, usurped the throne of Tripoli on June 11, 1795, and reigned as Bashaw until 1832. The deposed Bashaw died in August 1795. Ahmed, the Bey, retired to Alexandria. In 1804 the Americans, during their war with Tripoli, endeavoured to establish Ahmed on the throne, but failed. He died in exile.

[2] See letter, December 20, 1792.

When the last battle was fought between the Turks and the Moors, before the princes of Tripoli fled to Tunis, the contest of that day was expected to end in favour of the Turks. The frighted Selima, with two infants, fled from the Messeah to seek a safer retreat, and was conducted to the mountains by an Arab chief, of the tribe of the Benoleeds, who promised to protect her till he could put her safely into the hands of her lord, whom she had scarcely the hope of meeting again. Selima had no doubt of the chief's power, and the strength of his Arabs to shield her from the hand of the enemy ; but her courage forsook her at the thought of the state of Tripoli, where the Turk's tyranny precluded the approach of any Moor of distinction, but at the imminent hazard of his life. Among the defiles of the mountains, the afflicted Selima and her two little boys, her only solace, passed the tedious days, waiting for Sidy Mahmoud's arrival, during a long twelvemonth. The circumstance of her retreat prevented her meeting with Sidy Mahmoud on his immediate return, as it was necessary for himself to fetch her from the Arab, who so generously guarded her with all her property, during an interval of time so full of danger.

The Bashaw is not expected to live to return to Tripoli ; he is very ill at his country residence in the suburbs of Tunis, where he has lost by the plague, which has visited that country lately, a favourite eunuch, named Muzzouk, who had been with him many years in Tripoli. They say the Bashaw never held up his head after he heard of the death of his unfortunate Queen, Lilla Halluma.

I am sorry for Sidy Useph and the Tripolitans, that the former remains sovereign of Tripoli, as I fear it will but aggravate his crimes, and add to the distresses of the country.

I have subjoined to this, for your information, a few Moorish words with their meanings, but I believe I have inserted none in my letters without explaining them.

APPENDIX

Moorish Words.	Translation.
Ash harlic ⎫ Asslam ⎬	. How do you do ?
Asselmic .	. Peace be with you.
Salem alicum	. Be there peace between us.
Alicum salem	. There is peace between us.
Arrosa .	. Bride.
Wield .	. Son.
Ben . .	. Son.
Benitee .	. An endearing name for child or friend (my girl).
Ragil .	. A man.
Merte .	. Wife. *Merte el Chiaia*, the Chiaia's wife.
Shittan .	. An evil spirit.
Mahboul .	. Mad.
Ursul .	. The only one. (Rasul = the prophet.)
Allah .	. God. *Allah, Allah, ursul el Allah*, God is God, Mahomet is his only Prophet.[1]
Halloo .	. Sweet.
Halloowa .	. A sweetmeat made of almonds and honey boiled to a thick paste.
Cobah .	. Cupola (more probably Qubba).
Cobah .	. The morning star.
Gibel [2] .	. Mountain.
Gibeleene .	. Mountaineer.
Uras .	. Head (Ras).
Uras el Bashaw .	. By the Bashaw's head.
Uras enti .	. By your head.
Feizàr .	. Quickly (*Fi s'aa*).
Holsa .	. Bread ⎫
Traia .	. Bring ⎪ *Traia holsa fiel housh el Hamet.*
Housh . .	. House ⎬ Bring bread to the house of Hamet.
Ciel . .	. Into ⎪ (*Fiel*)
Liet . .	. Milk (*halib*).
Mille .	. Salt (*melh*). ⎫
Harda .	. This. ⎬ *Harda mush mille.*
Mush .	. Not, none, or nothing. ⎭ This man has no wit, or no salt in him.
Matamash .	. There is none. It is not here.
Empshie .	. Go.
Empshad .	. Gone (*Masha*).
Barsh el Mar	. The coast or seaside (*shatt el bahr*).
Hardi .	. Here it is.

[1] These words are sung before the dead as they are carried to the grave ; and they constitute all that is necessary to be said by an apostate, when he embraces the Mahometan faith.

[2] *Gibraltar* derives its name from Gibel-Tor, the Mountain of Tor, a chief of that name. (T.)

Moorish Words.	Translation.
Toma .	. Take it (not Arabic).
Ween .	. Where is it ?
Ash nu harda	. What is this ? What is the matter ?
Aga . .	. Captain in the army.
Rais. .	. Captain in the navy.
Selicta aga .	. Sword-bearer.
Chasnedar .	. Treasurer.
Chassne .	. Private treasury.
Mavelivi ⎫	
Chedri ⎪	. The names of four different communities of Shriefs belonging
Seyah ⎬	to Mecca.
Bickteshu ⎭	
Shrief .	. A churchman of an order belonging to Mecca.
Gazell .	. Divine love.
Esma [1] .	. One of the thousand and one names the Turks give the Deity.
Gatuss .	. Cat.
Eyen gatuss	. Cat's eyes (a green plum).
Toro .	. Bull.
Eyen toro .	. Bull's eyes (a bloom plum).
Gazzel .	. Antelopes, or the African deer.
Eyen gazzel	. Gazzel's eyes (a large dark plum).
Zein. .	. Handsome, beautiful.
Shair .	. Justice. Shair Allah, justice in the name of God.[2]
Toba .	. Forgiven.
Tobah Allah	. Forgiveness, God.
Allah barick	. God prosper you.
Hadgi .	. One who has been to Mecca. No Mussulman is a Hadgi till he has performed a pilgrimage to Mecca.
Kebbier .	. Great, grand.
Kebbierra .	. Greatest, grandest, as Lilla Kebbierra, Queen of Tripoli.
Corali .	. Turk (Cologhli).
Coralis .	. Turks.
Seid . .	. Lion.
Kief. .	. So. Kief kief, so so.
La . .	. No.
Ay . .	. Yes.
Fisby .	. Charity. Fisby ye Lilla, charity, ye lady.
Arrah .	. This minute (Halla).
Hada hower	. Presently, by and by. (That is him.)
Yassa .	. Enough (Berber).
Hada yassa	. That's enough.
Sahabti .	. Dear friend (my friend).

[1] Gazell-Esma, is a salutation given by one of the above order when they meet a fellow Shrief, an Imam, or a Marabut, but used to no other Mussulman.

[2] The Moors vociferate these words when they appeal to the Bashaw to redress their wrongs. (T.)